Digital Social Work

Digital Social Work

TOOLS FOR PRACTICE WITH
INDIVIDUALS, ORGANIZATIONS,
AND COMMUNITIES

Edited by Lauri Goldkind
Lea Wolf
and
Paul P. Freddolino

OXFORD
UNIVERSITY PRESS

Oxford University Press is a department of the University of Oxford. It furthers
the University's objective of excellence in research, scholarship, and education
by publishing worldwide. Oxford is a registered trade mark of Oxford University
Press in the UK and certain other countries.

Published in the United States of America by Oxford University Press
198 Madison Avenue, New York, NY 10016, United States of America.

Library of Congress Cataloging-in-Publication Data
Names: Goldkind, Lauri, 1969– editor. | Wolf, Lea, 1970– editor. | Freddolino, Paul P., editor.
Title: Digital social work : tools for practice with individuals, organizations,
and communities / edited by Lauri Goldkind, Lea Wolf, Paul P. Freddolino.
Description: New York : Oxford University Press, 2018. | Includes
bibliographical references and index.
Identifiers: LCCN 2018018656 (print) |
LCCN 2018033643 (ebook) |
ISBN 9780190871123 (updf) | ISBN 9780190871130 (epub) |
ISBN 9780190871116 (paperback)
Subjects: LCSH: Social work education—Technological innovations. |
Social service—Technological innovations. | BISAC: SOCIAL SCIENCE / Social Work.
Classification: LCC HV11 (ebook) | LCC HV11 .D564 2018 (print) | DDC 361.3/2—dc23
LC record available at https://lccn.loc.gov/2018018656

9 8 7 6 5 4 3 2 1

Printed by WebCom, Inc., Canada

Lauri Goldkind: For Jason, the kindest, most patient, and smartest technologist I know.

Lea Wolf: For AWF, ISF, and EAF: May each of you find joy in this brave new world.

Paul P. Freddolino: To all those who have struggled to learn how to use these new tech tools . . . and been victorious.

CONTENTS

PART III } **Communities**

ACKNOWLEDGMENTS: OR, A NOTE FROM LAURI GOLDKIND

Projects such as this do not happen in a vacuum, and our book is no exception. I clearly remember the generosity of Dr. Tom Packard, who is now emeritus at San Diego State University, offering to chat with me about teaching macro practice to social work students after I found his name and syllabus online. He pointed me to the great book of case studies by Fauri, Wernet, and Netting (2007), and I have used cases in my classroom ever since. Tom, thank you for being such a generous teacher, inside and outside the classroom.

Another group of people who deserve extra special thanks for their help above and beyond in bringing this book to fruition: Andrew Wong, the president and founder of AJW, Inc. Andy makes data sharing happen. He was kind enough to get on the phone with two random ladies from New York, walking us through the original story of the Shared Youth Database in San Francisco, and connecting us to the super smart Chris Kingsley.

David Follmer, the magnificently smart human and publisher at Lyceum Books, was willing to indulge smart-mouthed scholars with a single nod. David introduced us to the excellent Brent Jacocks who is one pleasant person, and a very talented editor.

I would be remiss if I also did not mention all of the mentors who have held me up: Margy Gibbleman, Marc Glassman, Meredith Hanson, John McNutt, and Bill Meezan; some of you I miss dearly, all of you have lit the way forward. While I have not always agreed with everything you have suggested, your smart, seasoned advice and splashes of dark humor have sustained me. I am deeply indebted.

Lastly I thank my family—without whose support the wheels do not turn.

May the force be with you now and always,

Lauri Goldkind

January 22, 2018

CONTRIBUTORS

About the Editors

Lauri Goldkind, PhD, LMSW, is a graduate of SUNY Stony Brook and the Wurzweiler School of Yeshiva University. She is associate professor at the Graduate School of Social Service at Fordham University, New York, NY. She has a long-standing interest and practice background in nonprofit leadership, capacity building, and organizational development. At Fordham she has created one of the few electives on technology-enhanced social work practice in the country. Her prior experience has centered on youth development, education, and juvenile justice. She was recently named editor of the *Journal of Technology in Human Services*. Her current research focuses on information and communication technology tools in nonprofits and social justice and civic engagement within the human services sector.

Lea Wolf, LMSW, is a social worker who lives and works in New York City. A graduate of Stanford University and New York University Silver School of Social Work, she is interested in human resilience and in strategies to cultivate it, especially peer support and creative expression. A fan of the diversity of practice in social work, she works with individuals and groups, engages in research, and has designed and evaluated human services programs. Her published work addresses arts-based interventions across sectors, social activism, and the nexus of social work and technology.

Paul P. Freddolino, MDiv, PhD, is professor of social work at Michigan State University and director of distance education and technology in the School of Social Work. His research and publications have examined the use of various educational technology tools in social work courses; comparisons between on-campus, distance, and online classrooms; and the impact of distance education programs on community agencies. He served on the Council on Social Work Education's Commission on Accreditation, where he chaired the e-Learning Subcommittee examining national standards for distance and e-learning programs in social work. He is also actively engaged in research related to the use of technology tools in social work practice. Current projects focus on technology for stroke victims and people with dementia and their caregivers.

About the Authors

Lauren Aaronson has spent nearly 20 years helping to transform New York City's most complex social services programs. She is assistant deputy commissioner for business process innovation at New York City's Human Resources Administration (HRA), the nation's largest social services agency serving over 3 million of the city's residents. Currently she is the leader of the HRA-wide benefits re-engineering initiative, which strives to improve client and worker experience through the use of modernized technology and simplified business processes and policies. Previously she served as the director of client solutions at NYC HHS-Connect, the city's enterprise transformation program focused on using technology to break down information silos and enable data sharing among the city's eight health and human services agencies.

Kristin Battista-Frazee is a marketing professional, social worker, and author of the memoir *The Pornographer's Daughter* (2014). She started her career as a geriatric social worker and parlayed her interest in improving people's lives into legislative and communications work on Capitol Hill. She has also served in marketing and communications' roles at corporate startups, nonprofit organizations, and advocacy organizations dedicated to raising awareness about mental health issues, providing online graduate degrees and continuing education, and improving policies to support behavioral health providers. She has written articles and blogs for *Huffington Post, New York Journal of Books, ELLE Magazine* (Australia), *NASW News,* and *Social Work Today* to provide book reviews and cover mental health and pop culture topics. She holds an MSW from Columbia University.

Emily Carter, LMSW, is an alumnus of Fordham University's Graduate School of Social Service.

Janice DeRito, LMSW, is an alumnus of Fordham University's Graduate School of Social Service.

Thomas P. Felke, MSW, PhD, is assistant professor in the Department of Social Work within the Marieb College of Health & Human Services at Florida Gulf Coast University. He has been conducting research and evaluation efforts using geographic information systems (GIS) technologies for almost two decades. His work has led to the establishment of child care centers in Connecticut and the first ever senior center in Naples, Florida. He has published on the topic and given presentations at local, state, and national conferences. He has taught a social work elective focused on the application of GIS technologies to social work research and practice for the past 10 years. He also provides GIS training to faculty and students at social work programs across the United States.

Dale Fitch, MSSW, PhD, is associate professor and director of the University of Missouri School of Social Work. He worked for 15 years with the homeless, youth in residential care, and medical social work. His research focuses on the use of information systems in human services agencies. He is the former editor in chief for the *Journal of Technology in Human Services* and was recently appointed as the subject matter expert for technology in social work for the *Oxford Encyclopedia of Social Work*. He was also recently appointed as a core faculty member in the University of Missouri Informatics Institute, where his research will focus on big data machine learning algorithms for social worker case notes.

Stephen Goldsmith, PhD, is the Daniel Paul Professor of the Practice of Government and the director of the Innovations in American Government Program at Harvard's Kennedy School of Government. He currently directs Data-Smart City Solutions, a project to highlight local government efforts to use new technologies that connect breakthroughs in the use of big data analytics with community input to reshape the relationship between government and citizen. He previously served as deputy mayor of New York and mayor of Indianapolis, where he earned a reputation as one of the country's leaders in public–private partnerships, competition, and privatization. Stephen was also the chief domestic policy advisor to the George W. Bush campaign in 2000, the chair of the Corporation for National and Community Service, and the district attorney for Marion County, Indiana, from 1979 to 1990. He has written *The Power of Social Innovation, Governing by Network: The New Shape of the Public Sector, Putting Faith in Neighborhoods: Making Cities Work through Grassroots Citizenship, The Twenty-First Century City: Resurrecting Urban America*, and *The Responsive City: Engaging Communities Through Data-Smart Governance*.

Kimberly Grocher, LCSW, holds an MSW from Howard University in Washington, DC. She has completed two years of postgraduate training in psychodynamic couples' therapy at the Training Institute for Mental Health in New York City, and is a doctoral student at Fordham University's Graduate School of Social Service. She has worked in community and corporate mental health settings in the DC Metropolitan area, South Florida, and New York City. She is engaged in research concerning the use of media and technology to enhance mental health practice and policy and mind-body therapies to address mental illness in women of color. She has a background in media production and uses these skills to create social advocacy media.

Laurel Iverson Hitchcock is assistant professor in the Department of Social Work at the University of Alabama at Birmingham. She is interested in social work education, technology and social media, social welfare history, and public health social work. Her current work examines the use of technology in social work education, focusing on best practices and improving student learning outcomes. In 2012, she received the SAGE/CSWE Award for Innovative Teaching for her work incorporating social media into social work pedagogy. She is an active partner with #MacroSW, an online community of social workers. She has more than

10 years of experience as a social worker in the areas of healthcare and community mental health. She completed her MSW and PhD in social work at the University of Alabama, and holds a master's in public health from the University of Alabama at Birmingham.

Michael Jaonsch, LMSW, is an alumnus of Fordham University's Graduate School of Social Service.

Chris Kingsley consults nationally on projects directed at improving the public sector's ability to use data to achieve better results. He has written about, advocated for, and provided training on issues related to administrative data systems, information sharing, and privacy policy as part of the teams at Data Quality Campaign and National League of Cities. He has a decade's experience as a nonprofit program manager and independent research analyst and has authored reports on performance management, municipal social media strategies, citywide information systems design, and economic development. He is a graduate of Haverford College and the University of Pennsylvania.

Sofia Konvitz, LMSW, is an alumnus of Fordham University's Graduate School of Social Service.

Alice Krueger is the founder and president, since 2007, of Virtual Ability International, a cross-disability peer-support community in the virtual world Second Life, where she is known by her avatar name, Gentle Heron. Alice is a former educator and educational researcher who "went virtual" when her multiple sclerosis prevented her from participating in activities in the physical world. She holds a BS in veterinary medicine from Iowa State University and an MSED from the University of Iowa.

Lynette Kvasny earned her PhD in computer information systems from the Robinson College of Business at Georgia State University. Her research focuses on how and why historically underserved groups use information and communication technologies to improve their life chances. Her research has been published in leading journals including *The Information Society, Information Systems Journal, Journal of Computer Mediated Communication, New Media and Society, Internet Research*, and the *Journal of the American Medical Informatics Association*. Her research has been supported by the National Science Foundation, the Oracle Help Us Help Foundation, Verizon Wireless, the Penn State Africana Research Center, and the Penn State Children, Youth and Family Consortium.

Andrea LaMarre, MSc, is a PhD candidate in the Department of Applied Nutrition at the University of Guelph in Ontario, Canada. Her dissertation research explores eating disorder recovery for diversely embodied Canadians and their supporters. She uses qualitative and arts-based approaches (digital storytelling) to explore the experiences of these individuals and their families, thereby creating spaces for engaging in productive dialogue among healthcare providers, policy makers, and those with lived experience. Through her research she hopes to expand on the dominant discourses about what it means to have and to overcome an eating disorder and how this may look different depending on one's social location. She is a Vanier Doctoral Scholar (Canadian Institutes of Health Research) 2014–2017.

Vu Le is executive director of Rainier Valley Corps, a nonprofit in Seattle, Washington, that promotes social justice by developing leaders of color, strengthening organizations led by communities of color, and fostering collaboration between diverse communities. He is the former executive director of the Vietnamese Friendship Association and author of the nonprofit humor blog Nonprofit with Balls. He holds an MSW from Washington University in St. Louis, Missouri. He was a Dan Than Americorps member for 2 years. He is involved with blogging because he believes there is a lot of injustice in our world that can be effectively addressed by getting everyone to work together.

Abraham Lincoln Lee is a former foster care worker, licensing supervisor, therapist, and licensed clinical social worker from Chicago. He moved into the technology side of the health and human services practice in 2001, and has been instrumental in the implementation and design of technology solutions specifically for social workers and their clients. With an MSW from Washington University in St. Louis (George Warren Brown School of Social Work), Abe is a reformed luddite who continues to focus on working with those with the most need, such as orphan survivors of the AIDS pandemic in southern Africa through a Charity called Hands at Work (http://www.handsatwork.org), and identifying mobility solutions for social workers and their clients at his current position as director of product management at Diona Mobility Solutions (http://www.diona.com; http://ngo.diona.com).

Joyce Y. Lee earned her master's degree in social work at Columbia University. She worked as a licensed social worker for 2 years before joining the joint PhD program in social work and psychology at the University of Michigan. Her three broad research interests are studying family systems from a developmental perspective; using big data from social media to examine fathers' and mothers' parenting attitudes, beliefs, and practices; and developing, implementing, and evaluating technology-based parenting interventions for fathers transitioning into parenthood. Her aim is to triangulate these three research areas to promote the ongoing involvement of fathers, especially those from low-income communities. Her research is rooted in her work with low-income families in a community-based youth empowerment program, as well as her ongoing clinical work with a wide range of fathers.

Shawna J. Lee is associate professor and director of the Parenting in Context Research Lab at the University of Michigan School of Social Work. She is a faculty affiliate at the Center for Human Growth and Development and at the Institute for Social Research, Research Center for Group Dynamics. She completed a joint doctoral degree in social work and psychology at the University of Michigan and postdoctoral training at the Columbia University School of Social Work. She has published more than 45 works focusing on child maltreatment prevention, fathers' parenting behaviors, father–child relations, and the effects of parental corporal punishment on child well-being. Recently she collaborated with Manpower Development Research Corporation (MDRC) to create the DadTime parenting app. She is pilot testing Text4dad, a text-messaging program for expecting and new fathers.

Carla Rice, PhD, is professor and Canada Research Chair at the University of Guelph in Ontario, Canada: A leader in the field of embodiment studies and arts-informed research in Canada, her research explores cultural representations of bodies of difference. She founded Re-Vision, the Centre for Art and Social Justice at the University of Guelph, a funded research program that works with misrepresented and aggrieved communities to challenge stereotypes. Through the Re-Visioning Differences Media Arts Laboratory, she continues to explore ways that arts-informed research can create opportunities for marginalized communities to transform stereotypes, advance social inclusion, and improve health equity. Notable books include *Gender and Women's Studies in Canada: Critical Terrain* (2013), and *Becoming Women: The Embodied Self in Image Culture* (2014).

Melanie Sage, PhD, LICSW, is assistant professor of social work at the University at Buffalo. Her research focuses include the use of technology in social work practice and education. She is coauthor of the upcoming text *Teaching Social Work with Digital Technology* and a board member of Human Services Information Technology Applications, an international organization focused on the ethical and effective use of technology in human services and publisher of the *Journal of Technology in Human Services*. Her interests include the use of social media in education and social work practice, and she has published in the area of ethical use of social media for social workers.

Jonathan B. Singer, PhD, LCSW, is associate professor of social work at Loyola University Chicago. He earned his MSW from the University of Texas–Austin and his PhD from the University of Pittsburgh School of Social Work. He is founder of the *Social Work Podcast* (www.socialworkpodcast.com) and the Google Plus community Social Work and Technology. Episodes of the podcast have been downloaded over 2 million times by 1 million people in 181 countries and territories. He is author of 45 publications and coauthor of the 2015 text *Suicide in Schools A Practitioner's Guide to Multi-level Prevention, Assessment, Intervention, and Postvention.*

Andrew Tepper has directed Music, Theater Program and Meditation programs in psychiatric hospital settings for over a decade. In his music program, he runs a recording studio to engage clients in the psychotherapeutic process through music production. He also provides individual psychotherapy; and facilitates group psychotherapy for adults, adolescents, and children. He has consulted as a facilitator for the Eileen Fisher Leadership Institute and currently is in private practice at the Riverwalk Group in Stamford, Connecticut, and Katonah, New York. Additionally, he is cofounder of Enhanced Mood, LLC, which is developing an app to help calm users in crisis. He holds an MSW from Columbia University School of Social Work and a BA in psychology from Bates College.

Chelsea Tussing, LMSW, is an alumnus of Fordham University's Graduate School of Social Service.

Tova B. Walsh, MSW, PhD (University of Michigan), is assistant professor at the Rutgers University School of Social Work and faculty associate at the Institute for Digital Innovation in Social Work. Her research focuses on identifying effective strategies to support emerging competencies in early parenthood and promote nurturing parent–child relationships among parents who face barriers in initiating or maintaining positive involvement with their children. She is currently examining the parenting support needs of new fathers and military-connected parents and collaborating to develop and test parenting interventions for these underserved groups. In her intervention work, she seeks to capitalize on existing technology or create new technology to more effectively reach the target population and address their specific needs. Her research draws on her experience working in low-income communities as a home visitor to families with children from ages 0 to 3.

Lap Yan is a doctoral candidate at the Fordham School of Social Work. He has an MBA in finance and marketing from New York University's Stern School of Business. He has worked as an architect and construction manager in New York. He is also a 23-year veteran of the US Marine Corps who was deployed to Operation Iraqi Freedom in 2003 and was part of the First Marine Expeditionary Force march to Baghdad. His research interests include the military–civilian divide and the effect of the all-volunteer military on this divide, as well as online education and the efficacy of this movement to nontraditional classrooms.

Karen Zgoda, MSW, LCSW, is instructor in the School of Social Work at Bridgewater State University and Simmons College. She has been nominated for the Presidential Award for Distinguished Part-Time Teaching and serves as teaching and technology faculty advisor for the Teaching and Technology Center at Bridgewater State University. She has been hosting online social work chats since 2000 and is currently a chat partner and host for the #MacroSW Twitter chats focused on macro social work practice. She previously wrote the SW 2.0 technology column for the *New Social Worker Magazine* and served as an AmeriCorps *VISTA member and project coordinator at CTCNet working on digital divide issues. Her research and pedagogical interests include technology in social work and education, macro social work, social policy, and research methods. She began her PhD in public policy at the University of Massachusetts–Boston in fall 2017.

Digital Social Work

1 }

Introduction

"We live in a society exquisitely dependent on science and technology, in which hardly anyone knows anything about science and technology."
—Carl Sagan, *1934–1996*

Social Work and Technology

This book is the product of 5 years of thought about the relationship—still nascent—between social work and information and communication technologies (ICTs). This text does not aim to describe why social work has lagged behind other sectors (like business or medicine) in embracing the technological change that has exploded in the last quarter century (Perron, Taylor, Glass, & Margerum-Leys, 2010; Zorn, Flanagan, & Shoham, 2015). We agree with the consensus of published literature, which affirms that limited resources, ethical and legal considerations, lack of training, and social work's historical emphasis on face-to-face communication have all contributed to this lag (Wolf & Goldkind, 2016). This volume looks forward, assembling the experience and expertise of practitioners working at the potent interface between social work and technology. The cases collected here illustrate new strategies, questions, and possibilities for our field, for those we serve, and for the society in which we share.

In this book, you will discover real-world examples of how technology can enhance the familiar components of social work practice—from therapy and psychoeducation to community building and fundraising—and how technology is creating novel forms of intervention, using new tools, like avatars, geographic information systems (GIS) mapping, text messaging, and large data sets. As Reisch and Andrews write, "the power of example seems to be universally effective in triggering deep learning" (2002, p. 2), and the case examples gathered here offer instructors, students, and practitioners the opportunity to think both creatively and critically about the potential of technology, the values that animate social work, and the realities of a changing culture. It is our hope that this book will provide tangible and thought-provoking examples that you can use in practice or in your classroom to activate (or enliven) the very necessary dialogue about the use of ICTs at micro, mezzo, and macro levels across fields of social work practice. Because most of our readers are likely to practice in the United States, the cases focus on technology in North American settings. If you are in a different part of the world, we urge you to consider how social work practice in your own geographic location may be different, or how a culturally distinctive pattern of technology use might inflect your work.

No one can opt out of the implications of technology. Any contemporary practitioner who engages in billing, e-mailing or texting with clients, record-keeping, supervision, or social media–based activism, or who uses data to assess community needs will confront evolving questions of ethics, appropriateness, and efficacy (Barsky, 2017; King, Goldsmith, Goldkind, & Wolf, this volume). Every arena of our discipline has been prompted to evolve by technology: technology is used to deliver social work education, it is reformulating the rules of research, it offers new approaches for individual and group work, and it continues to manufacture new tools for activism and community-based practice (NASW et al., 2017; Panos, Panos, Cox, Roby, & Matheson, 2002). We hope the cases in this volume inspire those who use this text to reflect on both the potential and the attendant responsibility of using technological tools to realize the essential values of social work.

Social Work and Technology: The Lens of Standards

The effort to articulate and advance the role of technology in the human services was spurred by individual advocates, starting in the late 1970s. Conducted by Gunther Geiss, a professor of social work at Adelphi University, a 1978 survey of faculty at schools of social work in the United States sought to identify those who were using computers or designing technology to augment their work. The more than 80 positive responses fostered a network connecting those with professional expertise that combined technology and human service. In the 1980s, committed individuals began to coalesce, and the decade saw the founding of husITa (Human Services Information Technology Applications), a virtual international association to promote the ethical and effective use of ICTs in the human services. In 1982, Dick Schoech published the first book to explicitly describe the potential of technology for social work and allied disciplines: *Computer Use in Human Services: A Guide to Information Management*. The dialogue widened across social work in the 1990s, as technology continued to emerge as a tool for education, for professional community, and for the provision of clinical services in social work. Accelerating professional use of ICTs prompted the formal structures of the discipline toward the fitful acknowledgment of an evolving culture. This response— slow and far from systematic—can be traced in training curricula and in standards for education and practice.

The goals, aspirations, and anxieties of a discipline are visible in the standards it creates to govern training and practice, and in an era when other professions—including medicine and nursing—were actively debating the role of technology in education (AAMC Institute for Improving Medical Education, 2007; National League for Nursing, 2008), social work demonstrated ambivalence about the incorporation of technology into professional training. The 2001 Educational Policy and Accreditation Standards (EPAS; Council of Social Work Education [CSWE], 2001) made minimal reference to emerging uses of technology. "Developing and applying instructional and practice-relevant technology" was listed as one of many possible goals that social work programs could include in their mission (EPAS AS 1.2), while administrators were encouraged to "pursue . . . exchanges with the practice community and program stakeholders . . . by developing and assessing new knowledge and technology" (EPAS AS 2.1; CSWE, 2001). The first standards to address technology directly, these included a single additional directive, specifying that programs must "have access to assistive technology" (EPAS AS 3.1.5).

This decade also saw the release of the first practice-focused standards guiding the use of technology in social work. The 2005 *Standards for Technology and Social Work Practice* (NASW, 2005), a collaboration between the National Association of Social Workers (NASW) and the Association of Social Work Boards (ASWB), recognized the growing use of technology among practitioners. These standards articulated the persistent, discipline-wide perception of technology as a threat to the relationships at the heart of social work, stating, "The potential for harm or abuse of vulnerable people can be increased because of the lack of a face-to-face relationship with the social worker" (Standard I, p. 7). An attempt to set forth protocols limiting potential harm to clients and to practitioners, the 2005 practice standards treat technology as a force disrupting recognized procedure with risk. They do not address the context of an evolving culture, changes in client expectations, or the ways in which technology could reconfigure social work's approach to creating change.

Three years later, the next generation of educational standards, the 2008 EPAS, failed to note the acceleration of technology—within or beyond the parameters of training. Revised to focus on the desired competencies to be demonstrated by professional social workers rather than on specific curricular input, these standards do not include any reference to the role of technology or to the responsibility of social workers to be aware of the ethical or effective use of technology with client systems. Even the most relevant of the 10 specified competencies—which requires social workers to "respond to contexts that shape practice" (EPAS EP 2.1.9)—makes no mention of the ICTs that were shaping social work education and practice or the larger social environment. Technology, in this iteration, is vague: The EPAS note that programs need to include in their content, goals, and context additional factors such as "new knowledge, technology, and ideas that may have a bearing on contemporary and future social work education and practice" (EPAS Educational Policy 1.2; CSWE, 2008). The only other explicit reference to technology echoes the standards of 5 years prior, requiring that each program describe "its access to assistive technology" (EPAS AS 3.5.6).

The most recent revisions to these two guiding documents—the 2015 EPAS and the recently published *Standards for Technology in Social Work Practice*—reflect significant development (CSWE, 2015; NASW et al., 2017). Educational standards have evolved to acknowledge the significance of technology in the lives of academics, social work professionals, and consumers by including it in the context of professional behavior and knowledge acquisition. These current standards present tech as an integral part of Competency 1: Demonstrate Ethical and Professional Behavior:

> Social workers also understand emerging forms of technology and the ethical use of technology in social work practice. Social workers . . . use technology ethically and appropriately to facilitate practice outcomes. (CSWE, 2015, p. 7)

The standards note that the "explicit curriculum, including field education, may include forms of technology as a component of the curriculum" (CSWE, 2015 p. 11), thereby documenting the recognition, by educational policy, of the extensive use of various forms of technology in social work education in the United States. Perhaps the clearest indication of this infusion of technology into social work is the note that even field education, a program considered unique to social work, "may integrate forms of technology as a component of the program" (Educational Policy 2.2; CSWE, 2015, p. 12).

The newly published *Standards for Technology in Social Work Practice* (NASW et al., 2017) open by acknowledging, "Technology has transformed the nature of social work practice and greatly expanded social workers' ability to assist people in need" (p. 7). While they reiterate the 2005 discussion of the complexity of jurisdiction, the dangers to confidentiality presented by technology, and the unreliability of information obtained online, these standards formally dismiss the idea that technology endangers practitioners and clients, stating, "These guidelines are not intended to suggest that the use of technology is inherently riskier or more problematic than other forms of social work" (p. 8). Though they address a context in which technology has yet to be fully integrated into service (continuing to describe the use of technology as a specialized practice context), the scope of these standards has expanded to include social media, how culture mediates technology, and the need to include questions about technology use in client assessment. This document acknowledges the degree to which technology pervades human interaction, describing the practice dilemmas that occur in a world where both clients and practitioners seek information, recreation, and community in virtual space, which may pose boundary issues, render information less impartial, and complicate professional interaction with colleagues.

Standards are a complex phenomenon, addressing the interface between actual conditions and the ideals of principle, poised between a catalog of present reality and the attempt to anticipate one that does not yet exist. The 2017 *Technology Standards* describe the particular difficulty of regulating the hyperdynamic phenomenon of technology use, noting their own impermanence: "As new forms of technology continue to emerge, the standards provided here should be adapted as needed" (p. 8). As the standards that guide social work continue to develop, we would advocate that future iterations be based on the assertion that the use of technology on behalf of clients has become a primary ethical obligation, and that those programs which train professionals must assemble curricula to prepare social workers to do this both "appropriately" and "ethically." We hope that as you encounter the examples of technology-enabled social work gathered in this volume—of mapping human need using data or GIS, of ICTs allowing clients to discover new forums for community and to construct new kinds of autonomy, and of mobile technology that can improve the interface between individuals and public services—you will think about how they support this conceptualization.

How Technology Can Help Us Move Toward Social Justice

Social work is framed by the imperative of social justice, or the ongoing project of working toward equitable distribution of resources and eradication of systemic disenfranchisement. Indeed, the technology-enabled interventions described in this book—when ethically and effectively deployed—are congruent with autonomy and justice. For example, as you will see, technology-enhanced practice can offer individuals the opportunity to create and control their own narratives and to participate in communities of their own choice and creation. Technology can engage and inspire hard-to-reach populations, offering access to evidence-based treatment and resources for remote clients. Technology can offer better predictions about areas of need and can model the best responses to crises at the individual or community level. It can manufacture awareness of social imperatives in an instant, broadcasting messages around the globe.

However, in order for technology to foster meaningful social change, access must be distributed equitably across populations. A developing body of literature documents the impediments to this distribution, including socioeconomic obstacles, the impediment of physical barriers in hardware or software, cultural bias in design, and lack of technological literacy (Kvasny, 2006; Vernon, Lewis, & Lynch, 2009; Hawkins & Oblinge, 2006; Krueger & Stineman, 2011; Kahn & Kellner, 2004). With this book, we intend to encourage social workers to consider technology as a social justice issue. As you read, ask yourself, Under what conditions can technology become the most powerful tool for the most people?

We do not suggest that social workers be required to learn to program in Linux or Python or even know what "open API" means (although we dare you to look it up). However, we believe that we are at a point of inflection at which new realities—such as the availability of supportive community and health information online, the emergence of public–private partnerships to provide benefits and entitlements, and the accelerating use of data for resource allocation—pressure the field of social work to rearticulate its mission and assert its value. With this imperative in mind, social workers must acquire the vocabulary and the skills to advocate for what the field—uniquely—can offer. As social workers, we possess capabilities that could enable us to act as translators and collaborators among programmers, policy makers, service users, and community members. We are trained to synthesize viewpoints, using a person-in-environment approach, and we are ideally positioned to introduce an ethical basis into the design of hardware and software initiatives that—without our input—may eventually only reify social inequalities. There is abundant evidence of the need for the ethical perspective that social work can provide: the failure of Google to diversify its workforce; Facebook's unwillingness to monitor hateful, violent posts; and the use of potentially discriminatory data-based algorithms by many courts to adjudicate justice. A major part of our new competence must be directed at claiming a place at the technology table—and fulfilling our responsibility to use it to ensure progress toward equality. Social work must inform the human–machine interface.

The How of Technology-Infused Social Work: Case Studies

Since the profession's inception, social work educators have used cases for teaching students about practice realities (Reynolds, 1942; Towle, 1956). There are many types of cases, ranging from brief, hypothetical vignettes to historical book-length accounts of complex situations (Evans & Evans, 2001). Traditionally, however, cases have most often been used to illustrate theoretical concepts or to depict practice situations and appropriate professional responses (Wolfer, Freeman, & Rhodes, 2001). Case method teaching is frequently recommended as a means for promoting critical thinking skills and better preparing students for professional practice by providing them with opportunities to exercise judgment and engage in decision-making. Rather than presenting information, case method teachers rely heavily on a variation of Socratic questioning to facilitate in-depth discussion of cases (Welty, 1989).

The term "case study" covers a wide range of problems posed for analysis, but most case studies are either based on real events or are a plausible construction of hypothetical events. They tell a story involving issues or conflicts that need to be resolved—although most do not have one obvious solution. The information contained in a case study may be complex (including charts, graphs, and relevant historical background materials) or simple (a human story that illustrates a difficult situation). Whether it is based on a real situation, a hypothetical situation, or a composite of the two, "a good case presents an interest-provoking issue and promotes empathy with the central characters" (Boehrer & Linsky, 1990, p. 45). Most cases take one of three basic forms: (1) appraisal or issues cases in which students are asked to identify the problem and then perhaps analyze it, (2) decision or dilemma cases that present problems or decisions to be made by the central character, or (3) accounts of events or situations that students are asked to dissect and discuss (Ramburuth, & Daniel, 2011).

What: The Cases

The locus of the cases in this volume, which are organized by micro, mezzo, and macro practice, is the United States, although the technologies are generally accessible worldwide. The cases will complement the content of most generalist practice textbooks at both the Bachelor of Social Work (BSW) and Masters of Social Work (MSW) foundation level, and specific chapters address populations and issues relevant across curricular areas (see Appendix C, for suggested links between chapters in this volume and specific chapters in popular generalist practice texts). Most provide examples of technology-enhanced social work using applications such as Tumblr, Second Life, and mobile apps that almost anyone can use and many already do. Several of these cases demonstrate how more complex technologies—such as geographic or management information systems—can be harnessed to make social work interventions more effective. Importantly, these cases show that the benefit offered by a technology does not correlate with its cost or complexity; easy-to-adapt technologies can be relevant and powerful tools of change. Social workers must, however, cultivate the skill of matching the technological tool to the task, which requires the use of long-established, non-technological processes, including needs assessment, goal setting, and cataloging of resources. Many of the cases in this book are arguments for a social work practice able to access a powerful hybrid of digital and analog skills. These examples suggest that, in the absence of real-world interaction and analog activity to support their use, digital tools stall.

Much of the debate about technology and social work has focused on the potential of ICTs to undermine the relationship, or the human interaction that is often described as the vehicle for change within social work. Importantly, then, many of these case studies illustrate how technology has enabled individuals to discover novel pathways to life-enhancing connection with others: facilitating the discovery of communities of affinity, virtual spaces that foster learning and development, and professional networks. Each chapter closes with a consideration of the ethical issues and social justice implications of the technology it describes, raising critical questions and making the connection between technology and the fundamental values of social work.

Chapter Summaries

THESE SUMMARIES OFFER A PREVIEW OF THE
CHAPTERS AHEAD

Chapter 2: Promoting Real Abilities in a Virtual World

Alice Krueger offers a compelling example of the power of virtual worlds to convey skills, to enable learning, and to offer opportunities for social interaction, focusing on persons with disabilities. The case features a young adult in his early 30s with Down syndrome who, after aging out of educational and supportive services, found opportunities to socialize and acquire new transferable skills in the immersive environment of Second Life.

Chapter 3: Where I Was and Where I Want to Go: Digital Music and Therapeutic Songwriting

Andrew Tepper, Lea Wolf, Chelsea Tussing, Emily Carter, Janice Derito, Michael Jaonsch, and Sofia Konvitz explore digital music—specifically collaborative songwriting using a computer as a tool of composition—as a modality for therapy with adolescents in a psychiatric hospital setting. This technology-enabled intervention incorporates the traditional elements of a therapeutic process—engagement, backward reflection, goal setting, and eventual termination—to explore family relationships, strategies for coping, and meaningful plans for the future.

Chapter 4: mDad: Helping Dads Be Better Parents with Mobile Phones

Shawna J. Lee, Tova B. Walsh, and Joyce Y. Lee discuss innovative technology-based approaches to reach, engage, and communicate with clients, focusing on mobile apps that help to initiate and sustain behavior change. The case study, which describes mDad, an app developed to deliver support and services to new fathers, shows how the ubiquitous and accessible app-enabled cell phone can engage a population that traditional parenting programs sometimes fail to reach.

Chapter 5: Online Support for Youth Transitioning from Foster Care to College and Adulthood

Lynette Kvasny, a former foster care youth, focuses on how social media can provide opportunities for these youth to seek and provide support as they transition to adulthood. Using the example of her own journey from foster care to college and a case study that describes how foster youths use Tumblr to locate information and community, Kvasny examines how peer interaction via social media can provide a new emotionally relevant and culturally appropriate resource to marginalized populations.

Chapter 6: Digital Storytelling: Tools, Techniques, and Traditions

Melanie Sage, Jonathan B. Singer, Andrea LaMarre, and Carla Rice show how digital tools—including audio, video, art, graphics, photographs, and words—can enrich storytelling, a primary human activity vital to the practice of social work. The case example describes young women in eating disorder recovery, making and sharing stories that explore individual identity, countering stereotypes associated with their diagnosis, and offering a complex narrative of what recovery means to them.

Chapter 7: Using Data to Improve Client Services

Using a universal example—a committed social worker whose work on behalf of a client is impeded by a lack of access to relevant information—Dale Fitch offers models for thinking about how integrated data management and case services systems can be designed to maximize access to information for all staff within a social service agency. He concludes by providing social workers some practical tools to improve the use of information systems in the human services.

Chapter 8: Getting Big Data to the Good Guys: The Promises and Challenges of San Francisco's Shared Youth Database

Public agencies increasingly look to share data, creating integrated systems that offer undeniable social benefit including higher productivity, improved services, better policy making, increased public safety, and evidence-based allocation of resources. However, data sharing poses ethical risks, including the loss of privacy and confidentiality, elision of informed consent, and reification of existing inequalities. In this chapter, Chris Kingsley, Stephen Goldsmith, Lauri Goldkind, and Lea Wolf describe the example of the Shared Youth database in San Francisco, examining the complexity and the potential of one city's data-driven effort to better serve youth at risk.

Chapter 9: The Use of Geographic Information Systems for Social Work Education, Research, and Practice

A technology that allows social workers to chart social problems in spatial terms, geographic information systems can be used to map phenomena such as poverty, food insecurity, or homelessness. Author Thomas Felke provides an example of how of one senior service coalition used GIS to inform the process of deciding on a location for a senior access center, describing the potential of this technology to empower advocacy and enhance planning in the context of social and human services.

Chapter 10: Social Media in Agency Settings

Around the globe and around the clock, people are engaged with social media. Their ubiquity has compelled many agencies to adopt social media without identifying goals, selecting an appropriate platform, or planning for evaluation. Authors Kimberly Grocher, Lea Wolf, and Lauri Goldkind address how social media platforms can serve distinct purposes for a nonprofit agency—including advocacy, fundraising, and education.

Chapter 11: Blogging: A Tool for Social Justice

Vu Le, Lea Wolf, and Lap Yan delve into the blog as a tool of interactive communication. Le, the author of a popular blog that meditates on (and often critiques) the nonprofit sector, discusses best practices for blogging and describes how to use a blog to mobilize people to real-world action.

Chapter 12: The Safety Net Gets Much Closer: m-Government and Mobile Benefits

The digitalization of the interface between citizens and government (often referred to as e-government) has emerged onto mobile platforms (mGov), prompting public agencies to implement electronic strategies that provide more effective service to citizens. Authors Abraham Lincoln Lee, Lauren Aaronson, and Lap Yan describe the case of a public–private partnership in New York City designed to streamline the application process for public benefits. The case documents how technology—here in the form of both a mobile-friendly website and a mobile app—can enable a more efficient and humane interface between government and those who depend on the services it can provide.

Chapter 13: #MacroSW: A Twitter Community of Personal Learning and Practice

Authors Laurel Iverson Hitchcock, Karen Zgoda, and Kristin Battista-Frazee address the growing numbers of online communities that are informing social work practice, focusing on #MacroSW, a collective that uses Twitter chats to create dialogue around issues relating to macro-level social work practice. The authors describe #MacroSW as one example of a virtual community that could be incorporated into a personalized learning network consisting of individually curated online resources that allow social workers to expand their professional networks, to encounter new topics and ways of thinking; and to connect to resources that challenge and enrich their practice.

ADDITIONAL TOOLS

This volume is designed to make it easy to incorporate meaningful technology content into courses across the social work curriculum. Tools for classroom use include assignments at the end of each chapter, as well as a chart of possible assignment types (Appendix A), designed to assist instructors in generating further exploration by students.

For ideas on how to incorporate content from this volume into the curriculum, Appendix C suggests links between chapters in this volume and specific chapters in popular generalist practice texts.

PART } I

Individuals

Promoting Real Abilities in a Virtual World

Alice Krueger

"One of the great things that any community can do is not teach tolerance, but live tolerance, not talk respect, but live inclusivity."
  —Michael Pritchard, *1949–present*

You sit down at your computer, click the icon on your desktop, enter your username and password, and log in. Immediately the sound of salsa pulses toward you from your neighbor's home. You glance through your living room window and see him dancing with a tall brunette in a violet dress. Turning slowly, you admire your newly acquired mahogany furniture atop a lush cranberry-hued Aubusson rug. You pull open the heavy oak front door and emerge to stride down your front walk between rows of colorful purple and white pansies. Another neighbor waves and calls out a cheerful greeting. You are distracted by the large black crow with beady yellow eyes sitting on her shoulder. Cawing merrily, the bird flaps into the bright sunlit sky, ignoring a descending cloud of azure butterflies lighting on the birdbath. A unicorn strolls down the street, dipping his horn to you in silent greeting, and you wave back. Welcome to the virtual world!

Background

As immersive incarnations of human imagination, virtual worlds offer unique opportunities for interaction, unencumbered by the limitations of the real world and presenting limitless possibilities for the practice of social work. A virtual world is a shared quasi-three-dimensional environment accessed via a computer screen. Like the physical world we inhabit, virtual world environments are experienced synchronously by their residents and are both persistent and mutable.

In *structured virtual worlds* such as World of Warcraft and EverQuest, which are created by game designers, users become immersed in goal-oriented fantasy and role-playing scenarios with "specific participatory agendas and payoffs" (Vernon, Lewis, & Lynch, 2009, p. 177). *Unstructured virtual worlds* are open environments that can be shaped by user choice and action; they offer numerous creative and economic opportunities to participants.

Although some use the terms interchangeably, "virtual worlds" differ from "virtual reality." Virtual worlds are complete universes created by technology; virtual reality is one type of technology that can be used to access and participate in these invented spaces. The hardware requirements for participation in a virtual world are basic. Unlike virtual reality, which requires specialized equipment that may be both complex and prohibitively expensive, entering a virtual world requires only a computer equipped with a decent graphics card.

Presence is a sense of being in the virtual environment, a perception of being physically present in a non-physical setting. *Immersion* is the perception of presence created by a particular technology. Readers become immersed in a good book, and viewers get immersed in movies. Persons active in virtual worlds become immersed in the virtual experience as the virtual world technology replaces physical world sights and sounds with virtual ones. Because immersion is a feature of technology, it is objective while presence is subjective (Mestre, 2005). Technological immersion factors have been shown to have a medium effect on the user's sense of presence in a virtual environment (Cummings & Bailenson, 2016). Furthermore, the sense of presence in a virtual world has been shown to affect users' emotional states (Shaw & Warf, 2009; Young, 2010).

The avatar is a digital artifact that embodies the virtual world participant (Taylor, 2002). Virtual world participants choose or create avatars to represent themselves inside the world. An avatar may be anything from realistically human to far-out fantastic (see Figure 2.1), and depending on the particular virtual world, the user may be able to change his or her avatar's appearance at will. Creating an avatar gives the user a personal sense of presence. The avatar conveys the user's presence to others (Benford, Greenhalgh, Rodden, & Pycock, 2001). Many virtual world participants choose avatars that enhance their physical appearance, making

FIGURE 2.1 Realistic human avatars and fantasy avatars in the virtual world Second Life.

themselves appear thinner, younger, and more muscular, for example. Avatars can be made to move through the virtual environment under the control of their users. The avatar is the feature that most readily distinguishes a virtual world from virtual reality (Schultze, 2010).

Through an avatar, a user can communicate with other avatars (more correctly, avatar operators) using text or speech and can interact with objects in the environment. Even when they are not photo-realistic, virtual world avatars and scenes are interpreted by most users as representational of the intended physical (or fantasy) world.

Institutions creating educational or service environments in virtual worlds such as Second Life invest heavily in development time. Because typical information technology departments are often unfamiliar with how to set up virtual environments, these institutions may need to hire development contractors familiar with creating venues and environments in virtual worlds. Additionally, there is a time investment for staff unfamiliar with teaching or counseling through an avatar to learn how to operate virtually, as well as the not-insignificant learning curve required to become competent in operating the avatar controls and capabilities.

Although there are international (World Wide Web Consortium, 2016) and in the United States, federally mandated accessibility standards for websites (US General Services Administration, 2017), there are currently no accessibility standards for virtual worlds, though a proposal was put forth in 2011 (Gelisen & Sivan).

Second Life

Established in 2003, Second Life is one of the oldest and largest virtual worlds. It is a product of Linden Lab (www.lindenlab.com), a for-profit technology company based in San Francisco, California. Second Life currently hosts approximately 900,000 active users monthly; these users access the virtual world from computers all around the globe.

User demographics can be difficult to discern; Linden Lab currently offers only economic statistics for Second Life. Demographic data are rarely collected on those signing up for social media or virtual world accounts, and often the data that do exist are proprietary. Pearce, Blackburn, and Symborski (2015) used a variety of non-virtual-world social media outlets to recruit members of virtual worlds to respond to a demographic survey. Their data show that among respondents most virtual world users were between 29 and 47, and there was a higher percentage of females than males. Virtual world users had a higher level of education than the general population. Respondents were mainly from the United States (although this could be due to the survey's recruitment process). Although virtual world use is often thought to be more popular among younger people, it was found to be both acceptable and feasible for older people in healthcare applications (Cook & Winkler, 2016). The average age of participants in Second Life (known as residents) is between 30 and 40, and the population is getting older (KZero, n.d.).

Because the content of the Second Life virtual world is user developed, and each user determines his or her own goals for being there, it is continuously evolving. Most residents do not consider Second Life to be a game. They may be in the world for a wide variety of reasons: to be creative, to attend college or informal classes, to receive technical training (e.g., to watch medical personnel model the mechanics of a particular treatment), to be playful (one Second Life resident described the world as a "mash-up of Barbies and Legos"), or to socialize. Institutions come into Second Life to do research, to educate, to provide services, and to establish brand presence.

Individuals can set up a Second Life account and access the world for free by downloading a user interface (viewer software) onto their desktop, and there is no limit on the time they can spend in-world. However, purchasing a higher level of membership allows users to own a small virtual house, to receive weekly game money, and to access expanded support and exclusive experiences. A virtual economy operates within Second Life, in which Linden dollars can be earned or purchased with real-world currency (Vernon et al., 2009). Virtual land can be purchased from Linden Lab or from in-world developers, or it may be rented from virtual landlords. Residents can purchase items in-world or through an on-line marketplace (https://marketplace.secondlife.com). It is also possible to earn money in-world. Games and contests are popular. Live musicians and DJs can earn tips, and employment opportunities include working in virtual retail stores, hosting events, teaching classes, and providing other services. Talented individuals can create virtual items for sale in-world or on the marketplace. The economy of Second Life was valued at about $US 60 million in 2015 (Charara, 2016).

Second Life is a public environment, open to everyone over the age of 16 who has a powerful enough computer to run the program. Sixteen- and 17-year-olds are restricted to G-rated (general) areas and cannot travel into or search for events in the moderate or adult areas, which may contain sexually explicit or intensely violent content or content that depicts illicit drug use.

Social Work and Virtual Worlds

The potential of virtual worlds to enable innovative social work practice is unlimited. Anstadt, Burnette, and Bradley (2011) suggest that virtual environments may offer a powerful solution to the persistent concern of access by diverse populations—to services, supportive community, and education. Virtual environments have been used for a range of purposes congruent with the values of social work: to provide immersive simulation of the experiences of schizophrenia and autism; to teach life skills to individuals with developmental delays; and to provide therapies to combat phobias, treat social anxiety, and lessen the symptoms of posttraumatic stress disorder (Levy et al., 2016; Reger et al., 2011; Standen & Cromby, 1995; Yuen et al., 2013).

For social workers, virtual worlds offer therapeutic venues, opportunities for research, and a tool for education and training. For two decades, virtual worlds have been used to enrich social work education and training; positive outcomes have been reported for more than a decade (Vernon et al., 2009). Social work students have been shown to benefit from coursework in the virtual world (Reinsmith-Jones, Kibbe, Crayton, & Campbell, 2015), for example, by acquiring interviewing skills (Tandy, Vernon, & Lynch, 2016) and developing cultural competency (Anstadt, Bruster, & Girimurugan, 2016). Virtual worlds offer social workers novel opportunities to conduct research, and researchers have conducted studies with participants in virtual worlds as subjects. For social work professionals who are working in virtual settings, Smyth (2015) offers suggestions that are guided by the same values that inform real-world practice, including following the *Code of Ethics* (NASW, 2008), establishing boundaries, respecting confidentiality, and establishing community. Zgoda's (2011) call to "go where the client is" means that social work professionals must begin venturing into virtual worlds.

A growing body of literature documents that Second Life offers a platform that can effectively deliver an array of meaningful experiences to users across every aspect of practice. Social work professionals have long been involved in Second Life, advancing education and research, delivering services, and offering informal support (for example, see https://njsmyth.wordpress.com/category/virtual-worlds). The Counselor Education in Second Life organization (http://sl.counseloreducation.org) has offered professional development in Second Life, including opportunities for continuing education units (CEUs). Social work professionals have presented at virtual conferences held in Second Life, and social work students have been shown to benefit from coursework in the virtual world (Reinsmith-Jones et al., 2015).

A range of providers, agencies, and advocates has established a presence in Second Life, and they continue to proliferate. Nonprofit organizations have virtual outposts; teaching hospitals offer information, coursework, and demonstrations; and schools of social work conduct lectures, discussions, and role-plays. Population-specific organizations and initiatives, including Virtual Ability (a nonprofit featured in the case study later), Alcoholics Anonymous, Brigadoon Explorers, and ADD/ADHD 2.0, can be found in Second Life (Vernon et al., 2009).

People with Disabilities and Virtual Worlds

Although there is a dearth of research on virtual worlds, preliminary literature reveals the effectiveness of telecommunication and computer simulation for certain clients in mental health and human services (Anstadt et al., 2011). Individuals with disabilities are active participants in virtual worlds, making creative use of their potential (Stewart, Hansen, & Carey, 2010). K. Smith (2010) writes that "virtual worlds serve as a form of augmented reality where users transcend physiological or cognitive challenges to great social and therapeutic benefit" (p. 2).

Long a significant constituency in Second Life, people with disabilities use the virtual world to seek information and support, to find entertainment, and to negotiate or confound stereotypical representations of their body or capacities (Stewart et al., 2010). Within Second Life, users can access referral and online counseling provided by in-world agencies, both volunteer and professional. People who experience a spectrum of stressors—associated with bereavement, cancer, depression, caretaker fatigue, bipolar disorder, or autism—can seek resources, consulting professionals or peers, or formal educational opportunities in-world (Lubas & De Leo, 2014; Parsons, 2008). For those whose disability isolates them, such as people with neuromuscular disorders, Second Life can become a primary conduit to social interaction (Krueger, in Vernon et al., 2009). In addition to unlimited opportunities for socialization, Second Life allows users to create their own avatars, importing their own 3D assets to populate and define a virtual universe. Literature describes powerful outcomes resulting from this engagement: Second Life communities, groups, and activities can augment self-worth and convey feelings of empowerment. Stewart and colleagues (2010) report that, for those with disabilities, "participation in virtual worlds enriches the overall quality of life . . . and may enhance their physical, emotional, and social adjustment." (p. 1).

Second Life is host to a variety of models for therapeutic work with people with disabilities. Preliminary research demonstrates the effectiveness of computer simulation with certain clients in mental health and human services (Anstadt, Bradley, Burnette, & Medley, 2013), and researchers describing such interventions believe that virtual worlds such as Second Life can provide therapeutic value equal to or greater than that of in-person therapeutic encounters (Kandalaft et al., 2013; Stein, 2007). Documented benefit includes improvements in both social and cognitive function. Role-playing has been demonstrated to enhance social work clients' socialization skills and emotional well-being (Anstadt et al., 2011). Virtual worlds have enabled individuals with high functioning autism to practice difficult or challenging social interactions in a less anxiety-producing environment than the real world (Didehbani, Allen, Kandalaft, Krawczyk, & Chapman, 2016). Brain scans of patients with chronic stroke and cerebral palsy who were treated in the virtual realm show changes in the reorganization of neural networks in the brain, along with better hand function and other skills (Gatica-Rojas & Mendez-Rebolledo, 2014).

People with certain kinds of impairments may have a more difficult time becoming functional in a virtual setting. There are four main impairment categories that affect participation in a virtual world:

- Inability to use a keyboard or mouse for computer input
- Inability to see or comprehend print/text information
- Inability to speak or hear
- Inability to learn, remember, concentrate, or understand new information

However, many people with disabilities use a wide range of assistive technology tools, such as alternative keyboards, screen magnifiers, voice input, transcription and translation tools, and screen readers, to overcome these obstacles (Kreuger, 2013). Some modification tools are built into the user interface. Many people with more severe physical and sensory disabilities access their computers with a wide variety of assistive technology devices. Some who are unable to use their hands for typing are toe typers. One uses a trackball operated with her foot. Some who cannot use their hands use eye gaze detection and an onscreen keyboard to type, while still others use voice recognition technology to type text and to direct the motions of their avatar. Some community members affected by paralysis control their Second Lives with movements of a single thumb, sip-and-puff switches, or a streaming alphabet onscreen whose letters are selected by purposefully bumping into a chair-mounted switch. Individuals with dyslexia use speech-to-text software to dictate text messages to deaf individuals. Blind users connect to a text-only version of Second Life and access information about their avatar's environment using their screen reading software (Krueger, 2013).

One problem not often seen in other forms of Internet-based communication is sensory discomfort or overload caused by the technology. This can range from vertigo when flying (which can be avoided by teleporting or walking to a destination) to overstimulation by colors, movements, text flow, or sounds. In some cases, viewer software preferences allow the user to modify the virtual environment (e.g., particle emissions or sound volume) and thereby remove or tone down the offending stimulation. If the environment cannot be modified, the user can leave that venue (often a dance club) and go somewhere else. For social workers or others setting up an intervention or research site in the virtual world, gathering input through a design process that includes future users would be helpful to avoid offending constructions (Wallace et al., 2010).

Krueger and Boellstorff (2015) noted differences in embodiment for persons with lifelong versus late-acquired physical disabilities within Second Life. In many cases, people who have had a physical disability all their lives view that disability as an essential part of their embodiment (see Figure 2.2). For instance, a person who has used a wheelchair for her whole life may feel most comfortable using an avatar with a wheelchair. Someone on the autism spectrum might not relate to his avatar until he used animations to give it tics.

Persons with disabilities acquired later in life may initially create avatar bodies as they remember their physical bodies. Such persons often say that their current physical embodiment is not how they envision themselves. Later they may create

FIGURE 2.2 Able-bodied and visibly disabled avatars.

more body-accurate avatars, sometimes to work toward accepting the changes to their own body or to explore social acceptance of their disability. Virtual embodiment can be a way to relate to memory, change, and the perception of disability by others (Krueger & Boellstorff, 2015).

VIRTUAL ABILITY

The work of Virtual Ability, Inc. (VAI), a Colorado-based 501(c)3 nonprofit that is committed to enabling people with a wide range of disabilities in a supportive environment (http://www.virtualability. org), is supported through consulting, research, and other projects undertaken with government agencies and universities. In 2009, Virtual Ability was awarded the first Linden Prize by Linden Lab, the creators of Second Life (Linden Lab, 2009), in recognition of its tangible impact on its members in their nonvirtual lives.

The founders of VAI began exploring the potential of virtual worlds as a supportive environment for housing a community of persons with disabilities. They found that people with disabilities are often socially isolated, sometimes even physically isolated, yet a sense of being part of a community is as important to them as to anyone else.

Virtual Ability has maintained an international cross-disability peer support community inside Second Life for almost 10 years. Members may have one or more types of disability: physical, mental, emotional, developmental, or sensory (deafness or blindness). Skilled mentors with similar disabilities have been recruited by VAI to help members learn to connect via assistive technology and function in the virtual world. People with particular accessibility issues often prefer to be guided by someone who uses the same assistive technology to reassure them that it is possible to interface with the novel environment. Greeters encourage newcomers to persist through the initial learning curve and explore virtual places and events they will enjoy. The Virtual Ability website explains its in-world presence as

> more than just a "virtual place." It is a true community, where individuals who physically live across the globe come together for conversation, learning, social activities, expeditions, and fun. Some take courses; others teach. Some mentor, others are mentored. Members create or build virtual architecture, write books or poetry, perform in plays, DJ, dance, play games, raise virtual gardens and virtual animals, or experience adventures of every type . . . all in a virtual world, from the comfort of their own computer. (Virtual Ability, 2017)

About a quarter of Virtual Ability's members are disability allies, including family members and friends of persons with disabilities, caregivers, researchers, and medical professionals.

The Virtual Ability community provides numerous types of support for its members. On its eponymous main island, a public new resident orientation course, designed using the principles of universal design and andragogy, is a frequent entry point for cohorts of university students as well as individuals with various assistive technology needs (see Figure 2.3).

The island was designed to maximize visual and experiential benefit for users with disabilities, including those using assistive technology. Early testing by individuals with disabilities yielded features including wide ramps usable by avatars in wheelchairs; bright, high-contrast signage for users with visual impairments; and flat, evenly landscaped walkways to accommodate users whose hand tremors would affect smoothness of motion. Training and education are available in time-limited increments in order to minimize fatigue. The island houses a large accessible auditorium for public events and two smaller classrooms (see Figure 2.4).

FIGURE 2.3 New Resident Orientation course.

FIGURE 2.4 Sojourner Auditorium, used for public events.

Any community member can seek information or assistance through the group chat function in Second Life. A community calendar lists various daily educational and entertainment activities. Members are encouraged to pursue their interests by joining and becoming active in other Second Life communities.

Virtual Ability's Healthinfo Island features a number of exhibits and displays that provide asynchronous information about various health and wellness topics. A fitness center with exercise equipment is open to the public. The Path of Support is lined with posters giving background information on the more than 120 groups that exist in Second Life to support individuals with a specific disability, including alcoholism, depression, or multiple sclerosis. Posters in the Research Pavilion encourage individuals to participate in institutional-review-board-approved research projects that will increase understanding about disability. Three residential islands owned by Virtual Ability offer virtual waterfront land for sale around a central public area. On Cape Able Island, an art gallery featuring works by artists with disabilities and the world's only authorized virtual "Deaf Chat" coffeehouse are found on public land. On Cape Serenity, a virtual public library offers only works by authors with disabilities. The intent of these public institutions is to showcase the accomplishments of people with disabilities.

Case Study

This case study provides one example of how virtual worlds can ignite and sustain the human potential for growth and change. Pseudonyms for persons in the physical world and their avatars in the virtual world are used throughout this chapter to protect their anonymity.

Ronald is a young adult in his early 30s who has Down syndrome. Families of children with Down syndrome may receive social work services in the hospital when the baby is born, including reassurance about his or her potential for a good quality of life, referral to existing community resources, and ideally direction toward Web-based communities and listservs offering peer support and relevant information. At the child's school the family may again receive social work services from an individualized education plan team member. However, it is rare for adults with Down syndrome or their families to receive social work services. In general, professional support for persons with Down syndrome and their families stops at adulthood, although the need for support related to skills of well-being continues throughout the individual's lifetime.

Ronald lives with both parents, who are supportive and nurturing. He was in public school special education classes until he turned 21. In school, it was determined that he would never be able to understand abstract concepts. However, with his parents' persistent encouragement, he learned to name many colors and a variety of domestic and zoo animals and to count reliably to three. Ronald has attained a lower-elementary skill level in literacy. He has also learned to type using a computer keyboard and to read simple words on the computer screen. His parents sit with him, interpreting any words he does not recognize on the screen.

Ronald has been employed for several years in a sheltered workshop, folding cardboard boxes for food products. He understands that a trouble ticket from work is a bad thing when given to him to take home, although he does not always understand why he receives them. He proudly brings home his paychecks for his parents to cash. At Christmas time, he spends some of his pay on "birthday presents for baby Jesus" (charitable donations through the family's church that his family helps him to make).

Ronald is over 6 feet tall and he weighs more than 200 pounds. His nose is flattened between broad cheeks, and he has a large tongue, making it difficult for him to speak intelligibly. He wears glasses with strong corrective lenses and bilateral hearing aids. He wears a perpetual smile until he accidentally does something wrong and feels confused by consequences he does not understand. Then he cries. His mother says he is like a "giant kindergartener."

Within his home, Ronald operates more or less independently. Working together consistently since he was very young, Ronald's parents have instilled rules, such as do not eat worms (when helping Dad with gardening) and do not lick the dog (when playing with the neighbor's pet). Posted notices around the home remind Ronald in words and pictures how to get dressed for the day and what to do after using the toilet.

Ronald enjoys being out in the community, making weekly visits to the library with his mother to choose simple picture books, often about animals, from the children's section. Grocery store trips are a highlight of his week, as he gets to choose some of the items to put into the grocery cart. The family has a large garden, where Ronald "helps" Dad with planting, weeding, and harvesting (with a lot of supervision). The family attends church every Sunday.

Ronald's appearance and behavior have led to active and passive shunning by members of his community. For instance, when he was hospitalized for surgery and then had to be at home for several months, nobody from church visited the family. When he fumbles an item in the grocery and drops it, managers often loudly insist that he be taken out of the store, although they would treat other customers less rudely. When the family goes to the beach, other families pointedly move their towels and beach chairs farther away from Ronald's family.

Six years ago, after hearing about Second Life from a family member, Ronald's parents created an account in the virtual world and made an avatar named Arthur. Though neither was familiar with virtual worlds, they were interested in investigating a possible social outlet for Ronald. Both had extremely limited experience with technology; only Ronald's father had an e-mail account. A Virtual Ability volunteer greeter met the new avatar as he entered the virtual world, welcoming Arthur and asking if he needed assistance. When Ronald's parents typed in-world that they had questions about the suitability of Second Life for their son with an intellectual disability, the greeter invited the author, as part of the executive team for the Virtual Ability community, to communicate with them and address their questions.

Ronald's mother was concerned about the unsavory reputation of virtual worlds. Both parents were concerned about confidentiality. They each spent significant time during the first few weeks using the Arthur avatar to chat by text with the author and others in the Virtual Ability community, gaining reassurance of their son's safety. They learned about safety features built into the user interface, such as the home button that allows an avatar to immediately retreat from any negative situation and return to a safe place. They read the terms of service and studied its assurances of personal data confidentiality and content areas designated general (G), mature (M), and adult (A). Virtual Ability's G-rated community standards coincided with their family values.

Ronald's parents began taking notes about what they learned to do in Second Life so that they would not forget all the new skills they were learning. They retain full control of Ronald's use of Second Life, because he cannot turn the computer on by himself, and they can turn it off at any point. They can take the keyboard and mouse away from him and move his avatar to a different location. They can interpret received text for him and translate his phonetic spelling for those to whom he types.

His parents posted a short description of Ronald's communication needs in his public profile to avert potential misunderstandings when he interacted with others in the virtual setting. They decided to tell those who met Ronald through his avatar that he had Down syndrome, that he could understand short typed sentences and would respond in text, and that he enjoyed animals and plants. They also said that, if there were any problems, they would be nearby in the physical world and available to assist Ronald.

When Ronald's parents felt reasonably comfortable that their son would be safe and that there were things he would enjoy doing in the virtual setting, they showed Arthur to Ronald, and demonstrated how to make him walk. They demonstrated how to type messages and how to click on images to make things happen (such as open doors, sit on benches, pet animals, or make fireworks shoot sparks).

Ronald quickly took over the computer and began operating the Arthur avatar. His enthusiastic use offered new challenges, and his parents immediately instituted a new rule: take turns. Otherwise they would not have a chance to use the keyboard. Now, every evening after supper, Ronald sits in front of the family computer and waits patiently for someone to turn it on for him.

Ronald soon became as independent in Second Life as he is in his home life. He knows how to water (virtual) flowers with a hose and play with (virtual) dogs, activities he enjoys at home. In Second Life he also gets to do things he is not allowed to do at home, such as mow the lawn and ride a bicycle. He knows how to change his avatar's clothing to match his activity. Arthur does not wear his church clothes when he is gardening, for example. Ronald would not consider dressing Arthur in his boots outfit to go to a dance, and Arthur wears his cowboy clothes only when riding a horse.

The family computer that Ronald uses does not have sound capabilities. He communicates with people whose avatars he recognizes by typing, often a string of single words either sequentially detailing his day's activities or describing what he is presently doing in Second Life. He seems to enjoy exploring the virtual world, particularly zoos, farms, and underwater areas with fish and whales. If he sees an avatar he does not recognize, he walks up to the avatar, types "hi do you type," and then waits for a positive response.

Ronald is a valued member of the Virtual Ability community in Second Life. Dozens of experienced community members have become friends and mentors within the virtual environment. They have learned about his interests and how to interpret his typing, and they are excited to interact, learning about his day or going exploring by his side.

Ronald has responsibilities within the community: he uses a hose to water the plants on Virtual Ability's islands and keeps the lawns mowed (virtually, of course). Early on, he was assigned a virtual apartment for which he chose décor that matches his interests (see Figure 2.5). The downstairs is planted as a garden. The upstairs is a menagerie with fish, birds, and a Cheerios-eating reindeer. He attends community dances and enjoys trying out the seating in the community's buildings.

Ronald has taken on a teaching role in Second Life, a social function rarely accessible to him in the physical world. After learning how to climb a tall tree, Ronald frequently shows newcomers how to do so. His mother marvels that he is teaching others skills he has mastered in Second Life. She reports that Ronald's receptive

FIGURE 2.5 Ronald's apartment.

and expressive vocabulary have both increased since he began interacting with other avatars regularly in Second Life.

Although the original intent of bringing Ronald into the virtual world was simply to provide social contacts, his parents soon realized that he could continue his education there. Zoo visits provide many learning opportunities. In addition to naming all the plants and animals and describing their colors and size, Ronald likes to count: "1 lion, 2 lion, 3 lion." Any larger number he calls "six," indicating too many to count. After much practice at virtual zoos, Ronald can now reliably count to four: "1 horse, 2 horse, 3 horse, 4 horse, six." Ronald's parents indicate that this enhanced ability to count has transferred to household chores, such as setting the table. He can now count out four plates, forks, and spoons.

In the virtual world, Ronald demonstrates and refines his agency. He expresses clear preferences as to how the avatar Arthur should appear. Given the opportunity to view his avatar as a miniature clown or an animal, he responds "no please" and quickly changes back to one of his human avatar selections. However, his avatar friends in Second Life include humanoids with blue or purple skin tones, a human-sized falcon, and dogs of various breeds. He accepts these nonhumanoid avatar friends, communicating with them by typing as he does with humanoid avatars.

Ronald blends physical world and virtual world interactions. If he is happy with a Second Life friend, he smiles and pats her head on the screen, leaving numerous fingerprints. He has lugged jack-o'-lanterns off the porch to show to his avatar friend on the screen. His mother barely restrained him from hauling the Christmas tree into the family room so the friend on-screen could admire it. When an avatar waves at Arthur, Ronald smiles and waves his hand back at the screen.

There is a physical world photograph of one of his Second Life friends on a large poster next to an image of her Second Life avatar. Ronald will sometimes stand in front of the image of his Second Life friend, typing a message. When it is time to go, he waves goodbye to the image on the virtual poster. Having never met this friend outside the virtual world, he ignores her physical world photograph.

Ronald is afraid of certain things in both worlds. At school, bullies were problematic. In Second Life, if he feels uncomfortable in a social situation, he knows how to teleport to a safe place with one click on the little house button at the top of the screen. Fires are frightening too. He has learned to call 911 if he sees a fire in his home or at work. However, a new rule became necessary when, after viewing a virtual bonfire in Second Life, he ran to his home phone to begin dialing. Mom stopped him just in time. She cannot imagine the local fire department's reaction if they pulled a hose from the fire truck into their family room only to be confronted by virtual flames.

Large avatars with sharp teeth are termed "monsters" in Ronald's vocabulary (see Figure 2.6). They clearly frighten him, and he moves his avatar behind foliage or buildings to peek out at them. If he is too frightened, he knows how to return to his safe home by clicking the little house icon on the user interface. He is trying to learn to be braver in Second Life. With his parents' encouragement, he tries to stay and look at the monster, sometimes changing his outfit to include a superhero cape.

Should the scary avatar happen to belong to one of his Second Life friends (who is unrecognizable to Ronald when appearing as a dragon or werewolf), he is encouraged to be braver and walk closer to the large avatar, which assumes a nonthreatening posture and stands very still. Those of his Second Life friends who appear as humanoid avatars will stand near the monster avatar, showing Ronald that there is no danger. This is an example of community problem-solving

FIGURE 2.6 "Monster" avatars in Second Life.

to support the growth of one community member in dealing with a source of discomfort.

Sometimes when Ronald and a friend are out exploring the virtual world, an unknown monster appears. Ronald will position himself between the monster and his friend and type "go" to tell his friend to meet him at the safe home spot. His parents say he exhibits a similar concern for the well-being of others in the physical world. This seems to indicate that he holds his Second Life relationships to be as real as those in the physical world and that he views his avatar as an extension of his physical self. This is part of the feeling of immersion experienced by virtual world participants.

One of the most promising results of Ronald's activities in Second Life illustrates the potential for transfer of skills acquired in a virtual world to the physical environment. Three years ago, Ronald's parents expressed concern that a change in bus schedule resulted in his being left off before work across a busy street from the workplace instead of in front of the door. They were worried about his crossing that street safely.

His Second Life friends, informed of these concerns, built a simulation of the street and his workplace, complete with moving vehicles (see Figure 2.7). One of his friends visited the simulated street every evening with him. With many repetitions, he was taught a four-part safety regimen: (1) stand at the edge of the sidewalk; (2) look carefully in both directions; (3) if you see anything moving, stop; and (4) if you do not see anything moving, go quickly across the street. Every time Ronald and his friends came to any street in Second Life during their frequent explorations, they acted out the four steps. After Ronald spent several months practicing street crossing almost every night in the virtual world, his parents

FIGURE 2.7 Virtual street scene with moving vehicles.

reported they were satisfied he was safe crossing from the bus stop to the entrance to his workplace. The skill, practiced and enforced in the virtual world, was now securely in his everyday skillset.

Ronald's use of the virtual world has been beneficial for his parents as well. They get to see their son interacting in ways that are impossible in their physical community. They have met parents of other adult children with developmental disabilities. This seems to have been particularly helpful for Ronald's father. He is now able to say to other dads at his workplace, "I have been horseback riding (or motorcycle riding, or scuba diving, or whatever the previous night's Second Life adventure involved) with my son." Ronald's growth in social skills and expressive vocabulary has strengthened his parents' resolve to continue their educational enrichment efforts.

Discussion

No comprehensive user data document the use of virtual worlds by persons with disabilities. Pearce and colleagues found in a 2015 demographic survey that the percentage of users of virtual worlds who self-report having a disability is higher than the nearly 15% of persons with disabilities in the general population. These data are almost identical to the results of an earlier study of players of online casual games (Information Solutions Group, 2008). This study indicated that in a computer environment somewhat similar to a virtual world, more than 20% of players are persons with disabilities. Additionally, persons with more severely limiting disabilities are overrepresented among gamers with disabilities (Information Solutions Group, 2008).

Ronald's story exemplifies some of the reasons why people with disabilities, including those with developmental disabilities, benefit from acting as avatars in a virtual world setting. They may have more agency in the virtual world than in the physical world. Social work professionals who intend to work with persons with disabilities should become familiar with virtual worlds. Not only are these places for education, support, and provision of structured interventions, but unstructured social interactions and community participation can be extremely beneficial to clients with some types of disabilities.

In fact, initial research by Loyola Marymount University (Gilbert, Murphy, Krueger, Ludwig, & Efron, 2013) surveyed persons with any kind of disability when they initially entered Second Life and then followed up with a repeat survey 3 months later. The measures in this study included several assessments of psychological well-being and adjustment. There was no treatment condition or stipulation for participation in the study; participants could do anything they wanted in the virtual world, spending as much or as little time online as they wished. The results of the study showed that persons with disabilities derived significant social and emotional benefits from being able to function as an avatar in a virtual setting. Depressive symptoms, trait anxiety, and loneliness decreased significantly, while measures of positive affect, life satisfaction, and self-esteem showed statistically significant increases. By removing stereotypes based on visually observable disabilities in the physical world, virtual worlds can provide a greater sense of social inclusion (Ford, 2001).

Stendal (2013) found that virtual worlds offer a variety of affordances for persons with lifelong disabilities in the areas of communication, mobility, personalization, social inclusion, personal development, and joint activity. Standen and Brown (2006) found that virtual worlds are a valuable tool for people with intellectual disabilities. Stendal, Balandin, and Molka-Danielsen (2011) contrasted novice and experienced users of Second Life, all with disabilities. They found that, while both groups experienced increased independence in leisure activities, social inclusion, and emotional well-being by participating in the virtual world, eight sessions were inadequate for the novice group to take full advantage of the affordances offered. It is notable that Stendal and colleagues' novice group was mainly composed of individuals with intellectual disability.

These findings and others corroborate anecdotal evidence from virtual world users and healthcare professionals of the numerous benefits to persons with disabilities of participation in virtual communities. As Ronald's case shows, persons with mild to moderate cognitive impairment are fully capable of using and enjoying a virtual world.

In general, the equipment needed to access the computer for any other use is adequate for working in Second Life. Costs for such equipment can be high, but may be covered by funding for education or employment use, such as through services of the state's department of vocational rehabilitation. Figure 2.8 shows adaptive equipment used to facilitate computer access.

Ethical Considerations

The social work *Code of Ethics* (NASW, 2008) applies to any environment in which social workers operate. Many ethical issues in the use of virtual worlds in social work are similar to those involved in using any Internet-based communication. Virtual worlds offer the opportunity for anonymous interaction, which can enable unethical conduct on the part of both social worker and client. Some researchers believe that the very nature of virtual worlds is deceptive (Pasquinelli, 2010). In the realm of social work this deception can change from playful to problematic in role-play. Acknowledged role-play, when both faux-counselor and faux-client are aware that the interaction is staged, is acceptable. However, one aspect of virtual worlds that is potentially dangerous for people seeking assistance with real problems and issues is that some fraudulent persons in the virtual world purport to be service providers although they are not trained or licensed.

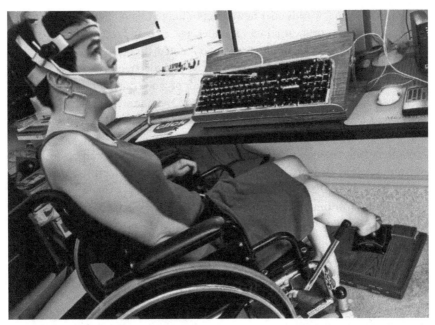

FIGURE 2.8 Assistive technology computer in use: a woman who types with a headwand and controls the mouse with a trackball under her foot.

Bullying exists equally in all worlds (Coyne, Chesney, Logan, & Madden, 2009). In the virtual world, bullying is known as *trolling* or *griefing*. The harmfulness of this negative behavior is exacerbated by the lack of text communication markers such as winks or smiles to indicate "just kidding." The victim does not know if the person making the mean-sounding statement is teasing or harassing. The perpetrator cannot immediately see the visceral reaction of the recipient of his or her message. Thus, teasing and joking in a virtual world must be done carefully and with clear intent to make it readily distinguishable from bullying. Social workers must be cautious in their use of humor in virtual settings.

Internet socialization encourages self-disclosure, which can lead to the well-known issues of financial loss, identity theft, and emotional distress. As social relationships form in virtual settings, participants may project idealized qualities onto the social partner. Bargh, McKenna, and Fitzsimmons (2002) recommend moving relationships forward in small steps and ensuring that such relationships are "founded on shared interests, goals, and values."

Any research conducted in a virtual world setting, including student research, must be supervised by an institutional review board to ensure ethical treatment of virtual research subjects, as they are in actuality human subjects (Grimes, Fleischmann, & Jaeger, 2010). When conducting research in a virtual world, especially when the research subjects are persons with disabilities, HIPAA requirements (US Department of Health and Human Services, 2016) for keeping personal health information private may apply, even if the information is provided by consent.

Typically, virtual worlds offer newcomers a limited set of premade avatars that do not reflect real-world variations in gender, age, race, and culture. Until recently, Williams, Martins, Consalvo, and Ivory (2009) noted, the default avatars in Second Life were all white, young, and Western. None of the current default avatars has a marker of visible disability such as a wheelchair or white cane. Although advanced users can learn to modify their avatars to make them more realistic, newcomers might find it helpful to be able to select a character appearance that is "more like me."

Avatars lack the body language and facial expressions common to human communication. Hearing people not on the autism spectrum do not usually realize how much they rely on body language and facial expressions for comprehension in ordinary communication. We acknowledge the lack of these comprehension aids when we communicate in text, inserting emoticons/emojis to explain the intent behind the typed words. For social workers, counselors, educators, and others who rely on interpreting subtle body signals to understand the intent, veracity, and meaning of words, virtual world text communications may prove inadequate.

Since virtual worlds are computer based and necessitate adequate Internet bandwidth to function well, access to virtual worlds is a digital divide issue and thus an ethical concern.

Neither advanced and emerging technologies (Wolf & Goldkind, 2016) nor disability studies (Bean & Kreck, 2012) are presently adequately represented in social work curricula for licensure. Lipschutz (2011) points out areas of the NASW *Code of Ethics* and *Standards for Cultural Competence* that should apply to working with persons with disabilities. These basic competency needs must be addressed before the profession can use venues such as virtual worlds to provide services to people with disabilities.

Social Justice Implications

In the case study, the virtual world is providing Ronald access to opportunities from which he would otherwise be excluded: He has the chance to continue to learn past the age of 25, beyond which age services typically do not exist, and he has daily access both to socialization and to activities that promote intellectual growth. Intentional or unintentional ableism, which fails to consider the interests of persons with disabilities (Connor & Gable, 2010; Hamre, Oyler, & Bejoian, 2006), may exist within the virtual world at the individual level (for instance, excluding a person who is a slow typist from a role-play community), institutional level (refusing to build accessibility tools into the virtual world), or cultural level (providing only able-bodied default avatars).

Social prejudices against individuals with disabilities in the physical world can limit their access to virtual worlds. Examples include caregivers denying an individual the assistive technology necessary to access a computer, officials creating policies that restrict access to online games for residents of care facilities, or virtual world developers believing that blind people would not be interested in virtual worlds because they are inherently visual environments.

As in the physical world, readily distinguished subgroups exist in virtual worlds, which engenders the potential for discrimination (Axelsson, 2002). Particularly widespread in virtual worlds is disdain for those appearing to be new or to lack basic virtual world competencies (Boostrom, 2008). This may exacerbate interaction issues due to disabilities that cause slow cognitive processing, slow typing, or slow reactions. Deaf people are still shut out of voiced conversations in virtual worlds unless someone is willing to transcribe into text what is said. As Carr (2009) writes, "online worlds and their various communities do demonstrate in new, clear ways, just how pervasive inequitable practices and discourses can be, and how difficult it can be to articulate and hence resist the power relations that are embedded within, and disseminated by, these same practices." Discrimination exists in all worlds.

For many virtual world participants, the borderline between the real world and the virtual world is not always distinct (Jakobsson, 1999). Many view the virtual world as an extension of their real life, not supplanting it but supplementing it. It is equally important to understand that, although an avatar is not a person, it represents one (Schiano & White, 1998).

Stendal (2013) notes that while virtual worlds enhance functioning for some persons with lifelong disabilities through positive affordances, the same features may present barriers to those with other disabilities. Second Life as originally created offered only text communication and became quite popular for deaf individuals. When voice capability was added in 2007, deaf individuals once again became as disadvantaged as they were in the physical world. However, voice capability enhanced the experience of individuals who had difficulty communicating in text due to upper extremity disabilities or dyslexia.

For people with disabilities, virtual worlds can be places for creativity, community, support, and activism (Krueger & Boellstorff, 2015). If virtual worlds are deemed to enhance the quality of life of persons with disabilities, access will become a social justice issue. Increasing the accessibility of virtual world software will become significant, and perhaps accessibility standards will be created for virtual worlds (Krueger & Stineman, 2011; Kruger & von Zigl, 2015). Persons with disabilities are less likely than those without disabilities to use the Internet (54% vs. 81%), and 2% have disabilities that make it extremely difficult to go online at all (Zickuhr & Smith, 2012). Only 41% of persons with a disability have broadband access compared to 69% of those without a disability.

Persons with disabilities who are denied access to virtual worlds for whatever reason and by whatever means will then have justification for demands for equal virtual opportunities. Additionally, lack of availability of social workers and other helping professionals familiar with virtual worlds and able to assist persons with disabilities and their caregivers in accessing and participating in them creates an additional element of inaccessibility and a further social injustice.

Questions for Discussion

1. Avatar Arthur's name and appearance in the virtual world differ greatly from those of Ronald in the physical world. Do you think Ronald recognizes his avatar as himself, or is his avatar simply another item in his environment over which he exerts control?
2. Since Ronald can recognize his friends' avatars despite clothing changes, yet does not read the names displayed above their heads, what features of the avatar might he be relying on for visual recognition?
3. Does Ronald appear to be able to distinguish between animate and inanimate objects equally well and in the same manner in the physical and virtual worlds?
4. What types of knowledge and skills learned in virtual world settings transfer most readily to the physical world?
5. What level of realism in a virtual world is needed to enable user immersion? Is this level of realism different for avatars and the perceived physical environment?
6. What are some effective ways to use virtual worlds in social work?
7. What user skills are necessary, particularly for persons with disabilities, to enable appropriate and effective use of virtual worlds in social work? What provider skills are necessary?

Additional Readings

Benford, S., Bowers, J., Fahlen, L. E., Greenhalgh, C., & Snowden, D. (1995). *User embodiment in collaborative virtual environments*. Retrieved July 1, 2016, from http://www.sigchi.org/chi95/proceedings/papers/sdb_bdy.htm

Burden, D. (2014). *5 key differences between virtual worlds and virtual reality*. Retrieved July 1, 2016, from http://www.hypergridbusiness.com/2014/08/5-key-differences-between-virtual-worlds-and-virtual-reality/

Damer, B. (2008). Meeting in the ether: A brief history of virtual worlds as a medium for user-created events. Artifact, 2(2), 94–107.

Dunn, D. S., & Andrews, E. E. (2015). Person-first and identity-first language: Developing psychologists' cultural competence using disability language. *American Psychologist, 70*, 255–264.

Madary, M., & Metzinger, T. K. (2016) Real virtuality: A code of ethical conduct. Recommendations for good scientific practice and the consumers of VR-technology. *Frontiers in Robotics and AI, 1*(3), 1–3

O'Toole, C. J. (2013). Disclosing our relationships to disabilities: An invitation for disability studies scholars. *Disability Studies Quarterly, 33*(2), 5–10.

Parrish, J. (2010). PAPA knows best: Principles for the ethical sharing of information on social networking sites. *Ethics and Information Technology, 12,* 187–193.

Søraker, J. H. (2010). *The value of virtual worlds: A philosophical analysis of virtual worlds and their potential impact on well-being.* PhD thesis, University of Twente, Netherlands. Ipskamp: Enschede.

Virtual Ability, Inc. (2016). *Testimonials.* Retrieved July 1, 2016, from http://www.virtualability.org/friends-and-family/

3 }

Where I Was and Where I Want to Go

DIGITAL MUSIC AND THERAPEUTIC SONGWRITING

Andrew Tepper, Lea Wolf, Chelsea Tussing,
Emily Carter, Janice Derito, Michael Jaonsch,
and Sofia Konvitz

"One good thing about music, when it hits you, you feel no pain."
—Bob Marley, *1945–1981*

Music—or the human urge to express feeling using rhythm and tone—pervades every culture and all history. Music is a tool to affirm individual identity and enact collective meaning. Our personal histories are encoded by music. From the moment they are born, babies identify music specific to their tradition and culture; adolescents affirm and display their emerging identities through musical choice; and until the end of life, adults report the power of music to evoke specific emotions, events, and sensations (Levitin & Tirovolas, 2009). Within the brain, music literally encodes experience: The mechanics of auditory processing are physically linked to the brain's ability to create memory (Schlaug, 2009). Music establishes primal recognition, manufacturing wordless connection with others who hear the same sounds. Pitch and tempo convey feeling across cultures, allowing us to recognize the emotional intention of others (Loewy, 2011).

The advent of ever more precise forms of measurement and brain-imaging technologies has revealed music's effects on the engines of our biology. In the brain, exposure to and engagement with music exercises attentional networks and executive function, excites the areas associated with emotional response, and stimulates the central nervous system (Schlaug, 2009).

Medically, music has long been recognized as a potent tool of rehabilitation, and increasingly powerful imaging technology is illustrating that music can provide an alternative entry point into a "broken" brain system and "fix" impaired neural processes or neural connections. This cerebral reconstruction offers clinical benefits to individuals with impairments in motor function, language, cognition, or sensory processing and to those who experience emotional disturbances as a result of brain injury. Music has been used successfully to induce cognitive repair in patients with stroke, Parkinson's disease, cerebral palsy, or traumatic brain injury. It can affect those physical processes that can be linked to emotional state, lowering cortisol levels, regulating heartbeat, and decreasing the perception of pain (Wolf & Wolf, 2011). In individuals with autism spectrum disorder and psychopathologies, literature documents positive outcomes for music-mediated therapeutic interventions (Hendricks, Robinson, Bradley, & Davis, 1999; Gold, Wigram, & Elefant, 2006).

In this chapter, we explore the power of music—specifically collaborative songwriting using a computer as a tool of composition—as a modality for therapy with adolescents. Both anecdotal report and emerging science confirm that music is central to adolescent life as a means to affiliate with peers, to negotiate an individual identity, and to regulate emotional states (Gold et al., 2006; Field et al., 1998; Lefevre, 2004; Olson-McBride & Page, 2012). Many qualitative studies and a few quantitative studies document that music-based intervention can foster positive gains in therapeutic programs for adolescents. As technology makes the tools for music composition more accessible, even to nonmusicians, this type of intervention can be used more broadly and benefit more people. The case study presented in this chapter describes how a social worker in a psychiatric hospital setting used the process of songwriting with a teenaged client to create a therapeutic alliance, to explore family relationships, and to make meaningful plans for the future.

Background: Computers for Music Composition

Audio input that has been transformed into a digital signal can be used to create, manipulate, and record sound. Digital music creation originated in the 1940s with magnetic audio tape, a technology that allowed musicians to record sounds and then modify them manually by changing the tape speed or direction (Vaughn, 2014). The transition to a computer-based production process dates to the 1960s, when increasing computational power enabled basic digital music-making (Burg, Romney, & Schwartz, 2016). The earliest music software ran on hulking computers housed at universities, including Stanford and Penn State (Fildes, 2008). Electronic music-making became popular for home use in the 1990s, as the hardware and software required for composition became more accessible and interfaces required less specialized knowledge (Bell, 2014).

Currently, most electronic music is composed at a digital audio workstation (DAW), a compilation of technological tools that allows users to record, edit, and produce sound and music (Walzer, 2016). Configurations vary from a single software program loaded onto a personal laptop computer to a dedicated unit or even a highly complex configuration of numerous components controlled by a central computer. Typically, a computer-based DAW comprises three pieces of hardware—a computer, a sound card, and at least one input device for adding or modifying data—plus at least one form of digital music production software. A microphone and audio speakers are also required if they are not built into the computer (Burg et al., 2016). The cost of acquiring a DAW can vary depending on the software and equipment incorporated and the needs of the user (Kuzmich, 2014).

In the early 21st century, a variety of digital music production software became available with a plethora of features, allowing consumers to personalize their music-production experience and to create music that sounds professionally produced. Recent digital music-production platforms include GarageBand, Sonar's Cakewalk, JavaFX8, LogicPro X, AVID's Pro Tools, and Logic Pro (Vaughn, 2014).

GarageBand, the software described in the case study that follows, is a digital multitrack recording application routinely used to produce professional-sounding music in a home setting, to create podcasts, and even to score movies (Howard, 2009). GarageBand provides a simple interface that allows a user to assemble and layer musical components. These musical ingredients can be created from an uploaded recording of a musician playing live or they can be selected from the program's extensive collection of prerecorded, loopable clips of drums, bass lines, guitar riffs, keyboards, and more. Loop-based programs such as GarageBand are user friendly and therefore less challenging for youth or first-time users. They are designed so that loops adjust to fit a user's selection of tempo and key, using automation to simplify the work of composition (Howard, 2009). In addition to recording features, GarageBand has various editing capabilities that allow users to individualize their music production experience, including special processing effects such as familiar sounds (such as a dog's bark) run backward, as well as the capacity to stretch and to otherwise distort sounds This musical output can be saved and shared; it can be burned to CD, e-mailed, or uploaded to the Internet.

GarageBand was developed for Apple by Gerhard Lengeling (Apple, Inc., 2017b; Future Music, 2011). Apple sought to create a simple, consumer-level music-recording and -editing program to ship with all Mac computers. First announced by Steve Jobs in 2004, GarageBand 1 was quickly followed by versions with upgraded features such as the ability to view music and make edits in musical notation and to integrate with iChat, which facilitated the software's use for podcasting. GarageBand is still preinstalled on Apple computers, which range in cost from approximately $1,000 to $2,400 for a laptop or desktop (Apple, Inc., 2017a), and the company continuously updates the software, fixing bugs and adding features. In 2011, Apple released a version of GarageBand for the iPad, iPhone, and iPad touch—making it even more accessible to consumers.

ADOLESCENTS AND TECHNOLOGY

For social workers who work with children and adolescents, acknowledging the role of technology in the lives of these digital natives is increasingly critical to effective practice. Access to and usage of technology have exploded in recent years, and many researchers have documented that youth are quicker than adults to adopt new technologies (Rainie, 2017). Madden and colleagues reported that, in 2013, 95% of US youth from age 12 to 17 were online, with their Internet usage facilitated by the potential of cell-phone access. Two years later, in 2015, Lenhart and colleagues reported that 73% of teenagers between the ages of 13 and 17 had access to a smartphone and 58% had access to a tablet.

Children and adolescents respond to technology-enhanced social work across a variety of technologies, treatment goals, and interventions. Studies have demonstrated statistically significant results for therapeutic interventions that use video conferencing, Internet skill-building modules, psychoeducation, and apps that direct self-care (Lightfoot, Comulada, & Stover, 2007; Muller, Roder, & Fingerle, 2014; Nelson, Barnard, & Cain, 2003; Nicholas et al., 2012; Pacifici, White, Cummings, & Nelson, 2005; Patten et al., 2006). Technology has shown utility with children from a variety of subpopulations and has proven to aid in the development of communication and social skills. Technology is often used as a "sticky" means to engage children and adolescents in educational programs, teaching adolescents the consequences of risky behavior, educating seriously ill children about the symptoms of disease and strategies to lower symptoms (Boydell et al., 2014; Cihak, Fahrenkrog, Ayre, & Smith, 2010; Danielson et al., 2013; Fernandez-Lopez, Rodriguez-Fortiz, Rodriguez-Almendros, & Martinez-Segura, 2013).

ADOLESCENTS AND MUSIC

Adolescence is second only to infancy in the rate and scope of developmental changes that take place (Department of Health and Human Services, n.d.). Between the ages of 10 and 19, young people experience acceleration in growth, development of primary and secondary sex characteristics, changes in body composition, and changes to the circulatory and respiratory systems (Steinberg & Silk, 2002). Brain images taken during this developmental window reveal that the prefrontal cortex (the area associated with judgment and self-awareness) is slower to evolve than are those regions that control emotion, desire, and action (Dahl, in Gopnik, 2012). Side by side comparisons of these distinct brain regions show that the two systems grow and develop asynchronously and independently from one another. The first, which includes those neural areas that govern emotional processing and sensitivity to reward, is acutely heightened during adolescence. The second, made up of those areas related to the ability to exert self-control and regulate impulse, matures slowly over time into young adulthood. As a result, while adolescents may be able to exhibit adult levels of intellectual capability, their levels of impulse control and self-regulation remain immature (Reyna & Farley, 2006). Thus, there is a "biologically-driven imbalance" that can foster the risky behavior and emotional reactivity typical of adolescence (Casey, Jones, & Hare, 2008, p. 112).

Music is vital to adolescents (North, Hargreaves, & O'Neill, 2000). Teenagers engage with music constantly, listening to, creating, or watching music between 4 and 5 hours a day—more than they spend watching television or hanging out with friends outside of school—according to a 2009 study by the American Academy of Pediatrics. Young people recite and dream lyrics, find transport and heartbreak in melody, and improvise riffs, bass lines, and beats collected through obsessive listening. The adolescent brain is highly plastic, especially in those regions sensitive to music and emotion, and it encodes lyrics and melodies, along with the emotional and social significance of music (Giedd et al., 1999). Because of this cerebral engraving, the soundtrack of adolescence runs in our brains for as long as we live. At 80 we remember the music from our teenage years more accurately and with greater emotion than the sounds from any other decade of our lives. Adolescents are intuitively aware that music can articulate and regulate how they feel, and they make purposeful use of music to assume control of their emotional state or mood (Saarikallio, 2007).

MUSIC-BASED THERAPEUTIC INTERVENTION FOR ADOLESCENT POPULATIONS

Adolescents listen to and make music with such constant commitment that some social scientists have argued that musical engagement is among the most reliable diagnostics of the onset of adolescence (Christenson & Roberts, 1998). Adolescents' self-initiated and increasingly intense exposure to music occurs during a period in which they experience (and need to resolve) a long list of developmental tasks, transitions, and dilemmas (Miranda & Claes, 2009). Adolescents are biologically prone to pursue risk, and art-based programs can offer critical learning opportunities (Ezell & Levy, 2003) in which risks that are positive, life-affirming, and safe provide the rush of success linked with purposeful activity (Hughes & McLewin, 2005). Importantly, because participation in this kind of activity or intervention is not limited by educational attainment or mental health need, these programs are an opportunity to escape from prior or recurrent experiences with failure and exclusion (Ecotec Research and Consulting, 2005). In terms of clinical practice, McFerran (2010) suggests that music therapies can answer the developmental needs of adolescents by offering them positive capacity to form identity and to cultivate resilience, connectedness, and competence.

Music is used to engage youth in a variety of therapeutic settings. Literature documents music's power to calm and lower stress levels, to enhance brain function, and to stimulate development in children of every age: from birth (music has been used successfully to regulate heart rate in premature babies and neonates) to adolescence and young adulthood (Wolf & Wolf, 2011). Generalizations are problematic, because music-based interventions vary greatly. While some are designed according to the principles of music-therapy—a discipline in its own right—others are programs in which therapists use music in programs of idiosyncratic design.

Clients, implementing professionals, families of clients, and facility staff are generally enthusiastic about music-based interventions, but their effects can be difficult to quantify. A majority of published studies address adult populations, and most studies have small sample sizes. Many evoke music's effects with qualitative description, and nearly all conclude that more research is needed.

Music-based therapeutic interventions in adolescent populations, though sparsely documented by quantitative evidence, are supported by biological science. In 1998, Field and colleagues documented that depressed adolescents listening to music experienced a significant decrease in stress hormone cortisol levels, and most shifted toward types of brain activation associated with positive affect. Gold, Wigram, and Elefant's (2006) meta-review of three randomized controlled trials of short-term music interventions performed with children and adolescents diagnosed with autism spectrum disorder found significant positive effects on verbal and gestural communication skills. In a randomized controlled study of music-based intervention with this population, family-centered music therapy showed a significant effect on social engagement abilities (Thompson, McFerran, & Gold, 2014). A 2004 meta-analysis of 11 studies including a total of 188 subjects reported that music therapy had a medium to large effect on clinically relevant outcomes among children and adolescents with psychopathology (Gold et al.). In a study of the use of music therapy techniques in group treatment of adolescent depression, Hendricks and colleagues (1999) documented a significant difference ($p < .0001$) between groups that used music therapy techniques and groups that did not. Results indicated that the use of these techniques was positively correlated with reduced posttest depression scores and increased posttest self-concept scores for adolescents enrolled in middle and high school.

The implementation of therapy using music as a modality can present challenges, however. In their study of music therapy to promote prosocial behaviors in aggressive adolescent boys, Rickson and Watkins (2003) detected no definite treatment effects, but highlighted outcomes suggesting that therapeutic music-making can enhance autonomy and creativity, which may help adolescents to interact more appropriately with others in a residential setting. However, the authors caution that such a program "might also lead to a temporary mild increase in disruptive behavior" (p. 283).

THERAPEUTIC SONGWRITING

Youth have moved rapidly to use technology tools for creating music via digital software. Writing their own songs offers adolescents the opportunity to express themselves through music via technology, potentially reducing resistance to therapeutic alliance (Olson-McBride & Page, 2012). In a survey of 477 professional music therapists practicing in 29 countries, Baker and colleagues (Baker, Wigram, Stott, & McFerran, 2008) identified the most common goals of therapeutic songwriting, finding many that line up in important ways with the needs of an adolescent client population:

a) experiencing mastery, developing self-confidence, and enhancing self-esteem;
b) making choices and decisions;
c) developing a sense of self;
d) externalizing thoughts, fantasies, and emotions;
e) telling the client's story;
f) gaining insight or clarifying thoughts and feelings. (p. 105)

In a randomized control study of 60 adolescents being treated for chemical dependency, participants in a songwriting activity experienced a positive effect on perceived locus of control and attitude toward self and recovery compared to participants assigned to other forms of intervention. Qualitative literature additionally documents positive outcomes for songwriting programs for adolescents with a diagnosis of anorexia nervosa (McFerran, Baker, Patton, & Sawyer, 2006), bereaved adolescents (Dalton & Krout, 2005), young people in hospice care (McFerran & Sheridan, 2004), and adolescents in secure juvenile detention (Baker & Homan, 2007).

Case Study

The following fictional case study takes place in a private psychiatric hospital near a major metropolitan area in the Northeastern United States, and it describes the potential of electronic music as a tool for therapeutic interaction. This case study shows an adolescent patient working with a single therapist in a resource-rich music studio, a treatment scenario that may be unavailable in many locales. Therefore, it is important to note that effective art and music-based interaction can happen with groups, in empty rooms, and without recording equipment. However, trained professional facilitators (therapists or musicians), working instruments, and the ability to record creative work are effective incentives to engaging a skeptical or musically inexperienced treatment population (S. Lee, personal communication, 2017).

The hospital in which the case study takes place provides acute care to patients of all ages, most of whom arrive in crisis. The patient population is socioeconomically and racially diverse, comprising some lower-income patients who live in the nearby urban areas and some middle-class patients who arrive from surrounding suburbs. The length of stay is decreasing, from an average of 2 weeks to about 10 days. The majority of the patients who use the music program are involuntary admissions, brought to the hospital by parents or referred by a school or group home. Their arrival is often precipitated by a major life event: an episode of dangerous behavior, a romantic breakup, an attempt to run away, or a spate of aggression. All arrive at the hospital with the goal of stabilizing their mental health.

Adam Treadwell, the fictional therapist, is a social worker in his 10th year of work at a private psychiatric hospital. A music lover who trained in theater before obtaining his MSW, he has an innate ease with patients and a roster of skills to draw on in his interaction with patients. His ability to be authentic is critical to his success with adolescent clients; he cites his drama training as the origin of acute observation and listening skills that allow him to tailor each session to the needs and capacities of each individual. Adam listens to a lot of music, and his knowledge of contemporary music including rap, pop, and heavy metal allows him to quickly connect with his patients and lock into the conventions of genre when writing songs with them. His study of lyrics allows him to discover deep and honest expression, which he can introduce in a clinical context, using it to prompt interaction and reflection. For example, Adam cites the lyrics to L'il Wayne's "Drop the World," elucidating themes of alienation, depression, and even suicide. He describes these lyrics as the basis of a concrete therapeutic opportunity to employ with adolescents who are attempting to make sense of their own overwhelming emotions.

Adam is sitting in a music studio that he has created in order to work with patients—a medium-sized room filled by a cluster of computer workstations staggered around a recording booth. He looks up from his computer and sees a skinny African American teenager leaning against the doorway. The teenager asks,

> "Hey, are you the music guy?"
> "Yeah," replies Adam, "I am. What's your name?"
> "I'm Travis."

Treadwell starts his work with patients when they arrive at the music room. He engages them without knowing their clinical history, developing a relationship in the moment, based on careful listening and on staying alert to the dynamics of their interaction:

> "Hey, Travis. Yeah, this is the music room. I'm Adam. Are you into music?"
> "Yeah, uh, I rap a little. I make some beats. I came down here to play some basketball. But I, I wanted to come check this out [Travis trails off]."
> "You want to come in and do some music? You can listen to music or you can make your own. I do therapy, but with music."
> "What does that mean?"
> "Well, it means that, if we do a song, we have a conversation to see what you want to write about. We use the computer to make some music and you write some lyrics, and you record your song in there. [Adam indicates the recording booth]. Then we turn that into a CD that you can take with you."
> "Hey, uh, yeah. Let me tell the guys I'm not gonna play and I'll be right back."

Adam Treadwell makes music with patients who range in age from 7 to adult. He recognizes that music is already important to many patients as a proxy to experience or to express emotion; a social space to inhabit with peers; or a private zone, an accessible and immediate time-out from stressors. Use of the music room is voluntary, and the patient chooses what to do in that space. Some patients choose to write songs with Treadwell (sometimes producing up to 5 songs over the course of a 10-day stay); others choose less interactive options, using the space to take a break from their treatment by playing one of the instruments Treadwell has collected or by listening to music on headphones.

Treadwell is upfront with patients about the therapeutic intent behind the facilitated songwriting he offers. When Travis returns and takes a seat next to Treadwell, Adam addresses the topic directly:

> "I have this speech I give before we start, just to let you know what we're going to do here. So, I think that writing music is a great way to get stuff out, and I think it can really help to shift your thoughts around—help you get rid of some old ways of thinking that could be painful or not that productive and introduce you to some new ways of thinking. A lot of people have really gotten a lot out of writing songs like this, and I really hope that you will too. Are you ready to start?"
>
> "Yeah, yeah I am."

Treadwell designed this program over years. He was initially inspired by the way theater- or music-based activities immediately engaged children and adolescents and let them speak to events and emotions that might be slow to surface in the more static setting of talk therapy. In his years of practice, Treadwell has designed a variety of entry points to get kids talking. His focus is on helping patients to reframe their experience: to describe the past and to work to articulate meaningful alternatives for the future. He calibrates his approach based on his observations. Sometimes he initiates conversation with one of the many fill-in-the-blank Mad-Lib-style templates he has created. He also asks patients to write a letter explaining their feelings to someone in their life; this letter can evolve into song lyrics. Whatever his initial approach, Treadwell always inserts guided reflection into the process of song creation. His therapeutic process uses the formal device of song structure to urge the patient to imagine positive change by writing a first verse dedicated to the past, a second verse imagining the future, and a chorus that speaks to strategies of personal change. With Travis, Adam decides to explore the music that Travis said he had made outside the hospital.

> "Have you ever written a song?"
>
> "Yeah, I wrote a rap about my life."
>
> "That's awesome; let's start there. I just want you to know that I'm your music producer right now, but I'm also your therapist, so I hope it's cool with you if I speak to what I hear in a therapeutic way."
>
> "Yeah, I guess."

> "Want to start with music or lyrics?"
>
> "Music, definitely music."
>
> "You want to do it on your own, or together? I have a short video here that shows you how to use the software."

Treadwell plays a 90-second tutorial he has developed on how to use GarageBand and then opens the program.

> "Type your name in here. OK, so first you pick the feeling of the song, like how you want your head to move while you listen. Like this [he plays a slow pulse and nods in time to it] or this [a quicker beat]."
>
> "I want it like this," Travis demonstrates.
>
> "Ok, cool. That's like 97 beats per minute. I'm going to play you some sounds, and you pick what you like to lay on top." Treadwell clicks through a series of sound loops prerecorded in the software, each a single instrument, some recognizable and some electronically modified.
>
> "I like that one," Travis interjects.
>
> "Ok, that's a drum loop. I'm going to make it repeat, so it keeps going for the whole song. Ok, now, what else?"
>
> "What is there?"

Treadwell clicks through another set of programmed instrumentations.

> "I like that one!"
>
> "Ok, let's put it on top. Now let's listen."
>
> "That sounds awesome. Hey, I want to put my rap to that. Lemme write to that."
>
> "OK, I'm going to give you some headphones and some paper and pencil. You sit here and figure it out and signal me when you're done."
>
> "Like, uh, rewrite the rap I had before?"
>
> "Yeah, and I want you to try and balance the past and the future in what you write. Like first verse past and then next verse where you want to be in the future. What you see coming true for yourself."
>
> "OK." Travis puts on headphones and gets to work, head pulsing to the beat, mouthing lyrics and then pausing to write.

Not every interaction goes this smoothly, and not all patients can work independently as Travis has done. Treadwell sees patients who demonstrate obvious symptoms of mental health conditions—addiction/withdrawal, paranoia, and bipolar disorder are common—in the music room. For Treadwell, it is important to determine whether the patient can engage with the music activity in the moment. If patients are agitated, he urges them to return when they are calmer. Sometimes a patient encounters raw trauma in the process of making a song and is seized by emotion. Treadwell stays engaged with the patient, helping to him or her to de-escalate with prompts to deep breathing and quiet reassurance, orienting him or her to the present reality of a protected environment and repeating positive affirmation: They are brave, they are strong, and they are able to face their hurt.

"OK," Travis says. "I got it."

"Awesome," says Adam. "Let me see." He reads what Travis has written. "Hey, this is really great. Man, the past is difficult, huh? Not knowing your dad—you could write a whole song about that. You want to add to that part?"

"I dunno."

"Ok, maybe it would be good to talk about this a little. Put the pen down. What's that like for you, not knowing your dad, living with your mom and sisters?"

"It sucks."

"Yeah? Sucks how?"

"Well, I never get to see my mom. My friends have dads. That makes me feel like shit."

"Ok, well, so that's a feeling, an emotion. What's another way to say that? Another feeling word?"

"Mad. Like angry. Sad, I guess."

"That's great! How would you feel about adding that in? I think the rap would be even better if you add in your feelings—like 'Growing up without a dad, when I see that it makes me sad.'"

"Yo, that's cheesy."

"OK, so make it not cheesy. I want you to try that."

Travis thinks, erases, and adds some additional words to his lyrics.

"Here."

"I like it; this is really good, really powerful. You like it?"

"Yeah. I do."

"Ok, one more thing. This is a great first verse, and now I want you to think of a second one. And this second one, like we talked about before, I want it to be about your future. Let's talk: what do you see for yourself in the future?"

"Well, I have a job, and I'm still doing music."

"Yeah?"

"And a kid. I have a kid and a family, and we live together."

"That's a great goal. Those are all great goals. You wanna add those lines into a second verse?" Travis starts writing on a second piece of paper and a few minutes later slides what he has written over to Adam.

"Those look really good."

"Yeah, I like it. It's like I never thought of it like that."

"You ready to go into the booth and record?" Travis nods, and Adam sets him up. The booth looks and functions like a professional recording studio, and patients are often eager to try it out, imagining themselves inside the images they've seen of famous artists in the act of recording. When Travis emerges, he is elated.

"Oh my god, man, that was *FIRE*. I feel great. That was awesome!"

Travis's enthusiasm is contagious, and Adam feels himself grin. He has observed that, for many of the patients who engage in therapeutic song-writing, the experience of recording is joyfully cathartic.

"You want to hear it?"

"Yeah, but private. Not on speakers." Adam sets Travis up to listen to his song on headphones. He notes that Travis plays the song over several times and that he cries while listening, scraping his cheek with his sleeve to hide tears. Travis takes off the headphones.

"Hey, mister, can you put this on a CD like you said?"

"Of course, yeah. It'll take me just a sec. You know, I think that was really great. I think you did an incredible job. I'm really proud of you. You wanna come back? Keep working together?"

"Yeah. I mean like what?"

"Well, would you like to come back tomorrow and make another song with me?"

"Yeah, yeah, definitely. I'll write some stuff tonight. I'll be back, Hey, I'll see you tomorrow."

"See you, Travis, Great job man." Adam hands over the newly burned CD.

Travis grabs it and starts to race out of the room. "Thanks!" he yells over his shoulder.

If Travis returns with additional lyrics on the following day, Adam will use the momentum of a powerful initial session to explore Travis's feelings more deeply, looking at the content they have already developed and discussing other areas of Travis's life. He will use the formal device of song structure to encourage Travis to think of specific strategies for creating the future he articulated in the second verse of his song, asking him to write a repeating chorus that names ways he can travel from a painful past to a future that he desires—by finding alternative means to resolve conflicts, assembling a script to approach a difficult relationship, or enumerating practical goals on the way to a stable adult life. Each time Travis writes lyrics, Adam will use them as the frame for therapeutic discussion, and he will conclude each songwriting interaction by recording a CD and giving it to Travis.

After each songwriting session, Adam offers a report to the patient's treatment team outlining what came up while the patient was in the music room and describing how he or she responded to music-based activity. In conversation with the treatment team, Adam will have the opportunity to learn the patient's history and can enter a written note into the patient's chart. Like any social worker, Adam is ethically obliged to share information about abuse, trauma, or criminality that emerges during a session, a course of action he shares with his patients in the moment: "I think it's really important for your treatment to let your therapist know what came up today."

Despite the novel format of his interaction with patients, Adam's therapeutic activity adheres to the principles that shape any responsive interpersonal treatment. The range of activity options he has cued up in the music room allows him to meet individuals where they are; he uses song lyrics as a means to reflect back to his patients and to ask them to actively reframe their experience. The handover of a recorded CD represents a mini termination. When treatment proceeds predictably and both he and the patient are aware of an impending discharge, Adam is able to conduct a more thorough termination process, sitting with a patient and sharing the ritual of listening to their songs and reflecting on what he or she has accomplished. He offers praise for the music, emphasizing the emotional work it represents. If patients are discharged without warning, Adam always tries to mail them a recorded document of the work they did in the music room.

Evaluation is critical to ethical practice and to the survival of any program sponsored by an organization that faces the tension between a high-need client population and limited resources. Adam's program thrives because it generates positive feedback to the hospital administration, both from patient participants and from the staff who serve them, including therapists, program directors, and nurse managers. Though not ensconced by formal evaluation procedures, over 10 years, the feedback on Adam's program has centered on four principal themes:

1. Many patients are eager to participate and use the music room.
2. Collaborative songwriting provides valuable therapeutic outcomes.
3. The music program works as an incentive to encourage patients to engage with other aspects of a treatment plan.
4. Patients who are otherwise treatment resistant respond to therapy in the context of the music program.

After 10 years, Adam remains committed to this form of intervention, and his interest has expanded to include formal study of its therapeutic efficacy. In particular, Adam wants to quantitatively document his understanding that participation in this therapeutic modality can increase treatment compliance, decrease the time it takes to complete treatment goals, boost self-esteem, decrease depressive symptoms, and increase feelings of self-validation. Additionally, he hopes to expand this work beyond inpatient psychiatric care. His success with the inpatient population in the hospital has inspired him to reach out in other arenas, possibly to create an after-school program that could provide individual, group, and family therapy to adolescents. In any context, Adam is well aware that the chance to record music is a powerful hook and that music production offers an extraordinary platform to engage the possibility of therapeutic change.

Ethical Considerations

Social work interventions with young people, such as the music program described in the case study above, are guided by the *NASW Code of Ethics for the Practice of Social Work with Adolescents* (National Association of Social Workers,1993). Although this code is congruent with the NASW *Code of Ethics* and emphasizes many of the same principles, some provisions are specific to youth populations, for instance, the mandate that social workers must understand the multiple dimensions of adolescent life, as well as environmental conditions such as family dynamics and political and economic factors affecting adolescents. It directs social workers to "strive to empower adolescents," a mandate clearly reflected in a music program that provides young people with the tools to express themselves, to reflect on their experience, and to set future goals.

The principles of privacy and confidentiality are vital to effective practice, and technology challenges both. The *Code of Ethics* (NASW, 2008, p. 12) incorporates technology into its mandates, offering specific guidelines to protect privacy and confidentiality.

As technology redefines the way we generate, obtain, or exchange information, almost every dimension of practice requires scrutiny. While the visible functions of technology must be addressed, the mechanisms that power many software applications and platforms are invisible to the user and may pose risk to privacy and or confidentiality. Multiple authors cite examples of invisible technological processes that may put sensitive information at risk, including sharing documents through the cloud; using a remote server; or failing to secure a digital footprint, cookies, or a browsing history (Barsky, 2016; National Association of Social Workers & Association of Social Work Boards, 2005). Even some of the simplest and most ubiquitous administrative tools—such as calendar programs or automated reminders—can expose confidential information. The hospital where Adam works is required to meet the high standard of the Health Insurance Portability and Accountability Act (HIPAA), which guarantees protection of clients' privacy and confidentiality, additionally requiring that clients be informed of any potential breach of personal or health information, a risk made more likely by the use of technology in record keeping, transmission, and sharing. Adam Treadwell observes all hospital policies on privacy and confidentiality. To ensure data security, all patients' compositions are saved on a secured hard drive to which Adam has unique access. Adam is the only person who can unlock the music room, and it is kept locked when he is not working there. None of the computers in the music room are connected to the Internet, and all client work is routinely cleared from machines.

Competence is not a static set of skills or body of knowledge; rather it is a series of responsibilities: to research, to learn new interventions, and to document and propagate effective practice (Csiernik et al., 2006). Where possible, competence includes active research into proven interventions and practice that has been documented to be effective. To maintain competence and to ensure that he is using the best tools with clients, Adam continues to learn and research music programs, to keep current with software updates and to develop skills through online videos and tutorials.

Internationally, social workers recognize that a client's informed consent is required to initiate any form of engagement: from therapeutic or case management services and the release of personal information to participation as a subject of research (Reamer, 1987). In the United States, the NASW *Code of Ethics* is congruent with these historic and international norms (standard 1.02). Adam's model for songwriting with young people foregrounds informed consent: he outlines the process to clients and makes clear that, while the opportunity to make music with professional grade equipment is exciting, the activity is based in therapeutic goals. Adam's work is predicated on ongoing exchange between social worker and client, which, with every choice, empowers the young person—clearly reflecting the directive of the *Code of Ethics for the Practice of Social Work with Adolescents* that youth "should have opportunities for decision making and for participation in the design and delivery of services" (NASW, 1993).

Adam regularly faces an ethical dilemma associated with a technological culture: the young people he works with are often so excited about the music they have made in the music room that they want to post it to YouTube. From a therapeutic perspective, the CDs of songs created while in the hospital offer real potential to the young people who create them—often allowing them a mechanism to share both their accomplishment and their emotions with important people in their lives. Client self-determination is an important ethical principle, and the adolescent songwriters ultimately own the material they have created in the hospital. This ethical dilemma overlaps with hospital regulation. Informed consent has always been dependent on a client's understanding of the process in which they are engaged; however, technology places new burdens on the social worker to understand the technology they are using and its implications and to ensure that a client has the same understanding in order to enable autonomous choice.

Social Justice Implications

One oft-cited potential of technology is its capacity to offer greater access to proven treatment and services to populations long disenfranchised by geography, disability, age, or historic mistrust of traditional social work interventions (Danielson et al., 2013; Kvasny & Payton, in press; Lightfoot et al., 2007; Pacifici et al., 2005).

The music program is one proof of technology's potential to engage and inspire hard-to-reach populations, such as the adolescent described in this chapter, who are often resistant to traditional talk therapy. In fact, Adam's program was formalized due to demand from an especially challenging population. The hospital conducted a formal Likert scale survey of acute care patients, documenting their eagerness to participate in music-based therapeutic activity.

If technology is to enable human progress toward the goals of social justice, every individual must have access to the hardware required to engage with technology. Access to the physical tools of information and communication technologies (ICTs) can be limited by many factors, such as cost—computers are increasingly affordable, but home broadband access is not (Abdel Wahab et al., 2011); cultural attitudes toward technology use; and physical design of hardware components. In order to pursue the kind of music making described in this chapter, a young person, an individual practitioner, or a hospital would require a DAW. Hardware ownership has been demonstrated to correlate with income, and some populations are increasingly smartphone dependent. For them, music production may be out of reach, as the complexity of music composition is difficult to manage in a mobile format. GarageBand software can be acquired at low or no cost; there are many free and open production programs, and some music software products such as Fruity Loops are available for download at no cost for both Mac and PC computers.

While traditional design prevents some people with disabilities from using applications without proprietary modification, some literature documents that GarageBand can make music production accessible to people with disabilities. GarageBand has been incorporated in both music therapy and music education for clients and students with varying needs and disabilities, including learning disability, visual impairments, mild cognitive impairments, and emotional regulation difficulties. Walzer (2016) directs inexperienced users to consult free Web-based tutorials and guides to learn how to use a DAW or a software platform and to practice making music by starting with some of the preexisting sounds that come with the software.

Beyond the challenge of working toward equality of access to hardware, social workers must strive to establish individual capacity to use technologies or technological literacy. The once-prominent model of a digital divide, which posited access to tools as the primary barrier to technological equity across populations, has been replaced by a paradigm that emphasizes "the degree to which people succeed or struggle when they use technology to try to navigate their environments, solve problems, and make decisions" (Horrigan, 2016), sometimes referred to as *e-competence*. As shown by a recent Pew Research Center report, such capacity varies according to socioeconomic status, race and ethnicity, and level of access to home broadband and smartphones. An earlier Pew study used the example of searching for work to illustrate that, in contemporary society and markets actions required for social and economic survival are increasingly negotiated digitally, that distribution of access remains uneven, and that, "in many cases, Americans who might benefit the most from being able to perform these behaviors effectively—such as those with relatively low levels of educational attainment—are the ones who find them most challenging".

The music program can offer clients an introduction to the skills of manipulating technology, and a model, in Adam, of how an informed user can use software to create an object of pride—an impressive-sounding CD. While cultivating this initial knowledge of a single software program into professional skills would require both access to hardware and singular personal focus on the part of an adolescent, the model of technology as a conduit to self-expression, to a feeling of potency, and to achievement may ignite an eagerness in a young person to pursue the skills and knowledge that aggregate to lifelong technological literacy. Like many social work interactions, the collaborative songwriting offered by the music program is brief: but by empowering clients to make decisions, to manufacture their own narrative of the future, and to experience the power of technology to amplify their capacity, its benefits may resonate deep into adulthood.

Questions for Discussion

Writing music using a computer lowers the barriers to composition, and it offers a therapeutic opportunity. What other populations might this intervention be appropriate for and why? How would you structure a songwriting session with a client from your target population? Would these clients be excited by a technology-based intervention? What musical genres might you draw from to inspire engagement? Would it work to write songs in a group with this population?, and How would you structure that activity to maximize its therapeutic value?

Some providers of music-based intervention care deeply about both the artistic quality and the social value of the music that they use as examples, sample from, or support clients in making. Adam Treadwell encourages clients to be inspired by any music that matters to them. Does the quality of the music used in a therapeutic context matter? What if a client writes a "bad" song? Is a therapist responsible to discuss the lyrics in a song enjoyed or written by a client if the lyrics are violent, racist, or misogynistic?

Composing songs on a computer is a therapeutic activity that encourages a client to "author" a narrative about themselves. Are there other technologies that would offer a similar opportunity, in another medium? Research a technology that would allow a client to create a therapeutic self-portrait—in words, visuals, motion, or sound. Describe how you would go about conducting a session that would make use of this client-generated artifact. How would you instruct a client, model the technology, and reflect on content created by or with your client? What are the issues of access involved with this technology—its cost or the cost of the equipment required to use it? Are special skills required to make use of this technology? Can you think of confidentiality, privacy, or other ethical concerns?

Further Reading

Ahmedani, B. K., Harold, R. D., Fitton, V. A., & Shifflet Gibson, E. D. (2011). What adolescents can tell us: Technology and the future of social work education. *Social Work Education, 30,* 830–846. doi: 10.1080/02615479.2010.504767

Fletcher, A. C., & Blair, B. L. (2016). Implications of the family expert role for parental rules regarding adolescent use of social technologies. *New Media and Society, 18,* 239–256.

Hatzigianni, M., Gregoriadis, A., & Fleer, M. (2016). Computer use at schools and associations with social-emotional outcomes—A holistic approach. Findings from the longitudinal study of Australian Children. *Computers and Education, 95,* 134–150. doi: 10.1016/j.compedu.2016.0.003

Kagohara, D. M., van der Meer, L., Ramdoss, S., O'Reilly, M. F., Lancioni, G. E., Davis, T. N., & Sigafoos, J. (2012). Using iPods and iPads in teaching program for individuals with developmental disabilities: A systematic review. *Research in Developmental Disabilities, 34,* 147–156.

Lenhart, A., Duggan, M., Perrin, A., Stepler, R., Rainie, L., & Parker, K. (2015, April 9). *Teens, social media and technology overview 2015.* Retrieved from http://www.pewinternet.org/2015/04/09/teens-social-media-technology-2015

Montgomery, K. C. (2015). Youth and surveillance in the Facebook era: Policy interventions and social implications. *Telecommunications Policy, 39,* 771–786.

4 }

mDad

HELPING DADS BE BETTER PARENTS WITH
MOBILE PHONES

Shawna J. Lee, Tova B. Walsh, and Joyce Y. Lee

"I cannot think of any need in childhood as strong as the need for a father's protection."

—Sigmund Freud, *1856–1939*

Mobile technology is increasingly being used to deliver physical and behavioral health interventions (such as online health checkups and tracking of symptoms and outcomes) because it is affordable and easy to implement, especially among large populations. The design of mobile devices and their features allows for easier access to communication and health interventions by those with diverse abilities (Rainger, 2005). For example, smartphones now offer built-in accessibility features that allow individuals with disabilities to more easily engage in personal and professional communication: gesture-based screen readers for the blind, intelligent assistants for those with limited motor and physical skills, and texting with auditory components for those with reading difficulties.

Business people and researchers alike (Ramey, 2013, 2014) have developed innovative technology-based approaches and strategies to reach, engage, and communicate with people in their day-to-day lives. Among these strategies are those that help individuals initiate and sustain behavior change (Eapen & Peterson, 2015). In this chapter, we focus mostly on programs designed for mobile devices, such as smartphones and tablets.

These mobile intervention approaches are relevant to social work practice because they are a part of the larger growth of technology designed to improve physical and psychological health and well-being (i.e., eHealth or mHealth).

Background

Nearly all Americans own a mobile phone, and about 77% of mobile owners have a smartphone (Pew Research Center, 2017a). Smartphones and devices such as tablets are an increasingly important part of people's daily lives. One study that surveyed smartphone users twice a day for 1 week showed that the vast majority of participants (89% to 97%) used their smartphones to text, e-mail, and access the Internet. In addition, more than half reported using their smartphones for social networking, to take pictures and videos, and to read the news online (Anderson, 2015). When asked about how they feel about their smartphones, 46% of users reported that they "couldn't live without" them, and that their devices are helpful, represent freedom, are worth the cost, and allow them to connect (A. Smith, 2015, p. 1).

Mobile technology is appealing for personal and professional use because of its relatively low cost and functionality, allowing Internet access through 3G, 4G, and long-term evolution (LTE) high-speed wireless systems, often without requiring the expense of a month-to-month Internet subscription. Text messages may cost as little as a few cents. More recently, messaging has become free with the development of built-in instant messaging programs (e.g., iMessage) and apps (e.g., WhatsApp, LINE, and KakaoTalk) that can use both Wi-Fi and mobile networks.

CLOSING THE DIGITAL DIVIDE

For many years, there was concern about the *digital divide*, defined as differences in access to computers and the Internet attributable to income, age, and other demographic variables. However, mobile devices such as smartphones and tablets have helped to bridge this gap (Chang et al., 2013; Ginossar & Nelson, 2010). Research shows nearly equal access to smartphones and related devices across race and ethnic groups. For example, the rates of smartphone ownership for Asian/ Pacific Islanders (86.6%), Black African Americans (83%), and Hispanics (82.4%) are higher than those of non-Hispanic Whites (74.2%) (Nielsen, 2015). Recent reports also show high levels of smartphone ownership across different socioeconomic groups. For instance, the Pew Research Center (2015) reported that half of individuals who earn less than $30,000 per year, 71% of those who earn between $30,000 and $49,999 per year, 72% of those who earn between $50,000 and $74,999 per year, and 84% of those who earn $75,000 or more own a smartphone (A. Smith, 2015, p. 1).

Literature Review

Because eHealth and mHealth are recent areas of intervention and practice, it is not surprising that most of the relevant research literature has been published in the past decade. One particularly effective mHealth intervention for parents is Text4baby. Initially offering a text messaging service to provide mothers with text messages to promote health behaviors throughout pregnancy and the baby's first year (Evans, Wallace, & Snider, 2012; Jordan, Ray, Johnson, & Evans, 2011; Whittaker et al., 2012), Text4baby now offers an app.

Text4baby has reached more than 450,000 mothers, many of whom may have received little parent education through traditional means, with information about their child's health and development (Whittaker et al., 2012). The evaluation study randomized pregnant women to either receive an intervention (both Text4baby and usual healthcare) or to join a control group (receive only usual healthcare). Pre- and posttests were conducted before the intervention was delivered (baseline) and at 28 weeks after the intervention (follow-up), respectively. At both times, women were asked about their attitudes and actions related to health behaviors. Researchers found that women in the intervention group felt significantly more prepared to be new mothers between baseline and follow-up (Evans et al., 2012).

ONE UNDER-EXAMINED GROUP: FATHERS

While a number of technology-delivered interventions are available for parents, they generally focus on mothers (Baggett et al., 2010; Evans et al., 2012; Ondersma, Svikis, & Schuster, 2007; Thraen, Frasier, Cochella, Yaffe, & Goede, 2008; Whittaker et al., 2012). One notable exception is Text4baby, a program aimed at fathers. Some early studies showed that many men did not perceive existing products for expecting or new parents (including books, web sites, and apps) to be father friendly (S. J. Lee et al., 2013; S. J. Lee, Yelick, Brisebois, & Banks, 2011). For example, many products did not address issues that fathers felt were important to them, such as "not knowing what to do" with a baby. Furthermore, the authors believed that technology had the potential to address a number of barriers such as work schedules and feelings that such programs were intended for mothers only (Bayley, Wallace, & Choudhry, 2009) that hinder access to parenting services and programs for many fathers. Our research suggested that technology was an appropriate tool for men and fathers, many of whom reported that they already used technology and felt comfortable with that form of communication (S. J. Lee, Hoffman, & Harris, 2016).

TEXT MESSAGING INTERVENTIONS

In the eHealth domain, studies found that text messaging (or short message service [SMS]) can be used to effectively support positive health behaviors in patients with diabetes (Franklin, Waller, Pagliari, & Greene, 2003) and bulimia nervosa (Bauer, Percevic, Okon, Meermann, & Kordy, 2003). The combination of intensive therapy and a text messaging support system was associated with improved glycemic control in patients with Type 1 diabetes (Franklin, Waller, Pagliari, & Greene, 2006). Similarly, a text messaging intervention for individuals with bulimia nervosa significantly decreased the number of binge eating and purging episodes, symptoms of eating disorder, and night eating from baseline to post-treatment and subsequent follow-up (Shapiro et al., 2010).

Over time, eHealth interventions have been developed to address some of the most important issues that social workers address in practice, including helping consumers increase vaccination rates (Hart et al., 2011), quit smoking (Strecher et al., 2008), and reduce alcohol and drug use in vulnerable populations such as pregnant women (Ondersma, Grekin, & Svikis, 2011; Tzilos, Sokol, & Ondersma, 2011). The eHealth field is well established, and meta-analyses and review articles have discussed best practices for technology-based interventions in domains such as smoking cessation (Whittaker et al., 2009), physical activity (Rabin & Bock, 2011), and blood glucose control in diabetes (Liang et al., 2011), among other important outcomes (Fjeldsoe, Marshall, & Miller, 2009; Heron & Smyth, 2010; Klasnja & Pratt, 2012; Krishna, Boren, & Balas, 2009).

Klasnja and Pratt (2012) provided an overview of the growing body of work on using mobile phones to deliver health interventions, describing features that make them a promising platform for interventions and identifying five mobile-based intervention strategies used across different health conditions. Fjeldsoe, Marshall, and Miller (2009) found positive behavior change outcomes in 8 of 14 studies using mobile telephone SMS to administer health behavior change. Five additional studies demonstrated positive behavioral trends, but researchers noted that sufficient statistical power was lacking to demonstrate significance. Calculated effect sizes ranged from small (.09) to larger (1.38). Fjeldsoe and colleagues also noted that the broad range of study designs and variability in SMS characteristics limit their conclusions and that future studies should use adequate sample size and representative samples, as well as report process measures.

Similarly, Heron and Smyth (2010) identified and reviewed 27 studies that use palmtop computers (small enough to be held in one hand) or mobile phones to deliver psychosocial and behavior treatments for smoking cessation, weight loss, anxiety, diabetes management, eating disorders, alcohol use, and healthy eating and physical activity. The authors found that, although most of the interventions they reviewed reported statistically significant findings (in treating health behaviors and psychological symptoms), less than half reported outcomes that provide information with respect to clinical and practical changes. Because the specific types of significant outcomes vary depending on the study, Heron and Smyth noted that future studies should not only report statistical significance but also state the practical importance of intervention outcomes to facilitate the interpretation of study findings.

Krishna, Boren, and Balas (2009) reviewed 25 studies that evaluated mobile phone voice and text messaging interventions. Interventions that demonstrated significant improvement ($p < .05$) among participants in the intervention group compared to those in the control group were considered effective. The authors found that 12 of 13 studies examined and reported changes in clinical outcomes. Further, three studies that examined and reported changes in social functioning outcomes showed that mobile-based interventions significantly improved quality of life for individuals with diabetes and significantly increased self-efficacy among those attempting to quit smoking.

MENTAL HEALTH APPS

Efforts are being made to evaluate research on the efficacy of mental health apps. Although these apps are potentially effective, findings thus far are limited to a small number of studies that had small sample sizes, high dropout rates, or no long-term outcomes. In addition to addressing mental health issues, technology can be used to promote positive social relationships and well-being, including relationship satisfaction (Kalinka, Fincham, & Hirsch, 2012), prosocial behavior and reduction of aggressive behavior (Konrath et al., 2015; Rajabi, Ghasemzadeh, Ashrafpouri, & Saadat, 2012), and positive parenting and reduction of child maltreatment (Baggett et al., 2010; Evans et al., 2012; Ondersma et al., 2007; Thraen et al., 2008; Whittaker et al., 2012).

Mental Health Apps That Address Depression

The use of mobile technology to address psychological and social well-being or *psychosocial outcomes* is more recent and less common. Many applications, such as Breathe & Relax, are for-profit and proprietary and thus have a download fee but some are available free (e.g., PTSD Coach; Naeem et al., 2016; Prentice & Dobson, 2014). Some mobile apps may not have a download fee but advertisement provides an indirect source of income for the developers. So far, research with small samples has shown that mobile interventions can significantly reduce self-reported depressive symptoms and significantly decrease the likelihood of meeting diagnostic criteria for major depression over a course of 8 weeks (Burns et al., 2011); they can also be used to reduce symptoms of mental illnesses (Depp et al., 2010; Granholm, Ben-Zeev, Link, Bradshaw, & Holden, 2012). Apps have been used to promote happiness and emotional self-awareness (Morris et al., 2010; Parks, Della Porta, Pierce, Zilca, & Lyubomirsky, 2012). As shown in Table 4.1, there are many apps for mental health, some of which may be useful to help social workers work more effectively with clients. For example, for clients with depression who may find it challenging to accurately recall their day-to-day mood and symptoms of depression, an app such as Moodnotes (Thriveport, 2016) may be an effective tool.

Mental Health Apps That Address Alcohol and Substance Use/Abuse

Little research has been done to examine the use of mobile phones among individuals receiving treatment for alcohol and substance abuse. Nevertheless, available research suggests that this group has access to mobile phones and is willing to participate in mobile interventions. For example, McClure, Acquavita, Harding, and Stitzer (2012) noted that 91% of patients enrolled in substance abuse treatment programs own a mobile phone and 79% have access to text

TABLE 4.1 } Mobile Apps Related to Mental Health and Addiction

Name	Main Features and Functions	Primary Use*	Evaluation
MENTAL HEALTH			
Mental Illness: Facts https://itunes.apple.com/au/app/mental-illness-facts-on-anxiety/id332173994?mt=8	Learn about different mental illnesses, including anxiety, ADHD, autism, depression, bipolar disorder	I	No empirical research on app. Average customer satisfaction rating.
DSM-5 DDx https://itunes.apple.com/us/app/dsm-5-differential-diagnosis/id1008319988?mt=8	Learn about psychiatric disorders and diagnoses based on the DSM-5 classification and ICD-10 codes; interact with decision trees	I	No empirical research on app. High customer satisfaction rating.
Depression Test https://itunes.apple.com/us/app/depression-test/id666436210?mt=8	Self-assess depression based on the Patient Healthcare Questionnaire-9 (PHQ-9), monitor treatment response over time, and access high-quality depression resources online	P	No empirical research on app. High customer satisfaction rating.
Mental Health Scales http://www.mobileappsandmore.com/index.html	Use the app's mental health rating scales (e.g., Generalized Anxiety Disorder-7, Geriatric Depression-Short Form) to self-screen and share results with a clinician	P	Developed with certified psychiatrist. No empirical research or customer satisfaction rating.
Happify http://www.happify.com/	Change mood and increase happiness with fun activities and games, learn positive habits, and track emotional well-being (e.g., overall happiness, life satisfaction, positive emotions)	P	Preliminary data suggests users experienced significant change in emotional and cognitive well-being. High customer satisfaction rating.
Moodnotes http://moodnotes.thriveport.com/	Capture and track mood, improve thinking habits through journaling, learn about thinking traps, and increase self-awareness	P	No empirical research on app. High customer satisfaction rating.
ADDICTION			
Drug Addiction Facts and Tips http://appadvice.com/app/drug-addiction-facts-tips/1050050528	Learn about drug addiction, watch tutorial videos to obtain knowledge and awareness, and receive daily tips and quotes	I	No empirical research on app or customer satisfaction rating.
AA Big Book https://itunes.apple.com/us/app/aa-big-book-free-for-alcoholics/id990308161?mt=8	Read Alcoholics Anonymous (AA)'s Big Book, listen to podcasts, find nearby AA meetings	I	No empirical research on app. High customer satisfaction rating.
Addiction Journal https://itunes.apple.com/cz/app/addiction-app/id798673569?mt=8	Read most recent issues from the journal *Addiction*, receive notifications about new issues, search and bookmark articles, share links to articles with clients and colleagues	I	No empirical research on app or customer satisfaction rating.
Addicaid https://itunes.apple.com/us/app/addicaid-addiction-recovery/id847509209?mt=8	Aimed at moderation, management, and sobriety; find and rate meetings, track progress with the support of a community, and access additional resources	P	No empirical research on app. High customer satisfaction rating.

(continued)

TABLE 4.1 } Continued

Name	Main Features and Functions	Primary Use*	Evaluation
nomo http://meetnomo.com/index.html	Track number of minutes, hours, days, weeks, or years since sober; share clocks with accountability partners or clinician; track how much money was saved since sober; play mini-exercises to help refocus when tempted	P	No empirical research on app. High customer satisfaction rating.
Dependn' https://itunes.apple.com/kr/app/dependn-quit-weed-tobacco/id1093903062?l=en&mt=	Monitor addiction behaviors; track progress; export data and share with clinician; understand connection between repeated actions, their context, and feelings	P	No empirical research on app or customer satisfaction rating.

* I = informational; P = practical.

messages. One study showed that substance abuse patients are willing to be contacted by their clinicians via mobile phones, but mobile phone ownership was lower for homeless individuals and those recently released from prison, suggesting that mobile intervention may be less suitable for these individuals (Milward, Day, Wadsworth, Strang, & Lynskey, 2015). Approximately half of the substance abuse patients in this study also reported that using geolocation features of mobile devices for treatment would be unacceptable. Because this group is frequently associated with the criminal justice system (Fazel, Bains, & Doll, 2006), their suspicion of tracking features and their attitude about mobile intervention and frequently updating their contact information for ongoing treatment adherence should be further explored.

Review of the literature and app inventories has suggested that, although there are many commercial smartphone apps for daily self-monitoring, real-time self-assessment, and treatment of substance use (especially alcohol abuse), few actually address behavior change or recovery and most lack empirical evidence of effectiveness (Cohn, Hunter-Reel, Hagman, & Mitchell, 2011; Quanbeck, Chih, Isham, Johnson, & Gustafson, 2014). Download rates for these apps are noteworthy. For example, Sober Grid, a sobriety app that helps find other individuals in recovery, garnered 25,000 downloads within a month of launch (Horton, 2015). Nevertheless, large numbers of downloads do not always translate into consistent use. Such apps have been criticized for measuring their success based on app store ratings and download rates instead of measurable behavioral changes or treatment outcomes (Bogle, 2016). An app such as Sober Grid may attract users despite limited evidence of effectiveness because it is free and allows anonymity (Bromwich, 2015). Table 4.1 provides examples of mental health apps that address depression, alcohol use, and substance use issues.

Mobile Apps for Social Work Students

There are a number of mobile apps specifically designed for social workers and social work students, as opposed to their clients (see Table 4.2). Some of these

TABLE 4.2 } Mobile Apps for Social Work Students and Practitioners

Name	Main Function and Features	Primary Use*	Evaluation
Guide to Social Work https://itunes.apple.com/ WebObjects/ MZStore. woa/wa/viewSoftware? id=482157799&mt=8	Learn about the basics of the field of social work; take short quizzes on learned materials	I	No empirical research on app or customer satisfaction rating
Social Work Helper https://www. socialworkhelper.com / download-social-work- helper-app/	Access information, resources, and entertainment related to social work; search online directories to locate low-cost drug prescriptions, affordable day care, senior services, and support groups	I	No empirical research on app or customer satisfaction rating
Social Work Social Media https://itunes.apple.com/gb/ app /social-work-socialmedia/ id656114442?mt=8&ign- mpt=uo%3D4	Learn about ethical issues of using social media in social work by interacting with game-based case studies; can be used for preteaching or training activity	I	No empirical research on app or customer satisfaction rating
ASWB LCSW Exam Prep https://itunes. apple.com/us/app /aswb- lcsw-exam-prep-2017 -edition/id599395631?mt=8	Prepare for the ASWB Licensed Clinical Social Worker (LCSW) exam by creating customized practice tests, viewing detailed answer rationales, and reviewing results	P	No empirical research on app; high customer satisfaction rating
ASWB MSW Exam Prep https://itunes. apple.com/us/app/aswb- msw-exam-prep-2017-edition/ id777128952?mt=8	Prepare for the ASWB Masters in Social Work (MSW) Exam by creating customized practice tests, viewing detailed answer rationales, and reviewing results	P	No empirical research on app; high customer satisfaction rating.
Indeed Job Search https://itunes.apple.com/ us/app/indeed-job-search/ id309735670?mt=8	Find social work jobs by organization and location, personalize searches and save results, receive e-mail alerts with new jobs, and create a resume and apply to jobs	P	No empirical research on app; high customer satisfaction rating.
Social Work Feedback https://itunes.apple.com/us/ app/social-work-feedback/ id1052093701?mt=	Receive feedback from clients to improve social work services	P	No empirical research on app or customer satisfaction rating

*I = informational; P = practical.

apps provide basic information about social work, address ethical issues in social work practice, and provide tools to prepare for the professional licensure examination.

Case Study

The case study that follows describes a smartphone app that is being developed to improve resources for new fathers, who often face challenges that preclude them from participating in traditional parenting programs. It provides a practical and realistic example of the type of technology-supported tools that can be and are being developed to address specific programmatic and client-oriented needs. At the same time it alludes to the time and expense, as well as the knowledge, skills, and expertise required to use the app successfully.

The intent of the case study is to get students and practitioners excited about the new tools that are being developed by others in the field. It is also intended to encourage students and practitioners to make better use of existing technologies that may aid their clients by becoming and remaining aware of emerging tools with demonstrated effectiveness through continuing education, conferences, journals, and Internet browser searches for phrases such as "social work technology services and apps."

MDAD (MOBILE DEVICE ASSISTED DAD)

mDad is an interactive smartphone app, designed as a basic parenting intervention for fathers of new babies. Intervention goals are to increase fathers' knowledge of early child development, to enhance father engagement, to support early father–child relationships, and to contribute to a positive trajectory of father involvement. Content addresses child development across the first year of life and offers specific ideas for how fathers can engage with their baby and support their development. mDad also offers functionality to track and record father–child activities as well as infant physical and social development, through videos, pictures, and logs.

Authors Shawna Lee and Tova Walsh assembled a multidisciplinary research team including social workers and psychologists with expertise in father engagement, early child development, and parent support programs. In conjunction with a team from the University of Michigan Center for Health Communications Research (CHCR; http://chcr.umich.edu/) that specializes in developing and delivering Internet-based and mobile health interventions, we developed the content for the mDad app with two goals in mind: to provide evidence-based parenting education and to encourage fathers' direct engagement in supporting their child's development, health, and well-being. The CHCR team was responsible for development of the application software, tailoring technology and graphic design to achieve an accessible and father-friendly presentation. Based on our previous discussions with fathers and prospective fathers, content included humor and jokes as well as more "masculine" graphic design. We solicited recommendations from a fathering expert and a comedian to enhance the accessibility and presentation style of the app; their guidance led to more and better humor, as well as a casual tone suggestive of a dad talking to another dad.

INITIATING AND CUSTOMIZING USE OF THE MDAD APP

When new users initiate the mDad app, they complete a brief survey that allows for customization of app content. For example, all milestone information, activities, and games are developmentally appropriate for the child's age and targeted at the father's residential status (living at home with the child or in another location). The app is also designed so that fathers can use it independently or share it

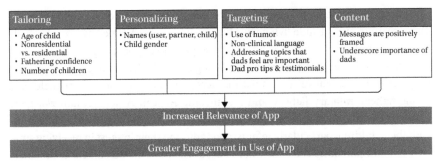

Tailoring	Personalizing	Targeting	Content
• Age of child • Nonresidential vs. residential • Fathering confidence • Number of children	• Names (user, partner, child) • Child gender	• Use of humor • Non-clinical language • Addressing topics that dads feel are important • Dad pro tips & testimonials	• Messages are positively framed • Underscore importance of dads

Increased Relevance of App

Greater Engagement in Use of App

FIGURE 4.1 The father-focused components of mDad.

with the child's mother or another significant person and together create a shared record of the child's development. Figure 4.1 illustrates the ways in which mDad content is both targeted to and framed for fathers and personalized to increase relevance and encourage greater engagement.

OVERVIEW OF APP FEATURES

The mDad app sends push notifications to users' smartphones twice per week offering brief hooks of information and links to more extensive messages within the app. Focusing on fathers' direct engagement, each message presents information relevant to the child's current developmental stage, accompanied by activities deemed appropriate by the child development expert on our team. Given that children can vary considerably in their development, our team strove to develop content that was general enough to apply to most children loosely based on their age. There is also a resources section within the app, where fathers can search for developmental information on topics of interest and locate relevant resources.

Once the father receives a push notification, the associated content (developmental information and activity ideas) lives in the app under the activities icon. Each week users are prompted to use the app to document their child's development and activities by creating logs and uploading pictures and videos. For example, fathers are encouraged to read stories or to record a game of peek-a-boo with the baby and upload the video to mDad. For nonresidential fathers using the app with the child's other parent or caregiver, the other parent or caregiver can help upload the recorded content and log developmental milestones on the app. By viewing this content, nonresidential fathers can stay connected and informed regarding their child's growth and development.

Target User and Needs

The target user is a new father. We were motivated to develop the mDad app by the recognition that fathers are an underserved population with regard to parent support and education. We particularly hoped to reach fathers who face barriers to positive involvement with their children or to accessing traditional parent services. These barriers may include living with their child on a part-time basis or not at all, feeling uncomfortable attending an in-person parent support program, or inability to attend parent support programs due to logistical challenges (e.g., work or military duty). In qualitative studies with fathers from diverse populations including young fathers, military fathers, and low-income African American fathers), men have expressed a desire to be positive parents; acknowledged challenges in engaging with their children, particularly infants; and indicated their interest in receiving support to build parenting skills (S. J. Lee et al., 2011, 2013). mDad content is designed to meet the needs of individual fathers from diverse populations with a variety of family structures. mDad can be accessed anytime, anywhere, at the user's discretion.

TRAINING AND COSTS

There is no specialized knowledge or training required to use this tool. The mDad interface is designed to be intuitive, and the content is designed to be accessible, using basic language and incorporating visually appealing design elements and video components. Development of the app required significant investment. Our team included one PhD-level developmental and clinical psychologist, and two PhD-level social workers. The technology team included multiple people with master's degrees in designing, developing, and implementing technology-based interventions. However, the only costs to an individual user are those associated with the data plan for their smartphone. An important advantage of technology-based interventions is their potential for scalability. That is, once initial development and testing is complete, there is the potential to reach a larger audience with relatively minor investment in infrastructure and minimal cost. Of course, as with any intervention, outreach is required so that people are aware that the product exists. There are likely to be significant costs associated with such outreach, but we are unable to provide estimates because our project has not yet reached that stage of development.

mDad can be used as a stand-alone intervention or it can be offered as an add-on by service providers or programs on fatherhood, either to increase engagement and prevent attrition or to reinforce training between sessions or after the programs are completed. It offers a means of delivering intervention and potentially providing access to fathers who otherwise would not be able to use it.

EFFECTIVENESS

Through an iterative development and testing process, we investigated content and functions that fathers would like to see in an app, developed the content and technical components, conducted acceptability and usability testing of beta mDad with fathers, and then refined the app based on what we learned (S. J. Lee & Walsh, 2015). Using a convenience sampling approach, we conducted several rounds of usability and acceptability testing. Usability testing examines the user experience in navigating through the features of an app to identify any challenges that users might encounter and determine whether technical refinements are needed (Kaufman et al., 2003). Acceptability testing assesses whether content resonates with the intended user.

Data were collected via in-depth one-on-one interviews to gather fathers' responses to mDad messages and other content as it was being developed; in-depth one-on-one interviews with individuals who used and provided feedback on beta mDad; and focus groups on the final version of mDad content, using screenshots taken from the app. Results showed that mDad content was relevant to the parenting experiences of fathers from diverse populations (S. J. Lee & Walsh, 2015). Fathers appreciated the ability to upload pictures and videos, but seemed to most enjoy the ongoing suggestions for direct activities and hands-on ways to engage with their child. They found the personalization and customization of the app to be a great strength and noted that mDad's father-friendly approach was markedly different from that of other parenting resources they had used (e.g., books and parenting websites such as babycenter.com). Moreover, they found the content well suited to their needs and interests as fathers of young children.

Usability and acceptability testing establish mDad as a promising intervention, but further study is needed to evaluate the efficacy of this approach. Figure 4.2 illustrates the theoretical model that we plan to test in future research.

MDAD FEATURES FOR FATHERS OF CHILDREN AT VARIOUS DEVELOPMENTAL STAGES

Fathers of newborn children to 1 year olds can receive 8 weeks of messages, content, and activities tailored to the age of their child (up to 14 months). As an example, Figure 4.3 presents topics for content provided to fathers of children 1 to 2 months of age.

To illustrate how content is varied to meet the needs of fathers of children at different ages, Figure 4.4 presents the topics for content provided to fathers of children 13 to 14 months of age.

All mDad content is personalized for each father and child. However, a limitation of our approach is that there are no content, resources, suggestions, or activities for children with developmental delays or other disabilities.

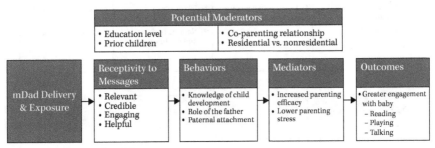

FIGURE 4.2 Theoretical model.

Age 1–2 Months			
Week 1	**Week 2**	**Week 3**	**Week 4**
1: Swaddling **2:** Feeding and bonding	**1:** Coping with crying **2:** Crying checklist	**1:** Sleeping **2:** Staying connected	**1:** Fatherhood: The emotional roller coaster **2:** Nicknames, baby
Week 5	**Week 6**	**Week 7**	**Week 8**
1: Reflexes **2:** Owen's vision	**1:** Bonding **2:** Fussy time	**1:** What the cries mean **2:** Colic	**1:** It isn't just baby talk **2:** It's just a phase

1–2	3–4	5–6	7–8	9–10	11–12	13–14

FIGURE 4.3 Content headings for child 1–2 months of age.

Box 4.1 shows an example of content that could be sent to a father who lives with his son Owen and is interested in ideas of things to do with Owen on a daily basis.

RESPONDING TO THE NEEDS OF DIFFERENT TYPES OF FATHERS

A nonresidential father, or a father separated from his family by military deployment can use mDad to stay current on his child's development and maintain feelings of connection while they are apart. He will receive push notifications

Age 13–14 Months			
Week 1	**Week 2**	**Week 3**	**Week 4**
1: Baby proofing **2:** Building an obstacle course for Owen	**1:** Exploring with Owen **2:** Outings with Owen	**1:** Teaching Owen to take turns **2:** Sensory play	**1:** Letting Owen play grown-up **2:** Imitation play
Week 5	**Week 6**	**Week 7**	**Week 8**
1: Changing sleep patterns **2:** Mobile Owen	**1:** Learning social cues **2:** Contagious emotions	**1:** Language development **2:** Naming body parts and common objects	**1:** Learning to name feelings **2:** It's just a phase

1–2	3–4	5–6	7–8	9–10	11–12	13–14

FIGURE 4.4 Content headings for child 13–14 months of age.

BOX 4.1 } Sample mDad Message for the Father of a 3-Month-Old Child

---

3-4 MONTHS, *READING TO OWEN*

Reading is a great way to help Owen develop language skills. It's also a wonderful way to bond with Owen and a ritual you can continue as he grows older. Here are a few suggestions:

Try a variety of books. In addition to any books you have at home, your local library is a great place to try out lots of books and see which ones you and Owen like the most. Personally, we prefer books that other babies haven't yet spit up on. Use mDad to log books you most like to read to Owen.

Make it interesting. Owen won't understand a thing you say, but your voice communicates more than the words. ("More than words" is not just a hit song from an '80s hair band.) Speak clearly and use lots of expression when you read to make it interesting for Owen.

Make up your own stories. You can tell stories to Owen about pretty much anything. (Well, almost anything. What happens in Vegas stays in Vegas.) For example, when you're getting Owen ready for bed, tell a story about how Daddy is changing Owen's diaper ("Once upon a soiled hiney") and putting on pajamas for bedtime ("dressed in foot pajamas tiny"). Tell Owen stories about things that happened to you while you were a child. If you speak with expression, Owen is bound to focus in on what you're saying. (This is also good advice if you run for office.)

---

describing the milestones his child is nearing and achieving, and this will help to ease the adjustment when he and his child are reunited. The app is tailored to the father's status as not currently living with his child; therefore, he will not receive suggestions for activities (which could serve as painful reminders of what he is missing). Instead, he will be prompted to reflect on and prepare for what he might do with his child the next time they are together, and if he is using mDad together with the child's mother or other caregiver, he will be prompted with ideas of questions to ask about what the baby may be doing.

A young father engaged in services to help him learn about his baby's needs and establish a meaningful bond with his baby could use mDad to support continued learning and relationship building between weekly program sessions. The app offers brief, discrete messages with information and activity ideas that a dad can turn to at any time, whether he is goofing off on his phone or looking for an idea of how to play with his infant. Having an interactive parenting resource that is available to him at his convenience may enhance his overall engagement and focus on fathering and help sustain his engagement in the program in which he is participating.

An experienced father might also use and benefit from mDad. The app is tailored to his status as a father of multiple children and will communicate with him in a way that acknowledges and respects his prior parenting experience. At the same time, the app can serve as a reminder of the wide range of child development, helping a father to understand the ways in which his new baby may differ from his older child(ren) in temperament or in the timing of reaching particular milestones. In addition, the app will offer activity suggestions that he can add to his repertoire and that may support his openness to discovery and new experience with his baby. However, as noted earlier, the initial development of mDad does not incorporate content or resources for children with developmental delays or disabilities. Therefore, much of the mDad content may not be useful to fathers of children whose development is considerably outside the range of normal child development.

THE DADTIME APP

After our initial work on the mDad app, we developed new ideas about how technology could be used for social work populations. We focused more narrowly on a population of relevance to social workers: low-income urban fathers with at least one young child. The DadTime app was created to address a different problem than mDad. Specifically, it can be challenging to keep participants engaged in social work programs and interventions. That is, participants tend to drop out or stop attending group or one-on-one sessions, especially when they experience barriers to attending, such as lack of transportation, inconsistent work schedules, and even lack of interest (S. J. Lee et al., 2016; S. J. Lee et al., 2011).

To address this issue, the team that developed the DadTime app sought a novel solution to help keep fathers engaged in a one-on-one fatherhood program that they had signed up for through local social service agencies. The DadTime smartphone app was developed with two primary goals. The first is to decrease fathers' barriers to participation in existing programs so that they attend all of the program sessions and receive a full dose of the fatherhood curriculum. The second goal is to provide curriculum "booster shots" that increase recall of the content and skills learned during the one-on-one fatherhood program sessions. The DadTime app is currently being tested in a research study to examine whether it helps fathers stay engaged (e.g., reduces attrition) in the one-on-one parenting program sessions. If successful, DadTime may eventually be a tool that social service providers can implement in conjunction with existing services to increase participants' program attendance and adherence to program goals. Thus, DadTime provides an example of how a social work agency or a social worker can use an app to augment existing programs at little or no cost to the agency.

Ethical Considerations

Social workers have the professional responsibility to respect the client's right to privacy and to protect the confidentiality of all information obtained from the client throughout service delivery (National Association of Social Workers, 2008). Given that technology-based tools, including mobile apps, allow for broad and ongoing data collection and information sharing with developers (and potentially third-party marketers and advertisers), it is important for social workers who often work with underserved populations—such as adults and children with mental illness (Crawford, Salloum, Andel, Murphy, & Storch, 2013; Rotondi et al., 2005), low-income ethnic minorities and undocumented immigrants (J. Y. Lee & Harathi, 2016), clients with a sexual abuse history (Kernsmith & Kernsmith, 2008), and individuals enrolled in drug court programs (Crunkilton, 2009)—to take extra caution in protecting client privacy and confidentiality by carefully screening apps they recommend to clients, discussing with clients how using the app could potentially compromise their privacy, and obtaining informed consent from clients prior to treatment (Carter, Liddle, Hall, & Chenery, 2015; Giota & Kleftaras, 2014).

Clients may face serious consequences when their mobile devices—containing personal information including pregnancy development, mood tracking history, health appointments, and medication intake routines—are broken, lost, or stolen. This is especially alarming when data are not adequately backed up or accessible on a secondary device. Clients may not have a way of retrieving previously entered information and thus taking necessary steps to protect further data breaches and hacks. Accessing stolen data from a secondary device allows clients to delete data remotely (Apple, 2016). Personal health information is valuable to cybercriminals who may use such data to obtain medical services, bill insurance companies in the client's name, leave inaccurate medical records, or track clients using geolocating—all of which could jeopardize the client's health coverage, credit ratings, social circles, and school and work life (Giota & Kleftaras, 2014).

As a preventative measure, social workers should encourage their clients interested in using mobile apps to carefully read the reviews, try apps that allow user access without entering personal information, delete apps no longer in use, and avoid sharing confidential information via text. Most importantly, social workers should inform clients to download apps at their own risk because there is currently no clear federal measure to ensure that apps deliver credible information and protect the storage and use of user data (Giota & Kleftaras, 2014). This may be challenging given that social workers are trying to encourage the use of mobile apps. To navigate this situation, social workers must do their homework before suggesting a particular app to a client. This entails visiting the mobile apps' website, reading peer-reviewed articles about the app's effectiveness (or lack thereof), and critically reviewing customer ratings.

Research shows that many parents use technology devices and social media at very high rates (Bartholomew, Schoppe-Sullivan, Glassman, Kamp Dush, & Sullivan, 2012). There is some public concern that parents' use of smartphones may be taking their attention away from their children, leading to less parental engagement and eventually poorer child outcomes (Browning, 2012; Hunt, 2015).

Social workers working with parents are in a unique position to reimagine these two domains—engaging with children versus spending time on smartphones—as complementary instead of competing. Both our work and a randomized experimental study of a mobile-phone-enhanced home-visiting parenting program (Carta, Lefever, Bigelow, Borkowski, & Warren, 2013) suggest that mobile apps have the potential to foster positive engagement and responsible parenting. Social workers can encourage parents to use parenting apps during the time they would routinely spend on their phone.

Social Justice Implications

Researchers and practitioners have noted that evidence-based interventions often do not reach the most underserved groups (Aguilera & Munoz, 2011; Gazmararian, Elon, Yang, Graham, & Parker, 2013; Ginossar & Nelson, 2010). Overall, the need for services outstrips the actual availability of such services (Chang et al., 2013), for example, for those living in rural areas with limited transportation or few service providers. Technology can serve as a tool to address these issues, and it has the additional benefits of usually being anonymous, especially for stand-alone informational and skill-building mobile apps that may be beneficial to those who are unlikely to engage in services due to stigma or other factors.

Providing social services that are culturally and technologically sensitive to the needs of the client is another social justice issue for social work practitioners. Social workers have the responsibility to develop skills and techniques to work with a wide range of people who are culturally and geographically diverse or from vulnerable populations (National Association of Social Workers, 2005). For social workers, this may translate to selecting mobile tools that are aligned with their clients' cultural background, language, and experiences as well as their reading and technological literacy levels. In addition, social workers are responsible for becoming competent in technological skills and seeking appropriate training so that they can stay current with new technology and provide ethical services (National Association of Social Workers, 2005).

Although emerging evidence suggests that mobile devices have helped bridge the digital divide (Chang et al., 2013; Ginossar & Nelson, 2010), some researchers have indicated that more attention needs to be placed on technology that addresses and accommodates low-literacy and non-English languages to prevent promoting disparities in access to service (Sly, Miller, & Jandorf, 2014). Despite the high level of mobile phone ownership, social work researchers and practitioners should consider that many individuals from low-income backgrounds may not have SMS services as part of their base rate mobile plans (Martin, 2012) or lack access to app stores for various reasons. Moreover, using SMS or smartphone apps requires a certain level of literacy and technical ability. Some interventions are best accessed on laptops or desktops, devices that are not nearly as ubiquitous as mobile devices.

Further, interventions using computers will likely require additional training for clients and maintenance of devices. To avoid replicating the digital divide, social workers can help clients build their skills so that they can successfully navigate the use of mobile tools in treatment. To that end, social work students should be trained to help clients improve their reading and technological literacy levels, identify effective mobile tools that they can use in conjunction with in-person services, and assess the strengths and limitations of employing mobile tools in their daily practices. Furthermore, they should be encouraged to take elective courses in other departments where they can learn to apply technological information to practice.

Questions for Discussion

1. Think of one underserved population that you are particularly interested in working with as a social worker. What existing technology-based tools could you use or what tool would you design? Consider the mode of intervention, the issue you would address, and the content you would include in your newly developed tool. What privacy or ethical concerns would arise, and how would you address them?
2. How might mobile-based interventions address the lack of parenting services and programs tailored for fathers and the barriers to participation in these programs, such as lack of awareness, scheduling conflicts, mother-oriented programs, and lack of organizational support?
3. There is little research to suggest that eHealth technology-based interventions have significantly reduced pressing health disparities, for example, in rural populations, populations with limited mobility, or populations that experience financial or other barriers to participation. Why have eHealth technology-based interventions failed to achieve their full potential for reducing or eliminating these disparities?

Additional Readings

Brauns, R., Catalani, C., Wimbush, J., & Israelski, D. (2013). Community health workers and mobile technology: A systematic review of the literature. *PLoS ONE, 8*(6), 1–6. doi: 10.1371/journal.pone.0065772. This article systematically reviews the literature on the use of mobile technology by community health workers, identifying opportunities and challenges to strengthen health systems in low-resource settings.

Reamer, F. G. (2013). Social work in a digital age: Ethical and risk management challenges. *Social Work, 58*, 163–172. doi: 10.1093/sw/swt003. This article gives an overview of current technology-based social work services, identifies ethical issues, and provides risk management strategies designed to help protect social workers and their clients.

5 }

Online Support for Youth Transitioning from Foster Care to College and Adulthood

Lynette Kvasny

"To be tested is good. The challenged life may be the best therapist."
—Gail Sheehy, b. *1937–present*

Social media and web technologies are changing the relationships of youth formerly in foster care with each other and with higher educational systems. Technology can assist current and former youth in foster care to achieve self-sufficiency and life skills prior to and after leaving the foster care system. By understanding the types of social support that these young people are seeking and sharing online, people and organizations in a position to provide aid and counsel can be better informed about what is working and what is missing from the services they offer. Technology has the potential to reshape the power dynamic by allowing former and current youth in foster care to inform improvements to long-practiced forms of intervention. Social work practitioners need to understand how and why people use developing information and communication technologies in order to more effectively serve this and other vulnerable populations.

This chapter focuses on how young people, emancipated from foster care, seek and provide peer social support through social media websites as they make their psychosocial adjustment to college and adulthood. Peer support enables youth currently and formerly in foster care to help similarly situated others by offering positive self-disclosure, role-modeling, and hope (Davidson, Chinman, Sells, & Rowe, 2006). Peer social support through social media websites, such as blogs, Facebook groups, discussion forums, and online support groups offers a means of tailoring information in ways that are culturally appropriate and emotionally supportive. I present my own personal journey from foster care to college as well as a case study of how youth in foster care use Tumblr to seek and offer social support to one another during their transition to and while in college.

Background

According to the Bureau of Labor Statistics (2016), 2.1 million (69.2%) of the 3.0 million high school graduates in 2015 enrolled in colleges or universities. The college enrollment rate for young women (72.6%) was higher than that of young men (65.8%), while that for Asians (83.0%) was higher than that of their White (71.1%), Hispanic (68.9%), and Black (54.6%) peers. For these high school graduates, the transition to college life begins as they shift their tassels from left to right. A few weeks later, they will arrive on campus full of confidence in their ability to meet the challenges and opportunities that the college experience will surely bring.

According to the Jim Casey Youth Opportunities Initiative, for the approximately 20,000 youth who transition out of the foster care system annually, only 10% enroll in higher education programs and less than 2% obtain a bachelor's degree. Most do not make it past their first year. "Youth in foster care often report that few people in their lives ever expected them to attend and succeed in college. These students seldom receive the kind of guidance and stable supports needed to prepare for and succeed in higher education" (Emerson, 2015, p. 7). Policy makers, the child welfare community, and higher education professional organizations have started to address this issue with calls for policy advances, practice innovations, and influential advocacy.

Foster Care Demographics

The US foster care system was designed to temporarily protect and nurture children whose parents were unable or unwilling to care for them until those parents were able to provide a safe loving home for them. According to the Adoption and Foster Care Analysis and Reporting System (AFCARS; US Department of Health and Human Services, 2016), in 2015 there were 427,910 young people in foster care. The average age of youth in foster care is 8.5 years old, and males (52% or 222,849) and females (48% or 204,999) are equally represented. Of the youth in foster care in 2015, 43% (182,711) were White, 24% (103,376) were Black, and 21% (91,105) were Hispanic of any race. On average, children remain in state care for nearly 2 years, and 6% have languished there for 5 or more years. Fourteen percent live in institutions or group homes rather than family settings. For the 243,060 young people in foster care in 2015, 51% (123,894) were reunited with parents or primary caretakers, but 9% (20,789) aged out of the foster care system without permanent families or skills to make it on their own. In most states, youth are emancipated abruptly at the age of 18. These young people are expected to live independently at an earlier age than the vast majority of their peers.

Research has shown that those who leave care without being linked to forever families have a higher likelihood than youth in the general population of experiencing significant problems transitioning to adulthood. As reported by Courtney and colleagues (2011, p. 6), "across a wide range of outcome measures, including postsecondary educational attainment, employment, housing stability, public assistance receipt, and criminal justice system involvement, these former youth in foster care are faring poorly as a group." The advocacy group Children's Rights reports that 47% of former foster children are unemployed, and of those with jobs, 71% report an annual income of less than $25,000. Youth who age out of foster care are also less likely than youth in the general population to graduate from high school and to attend or graduate from college. By age 26, approximately 80% of young people who aged out of foster care earned at least a high school degree or GED compared to 94% in the general population (US Department of Health and Human Services, 2016).

Social service agencies have focused primarily on protection and safety, but education has not been on the radar until recently (Nance, 2008). Education is particularly important because it offers economic stability and improved well-being in adulthood. Positive school experiences can counteract the negative effects of abuse, neglect, separation, and lack of permanency experienced by children and youth in foster care (National Working Group on Foster Education, 2014). However, the achievement gap between youth in care and the general population is staggering. According to the National Working Group on Foster Education, youth in care trail their peers in standardized test performance, high school graduation rates, and likelihood of attaining postsecondary education. School age children commonly experience higher rates of absenteeism and a number of moves while in foster care, which can significantly affect their educational experience. They are also twice as likely to experience an out-of-school suspension and three times more likely to be expelled. Fifty percent of youth in foster care aged 17 to 18 graduate from high school, and 84% want to go on to college. However, they face many challenges that make it difficult and sometimes impossible to achieve this goal. Only 20% of youth in foster care graduating from high school went on to college with 2% to 9% completing a bachelor's degree (AFCARS, 2016). Barriers to college completion include a history of trauma, lack of financial support, academic challenges, lack of preparation, and a culture of low expectations (Day, Riebschleger, Dworsky, Damashek, & Fogarty, 2012).

College Expectations and Success

Decades ago, Stern (1966) coined the term "the freshman myth" to describe the unrealistically high expectations of students in their first year in both academic and nonacademic domains. For many first-year students initial optimism wanes as the daily academic and social pressures of college unfold (Holmstrom, Karp,

& Gray, 2002; Karp, Holmstrom, & Gray, 1998). The college utopia that many students expected does not materialize as they face feelings of loneliness and difficulties making meaningful friendships (Larose & Boivin, 1998; Paul & Brier, 2001). Students on residential campuses are learning how to live independently, get along with roommates, and responsibly meet the demands of academic coursework. There are also the social pressures of drinking, dating, experimenting with drugs, and engaging in sexual activity.

A study by Smith and Wertlieb (2005) compared the social and academic expectations of incoming freshmen with students' experiences at the middle and end of their first year of college. While academic and social expectations were not statistically significant predictors of academic success, students with the highest social or academic expectations had lower first-year grade point averages than students with average or below-average expectations.

A high school–college disconnect in academic expectations is also reflected by college readiness indicators, such as standardized test scores, transcript analysis, and remedial coursework enrollment. According to the National Conference of State Legislatures (2016), studies of first-time undergraduates have found that 28% to 40% of students enroll in at least one remedial course. In addition, low-income Hispanic (41%) and African American (42%) students as well as students attending community colleges are more likely to need remediation than their wealthier White peers (31%). Remediation is costly for institutions, and remedial students, particularly those in math and reading, face dismal prospects for earning their degree. A US Department of Education study found, for instance, that only 17% of students enrolled in remedial reading and 27% of students enrolled in remedial math earn a bachelor's degree compared to 58% of students who do not require remediation.

College readiness, academic, and social pressures form a constellation of stressors that limit student success. Yet, in this growing body of literature, one vulnerable population is less commonly examined—college-bound youths aging out of the foster care system. In a *New York Times* article, Winerip (2013) writes, "By definition, foster children have been delinquent, abandoned, neglected, physically, sexually and/or emotionally abused, and that does not take into account nonstatutory abuses like heartache. About two-thirds never go to college and very few graduate, so it's a safe bet that those who do have an uncommon resilience."

Youth with experience of the foster care system who are in college today face many challenges, and academic success remains elusive for the majority. Youth are "heading out into the world with next to nothing—no family, no money, no support" (Guerra, 2015). Young people aging out of foster care often experience health issues and poor education and struggle with drug addiction, homelessness, and criminal behavior (Barth, 1990). They are also, on average, less prepared for college than their peers. Unrau, Font, and Rawls (2012) examined the self-reported college readiness of 81 college freshmen who aged out of foster care prior to or while attending a large 4-year public university. Findings show that youth aging out of foster care are similar to the general freshman population in their academic confidence and in several areas of coping. However, they are different from their peers in a few ways. They report being more academically and socially motivated and more receptive to student services in the areas of academics, personal counseling, and social enrichment. Conversely, they are less receptive to career counseling, have less family support, and perform less well academically upon entrance to college and after the first semester as freshmen. This performance gap persists through the first semester of college. Former youth in foster care are also significantly more likely than their non-foster-care peers to drop out of college before the end of their first year (21% vs. 13%) and prior to degree completion (34% vs. 18%) than their non-foster-care peers (Day, Dworsky, Fogarty, & Damashek, 2011).

Despite these challenges, there are a small number of youth aging out who do succeed. In their survey of 44 young adults who aged out of foster care and went on to successfully earn a college degree, Hass and Graydon (2009) identified a number of protective factors that positively contributed to the students' success: resiliency, a sense of competence, having few of the risk factors associated with mental illness or educational disabilities, a sense of purpose and bright goals for the future, social support, a strong sense of commitment to help others, and involvement in community service activities. Hines and colleagues (2005) also identified resilience as a key factor in college success.

Online Resources for Youth in Foster Care

College students use the Internet more often than the wider population (Ivanitskaya, O'Boyle, & Casey, 2006). With social media websites, students from marginalized populations can form communities that offer a sense of social belonging, trust, acceptance, and encouragement as well as useful information about services that help them to persist in college (Kvasny & Payton, 2018). Used in conjunction with counseling provided by mental health professionals and social workers who understand the role that growing up in foster care plays in producing psychological distress, peer support through social media can help to increase students' ability to cope with such issues as depression, isolation, financial aid, and food and housing insecurity.

While social media is not the magic bullet to curb long-standing disparities in the life opportunities of youth in foster care, they are a promising tool in the field of mental health promotion. For instance, Ziv (2015) highlighted the research of both social and medical scientists studying mental health using Twitter, facial recognition, and linguistics. Research at Johns Hopkins suggests that people experiencing psychological trauma use social media to share information and discuss issues that are causing them overwhelming stress. Montague and Perchonok (2012) report that, if they are tailored to the intended population, social media and video and cell phone technologies can be used to positively affect the health and wellness of historically underserved populations.

Selwyn (2004), Kvasny (2005), Brock (2007), and Kvasny and Payton (2008) posit that the use of terms such as "digital divide" to characterize marginalized communities' experiences with the Internet focus on users' presumed shortcomings in terms of technical abilities and access to the Internet as opposed to other significant factors such as disparities in the availability of relevant content and ability to create and use content. As Hargittai (2002) notes, "people may have technical access, but they may still continue to lack effective access in that they may not know how to extract information for their needs from the Web."

Before individuals can find content to meet their information needs, that content must exist online. In addition, they must have the technical and social competencies to create, curate, and share content. The availability of culturally relevant content is particularly important for marginalized communities because their unique needs may be overlooked by mainstream content providers (Kvasny & Warren, 2006). For instance, college students transitioning from foster care might seek tips and resources designed to help them navigate financial barriers as they transition into adulthood. Foster Care to Success (http://www.fc2success. org/our-programs/information-for-students), the oldest and largest national nonprofit organization working with college-bound youth in foster care, provides scholarships of $2,500 to $5,000, based on a combination of need and merit. The website of College Scholarships for Foster Children (www.collegescholarships. org/scholarships/foster.htm) lists national and state-specific scholarships available to current and former youth in foster care, and the Fostering Success Michigan National Postsecondary Support Map (http://fosteringsuccessmichigan.com/ campus-support), provides links and information on state tuition waivers, statewide education support programs, and 4-year campus-based support programs for students from foster care.

There are also a number of toolkits that cover issues such as finances, employment, healthcare, transportation, and relationships commonly experienced by college students emerging from the foster care system. The US Department of Education, in partnership with the US Department of Health and Human Services, the US Department of Housing and Urban Development, the US Department of Transportation, and the US Department of Labor, as well as youth in foster care and practitioners, developed a Foster Care Transition Toolkit (https://www2. ed.gov/about/inits/ed/foster-care/youth-transition-toolkit.pdf) to inspire and support current and former youth in foster care pursuing college and career opportunities. Similarly, a collaborative project of the Better Futures Project, Research and Training Center for Pathways to Positive Futures, and Portland State University produced "The Things People Never Told Me" toolkit (https://www. pathwaysrtc.pdx.edu/pdf/proj2-ThingsNoOneToldMe.pdf).

While there are a number of online communities for foster parents, campus professionals, social workers, and other service providers (e.g., Foster Care to

Success [http://www.fc2success.org] and Foster Care and Adoptive Community [http://www.fosterparents.com]), there are fewer online communities for youth in foster care. The most popular site is the Foster Club (https://www.fosterclub.com/), which provides a peer support network for children and youth in foster care. This website hosts a wealth of information including moderated discussion forums where young people can communicate safely, question and answer articles, message boards with resources on a variety of topics, contests, and biographies of famous people who were once in foster care. There is also a Facebook page (https://www.facebook.com/FosterClub) where youth can connect with peers. The Foster Care Alumni Association (http://www.fostercarealumni.org) connects the alumni community to transform public policy and practice, ensuring opportunity for people in and from foster care. This association has local chapters in 23 states and leverages the shared experience and expertise that come from being in foster care to improve the quality of life for those transitioning from foster care.

A Personal Journey

I am one of the uncommonly resilient youths who grew up in foster care and successfully completed college. I was in the care of a single guardian from infancy through the age of 18, and I was fortunate enough to grow up in an academically rigorous, well-funded school district in New York State. My personal pathway through college was fraught with limited information and guidance from my family, social workers, teachers, and guidance counselors. The social supports were in place, but as a 17-year-old high school graduate, I did not know how to ask for help. I had no idea how to select colleges or evaluate academic programs. Once I realized that you actually had to pay for college, I was overwhelmed with concerns about financial aid and affordability. I chose to go to Grambling State University based solely on the financial aid package. I had never visited the campus.

I rode a Greyhound bus from the New York Port Authority Bus Terminal to Grambling, Louisiana, and moved into my dorm room alone. Upon reflection, I do not think I had ever ventured beyond the East Coast. Once I got to campus, financial, food, transportation, and housing insecurities arose. While others have at least one parent to guide them and provide for their basic needs, I did not. When the Thanksgiving break arrived, I had nowhere to go. I am forever grateful to the friend who realized my unspoken predicament and invited me to spend the holidays with her family. I worked on campus as a data entry clerk as I struggled to pay the costs of college on my own. I joined the Air Force ROTC solely to earn college tuition money. It was a dreadful experience! When I went home at the end of my first semester, I packed all of my belongings. I knew that I was never going back.

Although I dropped out after my first semester, I was confident that I could make it at another institution closer to home in New York. I was an academically talented student from a well-resourced high school in Westchester County with teachers who had always encouraged me. I had excellent SAT scores and graduated with high honors. I never lost confidence in my academic abilities. School was always a place I loved because I felt empowered and brilliant in the classroom. I attended Mercy College the following fall semester, which was less traumatic because I had stronger social and financial support. I was able to complete my bachelor's of science degree in computer information systems with no major setbacks or complications.

In the decades since my graduation from college, institutional support for foster care youth transitioning to college has slowly emerged. Yet, in 2016, there are still 20 states that either lack campus-based foster care programs at four-year institutions or for which there are no data available (Zoppo, 2015). Only 11 states have statewide support programs, and less than half have tuition waiver programs. The National Postsecondary Support Map produced through research by Western Michigan University Center for Fostering Success (Figure 5.1) shows the states, shaded darker, with a statewide education support program and/or state tuition waivers for students from foster care. Colleges and universities have also been slow to develop programs that support these youth (Emerson, 2015).

While institutional support has been slow to develop, social media and Web-based resources that support communication and information seeking are more plentiful. A Google search on "foster care college" returns results that

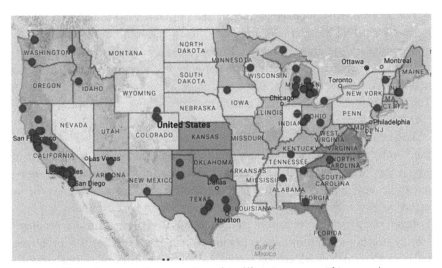

FIGURE 5.1 National postsecondary support map, http://fosteringsuccessmichigan.com/campus-support.

are primarily aimed at financial support in the form of scholarships and tuition waivers. Advice on preparing for college, applying to college, and succeeding in college is also available. Support for basic needs such as housing and meals and counseling for academic and personal issues are found less frequently. However, individuals can leverage the web for social support from peers. This type of online engagement is highly interactive and offers the opportunity for peers to construct and share information in their own voice. In the case study that follows, I provide empirical examples of how peers use the affordances of Tumblr to provide instrumental and expressive aid.

Case Study

This case study uses the framework introduced by R. Lee and Kvasny (2014) in their study of social media and social support for parents who have children diagnosed with rare chronic diseases. Social support is based on empathy and is found to be most effective when it comes from others who are socially similar and facing the same or similar circumstances (Cobb 1976; Thoits, 1995). Our analysis focuses on how content and the technological features of Tumblr, a microblogging and social media website that is popular among teens and young adults, are leveraged to provide instrumental and expressive social support to a psychologically distressed person.

Youth Transitioning Out of Care on Tumblr

A Pew Internet survey of social media use (Desilver, 2013) found that Tumblr is mostly used by young adults (13% of 18- to 29-year-old Internet users); men and women are equally represented. Tumblr users are often urban (7%) and educated (7%). In fact, 65% of Tumblr's audience is college educated. Hispanics and African Americans make up 29% of Tumblr's user base, which suggests that Tumblr is also an effective social media site for reaching communities of color (Plachecki, 2013).

I identified appropriate blog posts by entering the term "foster care" into the Tumblr search engine, manually sifting through the results in the order in which they were presented, and selecting posts with content related to aging out and college for analysis. I analyzed the Tumblr posts using a coding scheme based on two major categories: instrumental support and expressive support. *Instrumental posts* were those with advice on steps to alleviate stressors, problem-solving strategies, and information resources, including expressions of problems, referrals to service providers, opinions, and descriptions of related experience. *Expressive posts* were demonstrations of socioemotional support such as peer support, sympathy, compassion, spiritual advice, and encouragement. I used this coding scheme to determine how the affected communities were using social media for online social support. In addition to content, I categorized posts by the Tumblr features used.

INSTRUMENTAL SOCIAL SUPPORT

A number of Tumblr features are used to request and provide advice and resources to assist current and former youth in foster care as they transition to adulthood and college. The most common form of instrumental aid is the presentation of rather bleak statistics on the life chances of foster care youths. The blog post "Aging out of foster care and into poverty," for example, presents statistics from the US Department of Health and Human Services. This post uses the term "normal" to describe the support structures of children growing up with biological parents, implying that children in foster care have abnormal support structures that are inferior.

Following are some posts that relate to aging out of the foster care system:

> When most children become adults, they have parents to support them financially and emotionally—parents who have done so for the past 18 years. Foster care children aren't most children.
>
> Studies show that children who age out of foster care are different from the normal population in more ways than one. Aged out children are less likely to graduate from high school and college, less likely to be employed, less likely to be able to pay their rent, and more likely to be teen parents or convicted of crimes—all these things add up to lives of poverty.

One common way that students seek support is through "asks," which occur when Tumblr bloggers want to pose a question to their audience ("followers"). The following example is an anonymous ask seeking instrumental aid that was posted to a blog run by a group of rape survivors who give advice on coping, healing, and surviving sexual trauma.

> My foster mom used to make me have sex with a number of men when I was around the ages of 7–12 for drug money. I am now 18 and out of foster care, I'm in college to become a surgeon, I feel like I should be happy/proud of myself. Instead I still feel disgusting. It's hard to focus on my studies (definitely in med school) when all I can think about is what she did to me. Maybe it was my fault? I could of told my social worker but instead I stayed quiet.

The responder offers compassionate advice for behavioral change:

> First . . . LITERALLY NONE OF THIS is in any way your fault.
>
> Do I, as a foster care social worker, wish you had come forward? Of course, I do. Does that make any of what happened your responsibility? Absolutely not.

You know what I wish even more than you had come forward? I wish that whomever licensed your foster mom had seen that she was a predator seeking a paycheck and a victim. I wish that every foster care system in the country could find these placement providers and weed them out.

But that's a battle for another day.

Look, these thoughts that something we could have done would have stopped our abuse . . . they're understandable, and they have a purpose, but they aren't realistic, and they really aren't helpful.

We do this to ourselves because we want an explanation. We are entertaining a fantasy that our lives could have been different. . . . But I tend to think that a big part of recovery is just trying to sit still and accept what happened.

There's a place for anger. There's a time for honoring your wounds and tending to them. . . . I just . . . also think that acceptance is (for me at least) the biggest component of the recovery process.

So I would encourage redirecting your energy when you are able. (I say when you are able because sometimes we can't do that, and it's okay, and it's usually a sign that you *need* to be in that place of anger or hurt of whatever for a little while.) Basically, I think we need to listen to ourselves. I do believe that each of us has this internal sense of wisdom about what we need and what will help us, and the biggest trick is learning how to listen to your wisdom.

Reblogging is another Tumblr feature commonly used to share content that was posted by other bloggers. This helps circulate useful content while acknowledging the originator of that content. In the post that follows, a blogger shared a YouTube video of "ReMoved," an award winning documentary that details the experiences of children in the foster care system:

ReMoved and Remember My Story: This video project follows a little girl and her brother in their trip through the foster care system and court trials for their mother's custody. The reality of the children involved in the care system—how they react to life, feel about themselves—is often overlooked. What is focused on more heavily is the potential abuse of both the care providers and parents, the difficulties of case loads for social workers, and the outside perspective of addictions, gangs, and other deviant behaviour many foster kids resort to.

"Foster-care-survivors" reblogged this post and added commentary to engage their followers:

MAJOR TRIGGER WARNING in effect for these short films. I watched them, and they hit very close to home.

(For those who chose to watch:) Do you think the filmmakers did a good job capturing the experience? How was your experience different/similar?

Another Tumblr blogger talked about the video:

> "The sun comes up every morning, but do you know where? Each place it's somewhere different. It's hard to find East when you keep moving around, but at least it comes. It always comes."
>
> This part of the short film "Removed" really hit me hard. When I was in foster care that was one of the things I was always trying to figure out: which direction was where. Moving around frequently made it difficult to remember. . . . Once I gained a sense of direction I felt like I always knew where I was, even when moving into a completely different home. I felt secure.

Tumblr bloggers also leverage crowdfunding as a means of providing financial resources to youth in foster care. The blogger "parenting by proxy" reflected on the enjoyment that she received from getting care packages in college: In an attempt to bring that same joy to others, she asked her followers to contribute funds to stock and send care packages to former youth in foster care attending college:

> **Floating an idea to help aged-out teens**
>
> I loved care packages when I was in college. Once, a friend sent me a box containing loose confetti and candy bars, and it was basically the best thing that had ever happened. Care packages from my parents were more practical (socks, art supplies for class) and also beloved. I knew there was someone out there who took the time to go to the post office to ship me a little cardboard box of love, and I appreciated it.
>
> Would any of you be willing to spend $10–$30 on and send a care package to aged-out former youth in foster care who are living independently/attending college in the military? I think this would be a great way to demonstrate emotional support and create a connection with youth. Obviously, nothing can replace the presence of supportive parents, but social capital comes in all different forms.
>
> Like this post if you'd be willing to do that. If I get sufficient likes, I'll create a SurveyMonkey form to collect your info and that of interested youth, and then I'll match people up.

Forty-five Tumblr users "liked" the post and, by doing so, signaled that they were interested in offering instrumental aid.

Expressive Social Support

Expressive posts offer socio-emotional support, and include peer encouragement, sympathy, compassion, and spiritual advice. Often expressed by visual media and confessional writing. One example is from an untitled blog post that contains an image of a boy dressed up as a superhero, seated atop a skyscraper with the caption "Who has my back?" The boy's flowing red cape stands out sharply from the grey skyline. He is solitary, looking down at the cityscape below with his chin resting on his fist, face concentrated. The choice of a child superhero may signify that the blogger is facing significant challenges as he enters adulthood, and the contrast of a mighty costume on a child's body could describe the anxiety of taking on overwhelming life tasks.

Blogs afford users a space for confessional writing that shares poignant experiences by telling stories. The following confession from a woman who aged out of foster care discusses her inability to adequately handle "real adult questions" because she has no one to turn to. She shares her frustrations with similarly situated peers, who "like" her post as a means of showing that they identify with this situation. Hashtags are used to make it easier for other Tumblr bloggers to find content with similar themes.

> Note to self: need to invent a text-to-get-answers-to-real-adult-questions hotline for kids without parental resources. Because Lord knows if I know how to get/choose/manage a health insurance plan.
> #fostercare #this is foster care #foster care #fosteryouth #agedout

In a subsequent post, we see the blogger publicly making sense of her experiences as a former youth in foster care now enrolled in college:

> Some days it feels so hard to write or talk about anything foster/past related. The stigma of aging out and being in the system weighs on me hard.
> I live an entirely double life at school—with the exception of two friends, no one really knows my background. It is really easy to blend in some aspects, but in others, its hard not to feel left out. The university I go to is generally populated by very privileged, rich kids, so sometimes it blows my mind to see the dichotomy between their situations and mine. Nonetheless, I'm surrounded by people at school who never fail to make me feel loved and supported; in particular, I have a few staff members in an organization I belong to that generally look out for me, and I'm missing them a lot right about now. It is starting to feel painful to think I have two more weeks until I go back.
> I work everyday, trying to keep saving up money. My brother is locked up in juvie and hopefully I can visit him before going back to school. Still feeling the struggle of finding somewhere to sleep every night for the next two weeks, but I know I can keep staying with my old foster family if I really need to. I am so thankful to have them in my life still.
> #this is foster care #fostercare #foster care #agedout

The Tumblr confessional space is also powerful for showing the importance of resilience and mental healthcare in helping foster care to adjust to adulthood.

Growing up in foster care leaves psychological scars. The next blogger reflects on repressed memories and learned behaviors from her childhood in foster care, and how they manifest negatively in adulthood. She is seeking self-affirmation. In her post, we see the concept of "normal" being used to describe an idealized notion of family.

> I frequently realize . . .
>
> That the way I conditioned myself to live and act while in foster care, doesn't translate well into adulthood.
>
> It was my only way to ensure my personal survival in a world where nothing is yours and your livelihood depends on someone else's charity.
>
> For me, I'd try really hard not to be a nuisance, not to be rude, not to get in the way and to follow the rules lest someone gets annoyed at me and I have to move again.
>
> So I don't talk much if I don't feel I have something relevant to say. I apologize a lot. I stick to the rules and rarely deviate. I view myself as an inherently bothersome thing and in order to be tolerated, I consider other people before myself.
>
> I am always critiquing myself, forgetting that there's no need for that anymore. I can have an opinion now. I can have hopes and dreams and the drive to do what I want in life. I don't have to take shit and be neglected anymore.
>
> I've had a family for about 10 years now so I should be . . . normal, right? But I also spent the first 10 years of my life being ignored, neglected and beaten. I don't want to be a hurt, scared little girl anymore.
>
> All I want to be now is ME, the way I was meant to be. But its so hard when I have that little voice telling me that if I don't act a certain way, I'll be sent away again. And I believe it. Because I just don't know how to be . . . me.

Ethical Considerations

Social work practice with youth aging out of foster care is guided by the National Association of Social Workers (NASW) *Standards for Social Work Practice in Child Welfare* (2013), which interprets the core values of the *Code of Ethics*—"service, social justice, the dignity and worth of the person, the importance of relationships, integrity, and competence" (NASW, 2008)—in terms relevant to children and youth served by the child welfare system, including those who are or have been in foster care. One core principle of the *Code of Ethics*, social and political action (6.04 a), mandates that "social workers should engage in social and political action that seeks to ensure that all people have equal access to the resources, employment, services, and opportunities they require to meet their basic human needs and to develop fully" (NASW, 2008). This section of the code directs social workers to provide youth access to those resources that cultivate individual development.

Foster care youth in college and university settings are working hard at their own development, yet literature makes clear that they often do so with few resources. For example, for the 2015 annual survey of the Association for University and College Counseling Center Directors, of 518 responding directors, 4 reported responses similar to "University has set up department to serve foster students" and one reported "securing grant money" to serve foster students (Reetz, Krylowicz, Bershad, Lawrence, & Mistler, 2016, p. 75). Such statistics make obvious that youth coming from foster care into college will encounter a near-total lack of institutionalized support from the college that admitted them (Unrau et al., 2012).

Cultural competence is defined as a critical ethical mandate by the *Code of Ethics*. Social work with youth transitioning from foster care to college may need to reflect an awareness of the historic mistrust of formal social services and therapy by some marginalized communities and to recognize that, for these individuals, technology may provide a valuable alternative (Kvasny & Payton, 2018). Social workers have an ethical duty to acquaint themselves with supportive virtual communities, to direct clients to them as appropriate, and to understand the value that these supportive spaces provide to clients as critical tools of identity and making meaning.

Standard 11 of the *Standards for Social Work Practice in Child Welfare* emphasizes the responsibility to practice youth engagement within child welfare, articulating a special focus on how young people transition out of foster care. The code emphasizes a "successful transition into adulthood" based in a "planning process that focuses on the development of independent living skills and fully addresses topics such as housing, health insurance, education, employment, financial literacy, and permanency" (NASW, 2013, p. 22). Technology can be a source of information, a way to build marketable skills, and a conduit to the lifelong support of community. All social work emphasizes the importance of human relationships, and the earlier case study makes clear the power of technology to create community by enabling a novel form of virtual relationship. The collective social media space described above is an example of a social support built by the community it is meant to serve, demonstrating the empowerment that technology can confer to disenfranchised groups. Professional competence in contemporary culture includes the ability to assess and understand those technologies with which clients engage, a willingness to facilitate connection to virtual resources and technological skill-building, and the acknowledgment of technology's potential to enable clients and communities to define meaningful strategies of change.

Social Justice Implications

Access to social media and web resources is largely free of cost. Such access is more widely available and the technical skills to use these resources are more equitably distributed across advantaged and disadvantaged groups (Smith, 2016). Social media and the web are also powerful technologies for fostering peer support and communication. These technologies can help to diminish social inequities in access to college, enhance students' ability to find resources and persist in college, and help youth transition into adulthood.

While educational campaigns and culturally compelling interventions are being developed by social work practitioners, policy makers, state legislatures, advocacy groups, and university researchers, young adults are seeking social support from their peers. Their needs are not entirely being met once they are admitted into college and ongoing social support is needed to help them to persist toward completing a postsecondary education program. Online blogging communities offer collective spaces that facilitate the search for peer social support. These communal spaces are being used to supplement, and in some cases replace, professional counseling. However, the efficacy of computer-mediated communication among peers as a tool to provide meaningful support remains an open question (Bambina, 2007).

A growing number of colleges have created extensive local support programs aimed at current and former youth in foster care. These programs offer scholarships, year-round housing in the dorms for those who have no other place to live, academic and therapeutic counseling, tutoring, healthcare coverage, financial literacy workshops, campus jobs, and help with basic necessities. However, a college preparatory curriculum that is unique to youth in foster care is clearly needed to improve college readiness. At the policy level, the 2008 Fostering Connections to Success and Increasing Adoptions Act is useful because it provides states the option of extending federal aid programs for youth in foster care from age 18 to 21. This should help to reduce the financial burden placed on these young adults. People who serve youth in foster care, including foster parents, social workers, school counselors, college advisors, mentors, and all others, have a duty to become familiar with these types of institutional resources (Davis, 2006).

The Casey Foundation (2010) offers a comprehensive framework for improving students' success in postsecondary education through program enhancement for students transitioning from foster care (Figure 5.2). This framework calls on the collaborative efforts of students, community, and campus organizations to deliver programming in planning transitions; student engagement and leadership; and personal guidance, counseling, and support to help students across a number of domains including housing, academic and financial aid. This framework is multidimensional and collaborative, and it informs the development of sustainable programming based on rigorous data analysis and assessment.

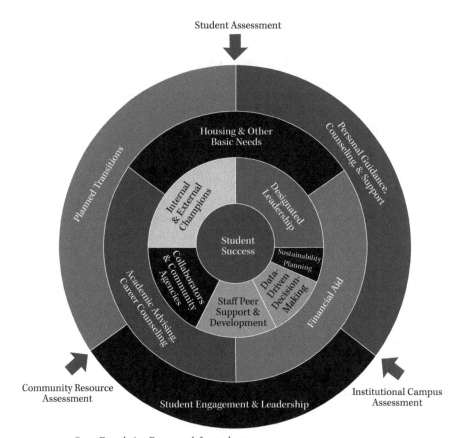

FIGURE 5.2 Casey Foundation Framework for student success.

Questions for Discussion

1. Choose a website that offers support to youth in foster care or those transitioning out and write a narrative essay that describes your response to the website. Write your initial impressions of the website, describe your step-by-step progression through the webpage, and finally record your impressions after you have completed your review. How does this final impression differ from your first impression? Does the webpage achieve its objective of providing useful, timely, and trustworthy information?

2. Imagine that you are a member of an advocacy group working to improve the access to college for youths transitioning from foster care. What recommendations would you make, and what policies would you want to see created or enforced?

3. Imagine that you are a social worker helping young people transitioning from foster care. Write a letter to a local high school

or the president of a local community college in which you make a case for academic, housing, financial, and other supports for college-bound youths.

4. Try blogging for a week. Visit Tumblr.com and follow the directions to set up your own blog. Write an entry that has a link to a site on the Web that you find important about youth in foster care and college. Along with the link, write a one- to two-paragraph or two commentary on this link: Write an additional post on the next 4 days. On day 6, spend an hour searching for additional blogs that might help former youth in foster care to become familiar with the blogging community. Note the type of content that they publish and the issues that they address. On the 7th day, write an entry analyzing your experience: What do you find worthwhile or problematic about writing a blog? How is it different from writing for print? How does your voice add to the existing blogging community? Do you think you might continue blogging in the future?

Additional Readings

Gottfried, J., & Shearer, E. (2016). *News use across social media platforms.* Pew Research Center. Retrieved from http://www.journalism.org/2016/05/26/social-media-and-news-2016-appendix-a-2013-and-2016-trends/

Nakumara, L. (2002). *Cybertypes: Race, ethnicity, and identity on the Internet.* New York, NY: Routledge.

New, J. (2015, October 9). Reaching vulnerable students. *Inside Higher Education.* Retrieved from https://www.insidehighered.com/news/2015/10/09/new-organization-study-ways-improve-mental-health-services-students-color

Scott, L., & House, L. (2005). Relationship of distress and perceived control to coping with perceived racial discrimination among black youth. *Journal of Black Psychology, 31,* 254–272.

Scott, L., McCoy, H., Munson, M., Snowden, L., & McMillen, J. C. (2011). Cultural mistrust of mental health professionals among black males transitioning from foster care. *Journal of Child and Family Studies, 20,* 605–613.

Seaton, R., Upton, R., Gilbert, A., & Volpe, V. (2014). A moderated mediation model: Racial discrimination, coping strategies, and racial identity among black adolescents. *Child Development, 85,* 882–890.

6 }

Digital Storytelling

TOOLS, TECHNIQUES, AND TRADITIONS

Melanie Sage, Jonathan B. Singer, Andrea LaMarre, and Carla Rice

"After nourishment, shelter and companionship, stories are the thing we need most in the world."

—Phillip Pullman, *b. 1946–present*

The art of storytelling has long been a multimedia affair. From cave paintings to Shakespearean plays to graphic novels, communications use combinations of audio, visual, and written texts offering complementary ways for adult learners to make sense of information. Although academics have long relied on books and journal articles as the most legitimate sources of knowledge, a growing literature about multimedia and multimodal learning identifies the ways that the brain processes and stores information better through the use of combinations of sensory information (Shams & Seitz, 2008), thereby enhancing comprehension. Using Bloom's Taxonomy (Bloom, 1956) and the updated Bloom's Digital Taxonomy (Churches, 2009), the social worker can understand the ways that manipulating and creating digital tools for storytelling can add value to communicating a story for both the author and audience.

Background

What is a story? A traditional story takes the audience on a journey, which usually has a beginning, middle, and end, but not always.

The sociolinguist William Labov (1997) identified four stages of a story: (1) an abstract or introduction; (2) orientation to time, place, activities, or characters; (3) complicating action or the story problem; and (4) resolution. The novelist Kurt Vonnegut identified six major narrative arcs or story shapes that are found in Western literature (Eilam, 2012; Vonnegut, 2006; Vonnegut & Simon, 2007).

He suggested that the New Testament and Cinderella have the same "happily ever after" narrative arc (life is good, tragedy strikes, and then a magical gift results in eternal happiness). Contrast this with the narrative arc of stories such as *Hamlet* (unclear whether events are good or bad), or season 4 of *Orange Is the New Black* (things go from bad to worse). While these stories are inherently descriptive, they can also be explanatory (e.g., origin stories) or persuasive (e.g., advertisement). Using stories to explain or persuade makes sense, since human brains turn information into stories, even where they do not exist. Journalists often report on youth suicide by writing the story bullying + final straw = suicide, even when there is no evidence of bullying and there has been a long history of known risk factors such as depression, anxiety, and access to guns. Photojournalism is so powerful because our brain takes the image and then creates a story around it. One glance at a powerful documentary photograph invites us to imagine the whole world of the character, from how he or she got there to what he or she has been through to what life may be like now.

Social workers can apply Labov's storytelling framework to the story of a policy, a research paper, or an individual's path through a system. Their jobs revolve around key players (characters), who may be individuals or organizations in a problematic story (or the postmodern version, a story that has been problematized), and they ideally help seek resolution. The last part—the resolution—tends to be the focus of education and policy. Practices and policies are taught with the goal of resolution, but we argue that there is great value in social workers recognizing the whole story, especially the parts that are rarely part of the mainstream narrative. The case study we present later in this chapter describes one way that digital storytelling can give voice to marginalized stories and challenge the traditional divisions between professional and consumer.

Storytelling is central to effective advocacy. Policies often change because a politician is emotionally connected to an issue and can tell a compelling personal story. For example, Senator Gordon Smith of Oregon became one of the nation's most important advocates for suicide prevention after his son died by suicide in 2003 (G. Smith, 2006). Initially overcome with grief and believing that he had put country above family, Senator Smith told colleagues that he was going to quit the Senate. They convinced him to stay and to use his considerable influence to pass into legislation two suicide prevention bills that had been languishing in committee for more than 10 years. The result was the Garrett Lee Smith Memorial Act, which has provided over $100 million dollars in suicide prevention funding since 2006. This narrative arc fits Vonnegut's "man in the hole" story, where the main character gets into trouble (the hole) and by resolving the problem (getting out of the hole) becomes a better person (Eilam, 2012; Vonnegut, 2006; Vonnegut & Simon, 2007). It resulted in the most influential suicide prevention policy in American history. This is why storytelling is central to effective advocacy.

WHAT IS DIGITAL STORYTELLING?

Digital storytelling is the use of any of a number of digital tools, including audio, video, art, graphics, photographs, and words, to communicate a story. The first uses of digital storytelling involved documentation of oral narratives. In the late 1980s, the Center for Digital Storytelling began training people to capture personal narratives so that they would not be lost from the historical record. The center developed seven elements of a digital story: (1) the author's point of view or perspective; (2) the question that the story answers; (3) the emotional content of the story that helps it to come alive; (4) the "gift of voice" that helps personalize the story's content; (5) the power of the soundtrack or sounds that support the storyline; (6) economy or using just enough information to avoid overwhelming the audience; and (7) pacing or story rhythm. A digital story may contain some or all of these elements. The definition of digital storytelling is very broad, but essentially it is a narrative constructed and communicated using digital tools.

Unlike storytelling in the 1980s, today's digital storytelling is inexpensive to produce, share, and consume. Often audio and visual stories are spliced together in interesting ways, leaving the story creator in charge of the content, pacing, and development of the point of view. A digital story in audio or video form is often 2 to 5 minutes long, about the length of a short news segment. Digital storytelling can also be a single picture or one-page infographic. Regardless of the medium or length, effective digital stories incorporate an emotional appeal to catch the audience's attention. For instance, Google has a digital evangelist who teaches storytelling to improve sales (Gallo, 2016). In 2015, Dave Isay, founder of StoryCorps, a project dedicated to recording and archiving stories, developed an app that walks people through the process of recording a digital story (http://storycorps.me). That same year, Isay started "The Great Thanksgiving Listen," which encouraged teenagers to spend Thanksgiving interviewing their grandparents and thereby capturing an oral history over a single weekend (https://storycorps.me/about/the-great-thanksgiving-listen/).

Digital technologies promote opportunities to share work with a wider audience and encourage collaboration and creativity (Purcell, 2013). Challenges to bringing digital communication to social work include clarifying the differences between formal and informal writing, understanding the audience, avoiding shorthand or simplistic communication styles common to some types of digital communication, assuring access to technological tools, and countering the view that digital communication tools are for fun and not for professional use (Purcell, Buchanan, & Friedrich, 2013). These are useful topics for instruction and discussion in the college classroom or social work setting.

TOOLS FOR DIGITAL STORYTELLING

Tools that would have once been locked away in the technology closet in a department's basement are now available on a typical smartphone. A camera, video recorder, and audio recorder, and even editing and presentation software either come with the phone or are downloadable as apps. A number of free or low-cost apps add additional utility to these tools. For instance, a photo and text-editing app such as ReType (sumoing.com/apps/retype) allows the author to overlay text in different formats on pictures. An audio-editing tool such as Voice Recorder (online-voice-recorder.com/) allows for parts of the audio to be clipped or combined. The video editing app Magisto (magisto.com) allows for advanced video editing and narration. Applications for capturing and sharing digital stories, such as the movie creator in Google Photos, are designed for and work better on mobile devices than desktop versions.

Table 6.1 lists tools and techniques that are currently used in telling a digital story. Because current programs will likely be discontinued or obsolete within a few years, you should focus on the program's function rather its brand. Some of these tools are free and others are not. Many tools offer free for educational use options.

App names and availability may vary by phone type (Apple, Android, and Windows). Potential users should also note that many free apps have paid services after download and/or trial-type frameworks that limit full functionality. In order to avoid unanticipated issues, potential users should become well acquainted with a tool's functionality and costs.

Desktop programs also offer editing capability. For instance, Audacity (sourceforge.net/projects/audacity/) is a shareware audio program that allows for advanced audio editing, including splicing, overlaying multiple audio tracks (such as a music file over a voice file), and other advanced effects. Videos can be edited with software included with computers, such as iMovie for Apple computers and MovieMaker for PCs.

Video editing is increasingly available online. Websites such as YouTube (youtube.com) and Vimeo (vimeo.com) allow digital multimedia (video, audio, images, and PowerPoint presentations) to be published free and also offer some integrated editing features. Some videos already uploaded to YouTube have copyright permissions that allow for remixing, which means that a user can incorporate content from another user in his or her own videos. Additionally, YouTube offers a free music and sound effects library with audio licensed under Creative Commons.

Live video sharing is now freely available online through tools such as Periscope (periscope.tv). A story author can adjust Periscope's settings to save a live recording after it is finished. Viewers can tune in live from their smartphones and share their love with the story author by tapping on the screen while watching. This is useful for live storytelling performances or for capturing narrative-style digital stories that will not be edited.

Authors of digital stories can use screen capture software such as Techsmith Jing (techsmith.com) or Screencastify to record a video of anything that is occurring on

TABLE 6.1 } **Considerations for Digital Storytelling**

		Considerations for Digital Storytelling		
Hardware	**Software**	**Techniques**	**Outputs**	**Ethics**
Smartphone	Phone apps	Record in quiet space	Health messages	Informed consent
Video camera	Storify	Test sound quality	Infographics	Institutional review
Audio Recorder	Piktochart	Use text to caption videos	Video shorts	Confidentiality
Laptop/Desktop	Powerpoint for slideshows	Train participants to use technology	Audio stories	Student privacy
Microphone	Audacity		Photo exhibits	Professionalism

their desktop, including a PowerPoint presentation and audio captured through a computer microphone or headset.

Infographics offer a unique way to combine images and text, typically to summarize important information in a multimedia format that is appealing, well organized, and shareable (see https://www.pinterest.com/pin/285345326364875526, for example). Although PowerPoint or more sophisticated graphic design software such as Adobe Photoshop and InDesign can be used for this purpose, Web-based infographic programs make the job easier and require little to no technical training. Popular free software for creating infographics includes VennGage (venngage.com), Piktochart (piktochart.com), and InfoGram (https://infogram. com). Most of these tools have added paid features but offer users the opportunity to create basic infographics free. Some of the tools also support data visualization by allowing users to enter spreadsheet-style numerical data to build charts and graphs.

Some websites enable creation of rich text (text with images) specifically for social media. VennGage and Pablo (Pablo.buffer.com) optimize images for the Pinterest, Instagram, Twitter, and Facebook. These rich text images are simple to create and easy to share, which can amplify the reach of your story.

Sometimes an author may wish to combine or curate (Mihailidis & Cohen, 2013) the stories of others to create new content. For instance, a digital story can be told about mental health stigma by capturing powerful tweets of others who have firsthand experiences with stigma alongside those of policy makers who are working on improving mental health systems. Free Web-based software called Storify (storify.com) allows users to organize tweets or other content and include their own words or pictures to help make sense of the story and then use a Storify-generated link to reshare the new story.

APPLICATIONS OF DIGITAL STORYTELLING

Digital storytelling is used across professional education programs and professions to enhance the digital literacy, storytelling, and communication skills and critical thinking of health providers. For instance, Community Health Worker students in Alaska used digital storytelling to create 2- to 3-minute consumer health messages about cancer; they reported that the content creation allowed them to share culturally respectful messages that promoted awareness and wellness (Cueva, Kuhnley, Revels, Schoenberg, & Dignan, 2015). Wexler, Gubrium, Griffin, and DiFulvio used digital storytelling as a suicide prevention program with Alaska native youth (2013). Over a 3-year period they produced 566 digital stories with youth. These served as digital hope kits for youth, who could watch them to remember key reasons for living. Digital storytelling was found to successfully engage undergraduate medical students in clinical reflection (Sandars & Murray, 2011).

Social work students and academics may find that digital storytelling is a successful tool for disseminating research findings or summarizing academic papers for new and wider audiences. Digital dissemination of research via social networks has been demonstrated to improve citation counts and scholarship views (Ovadia, 2014). Researchers who use social networking sites such as Twitter benefit from opportunities to disseminate research, discover new research, get feedback on forthcoming work, and network with other scholars. Stories can be shared through 140-character tweets with embedded URL and through images. For instance, in 2015 the Royal Society of Chemistry held a Twitter poster conference, allowing researchers to upload academic posters as tweets for scientific communication (Randviir, Ilingworth, Baker, Cude, & Banks, 2015). This not only expanded the audience but also challenged researchers to consider new digital outlets for their scientific stories.

A number of disciplines have used digital storytelling in their practice settings, which makes digital storytelling skills easily transferable from the classroom to the field. The act of telling and sharing one's story is a therapeutic tool. For example, one project studied the impact of digital storytelling workshops on members of a Latino community with chronic disease (Briant, Halter, Marchello, Escareño, & Thompson, 2016); participants each developed a 5-minute visual story about their experiences. The study participants said that the digital stories built community connections and healing; they felt good about sharing stories and potentially helping someone else. In several studies of digital storytelling as a health promotion strategy, consumers or others affected by a health issue shared their experiences as a way to process their own story and to offer it as a public tool for prevention or coping to benefit others with similar experience (A. Gubrium, 2009). These types of interventions have included a wide range of participants, from childhood cancer patients (Akard et al., 2015) to indigenous elders (Iseke & Moore, 2011). A noted strength of these techniques is that they offer opportunities to capture and share stories situated within specific communities, thereby improving dissemination of culturally informed health messages.

"It Gets Better" (IGB) was a video campaign started on September 21, 2010, by the sex columnist and publisher Dan Savage and his husband, Terry Miller, to address suicide risk in LGBTQ youth (Gal, Shifman, & Kampf, 2016). This campaign is a prototypical viral digital storytelling advocacy project in that people were inspired to make videos of their own stories, which were shared on a massive scale and became the focus of conversations at the individual, community, and national levels. Social workers who are looking to connect geographically diverse communities should consider the power of video testimonials such as IGB. Testimonials are powerful, because personal experience cannot be refuted and can provide a sense of connection and community among those who relate to the message. Social workers should be aware, however, that if all of the stories follow the same format (e.g., "it was bad then it got better"), the narrative can marginalize those whose experiences do not fit. A viral campaign is inherently decentralized, but planning a diversity of narrative arcs in the early stages of the campaign can serve as examples for future videos. The IGB project promised LGBTQ youth that their lives will get better, and early publications pointed to the project as a universal suicide prevention project. Neither of those claims has been substantiated by research. Social workers should therefore include an evaluation component for digital storytelling projects and avoid making unsubstantiated statements about the effect or benefit of a digital storytelling project on a population or problem area until the research has been completed.

STORYTELLING IN SOCIAL WORK

Storytelling is a vital skill for social workers, who tell and use stories in their work even though they probably do not conceptualize it as a significant part of their social work practice. In direct practice work, through the use of case notes and court reports, social workers tell the story of a problem, a crisis, and a resolution. When a child welfare social worker makes a case for removing a child from her home, the story must explain the circumstances, the specific risks to the child, the steps to mitigate the risks, and the plan for keeping the child safe. The story must be rich with detail and convincing enough for the courts to understand the need for serious intervention in the life of a family. Society connects so many meanings and stories to the word "family" that interruption of the family system is taken very seriously.

Stories are also important in clinical settings. For example, narrative therapy uses reframing and retelling of stories as a tool to help clients create new stories about themselves, see possibilities where they were not formerly present, and externalize the problem (Angus & Greenberg, 2011). A teenage boy may come to therapy with guilt related to his choice to study dance because of internalized cultural stories about its connection to mental models of masculinity. The therapist may help him consider where these stories have come from, to capitalize on the times when the dominant story has not been true, to externalize the problem of guilt by giving it a character name and finding ways to avoid it, and to retell and reinforce a new narrative about the brave role of young men who step outside a cultural expectation, thereby standing up for the possibility for all young men who want to dance.

Photovoice, another technique often used by social work practitioners or researchers, uses photographic images to tell a story and make meaning of a personal or community experience (Wang & Burris, 1997). For instance, youth who live in downtown Chicago may be given cameras and asked to take pictures of what "play" means to them. Through their unique knowledge of their community, they can collect images to launch discussions and make meaning, helping others understand the story. Conversely, Photovoice can be used in individual or family therapy; for example, a mother might be asked to assemble images that help explain what "happy" means as a way to launch conversations that may have been hard to share without a focused prompt.

Social workers in macro practice relate stories to policy makers, share stories of organizations, and disseminate public health messages to client populations.

In each of these cases, the social worker must master the craft of focusing the audience's attention on the most important moments, adjusting the length of the story to hold the audience's interest, and convincing the audience to care about the story. Dissemination is enhanced by using digital storytelling tools. Digital storytelling is a new kind of storytelling medium for social work. Although digital stories are not often seen in direct practice, audiovisual information might be incorporated into the standard casenote and court report. Foster care workers who support youth through lifebooks that record snippets of their histories are already experimenting with "digital lockers" (Gustavsson & MacEachron, 2008). A digitally recorded story about a trauma experience narrated by the child who experienced it is a common technique of trauma-focused cognitive behavioral therapy (Anderson & Cook, 2015). Macro social workers are embracing digital storytelling strategies, from creating infographic stories from annual reports to curating social media posts into discussion of social justice issues to collaborating on community projects to advance knowledge about social justice issues (Gelman & Tosone, 2010). The need for social workers to have digital competence is growing, and technology is finding its way into multiple areas of our practice.

Benefits of digital storytelling in the social work classroom include the opportunity for students to develop skills in content creation and curation, as well as the ability to quickly disseminate a story to a wide audience, to share a story asynchronously without using up classroom time, and to communicate with a public audience while still being mentored by a social work instructor. Students are shown to perform better and take their assignments more seriously when they take place in authentic learning environments with clearly transferable skills that have real-world application (Herrington, Reeves, & Oliver, 2014). By sharing digital stories in public spaces, students can practice the ethical use of technology in an applied environment.

Technology embedded in assignments offers opportunities for social workers to practice the media skills vital for engaged citizenship. Mihailidis and Thevinin (2013) argue that, as technology becomes ubiquitous, civic engagement gives way to digital participation and students become less connected to physical communities such as neighborhood meetings and voting efforts. Digital storytelling competencies allow students to engage as media creators, curators, and informed consumers in political and social justice discussions and thus move beyond the more passive digital participation of liking and reposting other people's content (Brady, McLeod, & Young, 2015; Young, 2015).

Case Study

In the following case study, chapter authors LaMarre and Rice look at a digital storytelling project that was codeveloped with participants to address issues in a community of people who identified as having an eating disorder. As with all marginalized communities, this community struggled with both the rigid and pathological stereotypes reinforced by the dominant society and the more nuanced and representative narratives generated by community members through their digital storytelling project. Creating the digital story was valuable because of both the *process* of clarifying and visually representing the narrative and the *product* that participants were able to share with people in the broader society. A central component of community organizing is meetings and workshops that challenge and rewrite dominant pathologizing narratives.

In the Western world, we have one dominant way of understanding mental states that people experience as distressing—the medical or psychiatric model (Ussher, 2010). When the representational field (or available ways of making sense of an experience) around mental distress is limited, individuals may feel unable to have their voices heard if their lived experience does not match the dominant stories or stereotypes that surround their diagnoses.

Digital storytelling, by putting technology into the hands of those with lived experience and inviting first-person accounts, provides a new way of talking through issues and problems in ways that do not fully map onto medical views. However, we cannot simply ask those with lived experience to share their stories without helping them to do so in a way that will not cause harm. Specifically, we are cautious not to ask people to divulge their innermost experiences without adequate framing or to lead them to tell stories in a way that re-entrenches problematic and narrow stereotypes about their experience. In our digital storytelling workshops we are cognizant of power dynamics between researchers and participants; dominant representations of issues such as eating disorders; disagreements among experts, advocates, and people with lived experience about what causes and alleviates eating distress; and interactional dynamics among workshop participants that can affect both process and product of digital storytelling.

NEEDS ASSESSMENT

Recovery is configured as the end point for any course of treatment; however, we lack a clear, consistent definition of what eating disorder recovery looks like (Bardone-Cone et al., 2010). More than 30 years of research has yet to yield a representation of recovery that fully accounts for the complexity and variability of eating disorders (LaMarre & Rice, 2015; 2016). Persistent stereotypes about eating disorders, such as that they affect only young, white, middle- to upper-class heterosexual women (Jones & Malson, 2013; MacDonald, 2011), are strongly ingrained in the social imagination (Saguy & Gruys, 2010) despite increasing recognition in the scholarly literature that eating disorders can affect anyone (e.g., Feldman & Meyer, 2007).

Stereotypes about who is at risk for developing eating disorders also affect who is seen as able to recover from them. In a society that treats some bodies as abnormal—notably those of people marginalized by ethnicity, class, ability, gender, sexual orientation, or size—individuals with such bodies may be framed as unrecoverable, (LaMarre, Rice, & Bear, 2015). In most studies, recovery is framed as residing only in people with a body mass index between 20 and 24, in people who score above a certain cutoff on scales designed using White Western samples, or in those who see recovery as the major element of their identity (Jenkins & Ogden, 2012). Rarely do explorations of eating disorder recovery entail a thorough consideration of different subjective experiences of recovery.

ENGAGING PARTNERS

Those with lived experience have not been silent; indeed, memoir-writing has become a popular way of chronicling recovery (McAllister, Brien, Flynn, & Alexander, 2014). Our focus here, however, is on (currently lacking) visual representations of recoveries. The myriad examples of those with eating disorders who present their recovery online through visual means, including YouTube videos and Instagram hashtags demonstrate their desire to engage with visual representations of recovery. We considered their engagement with these digital technologies as an indication that they would be open to digital storytelling as a method to explore and represent their own experiences of recovery.

EVALUATING POTENTIAL TECHNOLOGIES

There are many possible arts-based, visual approaches to research, including Photovoice, photo-elicitation, and documentary filmmaking (Boydell, Gladstone, Volpe, Allemand, & Stasiulis, 2012). These methods share a desire to place participants in the role of experts on their own experiences, challenging inscribed power dynamics that position researchers as in charge of the research. Arts-based research in general blurs the boundaries between the product of research and the process as a creative amalgamation of researcher and creator (Hodgins & Boydell, 2014; Rice & Mundel, 2018). Arts-based research methods share the possibility of undertaking research differently—and thereby building community and generating other benefits for participants who are actively involved in making representational decisions (Leavy, 2009; Rice, Chandler, & Changfoot, 2016). Digital storytelling allowed us to build a workshop structured using feminist educational methods and creative arts research, working with participants to create a collective, yet individual representation of recovery.

We view the process of developing and conducting the digital storytelling workshop as equally important to the products of the workshop. While the films themselves are impactful and have the potential to reach different audiences, from the general public to academics to healthcare workers (Rossiter & Garcia, 2010), what happened in the workshop is equally interesting, raising a number of tensions and subverting the oft-told reductive medical story of recovery through rich first-person conversations. Participants and researchers alike derived intellectual and emotional growth from the discussions that occurred during the workshop We did not have an explicit intention to build community and to impart therapeutic benefit—and in fact we challenge the idea that setting up this expectation would yield the desired results—but we certainly experienced the digital storytelling space as a venue where this kind of growth and community can and does occur (Rice et al., 2016; Rice, Chandler, Liddiard, Rinaldi, & Harrison, 2016). Digital storytelling invited us to engage with emotion, reflection, and collectivity in a deeper way than other forms of qualitative and quantitative social science research we have engaged in.

ESTABLISHING GOALS AND METRICS OF SUCCESS

It was less important to us that participants create conventionally beautiful, polished digital films than that they had the opportunity to deeply engage with one aspect of their lived experience. Again, the process of digital storytelling was as important as the films produced in terms of seeing the workshop as successful. Further, while we configured the workshop as a space to make films that speak back to dominant representations, this was not required of participants. We also found that participants were interested in trying to make their stories good for our research, but we continually reminded them that the point was not to make stories that fit neatly with our research This reveals an interesting tension around social desirability in social science research. While it is presumed that researchers care deeply about their participants' success, mainstream social science literature rarely acknowledges that participants might care deeply about *our* success. For us, success in digital storytelling is creating the best possible experience for a participant. It is our intention and goal to open space for stories—to allow for a disruption of hierarchy so that a new story can emerge (Alexandra, 2008).

IMPLEMENTATION

Author Rice has established a multimedia lab called ReVision: The Centre for Arts and Social Justice, complete with 15 MacBook computers and audio and visual equipment. The purpose of ReVision is to build a social inclusion and justice-oriented space to engage marginalized and misrepresented communities in arts-based projects. Its digital storytelling work was initially based in the approach advocated by the StoryCenter (formerly the Centre for Digital Storytelling; Lambert, 2010), but has since shifted to allow more flexibility and accessibility for diverse participants.

We consider each workshop to be an improvisation with arts-based tools (Rice et al., forthcoming). We see participants as partners in the research and art-making process, including the process of building and implementing the workshops. For example, we have trained interested members of disability arts communities to be paid facilitators for workshops (Rice et al., 2016; Rice, Chandler, Harrison, Ferrari, & Liddiard, 2015). Digital storytelling workshops allow us to work closely with participants over an extended period rather than meeting them once and presuming to know their stories. Having participants as partners forces us to think through the "us versus them" dichotomy that is part of the traditional research model and to reflect on our own subjectivities as they interact and intersect with disability and difference and the communities with which we do our work.

WORKING WITH COMMUNITIES

Even with the extended format of our interactions and our commitment to working with rather than on or for the communities our participants identify with, we can never truly know their experience as they know it. Further, we can never fully anticipate all accessibility needs in the workshop space. With each workshop, we have learned more about the complexities of accessibility and the impossibility of imposing one set structure for all people. Issues of technological accessibility and environmental changes to facilitate access (e.g., wheelchair accessible spaces) are only the tip of the iceberg; considerations such as the need to balance listening deeply with time limitations, differing politics among participants, and dietary needs affect the workshop design. We are continually engaged in a process of adapting the method to fit the needs of the group.

LOGISTICS

The workshop for this case study was part of author LaMarre's master's thesis project on eating disorder recovery. For this workshop, we had three participants engage in making digital stories. Because of the small size of the workshop, it was easier to tailor content and form to the participants and all participants had time to reflect on their experiences. The workshop took place over 3 days in January 2014. Largely based on the StoryCentre model (Lambert, 2010) adapted for research purposes by ReVision, the workshop followed five main components: (1) introducing the "representational field" to invite participants to explore how they relate (or do not relate) to the stories that they encounter in popular culture, media, scholarly texts, and literature about their experiences in the world; (2) telling our stories in story circle; (3) learning the technical aspects of digital storytelling, such as video editing software (Final Cut Pro X) and sound recording; (4) doing the technical work through open studio time with the assistance of the facilitator; and (5) screening the stories in a "world premiere" (LaMarre & Rice, 2016; Lambert, 2010).

Our goal at the end of the workshops, although not a requirement, is for participants to show their stories so that we can reflect on work well done and share experiences. How we achieve that goal depends on group dynamics, our read of the emotion in the room, the number of facilitators who help move the process along and their particular skills, and the desires and goals of the participants. If participants choose not to show their stories, we welcome this choice as well, but this has rarely happened.

While author LaMarre considers herself a part of the eating disorder community, this self-disclosure is not enough to counter the inherent power differential between participant and researcher. Therefore, she grounded the curriculum in the particular experiences of the participants making stories (LaMarre & Rice, 2016). She explored representations of eating disorders and recovery in academic literature, in historical documents, and in the popular media, and she conducted a preliminary analysis of her interviews with people in eating disorder recovery to see how participants were talking about their recoveries. When she presented these findings to participants, the group had an open discussion about how recovery is sometimes misrepresented in the media and by the general public. Participants identified, for instance, that sometimes recovery is framed in a way that made them feel as if they needed to do recovery "perfectly." Participants preferred to see recovery as an ongoing process or something that they would continue to work on for the rest of their lives. They feared that the way recovery was often framed made it impossible for them to admit to struggling in any areas of their lives in case this was viewed as a relapse. They also emphasized that only certain people were represented in what we see about recovery: thin, young, White, heterosexual, cisgender women from middle- to upper-class backgrounds (LaMarre & Rice, 2015a).

The following excerpt demonstrates some of the questions we asked of participants:

> Importantly, is it realistic to expect that all individuals will be able to come out of an eating disorder "like they were before" or even "better than" they were originally? What if you don't actually come to love your body?
>
> Our culture has taught us to expect a fairytale ending, but honestly that fairytale ending doesn't always happen; what would be the consequences of accepting messier endings? What if things weren't always wrapped up into a neat bow?

In this excerpt, although she was still in control of the workshop, author LaMarre used self-disclosure to present herself as being a part of the same community as the participants, thereby blurring the line between researcher and participant.

TECHNOLOGY

Following an exploration of the representational field, we invite participants to learn a video editing software program, Final Cut Pro X. We have noticed that introducing the technology early on can sometimes be anxiety provoking for participants who are less familiar with Apple computers; video editing software programs, and/or group-based learning. We have also found that, at times, introducing too much information too soon can lead to information overload and/or participants forgetting most of what was taught fairly quickly into the editing process. In this workshop, we balanced this tension between providing enough detail for those with technological expertise and just enough detail for those who are less technologically adept by offering a broad overview of the main elements of the editing program and then working individually with participants on the effects they wished to achieve in their stories. This individualized approach is possible only when there are very few participants and/or many facilitators.

A further technological hurdle is that of generating voice recordings that are satisfactory to storytellers. Rarely do people enjoy the sound of their own voices. We record our voiceovers in a sound booth, generally one-on-one. This can be a time-consuming approach, but it allows a speaker to redo takes. We try to reassure people that filler sounds and idiosyncratic gestures—including ums, clicks, and swallows—can be trimmed out of their audio tracks.

We have found that providing structure and a time frame enhances creativity. However, the time crunch of the digital storytelling workshop can be creatively and emotionally challenging for participants and facilitators alike. In the workshop with participants in recovery, a major issue was related to overcoming the pressure for perfection we sought to overcome. Whenever possible, researchers involved in our workshops experience the digital storytelling space as a storyteller *before* they facilitate so that they can better understand what they are asking of participants. Digital storytelling asks a lot of people—to engage in self-reflection, to find a moment in their life story to capture through image and sounds, and to learn both storytelling techniques and technological maneuvers. Further, it asks them to do this in the presence of others they have never met and in a short period of time. When we fail to create a safety space, we risk making participants unduly vulnerable. When we succeed, we engage participants in building collectivity with others who share similar experiences, we bring untold stories to the fore, and we work to dismantle dominant representations

Participants' stories varied, but were all centered on the theme identified earlier in the case study—the idea that recovery is imperfect and an ongoing process—and on breaking stereotypes around eating disorders and recovery. For example, one participant reflected on a conversation with a friend whose image of her did not match his stereotype of someone with an eating disorder: "I knew what he meant. I didn't strike him as shallow, vain, or fragile. As emotional, anxious, or self-doubtful. As someone who would idolize thin runway models. And he was right." Throughout her story, she linked her eating disorder to her need to be productive in a society that demands perfection. She showed images of herself at various stages of her illness and recovery. In her voiceover she talked about needing to let go of the idea that recovery is something to achieve in order to be happy in her life. It has been 3 years since the workshop, and she has reflected on how the story still feels true even though she has been through additional experiences in her life. She uses the story to shed light on how eating disorders are not the unidimensional cultural stereotype of being shallow, vain, fragile, emotional, anxious, self-doubtful, and tied up in ideals of beauty.

EVALUATION

As previously mentioned, it can be hard to define and measure success in the digital storytelling context. One measure of success is the degree to which those watching the digital stories experience a shift in their attitudes, values, or beliefs around a particular issue. If people who saw the story shifted from believing in the traditional narrative to multiple new narratives, opening up space for multiple stories of eating disorders and recovery, we would consider that success. After screening the stories of eating disorders, viewers shared their own struggles with eating disorders. We considered that successful, because it inspired conversation that would not otherwise have happened.

What we are less able to measure are the ways in which making the stories continues to affect the lives of the people who have made them. The community building and personal impact of the workshops cannot always be captured in numbers or words. We have heard from participants about how they have used the stories in their lives—to help loved ones understand their experiences, to educate healthcare professionals, and to feel a sense of connection to others who have experienced similar things. Some participants have maintained enduring friendships with other workshop participants, but sometimes the impact is more transitory. Sometimes, people's stories change after they have made their digital story, and they no longer wish to screen their stories. Permanency is not the point of making the story.

Ethical Considerations

The *Educational Policy and Accreditation Standards* (EPAS) published by the Council on Social Work Education (CSWE; 2015) recognize the growing need for social workers to gain technology competencies. Competency 1 sets out the expectation that social workers will "understand emerging forms of technology and the ethical use of technology in social work practice" (p. 7), including how to use technology to facilitate practice outcomes. To this end, programs accredited by CSWE must share the curricular approaches that they use to build student competence in this area. Although social work instructors vary widely in their skill and comfort with various emerging technologies, many resources are available online to enable them to provide best practices for using technology tools. Quality improves vastly when one makes use of best practices. For instance, an audio-recorded story that includes an interview requires a setting without distracting background with equipment situated close enough to the speaker for high-quality recording; audio recording on a desktop is greatly enhanced by using a headset with a microphone.

Often new technology learners will overuse animations or audio. The best outcome is achieved by using the right tools for the job (see Table 6.1).

Students and instructors need to be careful not to overestimate students' competence with digital technology. Student age or prior experience with technology does not necessarily prepare them to use technology for educational or professional settings (Šorgo, Bartol, Dolničar, & Boh Podgornik, 2016). This means that the instructor is responsible for teaching the tools and professional integration of technology. Some technologies, such as Twitter, bring forth complex questions related to third-party information ownership and the Family Educational Rights and Privacy Act (Brady et al., 2015; US Department of Education. 2015). Many of these complexities are addressed in the *Model Regulatory Standards for Technology and Social Work Practice* (Association of Social Work Boards, 2015).

Ethical ambiguity is inherent to working in the digital world with any marginalized population. Therefore, the organizer(s) must consider the consequences for the participants of challenging the status quo. In a qualitative focus group conducted by Yu, Taverner, and Madden (2011) about the risks of sharing digital health-related stories publicly, the researchers found that participants perceived the stories they viewed as very therapeutic and possibly a source of support for the storytellers. However, when considering whether they would share their own health stories, they spoke about fears related to embarrassment, reactions of others, and even their own safety. They suggested that digital storytellers involved in sharing personal stories should be given opportunity to use a false name or identity, offered financial incentives out of respect for their time, given emotional support around the issue they are sharing, and offered technical help to prepare them for sharing their digital stories.

In many ways, storytelling honors the unique position of the storyteller as creator of his or her own narrative and even as a community educator who shares his or her story in a way that may help someone else's understanding. This can be an empowering approach in practice. However, if researchers or practitioners play a role in the editing, shaping, and sharing (or deciding not to share) these stories, this process may end in disempowerment for the storyteller. The decision to remove or share a story may be based on concerns related to the participant's ability to consent, the social worker's perception of risk of harm or stigma resulting from the story, or for purposes of time or space (A. C. Gubrium, Hill, & Flicker, 2014). The practitioner is left to balance these considerations from a professional lens, but answers may be difficult.

Additionally, these techniques may be uncomfortable or unfamiliar to institutional review boards, which are charged with protecting the identities and privacy of research participants. The practitioner must be thorough in methodological explanations, including dissemination of information and informed consent that expands beyond the normal risks and benefits. The website *Transformative Storytelling for Social Change* (transformativestory.org) offers ethical practice considerations and sample informed consents for use when working in this research realm.

In the case study example, and in the research conducted by authors LaMarre and Rice, consent is conceptualized as an ongoing process. At the time of the workshop, participants are offered several levels of choice for consent, ranging from screening the stories in academic, educational, and/or community settings only to sharing them in all contexts, including posting online. We also ask participants if they would like to be contacted if their stories are shown, which allows us to recontact participants prior to each potential screening of the stories. Should participants decide they would like a story removed from our private digital archive or public-facing website or they wish to change the level of consent, we respond accordingly, while recognizing that others may have saved the story from its online space. This information and these options are shared with participants during the process of consent.

Social Justice Implications

Digital storytelling is a tool for social justice. Mass media communication was once controlled by a handful of news broadcasters and newspapers, often owned by a few conglomerate organizations, and referred to as *one-to-many communication*. Now everyone can share their stories through inexpensive digital tools in combination with free social media sites such as Twitter. This new *many-to-many communication* requires new types of learning in the use of technology (Pavlik, 2015), how to reach the desired audience despite increasing competition, and how to incorporate the values and ethics of the profession when using new media (Boddy & Dominelli, 2016).

We see digital storytelling as a wonderful methodological tool that allows us to deeply engage with participants and to destabilize power hierarchies between researcher and research subject and as an intervention into dominant narratives about particular experiences. Digital storytelling holds tremendous possibility for social work to advance social, economic, and racial justice. Social justice movements have always relied on stories to connect with the general population, as well as with legislators, agency administrators, or media outlets. Imagine 10,000 social work students going into their field placements with the ability to record audio and video and take photos, and have the knowledge to turn those into compelling stories. Imagine students entering the profession with the skills and confidence to support digital storytelling from people in oppressed and disenfranchised communities and using their professional power to take them to the halls of Congress. In fact, digital storytelling is one of the approaches identified in the Social Work Grand Challenge report to help achieve the profession's goals in the next 10 years (Berzin, Singer, & Chan, 2015). Digital storytelling is an ideal medium to use in communities that value storytelling and oral traditions, many of which are marginalized, silenced, and disenfranchised. Since every social worker is equipped with the minimum technology necessary to create and distribute digital stories—a cell phone—the only barriers to working alongside this essential skill are training and motivation.

Questions for Discussion

1. What stories have you heard your clients tell that you think would be important for legislators to hear?
2. What is the impact of thinking about case notes and court reports as storytelling? How can client voice be more fully integrated in these types of stories?
3. How can social media be used ethically to harness the power of digital storytelling?
4. In what ways can social work practitioners harness digital storytelling in their work with clients? What kind of training, agency permissions, and client permissions might be required? What other ethical issues related to ownership, storage, and documentation must be considered?
5. Think far in to the future of social work practice. What role might digital stories play in day-to-day social work?

Additional Readings

- Creative Commons (creativecommons.org) offers information about copyright and reuse of digital intellectual property.
- Educational Uses of Digital Storytelling (digitalstorytelling.coe.uh.edu/) offers a free 5-week Massive Online Open Course about digital storytelling, examples of digital stories created in the classroom, and other resources for educators.
- It Gets Better Project (itgetsbetter.org/) contains over 50,000 digital stories and messages to inspire hope for LGBT youth who have experienced bullying.
- Photovoice (photovoice.org) provides information and resources about the therapeutic and research use of storytelling with photos.
- StoryCenter (storycenter.org) offers examples of justice-centered digital stories and digital story workshops.
- Teaching Copyright (teachingcopyright.org) offers curricula and tips for educators and students about copyright issues.
- Telling Their Stories (tellingstories.org) is an oral history project that includes interviews with people who witnessed historically significant events, presented by the Urban School of San Francisco.
- StoryCorps App (https://storycorps.me/) is an app that walks people through recording a personal history/narrative. Users have the option of uploading their story to the Library of Congress.

7 }

Using Data to Improve Client Services

Dale Fitch

"It is a capital mistake to theorize before one has data."
　　—Sherlock Holmes, *by Sir Arthur Conan Doyle, 1859–1930*

Due to financial difficulties, Mr. and Mrs. Robert Jones were in danger of losing their home. This situation was compounded by their need to care for an adult disabled son who lived with them. Katherine Story, a social worker at a local human services agency that provided services to senior citizens, was able to provide resources to meet their needs. Katherine entered their case information into the agency database under Mr. Jones's name; she entered information on Mrs. Jones and her son into a separate table and recorded additional information on paper to be stored in folders in a file cabinet. Several years later Katherine received a phone message requesting additional assistance for Mrs. Jones and her son; Mr. Jones had died and their daughter, Rebecca Williams, would now be working with Katherine to conduct assessments and case management. When Katherine tried to access the previous files, she encountered a number of problems trying to access the information she needed and was forced to reenter Mrs. Jones's information all over again, along with information on her son and daughter.

We first introduced the Jones family, the subject of the case study in this chapter, in "An Alternative Database Table Design" (Fitch & Shaffer, 2007). This case is a useful illustration in the study of the use of information systems in human services that will be undertaken here. This chapter proposes a conceptual framework that addresses the roles of data, information, and knowledge in understanding information systems. The resulting conceptual framework explains how social workers can think about information systems from the perspectives of clinical social work, supervision, social work administration, policy, and community collaborations—all illustrated in the Jones family case study. The chapter offers models for thinking about how these systems can be designed for maximum utility and concludes by providing social workers some practical tools to improve the use of information systems in human services.

Background

Computers are now commonplace in human services agencies (Fitch, 2005). Some of these computers access agency information systems, while most access only common office applications and Web-based information systems the agency is required to use due to contracted services. As recently as two decades ago, most agencies did not have computers for their social workers; they were available only to administrative staff. If you were working in a large urban homeless shelter, in a residential treatment center, or as a medical social worker at a university teaching hospital, your access to information was dependent on what you carried around in a notebook or found on paper charts. Not having access to an information system would have been very frustrating—especially if you were interacting with colleagues from other disciplines who could access their case files online. Social work depends on access to information as a primary tool to make assessments or render decisions.

Our professional judgment depends on the quality of the information we possess in the moment. Dire consequences can result when relevant information is not systematically shared. An information system is a tool designed to store and to make available the information required to make decisions at every level. More often than not, at-risk or vulnerable family situations are marked by a breakdown in communication, when individuals who operate in complex systems fail to exchange what they know. These individuals are additionally charged with multi-faceted interventions with families identified as high risk or with clients receiving tertiary-level preventive services that extend across mental health, substance abuse, disability services, and/or residential care. In all of these circumstances, social workers and program managers depend on the quality of the information available to them in order to make critical decisions.

An information system comprises three distinct components: data, information, and knowledge (Checkland, 1999; Maier & Hädrich, 2011; Quinn & Fitch, 2014). Figure 7.1 shows the conceptual relationship among these components

Agencies often have multiple systems of information or ways of informing agency members. The *explicit* information system is the computer system that contains information about the clients served by the agency, which is accessed through a desktop computer or tablet. The *implicit* system of information consists

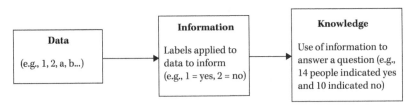

FIGURE 7.1 Data-information-knowledge conceptual framework.

of the paper records kept in file folders, Post-It notes, agency forms, evaluation reports, and the information shared at shift change or staff meetings. Several theories and methodologies help to make sense of this information and to categorize it most usefully. Taken together, these theories and methodologies can help social workers in an agency to diagnose their systems of information and thereby discover where a breakdown has occurred in the process of going from data to information to knowledge and then to recommend solutions that are systemic.

To be systemic means not only to address the immediate problem at hand but also to address design issues in the systems of information that can facilitate improved overall organizational decision-making. These design issues occur when some pieces of information are recorded on a paper form or analyzed by a separate spreadsheet application (after data have been entered again into the new application). While such systems of information may work well to meet the needs of one or two specific individuals, there is no unifying information system that makes the individually processed data accessible to people in the agency who need it to do their jobs. As a result, organizational decision-making suffers.

All professionals in every human services agency make decisions all day long. Since the implicit and explicit systems of information are duplicative and not coordinated, professionals can make decisions that are at odds with each other. For example, a decision to return a child home from care could be made not knowing that one caregiver is recently unemployed and the other is now receiving substance abuse treatment. All of the information was recorded somewhere—in a case note or a phone message—discussed at a team staffing, or left on someone's desk as a Post-It note, yet critically it is inaccessible to the person making the decision in real time about returning a child home.

Comprehensively, our thinking about information systems at the organizational level needs to address the ways data on individuals are recorded and then expanded upward as information to address knowledge management within a learning organization (an organization that encourages and facilitates the learning of staff and works to continuously improve itself) and ideally to support inter-agency collaborations. Across these levels, we need to challenge who can be involved in controlling these systems; control cannot be reserved solely for those in administration or information technology but must belong also to those who encounter and record the information based on client contact. Simultaneously, we must address whom and what purposes these systems serve; they cannot be for management, funders, or external reports only). As outlined in the discussion that follows, misconceptions of any of these imperatives either in the use or the design of information systems can hamper optimal organizational functioning and consequently threaten best client outcomes.

Our schools of social work need to examine how we prepare our students to be digital professionals in the 21st century. While our peer professions are educating their students via medical informatics and nursing informatics, research classes in the social work curriculum focus on some of the most complex aspects of knowledge generation, such as data analysis using Statistical Package for the Social Sciences (SPSS) or other advanced statistical software applications. With the traditional research class as their only formal exposure to the data-information-knowledge continuum, students fail to learn that all three of these components are ubiquitous in agency settings. Students need to learn how to use the data analysis tools available to and in use by their agencies (e.g., MS Excel).

In practice, we need to continuously train our staff to be aware of how they handle data. Do they enter the same data into multiple systems? Do they use tally sheets to track client outcomes? Are they spending more time managing paperwork than working with clients? If the answer to any of these questions is yes, we are depriving our clients of the time and resources that should be devoted to face-to-face interactions. We have machines that can manage data, but those machines cannot do the job of social work.

If social work is not involved in the design of technological and digital systems, we will be forced to use tools designed by others who may not have our profession's epistemological and values base. Data, information, and knowledge constitute systems whose boundaries must be determined and not left to assumption. If advocating for the rights of clients is the heart of social justice in social work, then the democratization of digital information access can rightly be viewed as one of those rights. Future research should and can seek to make those rights more explicit.

DATA

Data are the most fundamental units of an information system and yet they are often the element most overlooked. While data, quantitative or qualitative, are the primary focus of social work research classes, rarely is the topic of data or data management discussed in direct practice classes. Indeed, even in management or administrative classes, it is largely relegated to discussions about program evaluation or grant writing. Fortunately, some social work scholars, most notably Epstein, have tried to point out that human services agencies collect a vast amount of data and that some of these data are amenable to a whole range of uses from practice to research (e.g., Epstein, 1977, 2001; Freel & Epstein, 1993; Grasso & Epstein, 1993; Joubert & Epstein, 2005; Schoech, Quinn, & Rycraft, 2000).

Practice settings tend to value data that are entered into statistical software and to devalue other forms of data by assigning them to paper or leaving them unstructured in a Microsoft Word document in a folder stored in a file cabinet. Unless they are manipulated again, these unstructured data are of limited use. For example, client notes, including outcomes on service plans, may be recorded in a Word document. However, if a program manager wanted to know the outcomes for all the clients in a program, each file would have to be opened and every outcome recorded on paper or in another software application The need for digitally capturing unstructured data has been noted for several decades (e.g., Schoech &

Arangio, 1979; Semke & Nurius, 1991), especially because doing so may facilitate organizational processes (Coursen & Ferns, 2004).

Field research indicates that many agencies still use tally sheets to record client outcomes or copy and repeatedly paste data from one form to another for different reports despite the presence of information systems in the agency (Fitch, 2014). This seeming disconnect between the need to capture data digitally and what many social workers experience when using their agency information systems is quite perplexing. Part of this disconnect relates to how social work researchers and educators conceptualize the difference between data and information. Colloquially, and sometimes professionally, people interchange these terms as if they were equivalent. Technically, data are entered into spreadsheets in which the column headings indicate what the data concern.

Some of this conflation may be attributable to textbooks written before the differences between these entities were more clearly identified. For example, Geiss and Viswanathan's (1986) text largely focuses on shifting away from analog (paper, folders, etc.) to digital ways of handling data. However, data management via an information system was largely unaddressed. Furthermore, the role of the information system in helping an agency understand its organizational processes was totally ignored, as was the necessary alignment between storage of clients' data and how those data serve the agency. Agency personnel need to be extremely careful not to create data silos that force line workers to enter the same data into multiple applications.

INFORMATION

Information is so ubiquitous that how it is formed (data) and turned into knowledge is sometimes overlooked. Fortunately, Beer's viable system model (1985), based on organizational cybernetics, posits that information provides the means for communication up and down organizational levels as agencies seek to meet clients' needs and to survive in ever-changing environments. However, it is in the unpacking of those two processes, communicating both up and down organizational levels and communicating among the three actors—clients, agencies, and environment—that the disconnects between data, information, and knowledge are likely to occur.

Existing literature in this area often extends over several decades (e.g., Cnaan & Parsloe, 1989; Glastonbury, 1993, 1996; Glastonbury, LaMendola, & Toole, 1988; LaMendola, Glastonbury, & Toole, 1989; Rafferty, Steyaert, & Colombi, 1996; Steyaert, Colombi, & Rafferty, 1996). Research has focused on applications in hospital settings (Auslander & Cohen, 1992), child welfare (Benbenishty & Oyserman, 1991, 1995; Benbenishty & Treistman, 1998; Oyserman & Benbenishty, 1997), income support (Dearman, 2005), and school settings (Redmond, 2003). Although some of these texts provide a methodology for information system design, the issue of how social workers think about information in terms of its relationship to data and knowledge and the communication needs among the actors is usually underexamined. For example, missing from this literature is research in the larger information system field that addresses critical perspectives (Adam, 2002; Ulrich, 2003), as well as the issue of how power in agency settings is manifested through information system design (Burton & Van den Broek, 2009; Gillingham, 2011; Markus, 1983; Wilson, 1997). This latter issue is particularly important due to fundamental power imbalances between clients and agencies and between human services agencies and other organizations. For example, organizational dictates, by definition, flow down communication channels; returning upward communication channels are much more prone to blockage. Such blockage reflects a loss to the organization, particularly when this upward communication is attempting to convey information derived from practice data.

KNOWLEDGE

Beer's viable system model (1985) asserts that any information system should be assessed by whether it facilitates acquiring knowledge. A viable system can survive changing environments by having practices in place to ensure the flow of information, beginning with data, up through the agency. Such a system can process that information and then implement operational changes via feedback back down through the levels of the agency (see Figure 7.2).

An agency's information system should support the ability of staff to intervene in complex situations. In general, staff and programs become competent through learning activities, including formal training, education, and practice experience. Ideally, via an agency's information system, organizational processes should capture these learning activity outcomes and enable easy access, integration, and use of the enhanced knowledge and skills by staff. This capacity to use enhanced knowledge and skill, by means of a feedback loop, can then inform and improve multiple organizational processes, including direct practice and case management, program design, and policy development. This use of accumulated knowledge and skills enables the organization to become a functioning learning organization.

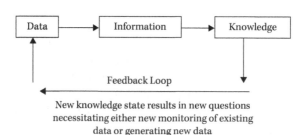

FIGURE 7.2 Data-information-knowledge feedback loop.

Ensuring that this feedback loop is operational is an essential aspect of systems theory: all of the components depend on feedback in order for the system to perform as designed. For example, in Figure 7.1, once we know that 14 people indicated yes and 10 people indicated no, it would be perfectly reasonable to use a feedback loop to ask the question why. Answering the question would entail gathering additional data, organized via information.

From an agency perspective, clinicians are making treatment decisions, program managers are deciding on the design of their programs, and executive leadership is deciding if the types of programs the agency is offering are helping it to achieve its mission. All of these decisions are based on information consisting of data entered into the agency's information system and hopefully fed back to the users as knowledge in a timely manner to enable their decision-making processes. This is a critical point. If the data are not gathered in an electronic database system, but are instead recorded on paper or shared only verbally, then the essential work of the agency is lost. If clinical outcomes, program design, or programmatic questions must be addressed, then a good portion of the data will need to be reproduced. Reproduction of these data takes time and money, resources that are not spent on directly helping clients, the primary mission of the agency.

These agency realities are reflected in our social work education programs. Although information systems in human services function meet all of these decision-making needs, there is a concomitant lack of empirical social work research on the use of these information systems. For example, the core social work curriculum on research and evaluation often require students to gather data, ignoring existing agency data even if these students are associated with an agency while they are taking the course. If research or evaluation classes are decoupled from the information systems that social work practitioners use in daily practice, we may be experiencing a fundamental feedback breakdown in the data-information-knowledge continuum in our profession.

SYSTEM BOUNDARIES FOR INTERORGANIZATIONAL COLLABORATION

When analyzing agency information systems, the boundaries for the system must be delimited because clients have lives before and after interacting with agency services (see Figure 7.3). Clients interact simultaneously with educational

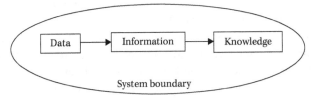

FIGURE 7.3 System boundaries for interorganizational collaboration.

systems, health systems, and any number of other community agencies and systems. Agency information systems were once referred to as management information systems (MIS) because they were designed for management purposes. However, beginning in the late 1980s, the notion of democratized information systems began to be viewed as the sole approach to improving organizational efficiency since it is at the operational level that line workers create the initial data. The human services are still uneven in terms of democratizing digital information access, and research has shown that the delimitation of system boundaries (including all information systems and systems of information) plays an important role.

Fortunately, there has been more social work research on interagency information sharing (see Figure 7.4) related to knowledge. This research has addressed the need for interorganizational systems in mental health (Bloomfield & McLean, 2003; Manderscheid & Henderson, 2004), welfare services (Harlow & Webb, 2003), substance abuse services (Hile, 1997), child welfare (Howell, Kelly, Palmer, & Mangum, 2004), homelessness (Peressini & Engeland, 2004), and juvenile justice (Savaya, Spiro, Waysman, & Golan, 2004). Paradoxically, the Internet has both facilitated and hampered interagency information sharing. Although it is much easier to share information between agencies using secured and encrypted file exchange systems, vendors have developed systems that sometimes group agencies into silos. However, if the underlying information is still digital and can thus be copied and pasted into other applications, this is still an improvement over paper records.

Well-designed information systems should be able to serve the needs of all agency personnel from line workers up to agency administrators, including members of community-based interagency task groups. Each of these individuals has to make work-related decisions every day based on the information available at the time and subsequently needs to know the outcomes of those decisions.

Case Study

The case of the Jones family provides many opportunities to catalog the difficulties Katherine Story, the social worker, faces as she attempts to provide services. Katherine is dependent on the information in the agency's information system to fully understand the Jones family's situation. However, information about the son, Sam, has been recorded in a different agency's information system. Finally, and unbeknownst to Katherine, someone in the community has made an elder abuse report on the family, and that investigative report is recorded in yet another information system. Therefore, Katherine needs to coordinate services, through the sharing of information, with other agencies in the community; this is especially important if abuse or neglect is suspected.

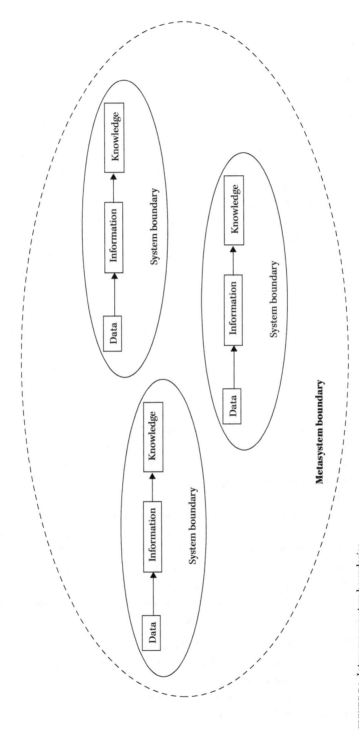

FIGURE 7.4 Interagency system boundaries.

The Role of Data

We know that data about the Jones family can be found in the information systems and the paper files in the cabinet. However, Katherine must find these data in order to access them. She will need to work with the agency database administrator either to create new structured data fields (e.g., separate tables of information for each family member) in the agency's information system and/or to convert existing unstructured data fields (e.g., text or comment boxes or Word documents) into structured ones.

While these two steps appear to be rather simple, they involve knowledge and expertise from requirements analysis and relational database management systems. Requirements analysis assesses the needs for information across a broad range of users (Byrd, Cossick, & Zmud, 1992).

The motivation for any such analysis should focus on the knowledge needed to make decisions in the organization (Fitch, 2007). All human service organizations should strive to answer one fundamental question: are we making a difference in the lives of our clients? This question is posed in different ways at various organizational levels:

- At the line level: am I making a difference in the life of my clients?
- At the supervisory level: are my programs making a difference in the clients they serve?
- At the executive level: is this agency making a difference in the community?

At the line level we typically have information associated with issues, interventions, and outcomes. At the supervisory level, there are questions about staff performance, clients with similar problem constellations, or the effectiveness of programmatic interventions. Questions at the executive level relate to all of these dimensions, but we are typically more interested in the data at a more aggregated level.

Determining what information is useful in making decisions largely influences where people go to find that information. Typically workers identify the following sources of information: interaction with others (conversations, e-mail, and telephone), observation, management reports, personal information repositories (notebooks), and finally the agency's management information systems.

The following questions can be posed to line workers, supervisors, and executive personnel in a requirements analysis process:

1. What information is used in making a particular decision?
2. What is the source of this information (on your desk, in your department, or elsewhere)?
3. If in the agency, how often is it collected?
4. In what format is it (forms, verbal)?

5. If analog (e.g., on paper or from meetings), how much of it depends on being at a particular place at a specific time?
6. How are client records accessed?
7. What volume of data is maintained?
8. What personnel are involved in obtaining this information?
9. How efficient is this task (duplicative information, lost information)?
10. What products result from this information?
11. Are these products used for decision-making?
12. What tasks in information production are not associated with decision-making?

A series of surveys, ideally accomplished through interviewing and observation, might be conducted to determine which data a system should capture and what functions the system needs to perform. Some requirements analysis textbooks use an ethnographic approach to understanding agencies and the functions of agency staff (e.g., Pedell, Miller, Vetere, Sterling, & Howard, 2014). Although agencies often assign requirements analysis to an outside consultant who is an information systems professional, in human services agencies, as in many domains, those most familiar with the work being undertaken and the data that it generates are arguably the best equipped to create a framework for building an information system. Social workers have the education, training, and experience to understand a human services agency more deeply than other professionals.

Unlike requirements analysis, relational database management should be undertaken only by professionals trained in computer science, information science, or related disciplines. Relational database management ensures that, while data are entered into tables that share similar components, each table is designed so that it can relate to the others. Such design reflects the interrelationships between the data entered in a system (how an individual is related to a family, for example) and can yield a system that is both flexible and amenable to future expansion. For example, instead of entering all the information about the Jones family in one table about the household, a properly designed relational database management system would have created separate tables of data for Mr. Jones, Mrs. Jones, and their son, Sam. The next step would combine the information about the Jones family in a separate table. In that way, once Mrs. Jones became the primary client, it would be much easier to reconfigure a new case around Mrs. Jones and Sam to reflect the new household. While Rebecca is Sam's sibling and a member of the family system, she is not a member of the household. This is the instance in which Katherine, as a front-line social worker, has expertise critical to effective system design: she is experienced with the distinctions between case, family, and household and with their implications for obtaining services.

Organizing appropriate tables for data and then joining related data through the concept of a family or household is not straightforward and requires knowledge about dependencies and referential integrity. However, an IT professional with the skill to program these mechanics may not understand the blended or transgenerational families that are encountered in the working environment of the human services. Forcing all members into a singular family or household table would not be appropriate. Therefore, social work practitioners should understand the rudiments of relational database management design so that they can work with trained professionals to design effective systems that serve the needs of every staff member in an agency.

The imperatives of requirements analysis and relational database management make it easier to understand why we do not have more robust information systems in the human services. A lot of time and effort is required to design these systems correctly. However, ignoring these design issues and forcing direct practice staff to repeatedly reenter data into multitude systems costs agencies much more than designing a good information system, especially if the underlying data could be used for multiple purposes (Gillingham, 2014).

The Role of Information

While a properly designed information system would help Katherine Story to find information about the Jones family more easily, such a system could also enable other capabilities. For example, direct practice workers are often asked to implement new evidenced-based interventions (EBIs) that will have specific outcomes. If the agency has an information system, then Katherine can enter the outcome data in a data form; otherwise, she will have to record these data on paper or in a word processing or spreadsheet application. As the new EBI is implemented across workers in the agency, they may observe that the outcomes account for what is happening with some but not all clients. Unfortunately, if there is no place to capture those data in the existing form, that information will be lost to the agency except by word of mouth. Even if workers push to have data fields added to the agency's information system, they are often told it will cost too much; as a result, the agency has failed to value the views and experience of those who work directly with clients and has lost valuable input on outcomes.

Katherine Story needs to implement a new housing service for Mrs. Jones and housing and disability support services for Sam Jones. Additionally, she has been contacted by an elder abuse caseworker who received a report on Sam Jones as a possible victim of neglect. She can implement an EBI housing program for Mrs. Jones, but she will need to coordinate services with a disability support worker in a different agency to implement an EBI disability support program for Sam. Furthermore, unless the outcomes for all of these interventions are communicated to the elder abuse worker, Mrs. Jones may face legal consequences and Sam may be placed in a group home.

The Role of Knowledge

Knowledge plays a key role in the Jones family situation. In the case study, Katherine made intervention decisions based on outcomes from her agency's prior work with the family. The EBI she implemented was chosen by her program manager based on a decision made about the outcomes across all the clients served by the agency, and the executive leadership for the agency decided on the types of housing programs they would offer as an agency. All of these decisions were based on information acquired from data entered into the agency information system. If data had not been entered into the information system, the executive leadership might well have made its decisions based on whatever knowledge or impressions were available. However, because she had outcome data to reference, Katherine could explain to the elder abuse investigator that reasonable steps could be made to minimize the risk to Sam Jones and that Mrs. Jones should be able to provide care for him if supportive housing services were in place.

The Role of Collaboration

Months after Katherine began her work with the Jones family, her local interagency task force on elder concerns met to discuss this and other similar cases in the community. Katherine had used the online referral system and had coordinated interventions with the disability support worker. Rebecca had also been allowed to access this system; thus she was aware of services needed by her mother and brother and could follow their progress. Even though Katherine was better able to capture the family information in her agency's information system, she had to reenter a lot of the same information into her community's Homeless Management Information System (HMIS). The HMIS initiative (https://www.hudexchange.info/programs/hmis/) is an important resource for homeless shelters and housing support agencies that lack information systems, and it allows networking of these agencies within a community to facilitate information and referral, service acquisition, and community-level outcome monitoring for homeless individuals. Unfortunately, however, if an agency serves other client populations, then workers must double (or triple) enter data into the HMIS and any other system the agency might use (Fitch, 2010).

Katherine found the interagency task force meeting an ideal setting to discuss the need to communicate information about the Jones family across different types of agencies and among the family members. Critical systems heuristics (Ulrich, 2003), which determines system boundaries by identifying who is involved and who is affected, is the best option for considering multiple perspectives in information-sharing situations. Critical systems heuristics then delineates those who are involved according to who is served and for what purpose, as well as who is a decision maker, which resources are used by the decision maker, and on what basis. Those who are affected establish legitimacy by acting as witnesses representing embodying values and worldviews. Ultimately it must be determined whether the information system is serving the needs of individuals or whether it is primarily serving administrative, financial, oversight, or contracting concerns. Extending the boundaries in one direction or the other reveals that housing services cannot be seen in isolation from disability support services, especially when issues of abuse or neglect are suspected. And beyond the nonprofit and public agencies that may be involved, extended family members will always play a key role in augmenting whatever services an agency may provide. Each of these agencies will have its own information system. The system boundary then becomes a meta-system as shown in Figure 7.4. A community collaborative on elder well-being might include a senior services agency, a mental health agency, and a healthcare provider. Most importantly, all the knowledge gained from these respective agencies is based solely on information initially recorded as digital data that *already exists* in their own information systems.

Ethical Considerations

Many social workers view technology suspiciously because they believe it is inherently impossible to protect the privacy and confidentiality of client information in electronic form, a critical ethical obligation. This belief is inaccurate. Threats to privacy and confidentiality can occur, but only when the technology tools and/or system have not been designed correctly. Health Information Privacy and Accountability Act (HIPAA) guidelines speak to the design of information systems that include many commonly used technologies. Social workers usually do not consider HIPAA guidelines on phone systems and fax systems. Our common acceptance of these analog technologies implies a trust that can be easily exploited by others. These technologies are hardly secure, as evidenced by YouTube videos on how to tap a phone or fax line. There are also videos on how to tap cell phones, but this involves more sophisticated technical skills and even those attempts can be thwarted if safe computing habits are employed. More information about the HIPAA technical guidelines (http://www.hhs.gov/hipaa/for-professionals/index.html) and the Health Information Technology for Economic and Clinical Health Act (http://www.hhs.gov/hipaa/for-professionals/special-topics/HITECH-act-enforcement-interim-final-rule/index.html)   is available online. In addition, there are many resources on HIPAA-compliant cell phones and texting (e.g., https://www.healthit.gov/providers-professionals/your-mobile-device-and-health-information-privacy-and-security).

Chief among many of the HIPAA-compliant technology features are remote wiping and the ability to disable a device if it is misplaced, lost, or stolen. Some devices have applications for automatic self-destruction of client files once they have been uploaded to an agency's secure server. It is impossible to remotely wipe a caseworker's notebook that has been left at a local coffee shop, but an electronic file can easily be wiped with a tablet or other device.

Unauthorized access to client information is another oft-cited privacy concern for electronic records. As discussed in HIPAA technology guidelines "permissioned access" in database design limits access to records within the database based on one's role in the agency. This access can be further stratified based on the client's record (i.e., some staff may have access to demographics or some services information, but are restricted from accessing medical or substance abuse information). Most importantly, those who do not have access will not know that the restricted information exists. Furthermore, permission can be controlled at the client and worker levels on a case-by-case basis. None of that is possible with a paper record.

Social Justice Implications

If an agency's information system is designed only for management purposes, then other employees in the organization are, in a sense, disempowered in that their informational needs for decision-making are not supported (Fitch, 2007). This latter type of disempowerment has significant social justice features in terms of an emancipatory information system design (Wilson, 1997).

An emancipatory design recognizes the differences in perspectives among line workers, supervisors, and executive-level staff. Instead of monthly reports created to meet the needs of funders, reports are produced that reflect client outcomes and inform the decision-making processes of all employees in the organization. In addition, an emancipatory design promotes more open communication channels in the organization. For example, operational or line staff may complete pages and pages of paperwork on clients only to summarize the same information on another piece of paper to be forwarded to a supervisor or manager for entry into a spreadsheet for tabulation purposes. It has long been argued that much of this information cannot be gathered within an information system because it is too nuanced or idiosyncratic.

To dismiss such information out of hand marginalizes the user and denies him or her the opportunity to make more information-rich decisions that could potentially benefit the lives of clients. Furthermore, if this information is not captured in an information system and the user is forced to record it on paper, perhaps on several occasions for different purposes, the agency is wasting time and money rerecording data instead of spending that time and money on services for clients.

Questions for Discussion

This chapter previously referenced the use of "requirements analysis" as an ethnographic approach well suited to social workers in understanding how information and information systems are used in agencies. Before delving into those specifics, it is helpful to keep in mind the motivating framework for any such analysis.

Too often we begin by focusing on data and the capabilities of an information system without exploring in detail the knowledge needed in order to make decisions in the organization (Fitch, 2007). There is one fundamental question all human service organizations strive to answer, or should answer, at some point in their existence: Are we making a difference in the lives of our clients? As previously discussed related to knowledge, this question is put forth in different ways by the various organizational levels. At the line level the question would be: Am I making a difference in the life of my clients? At the supervisory level: Are my programs making a difference in the clients they serve? And at the executive level: Is this agency making a difference in the community?

To answer these questions, a manifold of questions unfolds. At the line level we have various dimensions in which to assess progress with clients, typically information associated with issues, interventions, and outcomes. At the supervisory level, we have questions about the performance of various staff, clients with similar problem constellations, or the effectiveness of programmatic interventions. At the executive level, we have questions along all of these dimensions, but we are typically more interested in the data at a more aggregated level.

The question for staff then becomes, "Where do you find the information that helps you make those decisions?" instead of "What forms do you fill out?" Determining what information is useful in making decisions largely determines where people go to find that information. Typically workers identify the following sources of information: interaction with others (conversations, e-mail, and telephone); observation; management reports (these, however, usually only tell them what they already knew due to other information sources); personal information repositories (notebooks); and, finally, an agency's management information systems.

Synthesizing the decisions and possible sources of information, the following questions can be used in a requirements analysis process making sure to ask line workers, supervisors, and executive personnel the exact same questions:

1. What information is used in making a particular decision?
2. What is the source of this information (on your desk, in your department, elsewhere)?
3. If in the agency, how often is it collected?
4. In what format (forms, verbal)?
5. If analog (paper, meetings), how much of it is dependent on being at a particular place at a specific time?
6. How are client records accessed?
7. What volume of data is maintained?
8. What personnel are involved in obtaining this information?
9. Efficiency of this task (duplicative information, lost information)?

10. What products result from this information?
11. Are these products used for decision-making?
12. What tasks in information production are NOT associated with decision-making?

Further Readings

Bernstein, J. H. (2011). The data-information-knowledge-wisdom hierarchy and its antithesis. *NASKO, 2*(1), 68–75.

Carlsson, S. A. (2007). Developing knowledge through IS design science research: For whom, what type of knowledge, and how. *Scandinavian Journal of Information Systems, 19*(2), 75–86.

Carrilio, T. E. (2007). Using client information systems in practice settings: Factors affecting social workers' use of information systems. *Journal of Technology in Human Services, 25*(4), 41–62.

Checkland, P. (1981). *Systems thinking, systems practice.* New York, NY: John Wiley & Sons.

Checkland, P., & Holwell, S. (1998). *Information, systems and information systems.* New York, NY: John Wiley & Sons.

Fitch, D. (2006). Examination of the child protective services decision-making context with implications for decision support system design. *Journal of Social Service Research, 32,* 117–134.

Fitch, D., Watt, J. W., & Parker-Barua, L. (2014). Envisioning public child welfare agencies as learning organizations: Applying Beer's viable system model to Title IV-E program evaluation. *Journal of Public Child Welfare, 8,* 119–142. doi: 10.1080/15548732.2013.879089

Monnickendam, M., Savaya, R., & Waysman, M. (2005). Thinking processes in social workers' use of a clinical decision support system: A qualitative study. *Social Work Research, 29*(1), 21–30. doi:10.1093/swr/29.1.21

Rowley, J. (2007). The wisdom hierarchy: Representations of the DIKW hierarchy. *Journal of Information Science, 33,* 163–180. doi:10.1177/0165551506070706

PART } II

Organizations

8 }

Getting Big Data to the Good Guys

THE PROMISES AND CHALLENGES OF
SAN FRANCISCO'S SHARED YOUTH DATABASE

Chris Kingsley, Stephen Goldsmith, Lauri Goldkind, and Lea Wolf

"If all you have is a hammer, everything looks like a nail."
—Abraham Maslow, *1908–1970*

Chances are very good that the last call you received from a congressional campaign was highly targeted. A volunteer chose your seven-digit number, out of thousands, because an algorithm that compared dozens of data points on when you registered, how you have voted, and what kind of truck you drive suggested that you were persuadable. The pitch was further calibrated according to your magazine subscriptions and your credit history. The call was recorded by the campaign and analyzed alongside the outcomes of other calls being made concurrently to people who, the data suggested, were like you in order to better persuade the next voter. This is what integrated data look like on the campaign trail: dozens of linked data sets, sophisticated modeling, message testing, resulting in a significant edge over the politics of yesteryear—for candidates who can afford it.

By comparison, with few exceptions, the educators, counselors, and social workers hired by local governments to serve our communities' most vulnerable youth and families are working in a digital dark age:

- Street outreach workers helping a child find emergency shelter cannot determine whether he or she receives psychiatric care or suffers from physical health conditions;
- Juvenile courts cannot access students' academic records, even to verify school attendance and inform judgments;
- Planning directors cannot track clients' use of services across systems to coordinate care.

Background

A great deal of hardship follows from the inability of our public agencies to share information on their clients and, over time, to better answer questions about what works, for which families, and at what cost. The asymmetry between the sophistication of the marketing firms and political campaigns and the resources available to health and human services agencies is huge. Why is this so? And what can be done about it?

At the most basic level, crucial information on cases is recorded on paper or stored in impenetrable "legacy" databases written to aging standards. Much of this information architecture was developed with state or federal dollars that impose strict limitations on how systems may be extended, linked, or otherwise modernized. If the human and social services field had set out to design a system to preclude cooperation across agencies, it could hardly have done a more thorough job.

These limitations are not news to federal agencies, which have acknowledged the costs imposed by these limitations and taken the first steps to rectify the problem. In 2011, for example, the US Department of Education issued a clarification of the Family Educational Rights and Privacy Act (FERPA) that modestly liberalized the use of student data for research and evaluation. The Affordable Care Act provided generous federal matches for states to build infrastructure that integrates information across health and human services, and "interoperability" initiatives at agencies such as the Administration for Children and Families have provided a rough roadmap for administrators to pursue these opportunities. During the Obama administration, in particular, the White House and Office of Management and Budget at times tried to quarterback the painstaking work of rolling back unnecessary impediments to collaboration across federal and state agencies. Yet, for all this activity at the federal level, there are few examples of how local governments, which deal most directly with children and families and stand to benefit tremendously from better information on the needs of this population, have applied, researched, and mobilized the possibility of integrated data systems (IDS).

During the last 20 years, public organizations have shifted from a model that emphasized strict protection of information to one that emphasizes the use and integration of data as strategic assets for planning and management (Yang & Maxwell, 2011). State and local governments have developed an increasing number of IDS to link records across multiple agencies and contracted service providers. A defining feature of these IDS is their ability to combine and relate data across public agencies at the individual level and to aggregate data up to the level of the family, household, school, neighborhood, and larger geographies (Culhane, Fantuzzo, Rouse, Tam, & Lukens, 2010). In contrast to academic research data sets assembled for a single study, these IDS represent a permanent data infrastructure that can be used over time to inform and drive down the cost of research, program

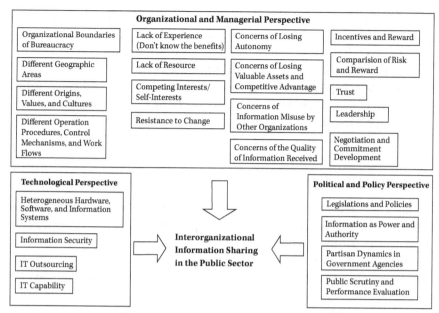

FIGURE 8.1 Organizational/management, technological, and political/policy perspectives.

evaluation, cost studies, and multiagency collaborations, ultimately improving service delivery to individual clients across a range of human services (Pardo, Cresswell, Thompson, & Zhang, 2006; Zheng, Yang, Pardo, & Jiang, 2009).

Integrated data systems pose challenges to individuals and organizations that go far beyond their obvious technological complexity. Designing, using, and learning from such integrated systems are human challenges, requiring innovation and collaboration across organizational and policy domains. As demonstrated by this chapter's case study of the San Francisco Youth Database (see Figure 8.1), the inception and maintenance of IDS are contingent on local leadership and the navigation of institutional cultures and politics (Yang & Maxwell, 2011).

TECHNOLOGICAL CHALLENGES

As in the private sector, government access to new strategies for data integration and use has been accelerated by the digitization of records and government processes over the past three decades (Zhang & Dawes, 2006). Every year, more elements of the workflow at public agencies are being digitized—from online report cards and attendance data in the public school arena to the public assistance application process for cash assistance and food stamps (Atabakhsh, Larson, Petersen, Violette, & Chen, 2004). Progress has been uneven, however, and challenges remain. Agencies' data are secured on many different computing platforms, some antiquated, with disparate data standards and schemas (Chau, Atabakhsh, Zeng, & Chen, 2001; Chen, Gangopadhyay, Holden, Karabatis, &

McGuire, 2007; Dawes, 1996; Fedorowicz, Gogan, & Williams, 2007; Lam, 2005; Pardo, Cresswell, Dawes, & Burke, 2004). Many public agencies struggle to attract and retain top-level programmers and analysts to maintain and integrate these systems (Akbulut, Kelle, Pawlowski, Schneider, & Looney, 2009). These techno- logical hurdles are persistent, but in cases such as the collective database on at-risk youth in San Francisco, staffing and coding may prove less of an obstacle to devel- oping integrated data systems than organizational challenges sometimes colloqui- ally referred to as problems of "trust and turf."

ORGANIZATIONAL CHALLENGES

Building IDS requires negotiating complex agreements between organizations with different origins, values, and cultures (Lam, 2005; Pardo & Tayi, 2007; Pardo et al., 2004). Furthermore, competing incentives among government agencies can make it extremely difficult to collaborate on time-consuming projects that appear tangential to their core mission (Fedorowicz et al., 2007). Integrated data systems are still rare enough that many government agencies have little or no ex- perience with them and small appreciation of the benefits that could accrue from sharing their administrative data. Thus, agencies may fail to realize that informa- tion relevant—or critical—to their clients is residing with adjacent agencies. Vague incentives for or promises of better collaboration carry less weight than the actual costs associated with overcoming the operational procedures, control mechanisms, and existing workflows that complicate participating in IDS (Canestraro, Pardo, Raup-Kounovsky, & Taratus, 2009).

Sharing of administrative data relies crucially on trust between the organizations involved, both interpersonal and as formalized through negotiation and doc- umentation (Akbulut et al., 2009; Canestraro et al., 2009; Dawes, 1996; Dehart & Shapiro 2016; Landsbergen & Wolken, 2001; Pardo et al., 2004; Pardo & Tayi, 2007). Just as good fences make good neighbors, the definition of thoughtful data- sharing agreements yields trusting partnerships when partners may legitimately fear a loss of autonomy or new liabilities from the misuse of information by an- other organization (Bellamy & Raab, 2005; Chau et al., 2001; Zhang et al., 2005). Getting past these fears requires a combination of executive authority, leadership, and patience (Willem & Buelens, 2007).

POLITICAL AND POLICY CHALLENGES

Legislation and policy have a strong influence on the sharing of informa- tion, knowledge, and data across organizations, especially in the public sector (Dawes, 1996; Gil-Garcia & Pardo, 2005; Zhang & Dawes, 2006). Legal and policy regulations can facilitate relationship building, risk reduction, and trust development in interorganizational information sharing projects by specifying how information can be used (Lam, 2005). Multiple players, such as privacy advocacy groups, government agencies, and legislatures, must be involved in creating protocols for data sharing and in determining what information to share in the public sector (Bajaj & Ram, 2003). Privacy policies, memoranda of agreement, and other formal working agreements can increase trust in government data sharing projects and thereby help to alleviate the concerns of the general public (Atabakhsh et al., 2004; Landsbergen & Wolken, 2001; Zhang & Dawes, 2006). Support from legislatures and policy makers is vital: without it, cross-boundary information sharing in the public sector loses the momentum of priority and will fail to garner the funding and resources that make such projects sustainable (Zhang et al., 2005).

Alternatively, laws and regulations may create barriers to cross-boundary information sharing because many have been designed explicitly to protect records, and multiple agencies are governed by mandates that prohibit or seriously limit their ability to share sensitive and regulated information in domains such as public safety and national security (Dawes, 1996; Gil-Garcia & Pardo, 2005). Often existing policies that create barriers to information sharing (Pardo & Tayi, 2007) predate contemporary technologies and capacities for intervention and may fail to accommodate emerging strategies that address the needs of individuals and communities. Hence, IDS must strike a balance between explicit statutory authority that defines the circumstances permitting and encouraging cross-agency data sharing (Lam, 2005; Landsbergen & Wolken, 2001) and the potential to create more effective and integrated policies and practices needed to address multifaceted social problems—such as those of children in foster care who encounter juvenile justice and families who interact with multiple public assistance and housing programs.

Ultimately IDS may have the potential to yield evidence-informed and evidence-based policy as well as to improve service delivery on the ground, certainly a win-win for all stakeholders. But realizing this promise will require rethinking fundamental issues of privacy, informed consent, and the ways in which aggregated data sets may reflect the concentration of biases or misconceptions resident in the original records. The following case study of San Francisco's Shared Youth Database highlights the active role and ethical choices that social workers will face as the use of data-based strategies of intervention accelerates and evolves.

Case Study

To social workers trying to verify young people's school attendance, to locate their foster care records, or to confirm their medications or psychiatric condition, it does not matter whether the inability to find the information they are seeking is the fault of bureaucracy, a restrictive interpretation of privacy law, or a technical bug. Whatever its cause, the missing information on their clients is a familiar, vexing, and urgent, problem.

Cities and counties trying to untie this knot of interrelated challenges that prevents effective information sharing must decide where to begin. Data integration efforts frequently start small, with one compelling use case or a single urgent question shared by several leaders already keen to work together. In San Francisco, the Department of Public Health's Shared Youth Database (SYDB) originated with a Substance Abuse and Mental Health Services Administration grant managed by Sai-Ling Chan-Sew, past director of Children's System of Care, that targeted high-need children and youth who were users of multiple systems. According to Dr. Tom Bleecker, who helped develop the initiative's research strategy,

> it had become clear that there were a number of shared clients between foster care, juvenile probation and mental health. There was some capacity to be able to talk about them, but a lot of it depended on informal relationships people had between departments. We often didn't know if the clients were shared or had services in more than one system.

To move beyond ad hoc discussion of hot cases and systematically identify at-risk youth, the heads of the Departments of Public Health (DPH), Juvenile Probation Department (JPD), and what is now the Human Services Agency (HSA) of San Francisco crafted an agreement with the city attorney's office that permitted the limited exchange of case information among agencies. Electronic files were exchanged using what Bleecker affectionately refers to as "sneakernet": CD-ROMs burned, distributed, and uploaded quarterly into a custom-built desktop application by hand.

The proof of concept worked. Even with its lack of real-time data, this kind of sharing enabled a new level of care for children interacting with any of the three agencies. Child protective services workers could find out if a child in an emergency situation had a probation officer or psychiatrist who should be involved in a response plan and case coordination improved. The system could also generate simple reports about overlapping clientele who, Bleecker noted, "were almost invisible populations before the database came along." He added, "the Shared Youth Database represents the potential for recognizing and focusing on the families that are most vulnerable, most troubled, and most in need."

Analyses of these new integrated data had immediate policy implications, as Dan Kelly, HSA's director of planning, described: A small number of residents in severe distress and a low percentage of those served accounted for a disproportionate amount of the city's dollars and attention. Moreover, plotted on a map of San Francisco, most of these multisystem clients' families "lived within walking distance of seven street corners in our city. . . . It's hard to realize how blind we were to the very concentrated nature of these issues." said Kelly. In response, the HSA began efforts to concentrate services in specific neighborhoods and to colocate services at community centers. Efficiency improved.

CHARTING THE TRAJECTORY OF SAN FRANCISCO'S
AT-RISK YOUTH

Figure 8.2 summarizes the data that resulted from the early implementation of the sneakernet system and the ways in which data sharing across agencies helped participants to understand the bigger picture of overlapping risk factors.

To build on the success of this relatively low-tech system, the city engaged the consulting and technology firm AJW Incorporated (AJWI) to migrate the SYDB from sneakernet to the Internet and to study the implications of the overlap among clients of these three systems. What could these three San Francisco agencies learn about their clients together that they did not know individually?

The SYDB contained few data on positive youth development outcomes such as school attendance, grade promotion, and high school graduation. However, the city could use the data for risk factor analysis to assess the increased chance of a *negative* outcome for multisystem youth: involvement in serious crime (see Figure 8.3).

Indeed, as determined by AJWI, "crossover clients" of multiple systems were at strikingly increased risk of committing a serious crime. According to the company's analysis, 51% of young San Franciscans involved in multiple service

FIGURE 8.2 Shared juvenile probation and children's mental health data from the Department of Human Services in San Francisco.

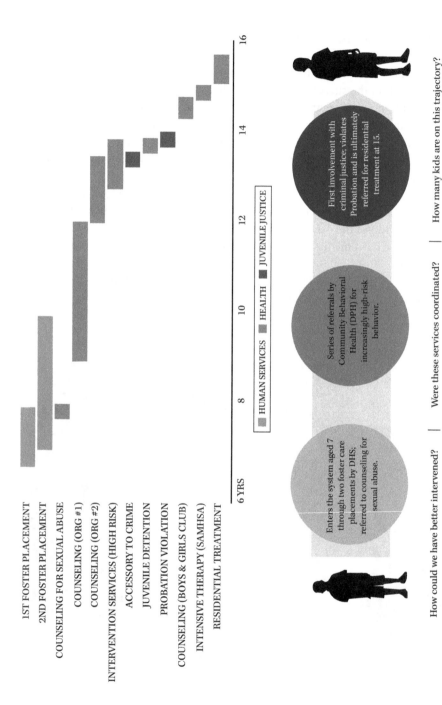

FIGURE 8.3 Risk factors for San Francisco youth.

systems had been convicted of a serious crime and a third had been served by all three agencies. The overwhelming majority (88%) of these youth committed the crime more than 90 days after becoming a crossover client, suggesting a critical window during which caseworkers might be able to intervene.

The report provided by AWJI included concrete data that heightened interest in the SYDB at, among other places, the district attorney's office. To Katherine Miller, policy director and assistant district attorney, the implications were clear: "When a youth shows up in that third system, the clock can't be ticking any faster at that point." What the city needed was a Web-based integrated case management system that could make these connections in real time, instead of once every several months.

LEGAL CHALLENGES

Unfortunately, in the legal review that followed San Francisco's decision to build out this expanded system, the city attorney determined that the justification used by the JPD to participate in the SYDB was unsound and instructed the agency to withdraw from the partnership and to revoke its data. The project partners were left with only this single study, albeit one that the district attorney's office found compelling enough to take leadership in the effort to change the city attorney's mind and rebuild the partnership.

In principle, the question of data sharing should be a matter of established law. In practice, interpretations of privacy statutes can be hotly contested, with legal counsel often arguing for the most restrictive interpretation. In San Francisco's case, a juvenile probation judge's court order was insufficient to authorize sharing of the department's records. A new data-sharing agreement would have to find a narrower justification for accessing JPD records on a case-by-case basis.

SYDB 2.0: REBUILDING THE PARTNERSHIP

The collaboration's early successes ultimately saved it. The report completed by AJWI before the JPD's exit was particularly compelling to policy makers and to the district attorney's office, which was convinced that the integrated database could be particularly useful for targeting prevention services: "We don't want to wait until a family is real far down this road before having these multi-disciplinary conversations," explained Miller.

The district attorney's office worked closely with the JPD to identify a permissible way to share records on youth at particularly elevated risk levels and equally closely with AJWI to ensure that the new SYDB could conduct that analysis from within the JPD's own information technology infrastructure. Administrative data on youth that do not meet these new elevated risk criteria are never moved outside of the JPD's firewalls. In 2016, after three years of negotiation, the JDP formally rejoined the SYDB.

While the three-year delay required to rebuild this legal scaffolding was frustrating to its original architects, it provided time for a culture of data sharing and collaboration to take deeper root in San Francisco. Both the mayor's office and the county board of supervisors subsequently endorsed comprehensive data-sharing initiatives in San Francisco. The DPH built a coordinated case management system and has increasingly looked for opportunities to bilaterally share data with the JPD and hence ensure continuity in mental health supports for youth known to both agencies. This blossoming of new initiatives owes some of its leadership and inspiration to the early success of the SYDB.

The SYDB itself has continued to evolve. In addition to welcoming back JPD in 2016, the partnership expanded to include the San Francisco Unified School District, which signed an agreement to share information on at-risk students. These data provide the kind of indicators of positive youth development that SYDB was missing, allowing schools to more effectively differentiate between students at low and high risk of dropping out. Critically, such data improved schools' ability to provide students with effective preventative services and to structure wraparound case management in collaboration with other agencies.

San Francisco is moving incrementally toward operating a real-time case management system across four of the public systems most crucially involved in the well-being of the city's youth and families. The remaining "million-dollar question," says Miller, is "once city staff have access to this information, what are they going to do with it?"

A first step, the system's stakeholders agree, is to communicate timely information that reflects a multisystem perspective on clients' risk and protective factors to families, teachers, and caseworkers. (Striking an appropriate balance between transparency and privacy will be important. Because families, social workers, and teachers each need different information, the flow of data across the SYDB is restricted by agency and by role.) Beyond that, the SYDB holds tremendous potential for helping city agencies determine which of their programs are most effective, where to target them, and how to coordinate responsibility among all who touch a family. The new SYDB will soon be able to provide a more complete de-identified research data set to public leaders and closely allied philanthropic initiatives such as San Francisco HOPE to evaluate the impact of their investments in the city's youth. As Dan Kelly explained,

> Rather than each of our different departments working in their own silos, throwing services at the part of the problem we can see—without a coordinated strategy or an evaluation of effectiveness across [departmental] outcomes, the Shared Youth Database represents the potential for recognizing and focusing on the families that are most vulnerable, most troubled, and most in need.

Ethical Considerations

The Shared Youth Database illustrates the evolution in our understanding and use of data. A once-static asset has become a live tool that potentially enhances our ability to anticipate or to map the interaction of forces and may increasingly shape the activity and priorities of the public sector. The case study presents the complex on-the-ground barriers to sharing information across agencies while illustrating how the merging of unique data collected by individual agencies may yield new insight and informed pathways for the coordinated delivery of resources to clients and communities.

At the same time, the technology and strategies of IDS raise new ethical questions that apply not only to lawyers or to those who write code but also to end users such as social workers and their clients. As in the case study, data sharing can fulfill the basic mandate of social work to "enhance human well-being and help meet the basic human needs of all people" (National Association of Social Workers [NASW], 2008), yet such novel use of data presents complex questions of privacy, autonomy, and consent. While the danger to long-established rights and protections cannot be ignored, there are costs associated with withholding technologies or their potential benefits from clients or sectors of society. The imperative, described in the NASW *Code of Ethics* (2008), to provide help, especially to "people who are vulnerable, oppressed, and living in poverty," dictates that any moral calculus must equally weigh the cost of failing to offer the coordinated and appropriate technology-enabled services to vulnerable populations.

As evolving methodologies for the collection and uses of data offer accelerating potential to agencies and actors, the discipline of social work will face the persistent challenge of translating existing ethical protocols to meet new realities of practice.

COMPETENCY

Within social work, competency is a core professional obligation, and the accelerating use of data across sectors dictates that individual social workers need to understand the collection, management, and analysis of data. As mentioned by Fitch (chapter 7), educational programs for social workers must ensure that these skills and competencies are not only taught, but applied to design, implementation, and evaluation. For individual social workers, competent use of technology for social work goes beyond the acquisition of technical vocabulary or the ability to operate hardware or software on behalf of clients to becoming conversant with guidelines for the ethical use of information and communication technology (ICT) tools (Barsky, 2017). Social workers must assume the responsibility of literacy—to anticipate the implications that attend the use of technology across contexts. Specifically, they will need to ascertain that existing technological tools (automated investigation of uses and access to data, forensic audits, and de-identification of data) safeguard client anonymity. More broadly, social workers must question how data collected by an agency will be used or shared, and they must commit to understanding the balance between the risks and benefits of such use. Going forward, social workers must remain alert to the ethical questions that proliferate around technology, with a focus on those that potentially impinge on individual and collective rights. Simultaneously, both individuals and the discipline as a whole must cultivate the ability to communicate clearly about these issues in treatment, policy, and advocacy contexts.

PRIVACY AND CONFIDENTIALITY

While privacy and confidentiality may be most simply understood in the context of micro-practice, or therapy with an individual, family, or group, the *NASW and ASWB Standards for Technology and Social Work Practice* (NASW and Association of Social Work Boards, 2015) explicitly address privacy concerns in mezzo and macro contexts, such as the case study's interagency data sharing example. The SYDB described in the case study offered clear benefit to clients—"[enabling] a new level of care for children interacting with any of the participating agencies" (Kingsley & Goldsmith, 2013)—yet concerns about privacy slowed its implementation. This example highlights the complex balance between clients' right to privacy and the potentially damaging implications of withholding beneficial processes, including improvements to services and enhanced efficiency. The principles of privacy and confidentiality are vital to effective practice (NASW, 2008); social workers must work to explicitly define privacy in a digital context and commit to protocols that safeguard protected information, even as agencies demand accelerating volumes of client data to realize their mission. Client records must be configured to limit the exposure of protected information when data are pooled, and a concern for security must inform the selection of platforms for electronic transmission, access, and storage of data. Additionally, the consequences of sharing data must be carefully considered so that one agency does not inadvertently identify clients for sanction by another agency.

As data proliferate, so does regulation. Social workers have a duty to acquaint themselves with the complex array of privacy mandates and measures that govern their work. These policies specify both how agencies uphold client privacy when partnering with peer organizations, funders, or stakeholders and how safeguarding privacy and confidentiality should manifest in interaction with clients. Social workers must join the public debate about the impact of technology on privacy to ensure that the implementation of powerful new strategies of data analysis do not erode the fundamental value of "respect for persons" (Gambrill, 2008a; Sedenberg & Hoffmann, 2016).

INFORMED CONSENT

Social work is predicated on the importance of a client's autonomous and informed consent, whether to services, use of personal information, or participation in research activity (Reamer, 1987). In the United States, the NASW *Code of Ethics* is congruent with these historic and international norms, and social workers are trained in the protocols that honor this imperative. Yet, as social work and other service fields begin to realize the potentials of data, legacy notions around consent are proving insufficient. At the mezzo level of practice, agencies are increasingly working to be able to share data and thereby more accurately depict needs and outcomes across communities and populations. The roots of informed consent in medical practice render it most appropriate for one-time time- and purpose-limited interventions; new strategies and applications, in which data are put to multiple uses over an unspecified period of time, are problematic.

Integrated data systems, which model and aggregate individual-case-level data to make predictions based on trend-level data, present particular challenges to obtaining informed consent (Dare, 2013; Gambrill, 2008a). In IDS, aggregation of data makes it difficult to trace clear relationships between data providers and end users, and data collected for one purpose will typically be used for another. Data live forever, and any form of consent must acknowledge the possibility that they "may be analyzed years after the point of collection and reveal new knowledge and generate new risks for an individual" (Sedenberg & Hoffmann, 2016, p. 15). Under those circumstances it is difficult—perhaps impossible—to maintain existing expectations of informed consent procedures (Gambrill, 2008b).

In historical terms, this incongruity between the paradigm of consent and emerging technologies is not unique. Since its origins in medical practice in the 1930s, informed consent has been a mutable concept, congruent with changing attitudes, practices, and technologies. Over the past quarter century, ICTs and data-driven research and prediction have propelled discussion of new models for consent in medicine and science. Evolving contemporary models of consent that attempt to incorporate changing technological realities emphasize the responsibility of those who collect and use data to define both methods and hypotheses as explicitly as possible for those from whom they seek consent. Any redefinition of consent protocol "in view of specific, contextual features of data science" must be based on a commitment to "operationaliz(e) the value of respect" (Gambrill, 2008a; Sedenberg & Hoffmann, 2016, p. 3)

In contemporary terms, these mandates require social workers to explicitly inform clients about what benefits any technology can provide, as well as to describe the risks of choosing to participate in services whose technological dimensions may be invisible (Barsky, 2017). Social workers must provide clients with clear descriptions of agency practice and its rationale, offering the opportunity to ask questions and to make choices. Historically, social workers have been ethically compelled to offer reasonable alternatives to technology—including sharing of client records among allied agencies—and to allow clients to withdraw their consent at any time, yet IDS pose challenges to such practice.

Social Justice Implications

The example of data sharing outlined in the case study vividly conveys the potential social benefit—better, more coordinated public services calibrated for delivery at moments of heightened risk—that results when public agencies can collaborate to pool their individual collections of data and to make informed decisions based on documented phenomena. Such initiatives reflect important and long-sought advances in the social service sector: cross-agency collaboration, effective sharing of previously siloed proprietary data, and evidence-based allocation of public resources. However, sharing of data also raises concerns, including the loss of privacy, the elision of informed consent, or the possibility that clients will be labeled high risk and targeted for scrutiny or interventions that they do not want or require. Social workers must accept the challenge of mastering both the mechanics and the ethics of data science to become informed advocates, ready to partner with technologists and decision makers to create information systems that support client populations.

Data are proliferating, and as they multiply, they are mined by businesses, government, and academic and research institutions as a newly powerful source of apparently objective information. Such use of data transforms individuals into a series of "quantifiable, encodable and machine-readable characteristics which enable them to be identified, classified, ordered or sorted" (Williamson, 2016, p. 127). Though this rendering of human reality in pure statistical terms appears compellingly objective (and continues to offer powerful and actionable insight across sectors), data are not neutral. Data collection—the sum of decisions about which data are collected, how they are collected, and about whom—reflects the values and biases of both individuals and society. A data set may exclude some groups and it may fail to recognize exceptions or to reflect the complexity of human interaction (Rainie & Anderson, 2017), thereby eliding the idiosyncrasies of individual identity and obscuring the role of social preference or prejudice. Thus, predictive decisions based on data reflect human bias and can render skewed or partial depictions of the reality they document.

As data become the primary tool of decision-making across sectors, they are used to predict future events via algorithms that aim to chart the statistically likely outcome of a confluence of factors (Pearsal, 2010). The integrity of the output of these algorithms is entirely dependent on their design, and advocates for social justice have increasingly focused attention on the designers and processes that create these technological engines of prediction. Algorithms that are based on training machines, for example, computers that develop algorithms based on reading vast numbers of case records, may compound the biases already present in the data by which they are trained. At best, a thoughtfully assembled algorithm can work to eradicate the unreliability of human decision-making or to reroute the prejudice that has long shaped the allocation of social resources. Ideally, data can reveal when an individual is most in need of support—as when the SYDB identified clients newly involved with three agencies as likely to commit a crime. However, data-driven decision-making among vulnerable populations is ethically charged because "significant burdens are likely to be borne by individuals or groups as a consequence of being identified as at risk" (Dare, 2013, p. 25).

Examples proliferate in which algorithmic decision-making reifies existing inequality. In documented cases of banks' predatory lending practices or unequal patterns in sentencing, bond, or parole decisions, algorithms are profiling individuals and communities, especially disadvantaging low-income individuals of color (Angwin, Larson, Mattu, & Kirchner, 2016; Coulton et al., 2015; Gangadharan, 2015). Social work must be alert to the challenges posed by evolving uses of data and must interrogate the models that underlie data analysis to tease out the cascading sequelae of structural inequality and to ensure that the algorithms in use are not simply "encoded opinions and biases disguised as empirical fact, silently introducing and underscoring inequities that inflict harm" (O'Neill, in Pazzanese, 2016). Social work must help to ensure that the needs identified by the analysis of shared data are addressed with meaningful resources and supportive services rather than with sanction.

The complex interplay of potential risk and gain is critical to the domain of social work. Interagency data sharing is a powerful step forward for the public sector, offering new possibilities for serving clients and communities in need. The ability to overlay data can yield vital public benefit: increased productivity, better policymaking, improved allocation of public resources, increased public safety, and better public services to citizens (Dawes, 1996). Social workers must work to realize these potentials while continuing to combat structural inequality by interrogating new models of individual privacy and autonomy and articulating new protocols for consent and machine decision-making.

Questions for Discussion

1. Imagine a client (a recent veteran, a victim of domestic violence or a substance user) who might be served by multiple public agencies. How would each of these specific clients benefit from data sharing across agencies? What would the risks of data sharing be to each client? How would you present the risks/benefits to each client in order to secure their consent? What might the concerns of these individuals be?

2. This chapter describes the concept of informed consent as fluid over time. Which technologies that you use require a new or expanded

version of consent? What are the implications for consent when you use a smart phone in practice, when your agency mines digital records for evaluation, or when you invite a client to a virtual support community?

3. Do you know if the agencies where you have worked have a policy on data sharing? Have you worked in an agency that shared data? What partners did they pool data with, and why? How were employees and clients made aware of the practice? If your agency does not share data, could they improve services by doing so? Which entities would make good data-sharing partners and why?

4. What knowledge, skills, or competencies related to data does this chapter inspire you to consider or to pursue? Why? Are such skills available to you in your training program, or in other programs to which you have access during training? How might you advocate for further training on data science or policy?

5. Which of the developments described in this chapter have the greatest implications for social work? What important issues does this chapter forecast for the field?

Further Readings

Cresswell, A. M., Pardo, T. A., Canestrato, D. S., Dawes, S. S., & Juraga, D. (2005). *Sharing justice information: A capability assessment toolkit.* Albany, NY: Center for Technology in Government.

Lee, J., & Rao, H. R. (2007). Exploring the causes and effects of inter-agency information sharing systems adoption in the anti/counter-terrorism and disaster management domains. In *Proceedings of the 8th annual international conference on Digital government research: Bridging disciplines & domains* (pp. 155–163). Philadelphia, PA: Digital Government Society of North America.

9 }

The Use of Geographic Information Systems for Social Work Education, Research, and Practice

Thomas P. Felke

"A map is the greatest of all epic poems. Its lines and colors show the realization of great dreams."

—Gilbert H. Grosvenor, *1903–1954*

Geographic information systems (GIS) are tools that allow social workers to conduct spatial analysis for various purposes. Spatial analysis can be defined as exploration of patterns, behaviors, and relationships using a set of techniques that include the geographical context of the data being analyzed. Social workers may use GIS technologies to conduct spatial analyses of poverty, food insecurity, or homelessness using data available from existing organizational sources or data that have been collected firsthand via a research project. Geographic information technologies seem to be a perfect fit for social work given its person-in-environment perspective "that highlights the importance of understanding an individual and individual behavior in light of the environmental contexts in which that person lives and acts" (Kondrat, 2008). While the adoption of GIS technologies as an instrument for the social work toolkit has been slow, the history of using maps in our profession is well defined and hopefully will continue to grow as more students are exposed to its potentials.

The earliest known use of spatial analysis dates back to the mid-1800s when Charles Picquet, a French geographer, developed maps using gradations of color to represent the cholera outbreak in the districts of Paris (Dempsey, 2012). The anesthesiologist John Snow undertook a similar effort approximately 20 years later by developing maps to document and analyze the cholera outbreak in London (Johnson, 2007). This work allowed Snow to determine that the cause of the outbreak originated at a water well, which led him to discover that cholera was a water-based disease. The advent of social cartography arrived soon after, most notably through Charles Booth's (1902) production of poverty maps in London. The period from the late 1950s through the 1970s saw the foundation and evolution of GIS technologies into their current form. The contributions of Ian McHarg with regard to map overlay, Roger Tomlinson in creating the first functional GIS in Canada, and the developmental work of Howard Fisher at Harvard laid the foundational groundwork from which GIS technologies have continued to mature (Chrisman, 2006).

The use of spatial technologies in our daily lives has become commonplace and pervasive. Individuals conduct spatial searches, such as pinpointing a particular site on a virtual map or obtaining directions between two locations using Web-based mapping on websites including Bing, Google, and MapQuest as well as through mobile applications that perform parallel functions. Approximately 1.9 million live websites incorporate Google Maps into their framework, allowing users to pinpoint locations across the globe (BuiltWith, 2016).

The practical applications of these technologies beyond travel and navigation are largely unappreciated, although GIS technologies have found a myriad of uses in various professions for decades. As an example, GIS technologies provide social workers with an opportunity to examine issues of interest for planning, evaluation, or advocacy.

The Environmental Systems Research Institute (ESRI), which produces the ArcGIS platform of products, defines a GIS as "an organized collection of computer hardware, software, geographic data, and personnel designed to efficiently capture, store, update, manipulate, analyze, and display all forms of geographically referenced information" (2002). Geographic information system software programs allow users to create maps by combining spatial data files with descriptive data files using a common identifier in each file. A spatial data file, commonly known as a shapefile, consists of several files that allow for the display of a digital representation of a geographic area such as a state, county, or zip code area. A table associated with the shapefile generally includes information such as the dimensions of the geographic area as well as a unique identifier for that geography. A descriptive data file, also including a unique identifier for the geography, contains information about the geographic area such as the demographics of its residents. With GIS software, these files can be joined using the unique geographic identifier to display the demographic information in the digital representation of the geography. Figure 9.1 shows two tables joined using a unique identifier (GEOID2 in the descriptive table and GEOID10 in the shapefile table) and the resultant map created through the join.

The availability of and accessibility to secondary data sets is a key requirement for proper use of geospatial technologies. A wealth of geographically referenced information is available to social workers from both original and secondary sources. Secondary sources have grown exponentially since the mid-1990s. In 1994, President Bill Clinton signed Executive Order 12906, subsequently amended by Executive Order 13286 in 2003, which established a plan for the development

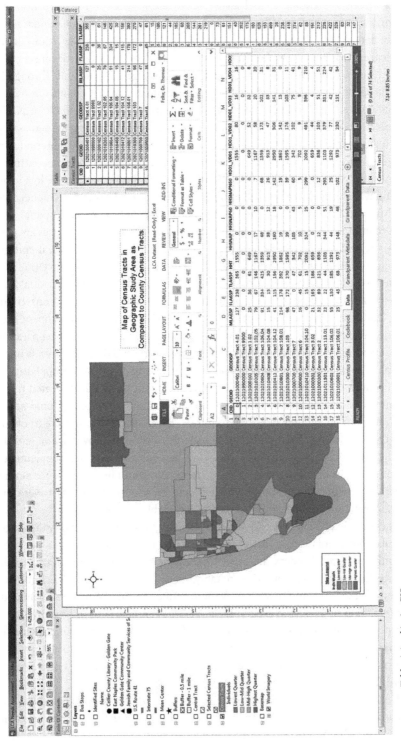

FIGURE 9.1 Tables joined in ArcGIS.

of an organized National Spatial Data Infrastructure through the formation of a National Geospatial Data Clearinghouse, along with the design of standards for spatial data to be shared universally. Spatial data, the digital representations of our physical environments, can be obtained from local, state, and federal sources. The US Census Bureau provides spatial data for a series of geographic units through its website. Geographic units include but are not limited to states, counties, zip code tabulation areas (ZCTAs), census tracts, and census blocks. Spatial data can also be downloaded from the Census Bureau for street networks, allowing for geocoding, which maps address data to geographic positions that are visually represented as markers on a map. State data may be available from agencies such as a department of transportation or a department of environmental protection, while local data may be available from a county planning division or a local law enforcement office.

Most states have at least one clearinghouse that has aggregated spatial data from multiple sources and made it available online. These clearinghouses are generally the result of partnerships among several entities including local colleges or universities. Examples include the Florida Geographic Data Library (FGDL), housed at the University of Florida's GeoPlan Center, and Pennsylvania Spatial Data Access (PASDA), which is a partnership of several agencies including Pennsylvania State University. The availability of data allows individuals to use desktop, or even mobile, GIS technologies to perform spatial analyses such as identifying patterns, understanding spatial relationships between variables, and detecting trends in geographically referenced data (ESRI, 2013). For example, an agency applying for grant funding to address food insecurity in the county where it is located might download related data to support its grant application. The agency could access the American FactFinder tool found on the US Census Bureau website to obtain county-level data on the number of households below the poverty line and the number of households currently receiving benefits through the Supplemental Nutrition Assistance Program (SNAP). These data could be obtained for several previous years in order to show the potential increase in these variables over time. This information could easily be converted into tables or charts.

The American FactFinder tool allows the user to quickly and easily create geographic representations of the data. These geographic representations can show potential program funders the exact location of the target population in reference to the agency location. Most notably, maps created using GIS technologies can build credibility and make it difficult to refute the current realities of an issue or population in a specific geographic area. This can be useful in breaking down stereotypes, both positive and negative, and destabilizing flawed arguments. In addition, research has shown that the use of maps as opposed to sole narrative reports to present information may increase user understanding and retention (Verdi & Kulhavy, 2002).

Data collected via intake and assessment sessions or during the conduct of research projects are geographically referenced through the various components of the client's home address. A complete data set of these client records might then be used to map client demographics at the state, county, city, or zip code level. Further, each individual client residence could be represented digitally through geocoding.

To illustrate the potential of geospatial technologies using these data, imagine a scenario in which a caseworker is conducting an intake and assessment in the home of a client with children. The worker may find during the assessment that the client is without reliable personal transportation, is experiencing food insecurity, and requires both before and after school care and clinical services offered on a sliding fee scale. The worker could use the address of the home and a spatial database of service providers to locate the required services within a reasonable distance from the home or at least on the local public transportation routes. The worker could leave a map of the service locations and transportation routes with the client by coupling the geospatial technologies with mobile printing capabilities. This type of scenario assumes that georeferenced agency data are available to the worker. Agencies such as the United Way, which have traditionally offered a hardcopy directory of local services, are now making this information available online in a searchable map-based format (see https://www.unitedwaylee.org/211-database, for example). An agency could create a map of households in need of services to illustrate its proximity to these households and therefore its ability to conduct outreach efforts to the target population. While a Google Maps search may assist in performing such a task, it is unlikely that a variety of social service agencies are listed on this platform.

A major drawback to the use of GIS technologies is the cost associated with the acquisition and management of software licenses and training (Felke, 2014). A basic license for the desktop version of ESRI's ArcGIS is $1,500 including software maintenance for the first year but requiring a maintenance subscription thereafter. The ESRI offers software discounts to nonprofit and educational institutions and has begun a program whereby users can pay $100 per year to use the full software as long as projects are personal and noncommercial (Fowler, 2016).

A recent review of popular GIS software options finds that ArcGIS, with 43% of the market, is the industry standard for desktop GIS software, but it is closely followed by several open source software options (GISGeography, 2016). Additional commercial GIS software options similar to ERSI's ArcGIS, are available (e.g., MapInfo Pro and Maptitude), but acquisition and maintenance costs are also similar to and in some cases higher than those for ArcGIS.

A number of noncommercial GIS software offerings have been made available on the Internet either as freeware (freely available software), trialware (trial version software), or open source software (software that can be modified by the user). Open source GIS software options include Geographic Resources Analysis Support System (GRASS) GIS, Quantum GIS, and several others. These programs are cost-effective alternatives to the commercial options available from ESRI, but they generally do not have the full functionality available from commercial software options.

Other alternatives for map creation are direct mapping websites or data warehouse websites that use embedded tools to conduct mapping. Many local, national, and international data warehouse sites now include these embedded tools to allow users to view descriptive data in a map layout and to print or create digital versions. The Centers for Disease Control and Prevention (CDC) offers a similar option via its online CDC WONDER (wonder.cdc.gov) tool. Users can create a map of specific health-related data such as cancer statistics, birth and mortality rates, and vaccine adverse event reporting. However, for some users the interface for the CDC WONDER tool may not be as user friendly as the American FactFinder product.

SocialExplorer (socialexplorer.com) is a direct mapping website that functions similarly to the embedded American FactFinder tool, but it is a commercial offering, requiring users to pay for an account to access advanced features and a larger number of datasets/variables. The site uses data primarily taken from US Census Bureau products, though other datasets focused on health, religion, and FBI crime statistics are also available. Users can create a storyboard of maps for comparative purposes, such as displaying longitudinal trends in the data. For example, maps of population data from each of the decennial censuses dating back to 1790 can be created.

The Housing and Transportation Affordability Index (htaindex.cnt.org) is another direct mapping website that allows users to create maps related to housing and transportation costs by geographic area. Data can be obtained at several geographic levels ranging from block groups to counties. The straightforward interface makes the tool very accessible to users at any level. The site requires users to set up a free account, but there is no fee for creating and downloading reports.

BatchGeo (batchgeo.com) is a website that allows users to supply a set of addresses in order to conduct geocoding. Users need only be able to format a list of address data according to the standards outlined on the website. The website examines and processes the address list against a national database of street addresses, providing a digital representation of the address data in the form of points on a map. The resultant map can be freely shared online via a website link. Advanced options such as more sophisticated formatting and exporting maps as image or Adobe Acrobat (PDF) files require a paid subscription. However, maps can also be exported free as Google Earth (KML) files that can then be used in the Google Earth platform or in standalone desktop GIS software program such as ArcGIS.

Training staff to use geospatial technologies is an additional expense outside of software licensing fees. The cost for training all staff to use GIS technologies effectively can be a major investment for some organizations, especially given the high rate of employee turnover in the nonprofit sector. However, the availability of group online training sessions eliminates costs related to travel and lodging. Staff members would have to commit a minimum of 7 working days (8 hours each) to complete the sessions in addition to outside practice work with the software.

The ESRI offers both foundational and advanced training. Foundational courses (offered online or at a training center) last from 1 to 5 days, and costs vary depending on the topics being covered and the length of the training. More advanced training is offered via hour-long online training seminars, 2- to 3-hour online Web courses, and instructor-led trainings that can be taken online or in face-to-face format. Some of the online training seminars and Web courses are free, while others require a maintenance subscription. To fully comprehend the ArcGIS software program, a set of four foundational courses is recommended. The total cost per attendee is $5,085, excluding travel and lodging, if no discounts are applied or available. Given turnover rates and job mobility in social services, such a large investment in staff training may be unwise.

There are other options available to agencies to decrease costs. More recently, GIS training has been offered through massive online open courses (MOOCs). These offerings allow students to complete self-paced training with some structure provided by the course developers. Providers including ESRI and Penn State University have offered these types of opportunities in recent years (Robinson et al., 2015). Evaluation data related to these offerings is not available, but average completion rates of approximately 6.5% have been reported in many cases (Jordan, 2014).

Clearly, there is more work needed if GIS technologies are to be included in the social worker's toolkit. These technologies can be used in any facet of social services, micro or macro, as well as in any social work practice setting. There is some interest among social work academicians and researchers in expanding the use of GIS technologies in social work research and practice. This is evidenced not only by the inclusion of technology in social work courses, as reported previously, but also by the creation in 2013 of a special interest group of social work professionals using or interested in the use of geospatial technologies. Thirteen presentations of projects that included the use of GIS technologies were delivered at the Society for Social Work and Research (SSWR) Annual Conference in 2016. The special interest group continues to meet annually at the conference and to expand into other technology groups that exist among the academic ranks in social work.

While these indicators are encouraging, it remains to be seen whether social workers will increase their capacity to use GIS technologies in practice. For this capacity building to occur, students and practitioners will need opportunities to develop the necessary skills in GIS for practical application to social work practice situations. The author believes the best strategy for increasing competency is through the inclusion of information about the technologies and the available tools in social work courses, both the core curriculum and electives. Within the core social work curriculum, instruction on GIS technologies would be a good fit for research methods or application courses, social policy courses, or micro and macro practice courses. A recent study identified 12 instructors across the United States who are teaching GIS technologies, with the majority including it as part of their core curriculum instruction and one, the author of this chapter, delivering a standalone elective course on the topic (Fedock, Klein, Litt, & Kapnick, 2015). The expansion of GIS use in the social work profession, though a slow process over the past two decades, has been encouraging. It is hoped that this trend will continue at a more rapid pace over the next several years.

Background

Modern GIS technologies initially focused largely on applications related to land use conservation and management. These efforts emphasized the geography rather than the residents within the geographic boundaries. However, practitioners from other professions who saw the potential utility of these technologies adopted them for a wide array of uses at local, national, and international levels. Specific uses of GIS technologies include the following:

- Public service planning and evaluation (Chang, Park, & Choi, 2016; Hansgen, 2016; Olajuyigbe, Omole, Bayode, & Adenigba, 2016);
- Disaster management (Amamoo-Otchere & Akuetteh, 2005; Ivanov & Yankov, 2016; Zakour & Harrell, 2004);
- Disease outbreak monitoring (Ailes et. al., 2014; Hershey et al., 2011; Wang, 2015); and
- Monitoring refugee situations (El-Atrash, 2016; Kemper, Jenerowicz, Gueguen, Poli, & Soille, 2011).

Though modern technological GIS applications were introduced into social work research and practice in the late 1990s, mapping was used in social work in the late nineteenth century. For decades, Jane Addams and her colleagues created sociological maps representing several demographic and socioeconomic characteristics of households in the area surrounding Hull House (Residents of Hull House, 1895). These maps, preserved in *Hull House Maps and Papers,* are precursors of those that can be created with much greater precision and analysis using modern technological advancements. Social work professionals have used GIS technologies in a number of planning and evaluation efforts since the late 1990s. This should not be surprising because the person-in-environment perspective validates the use of spatial technologies for social work education, practice, and research. This perspective emphasizes the value that is gained from an understanding of the environmental contexts that influence individuals and their behavior (Kondrat, 2008). Spatial technologies, specifically GIS, provide social work educators, researchers, and practitioners with the ability to examine a multifaceted set of environmental contexts from a macro perspective and to focus in on micro processes.

Hoefer, Hoefer, and Tobias (1994) first proposed the use of GIS technologies as a potential tool for social work research, planning, management, and administration. A few years later, the first manuscripts demonstrating the use of

GIS technologies to identify service gaps related to childcare services in Florida and Massachusetts appeared in the social work literature (Queralt & Witte, 1998, 1999). Since that time, GIS technologies have been used to examine issues such as access to maternity care (Gjesfjeld & Jung, 2011), access to drug treatment facilities (Kao, Torres, Guerrero, Mauldin, & Bordnick, 2014), the revitalization of urban neighborhoods (Kelley, 2011), and program evaluation (Wong & Hillier, 2001). The technology has also been used to define boundaries of neighborhoods to improve research methods and findings (Coulton, 2005; Foster & Hipp, 2011).

The use of spatial statistics to examine potential relationships between variables has been a more recent focus of GIS technologies in social work. Spatial autocorrelation and spatial regression are statistics than can be calculated to analyze the proximal relationship between variables in a geographic space. The results provide an understanding of whether or not clusters have occurred randomly due to chance. Hetling and Zhang (2010) used spatial autocorrelation to examine the relationship between incidence of domestic violence, poverty status, and location of agency services focused on domestic violence. Wiggins, Nower, Mayers, and Peterson (2010) used spatial autocorrelation to examine the relationship between certain population demographics and the density of lottery outlets at the census tract level. Yamashita and Kunkel (2012) examined the geographic access to healthy and unhealthy foods in a metropolitan area in Ohio. While the inclusion of spatial statistics has encouraged the use of GIS technologies, recent studies highlighting the potential for inclusion of these technologies in qualitative research projects (Teixeira, 2016) may further expand their appeal among social work researchers.

Case Study

The following case study demonstrates the potential application of GIS technologies to social work research and practice. Located in the southwest part of the state, Collier County, Florida, is an area of approximately 2,300 square miles with an estimated population of more than 330,000 residents (US Census Bureau, 2013). The county includes three established cities—Everglades City, Marco Island, and Naples—in addition to 19 unincorporated areas that have local recognition as communities (Figure 9.2).

Naples is a tourism and retirement destination that has consistently ranked among the top three cities nationally as having the highest number of millionaires per capita (Tribou, 2014). Nevertheless, a study commissioned in 2007 found that seniors were among the most vulnerable populations in this area (Collier Senior Resources, 2016). The Leadership Coalition on Aging of Collier County (LCA-CC), a partnership of community agencies, was formed soon after this report was released to collaboratively address the needs of seniors residing in Collier

FIGURE 9.2 Map of Collier County, Florida (Google).

County. Through the Department of Social Work at Florida Gulf Coast University (FGCU), the LCA-CC commissioned a study in 2011 to assist in identifying the most pressing needs of seniors.

Unlike most projects identified in the literature review, this project sought use of GIS technologies as a planning tool. During an initial planning meeting the primary outcome of the study was identified as the establishment of a senior access center in Collier County. No such entity existed in the county or the region, although the LCA-CC had developed plans to establish one. A traditional needs and assets assessment would include an analysis of existing demographic data for Collier County, a scan of existing community programs and services, focus groups with seniors, and key informant interviews with identified stakeholders. A spatial analysis of the demographics of seniors residing in Collier County and of the existing public transportation and street network was also proposed.

An initial meeting was held with LCA-CC members to outline the scope of the project and to define certain parameters including the age used to identify a senior and the geographic area for which the spatial analysis would be developed. It was important to define a qualifying age for seniors, because the data collected by the US Census Bureau vary depending on age. For example, data related to households receiving SNAP benefits is available for households including an individual aged 60 and older, whereas data on individuals living alone is available for individuals aged 65 and older. The LCA-CC resolved to define a senior as an individual aged 60 years and older so that variables for those aged 65 and over could be included in the study.

Identifying the exact geographic area to be included in the spatial analysis was critical, due to the size of Collier County and the resources available to the LCA-CC to establish a senior center. While the LCA-CC was concerned with the needs of seniors throughout Collier County, it became apparent that the geographic study area would need to be limited to the greater Naples area. At the outset of the study, based on feedback from LCA-CC members, it was determined that public transportation would play a critical role in the establishment of a senior center. The public transportation network did not extend far beyond the greater Naples area. Therefore, the LCA-CC identified four preexisting locations in Collier County, all within the greater Naples area, as appropriate to accommodate a senior access center. As a result, an area including the city of Naples and its immediate unincorporated border areas became the target geography for the needs assessment.

With the feedback from the LCA-CC members, the FGCU research team began development of a comprehensive demographic profile of the senior population in the geographic study area. The first step was the development of a basemap, which provides the general boundaries of the geographic study area. For this purpose, the author decided to use census tracts, which are "small, relatively permanent statistical subdivisions of a county . . . [that] generally have a population size between 1,200 and 8,000 people . . . to provide a stable set of geographic units for the presentation of statistical data" (US Census Bureau, 2012). The general intention of census tracts is to represent neighborhoods because they are relatively homogeneous with respect to population characteristics, economic status, and living conditions (Iceland & Steinmetz, 2003). Census tracts were deemed to be the best spatial representation of the area due to their ability to illustrate the individual areas of the geographic study area and the availability of data from the US Census Bureau for this level of geography.

To create the digital representation of the geographic study area, the author obtained a shapefile of all census tracts in Collier County for the year 2012 from the US Census Bureau website (http://www.census.gov/geo/maps-data/data/tiger.html). Since the geographic study area did not include all of Collier County, the author modified the census tract shapefile using ArcGIS (ESRI, 2011, v. 10.1) to include only those census tracts that fall within the geographic study area. A process of manual selection and extraction was used to isolate the needed census tracts from the original shapefile. The resultant shapefile included 53 census tracts from the initial set of 74 in Collier County (Figure 9.3). This basemap would later be used to execute a join process, as described earlier in this chapter, with the compiled descriptive dataset.

Additional shapefiles were obtained and added to the census tract basemap. A shapefile of the major roads network of Collier County, the highways that intersect the area, and primary state routes was obtained from the Collier County GIS Services Division. These shapefiles were added to the ArcGIS project as overlays

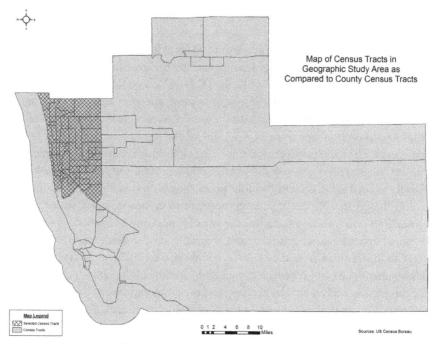

FIGURE 9.3 Census tracts of geographic study area.

to the modified census tracts shapefile. The street network shapefile was modified through a process known as clipping. In this process, a smaller shapefile, in this case the reduced census tract map, was used to clip a large street network shapefile in a digital approximation to match the borders of the census tract shapefile. The same clipping process was used on the shapefile of the major highways and state roads that intersect the geographic study area.

To complete the digital representation of the area transportation network, two shapefiles of the public transportation system, one for the transit routes and one for the route stops, were obtained from the Metropolitan Planning Organization (MPO) for Collier County (http://www.colliermpo.com/index.aspx?page=69). The transit route shapefile was not ultimately included in the project file because it closely approximated the major road network and therefore could not be clearly viewed. The route stops shapefile, consisting of points rather than lines, could easily be identified on the map. This shapefile was modified using the clip process outlined previously and then added to the ArcGIS project as an overlay to the census tracts layer. A final layer of the four locations originally identified by the LCA-CC as possible sites for a senior center was also added to the project file. These locations were added through the geocoding process whereby street address data are digitally represented as a point along a digital street network (ESRI, 2010). The shapefiles were added as layers to an ArcGIS project in order to create the complete digital representation of the geographic study area (Figure 9.4).

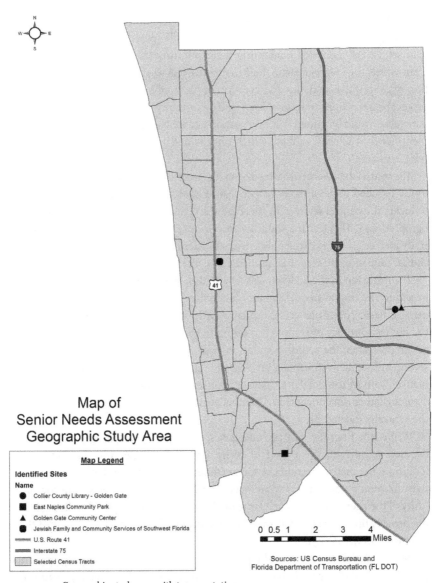

FIGURE 9.4 Geographic study area with transportation.

Once the spatial data set was modified and assembled, work began on building the descriptive data set for the spatial target area. All descriptive data for this project were extracted from the 2012 American Community Survey (ACS) 5-year estimate data set (http://www.census.gov/programs-surveys/acs/data.html) using the American Factfinder tool. The 5-year estimates are a strong option for analyzing very small populations such as at the census tract level (US Census Bureau, 2013). A further rationale for the selection of this data set was the availability of a broad range of age-specific variables focused on individuals aged 60 and older. Data for 78 discrete variables were downloaded and compiled into one data set using Microsoft Excel. The Microsoft Excel file included two worksheets: the data set, and a codebook containing descriptions of the variables and the tables from which they were drawn. The Microsoft Excel workbook allowed for calculation of descriptive statistics and creation of pivot tables, which were later used in project presentations to stakeholders and community members. Knowing that this data table would be joined with the spatial data table, the author included a unique identifier for each row of data, which represented a specific census tract found in the target area.

The spatial data were first analyzed to locate key features and orient stakeholders to the reduced target area. A geoprocessing tool found in ArcMap was employed to locate the central feature, in this case the central census tract, of the target geographic area. This feature, slightly east of center in the target area, was both centrally located in the existing public transit system and home to one of the potential site locations for the senior center (Figure 9.5).

The next step in the analysis was to visualize the descriptive data that had been joined to the digital map. The author visualized each variable in the digital map using a basic count per census tract in order to identify the census tracts with the highest number of seniors according to each variable displayed. In the target geographic area, the senior population (age 65 and older) totaled approximately 58,000 individuals (48% male; 52% female). The largest concentrations of this population were in the northwest corner and central southern sections of the target area. A smaller but concentrated band of seniors was located in the target area near the centrally located site.

While this map did not provide any specific analytic findings that might be deemed significant, the power of using GIS technologies was apparent. After looking at the maps, several LCA-CC members remarked that they were not aware that the senior populations were located in certain areas. After seeing the proximity of the agency location to a large pocket of the senior population living below the poverty line, one LCA-CC member stated, "I had no idea that so many of them were right in my backyard."

Not all initial reactions to the power of GIS were positive. During an initial presentation of the spatial analysis results at a project update meeting, a community stakeholder scoffed at the data and maps concerning senior poverty in the area: "This is Naples; there are no poor people in Naples." The author outlined the data and methodology used to create the maps as a means of addressing the comment. The stakeholder was then reassured by several others that the maps were in fact correct based on their direct service work with seniors in the area.

Several demographic and socioeconomic variables were illustrated via GIS using basic counts in each census tract of the spatial target area. Within the target area, there were an estimated 2,470 households with a householder aged 65 years or older and with income for the past 12 months below the federal poverty level. Spatially, the highest concentration of this population was located in the northeast

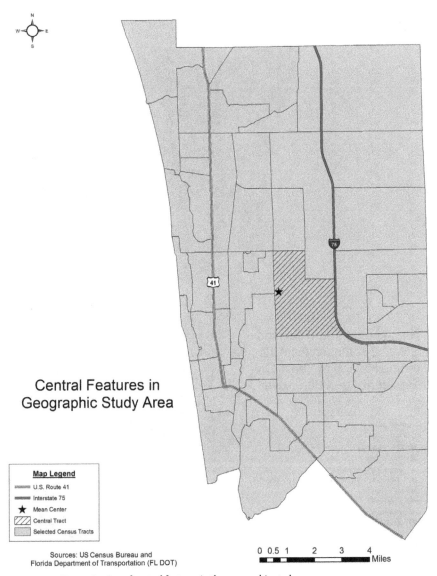

FIGURE 9.5 Determination of central features in the geographic study area.

corner of the target area with pockets also identified in the center and southeast corner. Additionally, there were approximately 1,200 households with at least one resident aged 60 or older that had received SNAP (Food Stamps) benefits in the past 12 months. Two pockets were identified, one located in the northeast corner of the target area and the other near the central site location, which was the Jewish Family and Community Services office building (Figure 9.6).

Among the most important findings were the data regarding the number of households consisting of seniors living alone in the target area. The data showed

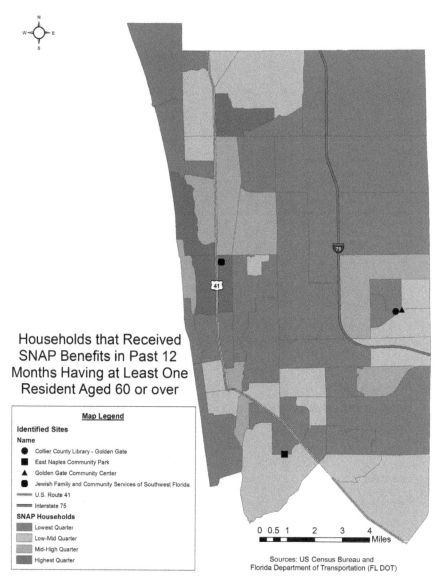

FIGURE 9.6 Households with a resident 60 or older receiving SNAP benefits.

that approximately 16,600 individuals, roughly 29% of the total senior population, were living alone. The number of senior females (66%) living alone was almost twice that of males (34%) living alone. These populations were found to be distributed evenly throughout the target area with a few exceptions based on gender. The highest pocket of males was located in the southern area, whereas three pockets of females were located in the central and northern areas. Taken as a whole, the highest densities were found near the central site location as well as on the northwest border. This variable assumed utmost importance because lack of companionship was the primary theme that emerged from the focus groups conducted with seniors in the target spatial area (Figure 9.7).

Using the total senior population by census tract as a base layer, a second geoprocessing tool was used to "buffer" the stops along the public transportation system. A buffer is an area of a predefined distance created around a map feature in order to conduct proximity analysis (ESRI, 2014). In this project, quarter- and half-mile buffers were created around the public transportation stops. Walkability research among the elderly identified these distances as the outer limits for seniors

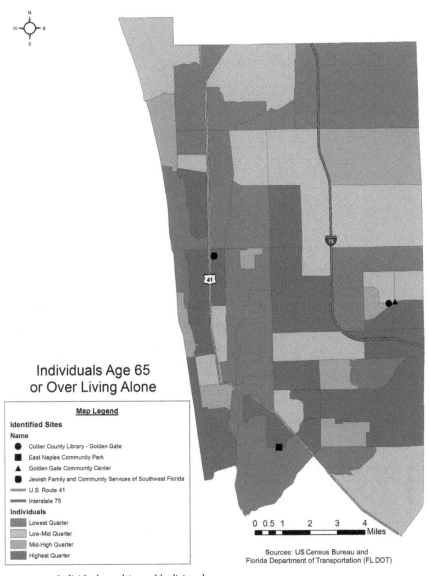

FIGURE 9.7 Individuals aged 65 or older living alone.

using public transportation (Hess, 2012; Kim & Ulfarsson, 2004). An additional 1-mile buffer was added for comparative purposes. The proximity analysis found that none of the four site locations were particularly accessible for individuals using the existing public transportation system. In most cases, minimum walking distances between transit stops and site locations were more than 1 mile. Two locations were found to have at least one transit stop situated within a quarter-mile although only in one direction of the transit loop (Figure 9.8).

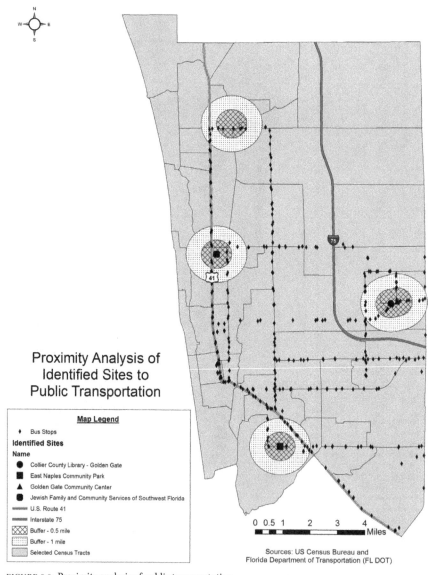

FIGURE 9.8 Proximity analysis of public transportation.

In summary, none of the four preexisting sites under consideration was located directly within a census tract with the highest population of individuals over 65, the largest number of individuals below the federal poverty level, the lowest median income, or the largest number of households receiving SNAP benefits. Census tracts located in the northeast and northwest corners of the target area were found to contain high concentrations of seniors who might benefit from a senior access center. However, the lack of an available site location, limited public transportation, and limited resources to build a new location were identified by LCA-CC members as major barriers for seniors residing in these areas. The centrally located site was the closest when evaluating the population according to each of these variables. This site was also the only location with a public transit stop within one-quarter mile. However, participants would either have to walk in the opposite direction of the center or to continue around the entire route.

Based on the findings of the spatial and proximity analyses, triangulated through data collected via the key informant interviews and focus groups, the author made a series of recommendations. Primary among the findings was the confirmation, despite public perception, that a population of seniors with incomes below the poverty level lives in the target area and that these residents do not have access to needed services because of either transportation barriers or a lack of basic services for low-income individuals. The findings also showed that a need and desire for social activities and companionship existed among seniors. Given its proximity to high senior populations based on the variables examined, the central location was recommended as the best site for a senior center with a second site located in the southeast corner if financially feasible. Finally, the author recommended development of alternate transportation options for seniors in the northeast and northwest corners of the target area so that they might benefit from participation in a senior center.

Based on the findings of the project, the Jewish Family and Community Services (JFCS) site was selected for the first senior access center in Collier County. The spatial analysis showed that this location was nearest to the section of the geographic study area with the highest rates of poverty and social isolation among seniors. Media coverage and public presentations of the study results, primarily the spatial analysis, led to JFCS receiving $250,000 to renovate its office building to accommodate the senior center. In January 2014, the 4,000-square-foot center began offering a weekly congregate luncheon and occasional social activities for seniors (Lopez, 2014).

The Collier County transit department took note of the recommendations concerning transportation preferences as reported via the focus groups. Public transportation was expanded to areas with high concentrations of seniors through modifications to the fixed route transit system and the expansion of ride share services. These alterations allowed seniors to attend activities without walking extended distances from off-site parking lots or riding traditional public transit routes that included multiple stops. The spatial analysis was used to assist in determining the modifications to the existing fixed routes.

The center opened officially in May 2014 to a membership much larger than initially anticipated. The prevailing thought at the time was that media coverage of the foundation and opening of the center increased the service estimates from an anticipated 150 to 200 seniors to more than 400. An outcome evaluation was conducted in 2015 to coincide with the center's first year of operation. Again, GIS technologies were used to analyze the areas from which seniors were attending the center. The analysis found that the center was reaching its intended target population: seniors residing in areas previously identified as having high concentrations of seniors living alone or below the poverty line were attending center-based activities. Further evaluation revealed a surprising result. Though the study catchment area focused only on the identified area within the Naples area, the spatial analysis showed that attendees were coming from areas well outside the study catchment area, not only from other areas within Collier County but also from southern areas of Lee County, which borders Collier County to the north. The tremendous response from seniors led to expansion of the center (with an additional 2,000 feet of space) and additional staff and programming (Marcus, 2015). A recent review of membership records in October 2016 shows the center is serving approximately 700 seniors annually.

A 5-year update to the needs assessment was undertaken in January 2017. The update examined needs in an expanded geographic area based on the current use of the center by seniors from outside of the original catchment area. In addition to basic demographic maps, spatial statistics were calculated to provide a more in-depth assessment of the current situation of seniors. The updated have led the agency to seek additional funding for the foundation of a larger senior center in the original catachment areas as well as for at least two additional senior centers to be developed in the expanded geographic area.

As the success of the senior center gained local and national media attention, regional social service agencies and even neighboring governments began to recognize the value of using GIS technologies as a planning and evaluation tool. As a result, the author has conducted additional studies in the region focused on affordable housing (Lysiak, 2015; Wolford, 2014), food insecurity (Varney, 2015), and community needs in the newly incorporated Village of Estero, Florida (Battle, 2015).

Ethical Considerations

The ability to display potentially sensitive data exposes GIS technologies to potentially increased ethical risks, including the failure to effectively preserve the anonymity of individuals, as well as the unintended impacts of reporting spatial analysis findings (Blatt, 2012). Geographic information system technologies allow the user to accurately aggregate data into discrete spatial units as well as to pinpoint specific locations on a map. While GIS technologies provide the ability to conduct analyses on a spatial basis, some analyses may prove problematic, given certain types of attribute data. For example, a user might create a map of geocoded locations of homeless camps to identify relationships or correlations based on the location of these camps; such a map could be used to bring harm either directly or indirectly to the individuals residing in these locations.

It can be argued that this risk is negligible if the map is not disseminated publicly. However, the use of network and cloud-based data storage versus local data storage may be problematic. It is now relatively easy to create and publicly share spatial data files through online mapping products such as Google Maps and BatchGeo. It could be insensitive and potentially dangerous to create maps including variables that an individual might not want made public such as health status or other socially controversial demographics. Curtis, Mills, and Leitner (2006) highlight this issue through their use of geospatial technologies to re-engineer mapped points provided by a local newspaper story in New Orleans concerning search-and-rescue sites in the aftermath of Hurricane Katrina.

The inherent risks of this approach are enhanced by the lack of clear standards for the creation, dissemination, and storage of these data. Although a set of standards and techniques has been developed to minimize some of the potential risks of using GIS technologies, the user must consider the potential repercussions of conducting and disseminating spatial analyses. The Urban and Regional Information Systems Association (URISA) has developed and approved a *GIS Code of Ethics* for its members, which was subsequently adopted by the GIS Certification Institute. The URISA code outlines GIS professionals' obligations to society, employers and funders, colleagues and the profession, and individuals (URISA, 2003).

In social work, the National Association of Social Workers (NASW) *Code of Ethics* addresses some aspects of technology use in social work practice, though in limited detail. Members from several of the national social work member organizations have recently undertaken the update of the "NASW and ASWB Standards for Technology and Social Work Practice," which was first developed in 2005 (NASW and Association of Social Work Boards, 2005). Neither the 2005 document nor the current drafts include specific mention of GIS technologies. Given the increased interest in the use of GIS technologies by social-work-related agencies and organizations, it may be wise to include these technologies in these standards.

Techniques to minimize risks are available if a researcher needs to geocode sensitive data. Geomasking, in which geocoded addresses are randomly dispersed within a defined spatial area, allows researchers to conduct appropriate analyses while providing necessary protection in terms of confidentiality and anonymity.

These techniques have been implemented and evaluated with positive results in studies that include sensitive health data (Allshouse et al., 2010; Hampton et al., 2010). A newly proposed technique called location swapping has also shown promise for ensuring the geoprivacy of individuals (Zhang, Freundschuh, Lenzera, & Zandbergen, 2015).

Studies using GIS technologies should be held to the same rigorous standards as more traditional research. Members of review boards at academic or service organizations and others assuming these roles in private and government agencies must be familiar with how GIS technologies are used to display, analyze, and visualize data, as well as the ramifications of their use to examine sensitive data. The current training level and general awareness of GIS mechanics and output among these individuals are unknown and may be an area for both study and education.

Social Justice Implications

The author believes that GIS technologies can be applied to any facet of social services to examine social justice issues occurring globally, nationally, regionally, or locally and that such application offers the potential to disrupt structural inequality. Displaying social issues within a geographic context allows for more efficient and effective planning, advocacy, and provision of services. As seen in the case study, the use of maps and spatial analysis builds credibility and provides a foundational underpinning that is difficult to refute. However, the use of GIS technologies in planning or evaluation projects creates potential ethical and political dilemmas whose intended and unintended consequences must be carefully considered during the project planning process.

Although commercial GIS software programs can be expensive, the wide array of freely available options make GIS an accessible tool. Online mapping tools, such as those discussed previously, require access to a computer and the Internet. Access may be available through a public or university library or other community resource. Education and training on these tools tends to be a larger issue. It is possible that community-based trainings can be arranged through continuing education programs via local community-based organizations or through university–community partnerships. Engaging in this type of training can empower residents to better understand their communities and to advocate for needed or enhanced policies, services, or programs. Residents have the best understanding of what is occurring in their communities on a daily basis. Coupling this knowledge with spatial analysis using GIS technologies could allow for the development of community plans of action that could be realized in partnership with local social service programs.

Questions for Discussion

1. The person-in-environment perspective is the overarching philosophy of the social work profession. Consider how the use of GIS technologies fits with this perspective.
2. Consider a social issue of interest to you. How do you think GIS technologies could be used to examine this issue? At what geographic level (block groups, census tracts, counties, states, etc.) would you recommend examining the issue? What data would you need in order to construct a meaningful analysis?
3. What potential ethical and political issues need to be considered when using GIS technologies to examine social issues, particularly at a local or state level?
4. The use of GIS technologies in social work is still developing. What strategies would you employ to gain buy-in from stakeholders for using these technologies?

Additional Readings

Blatt, A. (2012). Ethics and privacy issues in the use of GIS. *Journal of Map and Geography Libraries, 8*(1), 80–84.

Coulton, C. (2005). The place of community in social work practice research: Conceptual and methodological developments. *Social Work Research, 29*(2), 73–86.

ESRI. (2011, April). *Place matters in the helping professions: GIS for human and social services organizations.* Redlands, CA: ESRI Press.

Felke, T. (2007). Geographic information systems: Potential uses in social work education and practice. *Journal of Evidence-Based Social Work Practice, 3,* 103–113.

Hillier, A. (2007). Why social work needs mapping. *Journal of Social Work Education, 43,* 205–221.

10 }

Social Media in Agency Settings

Kimberly Grocher, Lea Wolf, and Lauri Goldkind

"Like all technology, social media is neutral but is best put to work in the service of building a better world."

—Simon Mainwaring, *b. 1967–present*

Social media can be a powerful tool for engagement, education, and promotion when used properly and with ethical consideration in a mental health setting. As competent social workers, it is our responsibility to stay abreast of social media and other tools that can enrich our clinical work with clients while being cognizant of the inherent risks and barriers. As the social work profession continues to incorporate social media into its practice and policy decisions, social workers need to establish resources and relationships to nurture a perpetually evolving skill set that supports just and meaningful practice.

Interactive Web-based media tools have reshaped personal reality. However, as our collective dialogue moves into virtual space and issues of identity, culture, and equality are negotiated via interactive media, we are witness to the parallel potential of these tools to reshape how organizations, civic entities, and communities present themselves and interact in the digital space. The Internet of the last century—called Internet 1.0—was a collection of Web-based pages that functioned like a library online, a one-way information system offering near-immediate access to a gigantic volume of static information. Web 2.0 (or Internet 2.0) is a conceptual leap beyond, an expansion into two-way transmission that allows users to communicate with each other, to establish networks, and to respond to what they encounter online by authoring their own content (Bizer, Heath, & Berners-Lee, 2009) and enable its immediate publication and exchange (Kaplan & Haenlein, 2010). Specific to the nonprofit sector, Web 2.0 offers tools that streamline or reinvent the processes of recruiting volunteers; raising awareness; providing education; mobilizing funds; and reaching out to friends, clients, and other constituents.

This chapter reviews the history and development of social media and explores how specific social media tools can help organizations to realize a variety of goals. The case study describes how one mental health organization has deployed a variety of social media tools as part of its strategic plan, identifying platforms that will help them to engage a client population, to launch a mental health awareness campaign, and to raise funds for a new initiative.

Background

The first recognizable social media site, Six Degrees (sixdegrees.com), was created in 1997, and the first major study of social media use is only 9 years old (Barnes & Mattson, 2008). While primitive, Six Degrees offered a virtual extension of real-life patterns of social connection. Based on the six-degrees-of-separation model, whereby any two individuals can connect in a maximum of six steps, it included message boards and allowed users to connect with each other and to send external messages (Boyd & Ellinson, 2007).

The first blogging platforms were launched in 1999, and in the next 3 to 5 years more recognizable social media sites—such as MySpace (2003), Friendster (2002), and Facebook (2005)—came online. Like Six Degrees, these early examples of accelerated connection within preexisting communities took real-life affinity groups into the digital sphere and accelerated their spread and reach. MySpace, for example, initially focused on music, offering members a space to highlight their works, a messaging tool, and the ability to invite new members.

Social media have introduced a new interactive communications paradigm for *all* organizations: public/government, private/corporate, and nonprofits. With the advent of Web 2.0, organizations had to reconceptualize strategy, with the goal of engaging constituents in ongoing two-way communication. Contemporary Web 2.0 social media tools, including microblogging tools such as Twitter and social networking sites such as Facebook and LinkedIn, are ubiquitous, and their accessibility allows organizations and their stakeholders to engage in dynamic dialogue (Goldkind, 2015; Goldkind & McNutt, 2014).

Although the spread of social media has significantly increased nonprofits' potential to communicate with stakeholders, including clients, volunteers, the media, and the general public (Lovejoy & Saxton, 2012), it is unlikely that they are using these resources to the maximum effect and questionable how, if at all, they are measuring and evaluating the effects of their social media use. Relationships are central to social networking and to interactive Web 2.0 sites (Goldkind, 2015; Waters, Burnett, Lamm, & Lucas, 2009), and one might imagine that nonprofit organizations, already practiced in relationship development at the client, donor, and volunteer levels, would be especially adept at exploiting the tools and the possibilities that have proliferated in this digital space. However, research on social media use by agencies and organizations suggests that this is not always the case (Goldkind, 2014). Although many of these tools are free, few aspiring professionals encounter them in graduate training programs; smaller agencies may not have the resources to allocate to staff who can oversee their implementation or maintenance; and organizational leaders often lack the vision to understand how a social media tool (or a constellation of social media tools) might help to realize organizational goals.

Investigations focusing on nonprofit social media use have been conducted predominantly in the disciplines of communications, marketing, and public relations (Roback, 2013). It is generally agreed that nonprofits have not realized the full potential of social media to meet organizational goals (Goldkind, 2015; Waters et al., 2009). In particular, it has been suggested that nonprofit organizations using social media may not yet have incorporated interactive two-way constituent communication—the hallmark of social media—thus limiting the yield of their communication (Lovejoy & Saxton, 2012). It has also been suggested that agencies should create social media ambassadors or champions to advance the use of this new tool—both internally and externally. Such proposed organizational changes reveal how social media have decentralized the tasks formerly associated with professional marketing and communications, diffusing responsibility across agencies and institutions. This decentralization of organizational messaging has been challenging for nonprofits to adopt and is rarely reflected in how they conceptualize their message.

Although employees of nonprofits are likely to use social media, familiarity with the medium does not necessarily translate into the ability or opportunity to use it in a professional context. In a study of agency-based social work supervisors, Goldkind, Wolf, and Jones (2016) found that personal use of social media did not correspond with professional use. With more training, this personal facility might translate into greater awareness of the potential of this tool to advance agency goals.

EFFECTIVE USE OF SOCIAL MEDIA

The term "social media" is deployed variously, often to evoke a phenomenon or to denote an ill-defined collection of the most popular online platforms. Yet the specific interfaces that characterize different types of social media tools may affect their utility. For example, while Facebook boasts an eye-popping 1.86 billion users worldwide, its broad reach does not mean that it is appropriate for all tasks.

For a nonprofit leader willing to prioritize the utility of a platform over its ubiquity, the framework articulated by Kietzmann, Hermkens, McCarthy, and Silvestre (2011) may prove useful in matching a tool to a task. These authors articulate social media as a honeycomb of seven building blocks: identity, conversations, sharing, presence, relationships, reputation, and groups. In their model, identity refers to the extent to which users reveal themselves, conversation to the frequency of communication between constituents and across groups, sharing is the extent to which information (data, images, stories, and gossip) is disseminated, presence is the extent to which constituents are aware of each other's availability online, relationships are how constituents connect with each other, reputation is the degree to which individuals trust each other's content, and groups are individuals' affiliations online (Kietzmann et al, 2011). For example, if an agency providing adoption services wanted to invest its social media resources in promoting and managing its reputation, under Kietzmann's model, it would prioritize LinkedIn as a social media tool, foregoing YouTube and other video- and image-sharing sites in favor of highlighting professionalism, integrity, and reputation within the community.

A myriad of new tools presents a range of options and choices for agencies interested in pursuing a social media program or campaign. Social media networks such as LinkedIn, Facebook, MySpace, hi5, Friendster, Google Plus, and Ning offer nonprofit leaders the option of engaging with constituents in new and more nuanced ways. Specialized social networking platforms allow for the sharing of specific types of data such as videos (YouTube, Vimeo, Vine, Ocho, and Metacafe) and photographs (Pinterest, Flickr, Instagram, Photobucket, and GifBoom). Blogs are online journals that involve a series of entries or posts and allow readers to comment on the posting (Goldkind, 2014). Video blogs (called V-Blogs) and photo blogs are also available. The blogosphere is a public opinion arena with more than 100 million blogs, and its interconnections cannot be ignored (Kietzmann et al., 2011). Lastly, by using microblogging or real-time updates known as tweets, everyone—celebrities to academics to political leaders—can share daily activities and updates. Founded in 2006, Twitter has more than 145 million users sending on average 90 million tweets per day, which consist of 140 characters or less (Madway, 2010).

FUNDRAISING WITH SOCIAL MEDIA

Social media, Web 2.0, and social networking technologies for connecting with like-minded people (Ogden & Laura, 2009) have become critical to nonprofits engaged in building new relationships and cultivating new donors. Social networking sites such as Facebook, MySpace, and LinkedIn dominate the social networking space, but there are other companies linking constituents online, some focusing on nonprofit, social enterprise, activist, or donor audiences. Facebook Causes, a registered 501(c)3, was created in 2007 and has since raised $21 million for 390,000 causes through the efforts of more than 100 million active users. Its founder, Joe Green, says the tool now processes $30,000 to $45,000 in donations every day—up from $3,000 just 2 years ago, with a median gift of $25 (Wasley, 2009). Saxton and Wang (2014) explored Facebook Causes account data from the *Nonprofit Times*' list of 100 largest nonprofits and found that fundraising success was not directly related to the organization's financial capacity but instead to its Web presence; social network factors appeared to take precedence over other economic explanations in predicting donor behavior. Research has found that online donors are also more likely to contribute to certain types of causes than others, especially those related to health. Facebook Causes and other giving campaigns such as the ALS Ice Bucket Challenge and the 2015 #FoodBankNYCChallenge are public examples of the success of this fundraising strategy.

In some cases social media have generated donations that supersede any conventional definition of fundraising success. The fraught political climate of early 2017 accelerated donations to a new extreme: in one weekend, inspired by a celebrity who posted a matching challenge on Twitter, contributors donated $24 million to the American Civil Liberties Union (ACLU)—approximately six times the organization's average *annual* fund-raising total (https://www.wired.com/2017/01/aclu-donations-twitter-celebrities). Yet this initiative did not originate with the nonprofit itself, and its success may have resulted from a unique combination of circumstances.

With potentially lower costs and better yield than traditional strategies, electronic media for fundraising have great appeal for nonprofits. Academic literature across all sectors—nonprofit administration, communications, public relations, and marketing—has not yet systematically assessed the effectiveness of these strategies. The literature that exists indicates that the success of social media in meeting fundraising goals has been uneven across nonprofits, suggesting that social media can support the recruitment of new contributors, but that donations tend to be smaller (Laird, 2010; Ogden & Laura, 2009; Saxton & Wang, 2014) than those solicited by traditional means within individual giving programs.

ADVOCACY AND SOCIAL MEDIA

Advocacy and social change have rapidly become linked with technology tools and Internet-based outreach (McNutt, 2008; McNutt & Boland, 1999). Proliferating rapidly, these strategies and tools are critical for nonprofit leaders to remain relevant in increasingly competitive climates. Internet-based interactive tools such as social media function as virtual hubs, facilitating engagement by individuals and organizations in advocacy campaigns (Guo & Saxton, 2012; Nah & Saxton, 2013). Social networking sites are driven by user participation and user-generated content (Tredinnick, 2006). These sites have the capacity to facilitate interactions among the users through the sharing of user-generated content in the form of text, audio and video files, and tools. Through interactions with stakeholders such as clients, donors, and volunteers on social media sites, organizations are seeking to develop relationships with important public communities.

The Internet can serve as a gathering place for those interested in activating change as well as a mechanism for connecting advocates. For organizations interested in creating and sustaining social change, social networking sites offer the ability to quickly and efficiently identify groups and allied organizations with common interests and agendas as well as empathic individuals. A multitude of organizations are engaged in advocacy work online, but one such agency, the Human Rights Campaign (HRC), has focused its social media investment on Facebook (http://www.Facebook.com/humanrightscampaign). Through data analysis and monitoring of posts, HRC has been able to identify topics and programs that generate the most buzz and to fine-tune its online offerings (Goldkind, 2014). As a result, HRC has seen tremendous growth in its fan base—an increase of more than 400% over 14 months—from 80,000 to more than 350,000 fans. Facebook also directs 30% to 50% of Web traffic to HRC's blog, consistently making it the top referring site. In the past 12 months, HRC added more than 23,000 new e-mail addresses to its list as a result of Facebook users taking action or submitting surveys posted on HRC's profile.

Other organizations are investing their social media resources in tools such as Instagram, Flickr, and Pinterest for sharing visual images, primarily photographs, online and linking them to other interactive structures, such as Facebook or MySpace. Photo sharing in the nonprofit space can be used to publicize conditions and causes affecting particular communities (Goldkind, 2014). As an example, Operation Smile is an international children's medical charity that provides pediatric plastic surgery and develops medical expertise across 60 countries around the world. This organization is the largest volunteer-based medical charity providing free cleft palate surgeries in the world. It uses a combination of Pinterest and Twitter to highlight its successes and to drive awareness of cleft palate and children's facial deformities. Between the two platforms it has garnered more than 13,000 followers.

These two cases and many others suggest that nonprofits are engaging in social media programs to promote advocacy causes and to promote civic engagement. However, the outcomes of these activities are not well understood (Phethean, Tiropanis, & Harris, 2013).

PSYCHOEDUCATION AND SOCIAL MEDIA

Almost 60% of Internet users reported searching for health information for themselves, making this the most common online health-related activity (Koch-Weser et al., 2010; Powell et al., 2011). Many people are using this channel, often before talking to clinicians, compelling agencies to offer direct access to health information online, replacing client dependency on traditional communication channels (Atkinson, Saperstein, & Pleis, 2009; Thackeray, Neiger, & Hanson, 2008). Social media outlets also offer providers an opportunity to reach traditionally underserved members of the population (Chou, Hunt, Beckjord, Moser, & Hesse, 2009). These tools are ultimately empowering for patients because they can provide the information required to improve self-care (Hawn, 2009).

Different forms of social media present different opportunities for health communication to reach a broad audience (Hawn, 2009). Social networking sites attract the largest portion of Internet users and are likely to continue to grow, making them an obvious target for maximizing the reach and impact of health communication (Chou et al., 2009). Blogs also present a tremendous opportunity for health communication. Bloggers have been observed to act as important communication stakeholders. Not only are they information disseminators but also play a crucial role in directing Internet traffic through opinions and hyperlinks. Communication among consumers and patients presents several advantages. Chou and colleagues (2009) found that age was the single strongest predictor of both social networking and blogging, which have the broadest reach and impact on the younger generation. However, social media are found to penetrate the population regardless of education, race/ethnicity, or healthcare access.

User interactions have a number of benefits for healthcare patients, who can compare care options and outcomes through social media platforms such as PatientsLikeMe. Such communication is increasingly understood as a critical way for the chronically ill to successfully engage in self-management (Hawn, 2009). Social media provide one route to greater patient satisfaction and to a more patient-centered healthcare system, offering a significant challenge to the paradigm of the physician–patient relationship (Hawn, 2009; Landman, Shelton, Kauffman, & Dattilo, 2010). Social networking sites such as CaringBridge and PatientsLikeMe create an online support system for patients with varying health issues (Chou et al., 2009). Participants have reported feeling empowered because they were better informed and experienced enhanced social well-being as result of participating in such platforms (van Uden-Kraan, Drossaert, Taal, Seydek, & van de Laar, 2008). Peer support is a critical adjunct to therapy—allowing patients to seek and to create a supportive community online (Khanna, 2008).

In terms of sustaining mental health gains, findings demonstrate a robust connection between Facebook usage and indicators of social capital for young adults. These online interactions do not necessarily remove people from their offline world, but they may be used to support relationships and keep people in contact, even when life changes and they move away from each other (Ellison, Steinfeld, & Lampe, 2007). Relationships formed or maintained in this community can help with long-term goals (DiMicco et al., 2008) in terms of jobs, internships, and other opportunities.

Case Study

Ms. Lee recently graduated with her MSW and is a full-time therapist at Choice Community Mental Health, an agency that serves children, adolescents, and adults in a diverse lower-middle class urban neighborhood. She started at the agency as a social work intern and was offered her current position following graduation.

NEEDS

During a recent all staff meeting, the program director informed the staff that the agency needed additional resources to meet a new local regulatory requirement. The city government would be offering grant funding to cover services to treat anxiety and depression in young adults between the ages of 18 and 21. Choice Community Mental Health (CCMH) wanted to apply for the grant, but had struggled to keep young adults engaged in services. Additional financial resources would be needed to supplement the city's grant in order to develop new programming specific to the young adults in the neighborhood. In order to begin addressing these needs, Ms. Lee's supervisor appointed a committee of clinical and administrative staff members to develop, implement, and evaluate a plan of action to address the clinical need (to engage young adults in treatment) and the administrative need (to procure additional financial resources). Ms. Lee was very excited to be appointed to the committee because she wanted to develop administrative skills in addition to her clinical skills.

PLANNING

The new committee met a week later and agreed to administer a short survey to its new and existing young adult clients diagnosed with anxiety and depression. The survey asked questions about three areas:

1. What are the most significant barriers to treatment?
2. What could keep clients engaged in treatment?
3. What additional help do clients need to support daily functioning?

The results of the survey indicated that the young adults identified both the stigma around mental health treatment and the symptoms (i.e., isolation, fatigue, and lack of motivation) as barriers to treatment. They reported that having access to support and information electronically or even on social media would increase their likelihood of engaging in treatment, since using mobile devices and social media were part of their daily lives. Finally, they reported that they needed additional help with establishing and maintaining social relationships and academic and/or career guidance.

The committee members were very motivated by the survey results and decided that the new programming initiative would include a group for young adults that offered concrete assistance with strengthening social skills and academic/career guidance in addition to support for anxiety and depression. They decided to leverage social media for clinical and administrative purposes.

Clinically, social media would be used to engage new and existing young adult patients by (1) creating and using the agency's social media pages to post psychoeducation resources about depression and anxiety and (2) posting general reminders about group sessions and encouraging patients to check in with their mental health providers on a regular basis. Administratively, social media would be used to launch a mental health awareness campaign to reduce mental health stigma and create a crowdfunding campaign to raise funds for staffing and space for the new young adult group program.

IMPLEMENTATION

Ms. Lee was eager to embark on the project and wanted to integrate her personal knowledge of social media into this professional forum. She began to think of the different social media platforms she used and her reasons for using them. She realized that each platform served a distinct function. For example, she primarily used Facebook to keep in contact with family members and friends, whereas she used LinkedIn mostly to establish and maintain professional connections. She brought her reflections to the team. Team members also considered how they used social media and concluded that each strategic goal should be matched to the most appropriate social media tool. The agency's social media pages (Facebook and Twitter) would be used to post information about depression and anxiety (psychoeducation). Facebook and Twitter would be used for general reminders about group sessions and notes encouraging patients to check in with their mental health providers on a regular basis. Administratively, social media would be used to launch a mental health awareness campaign to reduce mental health stigma (Instagram and Twitter), engage and collaborate with other local agencies and services in the community (Facebook, Twitter, and LinkedIn), and create a crowd-funding campaign to raise funds for staffing and space for the new young adult group program (Facebook and CrowdRise).

CHALLENGES

Ms. Lee and her colleagues quickly realized how much work this new initiative would require. Their first challenge was time management. Working in a busy community mental health agency, Ms. Lee found that it was extremely difficult to manage her workload—seeing patients, staying on top of treatment plans, preparing documentation and other required paperwork, and locating resources for patients—while simultaneously trying to develop and implement the agency's new social media plan. At the suggestion of her clinical supervisor, Ms. Lee recommended that the new social work interns should manage the daily postings on the various social media platforms. The program director quickly agreed.

Other challenges continued to crop up. The next major challenge was managing inappropriate contact by current patients. When they saw the signs posted in the waiting area announcing the agency's new social media presence, several patients used features on the social media platforms to "tag" or "check in" to the center, announcing to the public that not only were they were in this physical location but also that they were patients. The team quickly realized that this could have negative implications on patient confidentiality and could potentially violate HIPAA regulations. This problem was not discovered until the interns responsible for managing the social media accounts reported on their progress. Not only was there a delay in discovering these postings, but the interns (with no previous training on managing social media for professional purposes) responded inappropriately to many of the postings by welcoming patients to the center or expressing that they were looking forward to therapy sessions with them.

Ms. Lee and her colleagues realized that the interns and other staff would need to be trained to use social media for professional purposes. They would also need to develop a policy for handling patient contacts on social media, including defining appropriate and inappropriate contact.

Ms. Lee began educating herself on the professional uses of social media in healthcare, nonprofit, and social work settings. She found appropriate resources in scholarly social work and business journals, mental health and social work magazines, the *NASW & ASWB Standards for Technology and Social Work Practice* (National Association of Social Workers and Association of Social Work Boards, 2005), and social media pages and profiles of similar agencies and professional organizations such as NASW and the American Psychological Association. She discovered several important guidelines for using social media appropriately in the organization:

1. **Create a social media policy.** The policy should include the platforms to be used, the type of information to be shared on these platforms, plans for remaining compliant with HIPAA and other ethical considerations, evaluation methods and procedures, and an understanding of how social media fits into the agency's larger marketing and development plans.

2. **Determine the audience.** In this case, the agency determined that the audience included potential consumers, current consumers, and referral sources such as other agencies in the city.

3. **Consider the content.** Post material that correlates with the mission of the organization as a resource for current and potential consumers (e.g., articles from other reputable sources on addressing stress, finding jobs, or creating campaigns that challenge stigma around accessing mental health services).

4. **Provide training.** Staff should be trained and provided with guidelines on using social media professionally in addition to understanding the potential implications of their personal use of social media.

5. **Create a social media team.** Select staff members should be given time during their workday to maintain and update the social media sites on a consistent basis.

Impressed with Ms. Lee's initiative, the program director appointed her as the chairperson of the social media committee and agreed to reduce her clinical caseload to allow more time for her new role. Ms. Lee first met with the program director and other members of the management team to draft a social media policy for the agency. Once the policy had been drafted, the Social Media Committee created an editorial calendar similar to those used by journalists. On this calendar,

Ms. Lee scheduled her posts on each platform for the coming month. This allowed her make sure her posts were in line with current events, holidays, and themes. Once she understood the needs and concerns of the agency's clients, she was able to use her clinical experience and insights to inform the type of content that she posted.

Ms. Lee's self-taught knowledge of social media was useful, but she wanted more formal training to help with this new task. She began taking webinar courses from organizations such as the Foundation Center and sites such as Hootsuite. com to further develop her skillset.

Two months after Ms. Lee's initial appointment as social media manager, the CCMH's presence on social media was growing and becoming a useful resource, not only for the young adults served by the agency but for other age groups as well. During this time, the agency launched two major social media campaigns.

The first campaign, #MentalHealthCounts, focused on reducing the stigma around seeking mental health services. The Social Media Committee posted original content (created by staff) about the importance of mental health in the form of short articles, photos, and short videos produced using smartphones and other available technology. They also shared relevant content from other local mental health and healthcare agencies, initiating relationships based in digital collaboration or expanding existing collaborations into the virtual space. All of the posts were connected by using the hashtag #mentalhealthcounts in the post. Hashtags are a mechanism for creating bookmarks or keywords on social media, especially Twitter (Ma, Sun, & Cong, 2013). The campaign solicited interactive communication with the hashtags #tellyourstory and #igothelp, asking people to tweet their own experience of diagnosis and treatment. The campaign emphasized the power of retweeting powerful stories or posts.

When the campaign appeared on the CCMH social media websites, it quickly went viral and reached into the larger community, making it less obvious who might be a client of CCMH. The head of the City Council tweeted a personal story, a television actor from the area joined in, and a local firefighter tweeted about his brother's mental health diagnosis. These tweets garnered local media attention, spreading awareness through television news and attracting enthusiastic young adult consumers. Clinic therapists reported back that they were hearing about the campaign from their adolescent clients, for whom spreading the message was an empowering experience.

The second campaign, the Our Youth Our City Advancement Initiative, was a crowdfunding campaign. The goal of the campaign was to procure $10,000 in donations toward funding the CCMH's new young adult program. The social media committee created a profile on CrowdRise to promote the campaign. They provided a detailed explanation about CCMH, the agency's mission, and the goals for the new young adult program. They uploaded videos of CCMH's executive director and several clinicians speaking about the work of the agency in the community. Ms. Lee encouraged agency staff to brainstorm a list of well-known local personalities interested in mental health, and after coordinating with board members to make calls and call in favors, she posted two effective video clips: one of a celebrity chef talking about her own mental health diagnosis and the need for supportive care, and the other of a local news anchor delivering the message "Mental illness isn't a choice. Choose to talk about it." Ms. Lee promoted the crowdfunding campaign on all of the agency's other platforms, using graphics and links to drive potential donors to the agency's CrowdRise site.

EVALUATION

The program director emphasized the importance of evaluating the effectiveness of social media to justify the use of staff time. Ms. Lee appointed a committee member to track the numbers each week on each platform. This committee member looked at the number of followers or friends on the agency's social media platforms and compared the numbers from week to week to estimate and chart their growth. Other important metrics collected by committee members included the number of likes, comments, and reactions to the posts on each platform. Ms. Lee and committee members not only looked at the numbers, but also evaluated qualitative aspects, based on comments. They used the quantitative and qualitative data to determine which posts were more effective.

One of the nuances of tracking social media in a mental health setting is the difficulty of assessing efficacy and reach based on likes alone. Many consumers who visit a site or profile for information will not comment on or like the page/posts for fear of being identified as a patient or consumer. Facebook allows users with professional pages to see how many views their page has had without identifying who accessed the content. The Social Media Committee tracked Facebook view numbers as well as likes and comments. It also used Facebook Insights, Twitter Analytics, and InstaFollow to collect additional tracking information, such as how many times CCMH information was shared on other social media profiles and pages. Other critical evaluations included the following:

1. **Tracking the number of new patients referred through social media.** Online/social media was included as a referral option on the initial intake forms. Intake staff also tracked the number of new patients who said that they had heard about CCMH through a social media channel.

2. **Assessing progress of the CrowdRise campaign.** CrowdRise allowed the Social Media Committee to see real-time dollar amounts as well as the amount needed to meet their goal. They were also able to see who donated, enabling them to contact the donors, thank them, and begin building or further cultivating that relationship.

Ms. Lee and her colleagues realize that they are still in the early stages of using social media in their agency, but they are off to a good start. They have learned from their initial challenges and have created systems and policies to help them manage new issues as they arise. They have also created a culture that encourages staff to learn about new technologies to enhance their skillsets and pursue professional growth. It is evident that social media can be a tool that helps the team to engage consumers and provide them with information while contributing to the growth of CCMH. However, Ms. Lee and her team realize that social media should be used to enhance, not replace, the quality services CCMH strives to provide to its consumers and the surrounding community.

Ethical Considerations

The personal and professional complexities of social media require the amendment of many psychosocial, organizational, and communication theories and laws (McFarland & Ployhart, 2015). Organizations, including academia, need to be proactive in setting acceptable use policies for social media to prevent ethical and legal violations (Kimball & Kim, 2013) and to offer training that prepares social workers for the ethical challenges of using social media (Voshel & Wesala, 2015).

While technology offers obvious benefits to those who provide and those who seek mental or physical care, there are attendant concerns about the ethical implications of a changing practice. Increasingly, attention is focused on guarding the privacy of patients' health information and the risk of HIPAA violation, since social networks, by definition, facilitate communication among many parties simultaneously. The proliferation of virtual information also threatens a new flood of inaccurate or problematic information. The use of video and social media to transcend geographic barriers to delivering care also raises ethical questions. In all care sectors, there is concern that virtual communication can never adequately substitute for face-to-face care. Indeed, an entirely new regulatory structure is needed to support the high-tech transformation of modern healthcare (Hawn, 2009).

Confidentiality is probably the most common ethical dilemma for social workers who consider using social media to advance their clinical services. How do we protect our potential and current patient's identities? How do we protect our privacy? Are we violating HIPPA when we engage or respond to our patients on social media?

Barnett (as cited in Kolmes & Taube, 2014) noted that the use of social media by social workers to access client information is a clinical boundary issue that may violate an implied contract between the social worker and the patient. Zur

(2010) offered the following guidelines for social workers and other mental health professionals:

1. Articulate your general attitude toward Internet searches to your clients prior to searching for client information online
2. Ensure that there is a clinical rationale for the search.
3. Be aware that searching for client information online may yield results that can alter the therapeutic relationship.
4. Add a social media policy to the informed consent forms that clients review and sign prior to the first session.

The dual use of social media in both professional and personal communication results in ever-increasing claims of unprofessional behavior (Landman, Shelton, Kaufmann, & Dattilo, 2010). The risk of these claims can be mitigated by putting systems in place to ensure practitioner competence, client privacy and confidentiality, and informed consent; to avoid conflicts of interest, boundaries, and dual relationships; and to encourage practitioners to seek consultation and supervision (Reamer, 2013).

Despite these challenges, healthcare agencies are charged with a responsibility to understand how to best meet the needs of online information seekers (Atkinson et al., 2009). Cultural competence requires social workers and other practitioners to be cognizant of the role Web 2.0 may have in the lives of their clients (Giffords, 2009).

Social Justice Implications

Social work cannot ignore social media. Social media alert the public to issues of injustice and inequality and ignite discussion around issues of profound concern to citizens. Obviously relevant to the mission of social work, social media literacy is a professional skill worth advocating for during training and subsequent professional learning.

It is worthwhile to consider which populations have the skills and the technology to access the messaging on social media. Age is the variable most frequently correlated with social media use (Chou et al., 2009), and this has implications for the older generation. Social media may accelerate silos among populations, with like-minded groups coalescing and collectively ignoring conflicting fact or opinion. Social media have accelerated the rate at which content is generated and spread, and much of this content may be false, malicious, or harmful. Not all groups may have equal facility with social media. Independent practitioners or small group practices may not have the time or the money to adapt to the use of social media, particularly in the nonprofit sector. As social workers, we must look to our founding ethics and our long history of grassroots and community organization to ensure that we are creating opportunities to engage all people in need and to guarantee the distribution and use of all available tools and tactics.

Questions for Discussion

1. Discuss how social media are used in your agency or practice setting. Tie in the various components outlined in this chapter, including purpose and ethical considerations.
2. How are social media changing the way agency-based social services are accessed by consumers?
3. What are the advantages of using social media to engage with consumers and colleagues? What are some of the challenges?
3. With advances in technology, social media are constantly changing. What are some of the social media tools not included in this chapter that are being used in social work? How are they being used?

Further Readings

Boyd, D. E. (2008). Social network sites: Definition, history, and scholarship. *Journal of Computer-Mediated Communication, 13,* 210–230.

Brown, A. (2010). Social media: A new frontier in reflective practice. *Medical Education, 44,* 744–745.

Halabuza, D. (2014). Guidelines for social workers' use of social networking websites. *Journal of Social Work Values and Ethics, 11*(1), 23–32.

Judd, R. J. (2012). Ethical consequences of using social network sites for students in professional social work programs. *Journal of Social Work Values and Ethics, 9*(1), 5–12.

PART III

Communities

11 }

Blogging

A TOOL FOR SOCIAL JUSTICE

Vu Le, Lea Wolf, and Lap Yan

"The pen is mightier than the sword."
  —Edward Bulwer-Lytton, *1803–1873*

I write a blog called Nonprofit AF. You can laugh at the name, since it is a humorous blog detailing the fun and frustrations of the nonprofit sector. When I started it, it was meant to be something of a joke; now it is read by thousands of people each week, and I feel that, as a fellow social work professional, I have a responsibility to pass on the lessons I have learned to you: about blogging, about effective communication, and about influencing people. In this chapter, I delve into how and why to use the blog as an interactive communication tool and discuss blogging practices, including how to generate content, what the appropriate interval for posting is, how to use humor and pictures of baby animals, and how to use the blog to mobilize people toward action.

I do not claim to be an expert in social media nor am I an expert in blogging, and I cannot tell you much about search engine optimization (SEO), keyword searches, or nonfollow links. What I am telling you is based on my experience as writer of a blog and as a nonprofit professional. You may find experts who will disagree with any and all of my advice. As social work professionals, we must always think critically about what effective practices are. Use what works for you and discard the rest.

This chapter is a collaboration among several people who are interested in blogs for different reasons. As first author, I am a social worker who leads a nonprofit, Rainier Valley Corps, and I blog. For me, blogging has been a way to discuss ideas, build community, and elevate the profile of my organization. Lea Wolf is a social worker who is interested in how peer support works in cyberspace, especially around loss, bereavement, and human resilience. She has seen blogs convene people in a unique way and is eager to discover more about how and why they work. Lap Yan is a graduate student in social work at Fordham who is interested in how blogs collect and disseminate information that can enhance social work practice.

Background

WHAT IS A BLOG?

There is no single description that would sum up the entire funny-moving-sad-informative-distracting-opinionated universe of blogs, but as a simple definition: Blogs represent an infinite array of content published online, unified into a single medium by a shared format (Blood, 2000). Though blogs can be wildly different, the functional layout of every blog is the same: a blog is an interactive webpage to which an author or owner makes regular posts, displayed serially, in a fixed order. Each post includes the date of publication online, a time stamp, a permalink, and often the writer's name (Blanchard, 2004; Miller & Shepherd, 2004). Every new post is displayed above all older content, creating a reverse chronology of content over time (Herring, Scheidt, Kouper, & Wright, 2007). Each update (or post) typically provides space at its end to make comments, to post direct links to other blogs (including the commenters' own blogs), or to link to sites or stories on the Internet. This always-evolving web of links is a social network of interrelated, time-stamped posts, known as the "blogosphere" (Drezner, 2008; Kahn & Kellner, 2004). The comment section is what manufactures collective identity, connecting bloggers into a community and generating a kinship of shared knowledge and concern among the readers of a single blog (Efimova & Grudin, 2007).

A blog is a highly personal medium, permeated by a single author's interests, worldview, and style. Blogs are a new species of media, fusing public and private by launching the author into virtual public space (Miller & Shepherd, 2004). Some credit the spread of blogging in the early 2000s to an appetite for "real" information in a media-saturated, market-shaped, and brand-driven world. Possibly the exponential rise of blogs and blogging is tied to what readers perceive as the immediacy and spontaneity of the form, where the small details of living trigger insights, emotion, and new forms of association. Blogs trade in candor and (perceived) authenticity. In fact, a 2007 Internet survey of nearly 4,000 readers found that almost 75% of participants perceived blogs to be more credible news sources than traditional media outlets such as television and newspapers (Johnson, Kaye, Bichard, & Wong, 2007), operating outside of a sanitized or monetized information market. In its short life, the blog has quickly become synonymous with "the interpretation and dissemination of alternative information" (Kahn & Kellner, 2004, p. 6).

A BRIEF HISTORY OF BLOGS

It is difficult to identify the first blog, since its oldest roots may be in the confessional, the pages of diaries, or letters to the editor. But most attribute the origin of the media-borne concept to Jorn Barger, author of the "Robot Wisdom" webpage, who coined the term "weblog" in 1997 to reflect how he was logging what he discovered when he browsed the Internet (Blood, 2000; Jerz, 2003; Safire, 2002; Turnbull, 2002). By 2003, the condensed term "blog" became Merriam-Webster's word of the year (Wordpress, 2016). Though blogs are a familiar feature of the current mediascape, at their inception, blogs were typically published by their authors without any external editing or branding, and the blogosphere became the kingdom of unmediated content (Farrell & Drezner, 2008). In 1999, the software that later became Blogger emerged from Pyra Labs. Only four years later, WordPress, now the most popular blogging platform, launched, distributing easy-to-use editing tools that could be deployed by bloggers without any coding experience. Fostered by such accessible tools and the tradition of free access, blogging has grown exponentially. In 1999, there were 23 blogs on the Internet (Chapman, n.d.). By the end of 2011, NM Incite, a Nielsen/McKinsey company, tracked over 181 million blogs around the world. As of April 1, 2017, another popular blogging platform, Tumblr, hosted more than 341.8 million blogs. The simple first-person text blog of the 1990s is now a multimedia experience, incorporating images, audio, video, and live streaming, all of which can be uploaded from anywhere using a smartphone or mobile device (Kahn & Kellner, 2004).

WHY BLOG? WHAT MOTIVATES BLOGGING AND PARTICIPATION IN THE BLOGOSPHERE

Like tectonic plates on the move, blogs are a mighty environmental force. Many of the features we now take for granted in virtual space can be mapped back to the earliest incarnation of the blogosphere. For instance, our expectation that online interaction will be both immediate and personal may well be rooted in the first-person narrative of many blogs. Our assumption that online content will be interactive may have its origin in the comments section of blog posts, and the actual networked architecture of the entire Internet is generated, in part, by the practice of hyperlinking to other blogs and websites (Schmidt, 2007). Early participants in the blogosphere understood the Internet as a space for the expression of personal identity and opinion; they interpreted the immediacy of the medium as an invitation to interact, and they generated dialogue by creating links around the web (Blanchard, 2004; Miller & Shepherd, 2004;), replicating the zigzag, interconnected, wide-ranging energy of human curiosity and conversation.

We are just beginning to understand how and why blogs work. Across platforms, subjects, and styles, bloggers are motivated by the need to gather and disseminate information across an infinite array of content. Nardi and colleagues (2004) discovered five major motivations for blogging: documenting one's life, providing commentary and opinions, expressing deeply felt emotions, articulating ideas through writing, and forming and maintaining community forums. A 2008 study of 212 bloggers and their readers showed that ease of use, enjoyment, knowledge sharing, and social factors all motivated individuals to participate in the blogosphere (Hsu & Lin). Whatever a blogger's motivation, the form can flex to reflect it: blogs can function as personal diaries, provide political commentary, or disseminate technical instruction for giving a toast or constructing a bomb. Blogs can be a mechanism for authors to share intimate details or a platform for connecting like-minded individuals who want to gather information, sustain dialogue, and amass the momentum of community.

It may be this combination of immediacy, open access, perceived authenticity, and endless variety that explains why blogs have become powerful sociopolitical tools for traditionally disenfranchised populations. People in marginalized communities use blogs to assert identity and tell stories about themselves, replacing stereotypical or oppressive accounts dictated by others. For example, deaf bloggers write about the value of American Sign Language, call for the equal treatment of deaf and nondeaf people, and express their solidarity as a community (Hamill & Stein, 2011). Black British women "use blogs as a medium for discursive activism to challenge stereotypical raced and gendered representation in the mainstream media" (Gabriel, 2016, p. 1622). For individuals who routinely experience misrepresentation, blogs are a powerful means to craft an alternate narrative and to counter inaccuracies without the mediation of social gatekeepers or majority tastemakers.

BLOGS AND THE REAL WORLD: INFLUENCE AND ACTIVISM

Once, blogs were diaries made virtual and public. For example, the famous Justin Hall (called the founding father of personal bloggers) started a blog in 1994 at the age of 19 to share a complete catalog of his own consciousness— everything from nude photos and diary entries to his thoughts on the future of the Internet. But a quarter century later, blogs are grappling hooks deployed to make sense of contemporary issues and challenging real-world events (Kahn & Kellner, 2004; Sillesen, 2014). As early as 2002, bloggers detonated the story of then-US Senate Majority Leader Trent Lott, who had publicly praised US Senator Strom Thurmond, once a proponent of racial segregation. The mainstream media ignored the story until after the news was broken by bloggers, and the outcry that erupted forced Lott to make a public apology—in one of the first examples of how a conversation initiated by bloggers in virtual space could cross into the real world. Other public incidents, including the CBS network's apology for reporting a disputed story about President Bush's service in the National Guard and the resignation of *New York Times* executive editor Howell Raines over the reporter Jayson Blair's unrepentant plagiarism, confirmed the power of the blogosphere to influence public feeling and to enforce demands for action while elevating blogging into an acknowledged form of professional political engagement. In 2005 Garrett M. Graff was granted White House press credentials, the first blogger ever to be so recognized (Alonzo, 2005). We now expect that the inconvenient truths, questions, and revelations posted in blogs will affect (even blow up or shut down) political discussions, reveal scandal, and alter policy.

No one entirely understands how such a personal medium, spoken from such an individual perspective and doled out in such short entries, ignites real-world action and consequences. Academics can (and do) debate and dispute whether the online community generated by a blog meets the definition of a "real-life" community (Bausch, Haughey, & Hourihan, 2002). But the proof is in the participation: established, highly referenced blogs with many users offer tangible experiences of collective identity (Blanchard, 2004; Lai & Turban, 2008). Nonprofit With Balls is one proof. The case and discussion below make the point: well-written, provocative blogs with distinctive purposes and signatures can and do convene, inspire, and unite people. Blog readers who jump in, becoming regular commenters, see themselves as members of a community and get hooked, maintaining and increasing their participation in the virtual collective (Blanchard, 2004). There is even some evidence that participation in virtual communities transfers to the real world, increasing involvement with face-to-face communities and motivating higher levels of democratic participation and community activism (Bakardjieva & Feenberg, 2002; Blanchard & Horan, 1998; Wellman, Haase, Witte, & Hampton, 2001). Yes, it is hard to know if socially engaged people seek out blogs or if it is the blogs that inspire civic engagement, but blog readers tend to participate in politics more than nonreaders (Gil de Zúñiga et al., 2009).

CASE STUDY

Nonprofitwithballs.com started as a blog on the Social Venture Partners (SVP) Seattle's website. My organization, the Vietnamese Friendship Association, received funding from SVP as well as support around a variety of organizational development projects. Although SVP had regularly written blog posts, they wanted me to write from the perspective of an investee. I agreed because they are a funder. We called my column "Staff, Retreat!"

In the beginning, the blog was published twice a month and was read by a dozen people or so. As readership grew, I spun it off and started writing weekly, covering a variety of topics relevant to the nonprofit sector. It has often led to positive results that I never anticipated. The blog post excerpted below, for example, appeared on my site, Nonprofit With Balls, on January 20, 2015 (for the complete post, see http://nonprofitwithballs.com/2015/01/are-you-or-your-org-guilty-of-trickle-down-community-engagement). It has been read more than 75,000 times and shared more than 14,000 times on social media. It has led to hundreds of discussion threads on Facebook. Nonprofit colleagues across the country wrote reflections on it and organized discussion groups around it. Some even led in-person trainings or workshops on this topic. A few funders told me they use it in their training and staff orientations. Several colleagues wrote to express their appreciation for finally having a common term, "trickle-down community engagement" (TDCE), to describe and address this phenomenon.

FIGURE 11.1 Blog post on Nonprofit AF site January 20, 2015.

"Are you or your org guilty of Trickle-Down Community Engagement?"

In Seattle, if you're a person of color and you walk down a dark alley late at night and you feel like you're being followed, it's probably someone trying to do some community engagement: "Psst . . . hey buddy—Go Hawks!—you want to attend a summit? It's about economic inequity. We need your voice." "Daddy, I'm scared!" "Stay calm, Timmy; don't look him in the eye." "Come on, help a guy out! Here, you each get some compostable sticky dots to vote on our top three priorities! You can vote on different priorities, or, if you like, you put more than one dot on—" "Run, Timmy!"

This is why you should never take your kid down a dark alley in Seattle.

A while ago I was talking to a friend (another Executive Director, since all my regular friends have abandoned me because I make jokes about compostable sticky dots), and he said, "Have you noticed that everyone is getting paid to engage us communities of color except us communities of color?"

Sigh. Yes, I have noticed. I've been thinking a lot about this, and have come up with a term to describe it: **Trickle-Down Community Engagement (TDCE).** *This is when we bypass the people who are most affected by issues, engage and* *fund larger organizations to tackle these issues, and hope that miraculously the people most affected will help out in the effort, usually for free.*

There are several reasons why TDCE happens. First, the nonprofit sector has all sorts of unwritten rules designed to be successfully navigated only by mainstream organizations (See "The game of nonprofit, and how it leaves some communities behind.") Second, 90% of funding in the nonprofit world is relationship-based, which screws over marginalized communities, who have much fewer relationships with funders and decision-makers. Third, due to existing definitions, many organizations led by marginalized groups "don't have the capacity." They're "small and disorganized," they are "not ready to be leaders in these efforts." Fourth, community engagement has been seen as the icing on the cake, and not an essential ingredient, so it is always last to be considered. Fifth, many funders and decision-makers focus on sexy short-term gains, not effective long-term investments.

Look, I'm not saying anyone is intentionally trying to discriminate against certain communities. Everyone is well-intentioned. Diversity, equity, inclusion, and cultural competency have risen to the front of people's minds. Organizations are scrambling to talk about these issues, to diversify their board, to get community input. That is great and all, but it has only been leading to marginalized communities being irritated and frustrated. Every single week, we leaders of color get asked to provide input, to join an advisory committee, attend a summit, to fill out a survey. Because of this well-intentioned mandate to engage with communities, we get bombarded with requests to do stuff for free.

Trickle-Down Community Engagement is pretty dangerous, for several reasons. When people who are most affected by issues are not funded and trusted to lead the efforts to address them:

It perpetuates the Capacity Paradox. The Capacity Paradox is when an organization cannot get significant funding because it has limited capacity, so it cannot develop its capacity, which leads it to not being able to get significant funding, which means it can't develop its capacity. This greatly affects organizations led by communities of color and other marginalized communities. And then they can't be as involved, which leads to ineffective efforts to tackle issues. (See "Capacity building for communities of color: The paradigm must shift.")

It's annoying as hell. In every single issue, I keep seeing larger, well-connected organizations getting significant funding but are not effective at engagement. So they pester us smaller ethnic orgs to help. I was asked by a collective impact backbone org to be involved with planning a summit to engage communities of color. I advised them not to do it, and told them that I've been to far too many summits that suck (See: "Community Engagement 101: Why most summits suck.") Next thing I knew, they organized the summit anyway, asked my organization to help with outreach, and asked me personally to translate their outreach material into Vietnamese! All for free, of course! ("Run, Timmy!!")

It's intrinsically wrong. We, above any other field, must act on the belief that people most affected by inequities must be leaders in the movement. It is the right thing to do. Imagine a group of men leading an effort and making important decisions on women's issues like reproductive health, and then asking women to come give feedback at a meeting. Or a bunch of idiots who don't know anything about science leading a committee on climate change and asking scientists to come testify about global warming. These scenarios are ridiculous, which is why they happen in Congress.

Importantly, it doesn't work and is even counterproductive. If TDCE actually works, then we'd have little to argue about. But it does not. When the people who are most affected are not well represented at the table, well-intentioned but useless and sometimes even harmful stuff gets voted on and implemented. For example, at a meeting I was invited to someone said, "We need to put 100% of funding into early learning instead of splitting it among early learning and youth development" and I had to remind them that "Many immigrant and refugee kids get here when they're older than 5, so they'd be screwed if you only invest in early learning. We need to support the entire continuum of kids' development." (See "Youth Development, why it is just as important as early learning.") Unfortunately, by the time a mainstream organization finally gets to that community feedback forum or summit to get feedback on their well-intentioned but crappy plan or policy, it is too late.

WHY A BLOG?

In many ways, there is still a lack of respect for blogs. However, what I have seen is that people gravitate toward good content, no matter what medium it is delivered in. This has allowed some blogs to be taken as seriously as traditional media. Blog posts that resonate with people and those that are backed up with research and sources will be shared and cited, often to the same degree as newspaper opinion pieces or feature articles. A blog even has some advantages over traditional more "serious" media:

- *It is more personal, and thus more engaging.* Because a blog can be a type of online journal, people not only accept but also expect that blogs will be more personal. An individual voice is often what draws people to your work. The blog is by its nature first person, allowing the reader to connect not just with the topic but also with you as a human being. This can be extremely helpful, especially if you plan to use your writing to persuade people to take action or assume certain mindsets because these people are persuaded not only by what you say but also by who you are.
- *It is an instant communication tool.* It takes far too long for traditional media such as newspapers, magazines, television, and radio to affect the course of human events. With a blog, you can write something and publish it in literally minutes. When an unjust law is being voted on, for example, and we need to mobilize people to oppose it, immediacy matters. If I had submitted the content of the blog post

above to a magazine, I would still be waiting to have it reviewed, designed, and published. With the blog I could publish this post within a few days, and I was able to control the message and deliver it the way I wanted to. Since that day, it has been read more than 75,000 times.

- **It is more substantive than social media**. Facebook and Twitter are great as tools to spread the word, but not to deliver content. Blog posts are better vehicles to deliver thoughtful content. You can write longer, more detailed posts. Use Facebook and Twitter to help you promote the content you compose and post to your blog.
- **It is much more flexible than other media**. There are fewer restrictions and conventions for blog posts. Whereas most newspaper columns have the same word limit, my blog posts can range anywhere from 800 to 3,000 words. The content and tone also vary. One day I am talking about the importance of disclosing salary ranges in job listings, and the next week I will expound on the rules of dating in the nonprofit sector.
- **It is a tool for learning and reflection**. Whereas other media usually present information or persuade, you can use blog as a tool for learning. In the nonprofit settings where social workers toil away, opportunities to reflect can be severely restricted. But constant reflection is one of the most important tools of an effective leader. Use your blog to mull over the lessons you have learned, the successes you have had, and especially the failures. Not only will you absorb these lessons better, but you will help others who learn by reading your writing. (Share your scars and shin splints!)

LIVING THE LIFE OF A BLOGGER: HOW-TO'S, PLUSES, AND MINUSES

Here are a few things I learned after blogging for 5 years (take what's useful and jettison the rest):

- **Be consistent**. Post regularly, preferably once a week, on the same day. If you cannot do that, post once every 2 weeks, or monthly. Predictability builds anticipation.
- **Focus on quantity over quality**. Quantity trumps quality, no matter what your high school English teacher said. Posting frequently matters more than building an irregular archive of "quality" posts. Don't wait for inspiration to strike.
- **Stick to a routine.** Writing is a daunting task, sometimes torturous. You need a routine, including a regular time and place where you write and the will to stick to that routine, whether you feel like it or not. Once you begin typing, you will likely find that it gets much easier.

- **Determine your blog's goals and scope**. What do you want to accomplish with your blog? Is it to inform your audience of trends in the sector? Is it to capture hilarious adventures you are having as a social worker? Is it to mobilize people to take action around specific issues? Do you plan to target one particular topic or be more general? Nonprofit With Balls is a general blog focused on anything relevant to the nonprofit sector that I find interesting, and the goals are to expose people to new ideas, to provide them with the language and concepts they need to talk about complex subjects such as equity, to increase the sector's ownership of its influence and awesomeness, and to be a cheerleader and morale booster for the hardworking professionals in the sector. However, there are successful blogs that have narrower foci. Determine your goals and scope, but as your blog develops, these things may naturally evolve and change.
- **Decide who your audience is**. Early in my blog's history, my audience was mainly funders and potential donors. As I developed the blog, it became clear that a wider audience was reading. I decided to spin the blog off, focusing on everyone in the nonprofit sector, but mainly nonprofit and foundation staff. Before you start your blog, figure out your audience, but be prepared for it to evolve.
- **Have a consistent tone**. Nonprofit with Balls uses humor to talk about the nonprofit sector because one of the goals is to cheer up nonprofit professionals whose work is often very heavy. I also find that humor is an effective tool to use when delivering critical messages because it encourages people to be open to criticism and to seeing differing viewpoints. If you are not naturally hilarious, then maybe this is not the tone for you. The important point is to find a tone that fits with you and to use it consistently.
- **Find joy in the writing**. If you enjoy writing and believe in what you write, readers can sense that, and your writing becomes more enjoyable for them. You are not expected to be an amazing writer whose prose will sweep readers off their feet. Do not always take yourself so seriously. I insert pictures of baby animals in many of my blog posts and make a ton of references to popular TV shows—*Game of Thrones, Walking Dead,* or *The Golden Girls*. Try to have fun with your blog, even if you decide on a more serious tone.
- **Include images**. Images are helpful to break up the wall of text and help to draw readers in. One or two images per post will do. Use Creative Commons licensed images to avoid copyright issues. I am a fan of Pixabay.com.
- **Focus on substance over style**. If your content is not useful or substantive, it does not matter how awesome your blog looks. Focus first on writing consistent, high-quality posts. Ignore all the advice on search engine optimization, keywords, and ads until you have strong content.

- **Be thoughtful about accessibility**. No matter who your audience is, chances are you have readers with disabilities. Tiny fonts or noncontrasting backgrounds/text are difficult for many people to read. Using big words, obscure acronyms, or overly complex syntax just makes your writing off-putting to some and inaccessible to many. Add image descriptions to your images for readers who are blind or who have other visual impairments. For tips, go to http://livingwithdisability.tumblr.com/post/124066767358/all-about-image-descriptions

- **Be persistent**. Honestly, it takes a long time for your blog to establish a readership. Do not anticipate that people will find your writing so compelling that thousands will sign up after a handful of posts. Even if one of your posts goes viral, there is no guarantee that you will instantly develop a following. Be committed to writing 52 posts before you get more than a dozen readers. Most blogs fail because writers do not persist.

- **Forget about making money with your blog.** In a 2012 survey of 1,000 US bloggers, blogging.org found that 81% never made more than $100 from their blog (https://blogging.org/blog/blogging-stats-2012-infographic/). It took 4 years before I saw a dime in advertisements. My blog actually costs me money to run. Your more likely source of revenue will come *after* you have established yourself as a voice that people want to hear in person, and you can charge speaking fees for speeches. Even those opportunities are rare.

- **Interact**. How you communicate with readers and the examples you set will determine what kind of community your blog will create. Set good examples for your readers by being patient and understanding, especially in responding to constructive feedback. If you set a tone that disagreements are OK as long as no one attacks anyone's character, then you will create a community that does the same. Respond to comments and e-mails, and when you can, offer your readers useful counsel or connection. Word will spread about how supportive and awesome you are, and that will drive up your readership.

PLUSES AND MINUSES

As the readership of my blog grew, I inadvertently joined the ranks of people who are seen as having insights into the sector. So now I am invited out a lot—to give a speech, to facilitate trainings, to sit on panels, and to write articles and books. This has enhanced my own professional profile and served as a source of exposure and earned income for my organization, Rainier Valley Corps, a social justice organization focused on developing nonprofit leaders of color, strengthening organizations led by communities of color, and getting diverse communities to work together. The blog has been extremely helpful in informing funders—both local and national—about the work we do. On more than one occasion, the blog has directly resulted in funding from foundations and individual donors.

The positive outcomes of having a successful blog far outweigh any negative outcomes. But there are a few challenges:

- **It is time consuming**. To have a successful blog, you must blog consistently. I spend probably 8 to 15 hours a week on this blog, writing and responding to readers' comments, which is like a part-time job.
- **Demands on your time multiply.** As NWB grew in readership, I got a lot of e-mails from readers asking for advice about various challenges or for my opinions on various topics. I enjoy these interactions and always learn something new, but it can get overwhelming. And then there is the guilt of not being able to respond to everyone in a timely manner. I finally had to put up an automated-response telling people that it may take me months to respond to them. I also get more and more requests to do things, such as provide consulting, or give a speech, or be on a panel, usually for free. But I run a nonprofit full-time and I also have a family. I have been learning to say no more often.
- **Attacks happen.** I have gotten attacked a few times in the comment section, sometimes by trolls, but sometimes by people who have had bad experiences with nonprofits and see the opportunity to slam a punching bag. As your profile rises, be aware that not everyone will be your friend. Learn to not let it bother you. And in fact, getting angry responses may be considered a sign that you are reaching beyond the choir.

Q: HOW CAN A BLOG CHANGE THE WORLD? A: BY CREATING AND STRENGTHENING COMMUNITY

Research on blogs tells us that when people read a blog regularly, and especially when they make comments, they are building community. That has the potential to cross over from the virtual world into the real one. As NWB grew, colleagues gravitated toward it, interacted with the blog and with each other, and urged me to form a Facebook page where people could comment without the hassle of a log-in and password. This page now has about 34,000 fans. But because it was a company page, or a fan page, only I could post. Readers started e-mailing me to ask me for advice or to get my 34,000 colleagues to provide advice on the challenges of working in the nonprofit sector. I quickly realized I needed to create a group where any member could post—it is through the *interaction* that community is created.

So Nonprofit Happy Hour, the Facebook group, was born. It was announced on the blog, and within one day gained nearly 1,000 members; it has now shot up to more than 23,000 members. See Figure 11.2 for a screen shot from the Facebook

FIGURE 11.2 Nonprofit AF Facebook group.

Group where my community gathers. People share success stories, ask for and give advice on ineffective boards and irritating bosses and coworkers, provide recommended resources, and share jokes. Another group formed, one only for nonprofit executive directors or chief executive officers, current or past. This one, now at about 3,200 members, developed into an even tighter community. How do I know? I get regular feedback about how the sense of community generated has helped many people in the sector during difficult times.

By Documenting Effective Practice and Manufacturing Knowledge

I use the blog to capture the lessons we have learned at my organization, Rainier Valley Corps. Since I began to collect my thoughts and to reflect on the nonprofit sector in regular posts, I have grown professionally and the blog has definitely elevated Rainier Valley Corps' profile (two good things), but I believe that the blog, and the interaction it inspires, is really a living body of knowledge and an invitation to everyone to reflect on the work we do and to practice better.

Blogs and the communities they create can be extremely helpful in elevating and disseminating important ideas. As it builds community, the blog is also a way to gather and synthesize readers' thoughts. Some of the posts I write are crowdsourced, beginning with a question out to the Facebook community. On many occasions, I will write a blog post, get comments on it, and then incorporate the comment back into the original post. Constant feedback and engagement are the strengths of a blog.

By Influencing People's Behavior

One of the most rewarding outcomes of writing a blog is the feedback I get from nonprofit professionals as well as foundation staff. I get e-mails and Facebook messages from colleagues across the world telling me that, because of something I wrote, they did something differently. In the post about TDCE, I used my voice to call out a harmful practice, and I spoke out about how that kind of inequitable system leaves behind organizations led by communities of color, rural communities, LGBTQ communities, and communities of people with disabilities. To this day, people still cite this blog, and funders have told me they are being more thoughtful about their funding practices in order to avoid TDCE.

Ethical Considerations

While plenty of people accuse blogs of being self-indulgent and playing fast and loose with the facts, I would argue that blogging actually offers a novel strategy to realize the ethics and values that underlie social work. Here are the ground rules:

- **Insist on competence**. Competence, or knowing what you know and do not know, is a primary ethical principle. Social workers pledge to "develop and enhance their professional expertise" and "to contribute to the knowledge base of the profession," (National Association of Social Work [NASW], 2008). The immediacy, reach, and engaging quality of a blog may act to circulate information more quickly and widely than any local, proprietary, or specialized reporting. Blogs have the potential to focus attention on an issue or outcome across fields of practice, geography, and national borders, helping an array of social workers to "keep current with emerging knowledge relevant to social work" (NASW, 2008, 5.02C). Beyond that, our *Code of Ethics* urges us to turn our practical experience into understanding using research and documentation; a blog can be a novel strategy to report and reflect on practice and to share expertise in order to build and inform our larger social work community.
- **Don't shy away from advocacy**. Social workers are ethically compelled to "social and political action," which promotes "development of people, their communities, and their environments" (NASW, 2008). Blogs give us an immediate and accessible means to act on this principle *by* fusing the private and the public, the individual, and the collective—to build community by attracting readers and commenters who share an interest

or values, assembling a collective force for advocacy. Though the ideal of universal access to technological tools remains unfulfilled, social media—such as blogs—can offer social workers tools to work toward the ethical imperative to "promote conditions that encourage respect for cultural and social diversity within the United States and globally" (NASW, 2008).

- **Think and write ethically.** As social workers increasingly look to virtual space to engage in dialogue, we need a conversation about ethics: How do we locate the borders between self-expression, advocacy, and doing harm?
- **Beware revelation.** The Internet instantaneously translates any writing, commenting, linking, or posting into public record that lasts forever. It links person and action, with consequences that may affect job prospects, legal process (all online communication, text messages, and e-mail can be subpoenaed in legal proceedings), and social reputation. Social workers must take precautions when sharing personal information or opinion to avoid revealing sensitive or confidential information about self or others. This is doubly true for clients; no social worker should make them identifiable or vulnerable as part of blogging and they must ensure clients' literacy so that they can participate without harming themselves or others.
- **Practice respect for all peoples and communities.** Without the norms that regulate in-person communication, virtual dialogue easily becomes dramatic, extreme, or polarizing. Social workers need to reflect on and maintain a virtual presence that is congruent with their professional identity. Similarly, as social workers begin to assess clients' use of technology, they need to help clients think through the implications of speech online and to align their virtual activity with their identity in real life.
- **Become critical.** Blogs are a vital source of information, persuasive argument, and entertainment. Though many blogs are well respected, they are not subject to the standards of journal publication or traditional news journalism. As social workers use more and more technology to gain knowledge and to engage professionally they must cultivate the habits of critical thinking that enable them to assess and reflect on the information they encounter before using or sharing it.

Social Justice Implications

All of us are drawn to blogs for their power to communicate and to convene. Blogs, when used well, can play a critical role in mobilizing people to take action, to have conversations about race, to check in with one another after devastating national or global events, and to reexamine inequality in hiring and other practices.

Some blog posts can go further, urging specific actions. For instance, when Americorps funding was jeopardized by the new administration, NWB wrote a post—filled with pictures of kittens—asking readers to take a few minutes to call their legislators to preserve funding for AmeriCorps programs. Several readers reported they did just that. Others shared the post, and some indicated they were not even aware that AmeriCorps funding was in jeopardy. To call readers to action effectively, you must do these things:

- **Preview the landscape**. Do some serious research on the issue you are trying to address. If your blog post reinvents efforts that others have already been tackling or you miss important conversations that others have been having, you will be ignored, or worse, considered a barrier to the efforts you are trying to help.
- **Present the need**. Present the information you found, and make a case as to why this is important. Throw in the statistics that you found, along with links to the organizations that are working on this issue. Feel free to personalize the post with your own experiences and why this issue matters to you personally.
- **Propose the action**. People need tangible, feasible, time-bound actions that they can take immediately. Spell out the specific things that you want them to do. Otherwise, a few fired up readers will take initiative, but the majority will likely not do anything.
- **Provide the tools**. If you say "call your legislators," indicate which one(s) and at what phone number. Provide a list or a website where people can look up their legislators' names and contact information. Write out a sample script that people can use when they call. If you ask people to tweet about things, list out the hashtags they should use. But be strategic. A few resources are great, but do not provide a long list of links because that might overwhelm your readers and lead to inaction.
- **Prepare for counterarguments**. Do not assume that all your readers will agree with you. Some people will have opposing views on the issue, while others will agree with you but disagree with the actions you are proposing. Stay calm and try to find alignment where you can, and adjust your course based on feedback when it makes sense. Do not get into prolonged battles with people who are not engaging constructively because that will take attention away from your efforts.

Questions for Discussion

1. Will you blog? Why or why not?
2. What issues need your voice?
3. What can you learn from blogs that moves you to action?

Further Readings

Almog-Bar, M., & Schmid, H. (2013). Advocacy activities of nonprofit human service organizations: A critical review. *Nonprofit and Voluntary Sector Quarterly, 43*, 1–25.

Efimova, L., & Hendrick, S. F. (2004). In search for a virtual settlement: an exploration of weblog community boundaries. In *Association of Internet Researchers Conference*.

Efimova, L., & Hendrick, S. (2005). In search for a virtual settlement: An exploration of weblog community boundaries. In *Communities and Technologies* (Vol. 5).

Hartelius, E. (2005). A content based taxonomy of blogs and formation of a virtual community. *Kaleidoscope: A Graduate Journal of Qualitative Communication Research, 4*, 71–91.

Jackson, A., Yates, J., & Orlikowski, W. (2007, January). Corporate blogging: Community building through persistent digital talk. In *40th Annual Hawaii International Conference on System Sciences, 2007. HICSS 2007* (pp. 80–90). IEEE. Honolulu: IEEE.

Maratea, R. (2008, February). The e-rise and fall of social problems. *Social Problems, 55*(1), 139–160.

Nielsen. (2012). Buzz in the blogosphere: Millions more bloggers and blog readers. http://www.nielsen.com/us/en/insights/news/2012/buzz-in-the-blogosphere-millions-more-bloggers-and-blog-readers.html

Vaezi, R., Torkzadeh, G., & Chang, J. C.-J. (2011). Understanding the influence of blog on the development of social capital. *Database for Advances in Information System, 42*(3), 34–45.

12 }

The Safety Net Gets Much Closer

M-GOVERNMENT AND MOBILE BENEFITS

Abraham Lincoln Lee, Lauren Aaronson, and Lap Yan

"We must not innovate for citizens, we must innovate with citizens. . . . We have to create canvases for citizens to collaborate to tackle challenges and advance their communities."

—Anonymous

Despite recurrent cycles of debate and divided political opinion in the United States about the morality of expenditure on safety net programs, government spending clearly indicates our nation's investment in providing social support for the neediest populations. The US social safety net is a constellation of protections that subsidizes goods and provides services to insulate individuals from the sequelae of extreme poverty (Rebecca, 1998). The programs that provide these resources serve millions of Americans each year. A 2014 Center on Budget and Policy Priorities (CBPP) analysis, based on the Census' Supplemental Poverty Measure, shows that government safety net programs kept some 38 million people out of poverty in that calendar year (CBPP, 2015).

This chapter investigates how technology could result in far more effective execution of this government priority. The intervention described herein offers one example of a how an already familiar technology can be used to improve a single process for both clients and the government agency that serves them, offering increased efficiency, better outcomes, and a more satisfying experience of citizenship.

Background

Safety net or social insurance is defined by the International Monetary Fund's Organisation for Economic Co-operation and Development (OECD) as either public or private money used to redistribute resources from one group to another to support a disadvantaged population (OECD, 2016). Such programs vary widely in what support they provide and how they provide it. The OECD reported that nearly 20% of the United States' gross domestic product is spent on public expenditures for benefits programs (https://www.oecd.org/social/expenditure.htm). In the United States, several examples of this spending include the Supplemental Nutrition Assistance Program (SNAP), which provides food assistance; and Temporary Aid to Needy Families (TANF), which provides cash assistance. Within the federal budget, Social Security accounts for 24% of total spending, healthcare for 25%, and safety net programs (such as SNAP and TANF) for another 10%. Thus, according to the CBPP (2016), nearly two-thirds of the federal budget is focused on social spending (http://www.cbpp.org/research/federal-budget/policy-basics-where-do-our-federal-tax-dollars-go).

Though government-funded social supports represent a significant fiscal commitment, these programs also provide an important touch point between the citizenry and public agencies. For many individuals, obtaining these benefits represents their primary contact with government. Unfortunately, the initial contact between individuals and these public agencies—to apply for SNAP or TANF benefits—is often, if unintentionally, demoralizing (Keigher & Stevens, 2011). The city, state, and federal forms that must be submitted in order to be registered to receive benefits can be voluminous, complex, and difficult to understand. An application for benefits typically requires that the client locate and provide reams of supporting documentation, including adoption records, alien registration card, bank statements, birth certificates, benefits check stub, marriage license, baptismal certificate, and income tax records. The process of applying for support can be unnecessarily burdensome, intimidating, and time consuming for applicants. In a perfect storm of inefficiency, the applications, once completed, also demand a massive commitment of staff hours by those agencies charged with verifying eligibility. These mechanical burdens are magnified within those agencies that still deploy antiquated tools to complete the processing of applications and verification of documentation.

E-Government (eGov) Movement

Accelerating use of information and communication technologies (ICTs) by populations across the globe has transformed many types of exchange, including citizens' approach to and interaction with their governments ((http://cimic.rutgers.edu/~soon/papers/2010/ip2010.pdf). The digitalization of the interface between the citizenry and the agencies of government, referred to as e-governance or eGov, is directed at maximizing the interface between the public entities of the state and the private sector (including individuals, institutions, and business interests).

In the United States, the first eGov policy initiatives emerged in the early 1990s, spurred by an effort to improve access to government services and information. The first directive issued by the Clinton-era interagency task force on government reform known as the National Performance Review pointed to the potential of the Internet to facilitate exchange between individuals and government, targeting the improvement of service delivery via technology (NRC, 2007). A decade later, the E-Government Act of 2002, enacted on December 17, 2002, mandated "a framework of measures that require using Internet-based information technology to improve citizen access to government information and services, and for other purposes."

While the launch of e-government three decades ago aimed to provide more efficient service delivery and government administration, subsequent—and global—iterations of the e-government paradigm have emphasized its potential to enable and expand democratic processes and to enhance relationships among the state, its citizens, and the private sector (Dawes, 2008). Improved access to services, increased government transparency, and the publication of government data are seen as key drivers of reform, participation, and innovation. The United Nations officially recognizes "the role of information and communications technology in promoting sustainable development and supporting public policies and service delivery" (United Nations, 2016, p. 5) and has identified e-governance as a key driver of change in the worldwide 2030 Agenda for Sustainable Development.

While the ideal (and theoretical) end-state of e-government is a fully participatory democracy, the practical realities emerge in stages. Like many technologies, e-governance evolves from an initial stage characterized by one-way flow of information (originating with government and directed toward the public) into dynamic two-way interaction. Broadly, e-government 1.0 typically describes the digitization of existing information held by the government, presented to the public via static websites maintained by public agencies. From this initial stage, e-government develops to offer basic interactions in virtual space, through e-mail contact and forms, making it easier to perform the obligatory tasks of a citizen online (renewing a license, downloading an immigration form, or applying for a permit). Harnessing the interactive elements of Web 2.0 to increase citizen participation, e-government 2.0 represents a paradigm shift to the productive exchange of information. It engages the public in new ways: mobilizing dialogue via social media; increasing transparency by uploading real-time information and mapping; and providing open data, which can be used for research, for crowdsourcing solutions to common problems, or for creating innovative apps or widgets (O'Reilly, 2009). Ideally, this two-way interactive model will evolve to dynamic collective governance, where the administration of civic functions is collaborative, supported by a seamless flow of information that informs decision-making and problem solving (Chun, Shulman, Sandoval, & Hovy, 2010).

In the United States, the e-government paradigm increasingly characterizes current practice and strategy at all levels, from the federal government to state and municipal governments (National Research Council [NRC], 2007). Considerable resources have been developed to roll out across government agencies, although the development of some local e-government efforts has been slow or fragmented, and efficiencies may have plateaued following initial momentum (Baumgarten & Chui, 2009).

While the efforts of some public agencies and departments to transition to e-government may have stalled at the one-way flow of information, citizen use of e-government resources continues to grow. A 2005 survey of people in the United States found that more than 55% had made at least some use of these resources; that number had increased to 76% by 2014, with the largest group of users falling between ages 18 and 29 (United Nations, 2014). Currently the volume of interaction is enormous: in the first 90 days of 2017, US government websites (web traffic from around 400 executive branch government domains across approximately 4,500 websites) saw a total of 2.53 billion visits (analytics.usa.gov).

A variety of information and activities—some as pedestrian as viewing a weather prediction derived from government satellites on a smartphone or paying a parking ticket via a city website—make life simpler, yet many of the most-used and best-rated e-governance interfaces allow citizens to perform crucial tasks or to access vital information. In 2013, the International Revenue Service (IRS) reported that the electronic filing rate for individual income tax returns was approximately 83% (IRS Oversight Board, 2013), and in the first quarter of 2016, the government websites with the highest customer satisfaction ratings included the Medicare Prescription Plan Costs and the Social Security Administration Retirement Estimator (Lewan, 2016). In addition, the advent of e-governance has seen the release of stores of government data to the public. This open source view into the metrics that describe the American experience— from obesity rates to maps of environmental toxins to crime data—has given rise to innovative applications that connect overdose victims to the nearest person carrying naloxone, allow diners to check the health code violation history of local restaurants (https://www.whatthehealthapp.com), or provide a breakdown of the history and implications of pending legislation in cities across the country (Prizewire, n.d.).

THE MOVE TO MOBILE: MGOV

Since the early 1990s, the US government has promoted the use of the Internet to dispense information and to provide access to data and services to the public (Moon, 2002). Yet access to the Internet via broadband has been overtaken by use of cellular phones, in part because significant barriers have slowed the reach of Internet access (Rainie, 2013). Internet access from a home or public computer depends on significant infrastructure, which cannot be provided without substantial capital investment. In the United States, such infrastructure is supplied by private companies, which are willing to invest only in areas and neighborhoods that will obviously yield profit (Holmes, Fox, Wieder, & Zubak-Skees, 2016). As a result, many low-income areas lack Internet access whereas access via mobile is immediately available to all—independent of geography.

While participation in the digital realm trends upward, how people participate—specifically the devices they use to access the Internet—is changing. Today, 92% of adult Americans own cell phones, with 72% of those being smartphones (up from 35% in 2011; Pew 2016). Modern-day cell phones are relatively inexpensive, can work all day, and will fit inside a pocket. Cell phone hardware, infrastructure, and applications have become ubiquitous worldwide. A 2015 national survey noted the increasing number (then reported to be 13%) of smartphone-only adults—those who access the Internet only via a smartphone and do not have private Internet service at home—further stating that rates of smartphone adoption were equal to those of home broadband for the first time (Pew, 2015). Nationally, many disadvantaged populations—including those with a household income under $20,000/year and those adults with a high school degree or less rely entirely on a smartphone to access the Internet from home. As mobile becomes the conduit of choice for digital access, e-government is evolving to meet these realities. Mobile government, the natural, evolutionary extension of e-government, is defined as a set of strategies, services, and applications for improving benefits to the parties involved in e-government—including citizens, businesses, and all government units—all rendered accessible via mobile phone (Kushchu & Kuscu, 2003).

Only 57% of the people living below the poverty line have any home Internet access, and even fewer—only 48%—have high-speed access. Comparatively, 78% of people above the poverty line have home access, and nearly all of them have high-speed access. Many people with low incomes increasingly use mobile devices to access the Internet (33%, compared to 19% for people above the poverty line).

The explosion of mobile devices and the parallel expansion and "app-ification" and reliance on these new tools have created new opportunities for federal, state, and local governments. Schadler, Bernoff, and Ask (2014) argue that there is a mind shift in the mobile environment, in which a person expects, "I can get what I want in my immediate context and moments of need." This instantaneous feedback loop between vendors and consumers and senders of information and receivers has changed the paradigm of responsive communication and is creating conditions where new types of service delivery and workflow paradigms are the norm. Government cannot remain exempt from these accelerated patterns of exchange and expectation. Mobile government is defined as a set of strategies, services, and applications for improving benefits to the parties involved in e-government, an extension of the e-government paradigm to a mobile platform (Kushchu & Kuscu, 2003).

Case Study

The New York City Human Resources Administration/Department of Social Services (NYC HRA/DSS) is dedicated to fighting poverty and income inequality by providing New Yorkers in need with essential benefits. With a budget of nearly $10 billion, HRA is the largest public social service agency in the country, employing 14,000 people to provide more than 3 million New Yorkers access to income support through TANF, food security through the SNAP, shelter support through Emergency Rental Assistance, and additional benefits. These safety net programs, which help New Yorkers cope with a variety of serious needs, such as food or cash assistance, one-time emergency assistance to avoid eviction, services for the disabled or those living with HIV and AIDS, and temporary shelter to escape domestic violence, include the following:

- **Adult Protective Services (APS)** provides services for physically and/or mentally impaired adults to help at-risk clients live safely in their homes.
- **Home Energy Assistance Program (HEAP)** helps low-income homeowners and renters pay bills for heating fuel, equipment, and repairs. It is a means-tested benefit (individuals must meet income eligibility criteria to receive a financial subsidy to cover heating costs).
- **Employment Services** helps meet the needs of job seekers, workers, and employers. Clients receiving cash assistance are provided with job search support, training, literacy education, and resume writing. Employment services works closely with participants and employers to achieve worker success, improve on-the-job performance, and focus on reducing turnover by increasing the economic mobility of workers.
- **Cash Assistance** is New York's name for the TANF program. Families may receive up to 60 months of cash assistance based on demonstrated financial need. Families that have exceeded the 60-month limit or eligible single individuals may be able to receive case assistance under the state's safety net program. Clients are typically required to engage in work and/or training activities and may also be eligible to receive transportation and child care support to engage in these activities.
- **SNAP** provides food assistance for nearly 1.8 million low-income New Yorkers including families, the elderly, and the disabled. Formerly known as Food Stamps, the program is designed to help families and individuals supplement the cost of their diet with nutritious foods.
- **Homelessness Prevention (HPA)** helps to keep New Yorkers in their homes by collaborating with the Department of Homeless Services, the NYC Housing Authority, and many other organizations and city agencies. The goal is to prevent homelessness by assisting families and individuals maintain stable, affordable housing in their communities. Supportive services include rental assistance, legal services, and other intervention services.
- **HIV/AIDS Services Administration (HASA)** supports individuals living with AIDS or HIV illness who meet financial need requirements live healthier and more independent lives. It collaborates with eligible individuals to define plans that target necessary benefits and provide

support specific to their situation. Clients receive intensive ongoing case management and assistance in applying for public benefits and services.

- **New York City's 24-Hour Domestic Violence Hotline** (1-800-621-HOPE) supports victims of domestic violence by providing temporary housing, emergency shelter, and supportive services for themselves and their children.
- **Disability Access** provides support or accommodation to ensure that all eligible New Yorkers are given reasonable accommodations to needed services (from making appointments at times that avoid rush hour travel to providing an interpreter at appointments).
- **Long-Term Care** includes a number of different programs, all funded under Medicaid, that are designed to help eligible elderly or disabled individuals remain at home instead of entering a nursing home. This includes programs such as Medicaid-funded home care, which provides a home attendant and housekeeping services for individuals having difficulty with at least one or more activities of daily life, and the Managed Long-Term Care Program, which covers a number of more intensive services (e.g., case management, nursing, and home health aides).

BATTLING FOOD INSECURITY

The US Department of Agriculture (USDA) defines food insecurity as a condition in which a household reports disrupted eating patterns and reduced food intake, typically due to a lack of cash or access to resources (Wunderlich & Norwood, 2006). As shown in Figure 12.1, USDA's Economic Research Service (ERS) reported

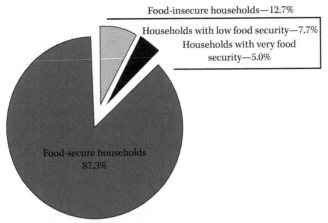

FIGURE 12.1 U.S. households by food security status, 2015.
Source: Calculated by ERS, USDA, using data from the December 2015 Current Population Survey Food Security Supplement.

that in 2015, nearly 13% of US households (more than 15 million people) were food insecure at some point. (http://www.usda.gov/topics/food-nutrition-assistance/food-security-in-the-us/key-statistics-graphics).

The NYC HRA manages New York City's SNAP, which supports nearly 2 million disadvantaged households every month to purchase nutritious foods. More than 40,000 new applications for SNAP are processed every month. Before updates in 2010, each household had to complete a 7-page application. After 2010, the HRA started accepting online applications for benefits via ACCESS HRA.

Applicants must complete a detailed form attesting to their current financial situation to receive SNAP benefits. Attestation requires documentation for verification, which can include pay stubs, housing rental agreements, birth certificates, and public school records (http://www1.nyc.gov/assets/hra/downloads/pdf/services/snap/eligibility_factors_and_suggested_documentation_guide.pdf).

Prior to 2010, potential clients were expected to complete an application and provide verification documents as requested, bringing the entire collection into a local office. If any verification documentation was missing, the application could be held until all documentation was submitted. The applicant might then have to take time from work, spending money on transportation and child care, to submit the missing documentation. In practice, this hurdle discouraged clients from completing the SNAP application. Before modernization of the process in 2010, 60,000 New Yorkers who applied for food assistance were being rejected due to missing or late documentation (New York City Public Advocate Office, 2003).

It was determined that the city would seek to improve the application process for benefits, facilitating the process for potential clients while creating a high-volume and low-touch way to receive supporting documentation more quickly and efficiently. Such efficiencies were intended to reduce the number of cases in which eligible applicants were rejected.

While New York City is on the forefront of leveraging technology to create an e-government model, fully modernizing any bureaucratic process takes time. Clients can still travel to a local SNAP office that provides access to a bank of computers or to a local community-based organization SNAP partner. Otherwise, they need a computer with Internet access to file for and claim benefits. Alternately, a robust smartphone can be used, although the website may be difficult to negotiate on small screens and across different platforms. Unfortunately, as mentioned previously, 31% of low-income Americans have no computer at home, and only 73% of this population owns smartphones. For many jurisdictions throughout the United States, social welfare organizations still rely heavily rely on paper-based processes, an inefficient, costly, and burdensome process for clients and the social welfare organization. Since modernizing in 2010, New York City has moved close to 80% of its applications to the ACCESS HRA channel (online), with 65% coming in outside of the SNAP office's computer banks.

ACCESS HRA

ACCESS HRA (www.nyc.gov/accesshra) was designed to provide enhanced user functionality and account management services. It has become New York City's one-stop client portal in support of HRA's clients. Clients and applicants are able to access the portal at home, as well as through self-service areas at HRA centers and some community-based organizations. This program reflects HRA's commitment to increase access for as many clients as possible, as well as to allow for remote access to upload documents.

As noted previously, there has been a shift in Internet connectivity from home broadband to smartphones (see Figure 12.2). It is that specific demographic—the smartphone-dependent population—that constitutes a significant proportion of the target population for local government programs that address food insecurity and financial stability. Additionally, a client needs assessment survey conducted by HRA showed that a majority of clients (62% of telephone respondents and 80% of online respondents) owned smartphones and were interested in using them to apply for benefits (80%) and to submit supporting documentation (74%).

The HRA sought to modify its existing workflow processes to capitalize on the ubiquity of the Internet in the daily lives of its constituents using specially designed mobile apps to supplement more desktop-friendly application processes that fewer

Several groups are shifting their home Internet connectivity away from broadband and toward smartphones

% of each group who have...

	Broadband at home			Smartphone, but no broadband at home		
	2013	2015	CHANGE	2013	2015	CHANGE
All adults	70%	67%	−3%	8%	13%	+5%
African Americans	62	54	−8	10	19	+9
Rural residents	60	55	−5	9	15	+6
Household income < $20K	46	41	−5	13	21	+8
$20K–$50K	67	63	−4	10	16	+6
$50K–$75K	85	80	−5	5	10	+5
Parents	77	73	−4	10	17	+7
High school degree or less	50	47	−3	11	18	+7

Source: Pew Research Center surveys

PEW RESEARCH CENTER

FIGURE 12.2 Shift in Internet connectivity, 2013–2015.

clients can access. It sought to address the issue of incomplete applications by simplifying the process of completing those applications remotely.

ONE APPROACH: A MOBILE FRIENDLY WEBSITE

The studies referenced earlier highlight the importance of creating interaction between government agencies and their clients (citizens and residents) through sites that are mobile friendly, often called responsive websites. Responsive websites provide instant access (assuming at least a 2G or 3G connection) to information and interaction with government entities. New York City and Utah are prime examples of a shift toward a digital government presence on the web. In each of these states, state and city governments are moving not only toward providing access to application online (eGov), but also toward considering how such applications can be completed via mobile devices (mGov). Neither platform is ideal yet, but the move toward an e-government strategy has begun with the creation of online portals that consider mobile first design.

ANOTHER APPROACH: A MOBILE APP

The NYC HRA initially focused on creating a mobile friendly web app, which is a program delivered through a browser interface rather than an application downloaded and installed on a mobile device. However, during the first round of beta testing, it became clear that a technology course correction was needed. Smartphones had built-in features such as notifications, messaging, GPS, and cameras that were rapidly improving to capture more memory-intensive photos. Additionally, there were inherent security issues associated with a web-based interface. For the soft launch, the deployment strategy shifted to an Android native app and the mobile responsive website for iOS users until the native iOS app could be deployed 3 months later.

The NYC HRA decided to contract with Diona Mobile Solutions for design and upkeep of the application (choosing to buy rather than build). This arrangement provided a solution that would be regularly tested and maintained on current updated operating systems. Diona will continue to consider the most relevant and appropriate design standards (material design standards for Android and human interface guidelines for iOS) to maintain and enhance ease of use.

In November 2015, NYC HRA's work with Diona culminated in the release of the NYC HRA Document Upload app for Android (https://play.google.com/apps/details?id=gov.nyc.hra.DocUploads&hl=en) and iOS https://itunes.apple.com/us/app/nyc-hra-document-upload/id1067439293?mt=8). The goal of the app was to create a mobile interface that would reduce the burden of document submission while increasing the likelihood of application approval. Clients who might once have had to visit multiple offices numerous times were now able to download the NYC HRA app from the Android or iPhone store, install the application on their devices, take a photo directly from a mobile handset, and begin uploading through the app interface. As deputy commissioner for business process innovation at NYC HRA, coauthor Aaronson reported that "working with Diona's mobility solutions opened up a new, cost-effective and powerful way for us to engage with the people we serve while improving the operational performance of important programs, such as SNAP."

For the official release, NYC went live with an app that would be usable by almost anyone (see Figure 12.3). In order to be able to operate the app the only requirement was that users be able to enter their name and a personal identification number to operate the smartphone camera.

Using both city and state notices and online next steps prompts, center staff and clients were informed of the mobile app option for completing their application from home by uploading their documentation with their phone. As of May 2016, more than 33,000 New Yorkers had downloaded and installed the app on their phones, and more than 200,000 images had been uploaded with the app (about 10,000 images for 1,500 cases per week). This resulted in a savings of about 4 minutes per document compared to images submitted through the mail or by fax. Since most cases require multiple documents, this can be a significant time savings per case for HRA workers, with an 85% success rate for automatic attachment of supporting documents to the correct case. The app is also saving time and money for clients, who no longer have to submit documents manually.

The NYC HRA continued down the mobile app path with a plan to implement a new self-service solution (see Figure 12.4). This new solution went live in April

FIGURE 12.3 NYC HRA document upload app.

FIGURE 12.4 The new self-service app (left: a walkthrough of the features of the new self-service app; right: the client dashboard, including payment details, appointments, and messages).

2017 and allows HRA clients access to their information 24/7. The NYC HRA will continue to accept paper applications when a client requests this option. However, the goal of its new digital strategy is to provide avenues of access beyond the traditional, thereby increasing the potential outreach to households in need. Currently, most clients submit their initial SNAP application online.

ETHICAL CONSIDERATIONS

The National Association of Social Workers Code of Ethics (NASW, 2008) includes the following ethical responsibilities to clients regarding informed consent and confidentiality:

> Social workers should provide services to clients only in the context of a professional relationship based, when appropriate, on valid **informed consent**. Social workers should use clear and understandable language to inform clients of the purpose of the services, risks related to the services, limits to services because of the requirements of a third-party payer, relevant costs, reasonable alternatives, clients' right to refuse or withdraw consent, and the time frame covered by the consent.
>
> Social workers should protect the **confidentiality** of all information obtained in the course of professional service, except for compelling professional reasons. The general expectation that social workers will keep information confidential does not apply when disclosure is necessary to prevent serious, foreseeable, and imminent harm to a client or other identifiable person. In all instances, social workers should disclose the least amount of

confidential information necessary to achieve the desired purpose; only information that is directly relevant to the purpose for which the disclosure is made should be revealed.

Today these standards often result in the creation of silos of information. In practice, organizations err on the side of caution and do not share information with other organizations, even when collaboration is necessary or recommended. This default is changing at the federal government level as more agencies move to a more positive consumer experience model. As one of the key federal agencies spearheading this change, the Center for Medicare and Medicaid Services (CMS), through its new emphasis on the "social determinants of health" has identified a need to be able to collaborate and share information across healthcare and social welfare organizations to address the client holistically in addressing day-to-day needs.

The concern for the efficacy of such interactions (sharing of personal information across agencies) in lieu of conventional wisdom regarding confidentiality is still a major stumbling block for agencies today. However, the value of being able to capture information one time and then coordinate that information across government organizations for the benefit of the client is becoming an acceptable ideal. Even the NASW is considering whether or not confidentiality rules need to be revisited.

The problem today lies more within the implementation of security parameters that will safeguard the client's information (cybersecurity). For example, one of the key aims of the Health Insurance Portability and Accountability Act (HIPAA) is the protection of healthcare information while sharing that information with other providers who are working for the client's benefit. To shift the focus in data sharing from policy to cybersecurity, states are starting to find new ways to cooperate with one another (from the creation of simplified applications for multiple programs to the reorganization of entire departments to inclusion of house agencies within a single department).

From an ethics perspective, sharing information across agencies with the informed consent of the client is becoming standard practice because the goal is to provide a positive consumer or client experience. In an era of budgetary constraints, automation of simple processes both reduces bureaucracy and improves efficiency while potentially humanizing the experience for recipients by reducing repeated requests for the same information. A client should have the option to allow information to be shared with multiple agencies but should also have assurance that the sharing of that information will be secured and not hacked.

Social Justice Implications

Government agencies are typically mandated to serve the people who live and work in their jurisdictions. Therefore, these agencies need to constantly consider how to best reach all of their constituents, removing any and all potential barriers to access to benefits and services. As a result, it is unlikely that government agencies will ever be able to move away from providing manual (paper-based access options. However, as mobile devices become necessities rather than luxuries, these agencies should move toward providing access to their services through these devices. Those populations most in need of government services and benefits tend to be dependent on mobile Internet access, which underlines the need for e-governance strategies to be maximized for use on mobile phones (Moon, 2002).

Questions for Discussion

1. What are some of the sociological or psychological barriers applicants or clients face when they use technology to interact with government resources?
2. What strategies have been employed today or could be employed tomorrow to move government agencies into a more collaborative mindset so that information sharing may become the norm versus the exception?
3. Informed consent and confidentiality are key tenets in social work. How does one assure adherence to such values while prioritizing the needs of their clients and improving ease of access to government services?

Further Readings

Borucki, C., Arat, S., & Kushchu, I. (2005). Mobile government and organizational effectiveness. In *Proceedings of First European Conference on Mobile Government* (pp. 56–66). Brighton, UK: Mobile Government Consortium International.

Dawes, S. (2008). The evolution and continuing challenges of e-governance. *Public Administration Review, 68*, S5–S198.

OECD. (2011). *Benefits and outcomes of m-government*. Paris, France: OECD.

McGrath, R. (2013, November). The pace of technology adoption is speeding up. *Harvard Business Review, 25*.

Rideout, V., & Katz, V. S. (2016, Winter). *Opportunity for all? Technology and learning in low income families*. New Brunswick, NJ: Rutgers University, School of Communication and Information.

Roggenkamp, K. (2003). *Development modules to unleash the potential of mobile government: Developing mobile government applications from a user perspective*. Berlin, Germany: Institute of Electronic Business.

13 }

#MacroSW

A TWITTER COMMUNITY OF PERSONAL LEARNING
AND PRACTICE

Laurel Iverson Hitchcock, Karen Zgoda, and Kristin Battista-Frazee

"A community is like a ship; everyone ought to be prepared to take the helm."
—Henrik Ibsen, *1828–1906*

YouTube channels for LGBTQ youth, Facebook groups for women with fertility concerns, listservs for people with rare or serious illness, and university alumni groups on LinkedIn offer specific and meaningful opportunities for learning and interaction with others having similar interests, concerns, and/ or identities. Since 1983, technology has fostered the development of online communities that allow members to communicate and form meaningful relationships using their laptops, tablets, or smartphones—or via public portals available at public libraries and schools (Leiner et al., 2012). Such communities can supersede the barriers of time, geography, and cultural expectations as individuals can participate in these collectives by choice from almost any location and at any time. Social workers can derive important benefit from communities that exist in virtual space: information and support or insight into worlds that clients inhabit and depend on. For many professionals, these shared virtual spaces are a valuable resource to incorporate into a professional learning network (PLN), offering a dynamic collection of research, news, and ideas for practice.

To explore these opportunities and their relevance to social work, we introduce the key features of online communities, technology tools and applications used to cultivate and shape those communities, and a case example of how online community life can inform and enrich social work practice.

Background

Online communities in social work date back to the late 1980s, when electronic bulletin boards and listservs were used to help social workers share resources, communicate, and network (Grobman & Mankita, 2016; Vest, Pruett, & Holmgren, n.d.). One of the earliest online social work communities is SocWork, a listserv created at the University of Toronto as a way for students of a policy course to learn more about computers. By the mid-1990s, social work educators used Internet-based tools such as e-mail and electronic mailing lists (Shorkey & Uebel, 2014). In 1995, Susan Mankita founded the first AOL chat group for social workers to connect social workers online to discuss social work practice, special topics, and ethics (Grobman & Mankita, 2016).

Social and digital technologies are pervasive in 21st-century life, across geographies and cultures. While there are inequalities in access, about half of the world's population regularly uses some form of social and digital technology to communicate, access information, and connect with resources (International Telecommunication Union, 2016). Globally, more than 50% of all people have Internet access, with rates closer to 80% or 90% in developed countries. Nearly one-third of the world's population (or 2.3 billion people) uses social media in some capacity (We Are Social, 2016). In the United States, approximately 70% of all Americans use some form of social media, with Facebook, Instagram, and Pinterest ranking as the top three platforms (Pew Research Center, 2017b). While there are disparities in access and device ownership in the United States, nearly 90% of teens and young adults (under age 24) have smartphones that they actively use for texting and surfing the Internet.

Access to the Internet and interactive devices has uncoupled shared space from sustained human interaction, raising concerns about growing human disconnection; eroding empathy (Carr, 2011; Turkle, 2012); and anonymous use of divisive and provocative language, including hate speech directed toward women, minorities, and other vulnerable populations (Blau & Caspi; 2010; Santana, 2014). Further, threats to privacy and confidentiality are increasingly concerning as reports of governments spying on citizens and companies selling consumer data proliferate.

By contrast, virtual spaces and online platforms allow diverse people who might never meet in the real world to connect, share, learn, work, and play asynchronously and across geographies. Online degree programs and free massive open online courses (MOOCs) for individuals across the globe provide access to new forms of education (Allen & Seaman, 2016). Social media apps allow people to share photos, comments, and videos in public and private groups, such as grandchildren sharing the days' events with their grandparents through a video conferencing app or citizens monitoring police activity. Nonprofit agencies and some government agencies are using online tools to become more transparent in their policies and practices and to make public benefits more accessible (Kanter, Fine, & Zuckerberg, 2010; Young, 2013; see also chapter 12).

ONLINE COMMUNITIES AS A RESOURCE FOR SOCIAL WORK

Many social workers fear that online communities and technology-mediated interactions devalue the importance of human relationships and the kinds of direct interactions where they can effect change (Mishna, Bogo, Root, & Fantus, 2014; Wolf & Goldkind; 2016). However, in this chapter we take the opposite view, arguing that online communities hold great promise for enhancing and complementing face-to-face social work. Especially for emerging generations of native users, technology offers a legitimate and meaningful means of social interaction. For example, one-third of America's marriages now start online, and 74% of Internet users access social media to stay connected to people important to them (Cacioppo, Cacioppo, Gonzaga, Ogburn, & VanderWeele, 2013; Pew Research Center, 2017b). Further, research asserts that no difference exists in learning outcomes for face-to-face versus online class offerings (Cummings, Chaffin, & Cockerham, 2015; Russell, 2001; Vernon, Lewis, & Lynch, 2009; Wilke, King, Ashmore, & Stanley, 2016).

Consider the growing numbers of online communities that are already informing practice. For example, the Google Plus community Social Work & Technology was started by a social worker, Dr. Jonathan Singer (n.d.), as a virtual space for practitioners who "believe that technology can and should be used by social workers to make the world a better place." This community has more than 1,200 members who share news stories, research articles, event happenings, photos, apps and other ideas about technology and social work practice. In addition, the e-mail listserv from the Association of Baccalaureate Social Work Program Directors (http://www.bpdonline.org/BPDMBR/BPDMEMBER/Resources/BPD-L_List/BPDMEMBER/Resources/BPD-L_Email_List.aspx) offers a good example of the connective powers of online community, providing a venue where members can connect with the organization and share ideas and consult about issues related to baccalaureate social work education.

From our point of view, social work risks becoming an increasingly irrelevant helping profession in the 21st century to the extent that practitioners who know and use technology in their personal lives shun it as a tool for strengthening their professional practice (Mishna et al., 2014; Wolf & Goldkind; 2016).

KEY FEATURES OF ONLINE COMMUNITIES

Online communities are "social aggregations," individuals who come together on the Internet to engage, which leads to the development of social interactions and relationships (Rheingold, 1993). In the last quarter century, there has been a rapid evolution in technology from computers using dial-up modems to webcams, microphones, and software platforms that allow for face-to-face contact and image-rich, real-time virtual communities such as Facebook, World of Warcraft, and Second Life. In order to make the best use of these emerging opportunities, it is important to understand the varieties of online communities. Several key characteristics—evolving membership, fluid identities, and global connections— offer special promise for enhancing social work practice.

Flexible Participation

Kim (2000) suggests that online communities are open, flexible, and dynamic; there is a membership life cycle in which user roles and activities evolve based on their sustained participation. Novice members spend most of their time learning about the community and its members, while regular members spend more time participating and contributing to the community. Leaders and elders are most involved in setting and enforcing group rules and norms, recruiting and socializing with new members, and organizing decision-making efforts. In order to recruit and engage new members and provide for the health and growth of the community, online groups must provide virtual content and tools that help to initiate and inform members at each specific stage. For example, while an online community may maintain private spaces for use only by members, it must have a public web page that introduces visitors to their group, communicates collective norms, and trains them for participation. Similarly, online communities support a wide range of members—from sporadic transitional visitors to committed core participants (Wenger-Trayner & Wenger-Trayner, n.d.). This flexibility creates a community in which both social workers and clients can become involved in a step-by-step process, gaining comfort and skills in individualized ways.

Online communities are also defined by fluid identities. Individuals can identify themselves through online profiles, avatars, photos, and user names from authentic to imaginative. While the real world typically limits a person to one identity, online environments allow multiple identities (Golder & Donath, 2004) that may or may not include real information (Sullivan, 2015). Such flexibility raises issues of authenticity, inclusion, deception, and privacy. However, at the same time, fluid identities permit and even encourage the creation of experimental or aspirational selves coupled with anonymity that avoids exposure and risk.

In-Depth Communities

While critics frequently suggest that online activity is characterized by short-attention-span browsing, virtual communities of practice (VCoPs) can bring together people who are passionate about something that they do in an environment that permits and encourages continued learning (Adedoyin, 2016; Hara, Shachaf, & Stoerger, 2009; Lave & Wenger, 1991). These communities can support practitioners in continuing professional education—physicians who want to learn to use social media in their practice or lawyers interested in family law—and they can generate deep connections and enduring commitment. Because they are no longer tied to geography, professionals can connect and engage with other similarly engaged individuals around the world, reducing professional isolation and improving clinical practice. Examples of VCoPs can be found in medicine, nursing, and social work (Rolls, Hansen, Jackson, & Elliot, 2016; Schwartz, Wiley, & Kaplan, 2016).

TOOLS FOR ONLINE COMMUNITIES

Similar to the role that physical boundaries play in shaping a geographical community, the design and functionality of digital tools influence how online communities develop and maintain their efforts. In addition to the four types of digital tools typically used by online communities—websites, message boards, listservs, and chat rooms—new tools are gaining popularity.

Websites

Many online communities live on websites, which are collections of webpages hosted on a public or private server. Users typically register for membership and then host their own pages to engage with other members. For example *Caring Bridge* (www.caringbridge.org) provides a virtual space for families with a seriously ill family member to share updates and communicate with others through customizable pages with access limited by privacy settings and user authentication. The National Association of Social Work provides an online community for its members through several websites such as Social Work Speaks (http://www.socialworkersspeak.org); the Social Work Career Center (http://careers.socialworkers.org); and Information for Practice (http://ifp.nyu.edu/), which creates an online community around the use of evidence-based practice.

Social networking sites (e.g., Facebook, LinkedIn, and Google Plus), which may be the most commonly used digital tool for online communities, are web-based software platforms that have tools for communicating and sharing information. Users (individuals or groups) can create a unique profile and then use the network's tools to interact with other users by posting written comments or photos, "liking" what others share, and controlling who they follow or who follows them through privacy settings. Social networking sites connect subject or hobby enthusiasts, host support groups, provide advocates with the tools to run awareness campaigns, offer psychoeducation, and link individuals or families with special needs. For example, Facebook is home to ADHD Kids Care Support Group for Parents with 43,086 followers; Cancer Support Community with 28,373 followers; Social Work, Human Rights, & Activism with 1,202 followers; and Anxiety & Depression Support Group with 146,017 followers.

Message Boards

These online forums are simple e-mail or posting tools located on a central virtual space that allows sharing information. Message boards are public or private, free or paid, and allow for anonymous comments. Discussions typically follow a hierarchical structure with an unlimited number of responses, commonly known as threads. These forums have been adapted for use in social work courses to facilitate greater interaction between students and teachers, but are becoming less common in professional practice as more nimble technologies become available.

Listservs

Listservs are easy-to-implement software programs that send out e-mails to a list of addresses. Members typically subscribe to a listserv and post messages through e-mail. They respond to each other by sending an e-mail to one address; the software then distributes the e-mail to everyone on the mailing list, either as an individual e-mail or in a digest format. Listservs have moderators who enforce group rules and norms. Many social work organizations have listservs including the National Association of Social Workers (NASW; http://www.socialworkers. org/pressroom/media/medialistserve.asp), the North American Association of Christians in Social Work (NASCSW; http://www.nacsw.org/Listservs.html), and the Nursing Home Social Workers' Listserv (https://clas.uiowa.edu/socialwork/ nursing-home/nursing-home-social-workers-listserv).

Chat Rooms

These virtual meeting spaces allow users to meet synchronously in real time. In the 1990s, America Online (AOL) chat rooms became popular, offering users basic texting tools by which to communicate (Dewey, 2014). Now many Web-based platforms such as Google Hangout, Facebook Messenger, and Skype offer public or private chats with video, audio, or text messaging. Some websites, such as 7 Cups (http://www.7cups.com) and the National Suicide Prevention Lifeline (http://chat. suicidepreventionlifeline.org), offer private chats with trained volunteers to provide therapeutic support or crisis intervention.

Virtual or Digital Worlds

These platforms offer users the ability to create an avatar, a multidimensional computer graphic, as part of their profile. In some virtual communities, such as Second Life or video gaming communities, users can use keyboards, mouse, microphone, and/or other hardware devices to control the actions, behaviors, and words of their avatars and thereby interact with each other. Communication can be text-based or audio. Community members can work together to design or directly influence the environment of the virtual world by creating buildings, locations, or sharing resources, as in Pokemon Go, Minecraft or Second Life. Virtual worlds offer interactivity that most closely resembles in-person interaction. Some therapists are using virtual worlds to treat posttraumatic stress disorder or to facilitate interaction for clients with disabilities (Reamer, 2013; Smyth, 2011; see also chapter 2). While avatars and virtual worlds are not yet commonly used in social work practice, some social work educators have used them to provide experiential learning experiences for students, especially to explore other cultures and practice skills (Anstadt, Burnette, & Bradley, 2011; Vernon et al., 2009).

Digital Learning Platforms

Technology has redefined the conditions that we assume are required for learning as part of formal or continuing education. In higher education, the traditional model, which prioritizes face-to-face interactions to transmit information, is being supplemented by content management systems, MOOCs, and social media platforms that allow users to organize groups. Ninety percent of all universities and colleges in the United States use some form of learning management system, such as Blackboard, Canvas, or Moodle, to deliver online content to students (Allen & Seaman, 2016). Online offerings range from Web-supported content in a traditional classroom to fully online courses and are supported by a variety of digital tools that allow students and faculty to connect, share ideas, and develop an online social presence. Further, recent research shows that college students commonly use Facebook to organize study groups and other types of support groups (Roblyer, McDaniel, Webb, Herman, & Witty, 2010).

Examples of virtual learning communities include commercial websites such as Lynda.com, Coursera (https://www.coursera.org), and edX (https://www.edx.org) and nonprofit websites such as the Screening, Brief Intervention, and Referral to Treatment (SBIRT) Education Learning Collaborative sponsored by NORC at the University of Chicago. Many disciplines and business associations/specialties have established online communities where participants can make professional connections, ask questions, or learn about new developments in practice or in regulation. Examples include healthcare practice (the Community Toolbox of the Kansas University Work Group for Community Health and Development [http://ctb.ku.edu/en]) and the federal government (Child Welfare Information Gateway [https://www.childwelfare.gov]). For social work professionals, there are several virtual communities: the NASW website Information for Practice, the BPD listserv, and the Social Work and Technology Google Plus Group. Eight-five percent of all social work educators use their institution's learning management system, immediately exposing new social work students to online communities as they embark on professional training (Buquoi et al, 2013).

WHY WOULD A SOCIAL WORKER JOIN AN ONLINE COMMUNITY?

Competent and ethical social work practice requires practitioners, educators, and students to stay up to date and share information about current issues, practice knowledge, and the latest research findings (Council on Social Work Education,

2015; NASW, 2008). One robust strategy is the professional learning network, which connects individuals to others who share interests and with whom they can share useful information. These networks are a well-established practice in education (Richardson & Manacebelli, 2011) and are emergent in social work. For example, a social worker can use social media to collect information related to professional interests, share this information, and collaborate with others on projects. A PLN allows a social worker constant access to a developing stream of targeted information, drawing from a variety of sources such as blogs, e-letters, interest communities, listservs, and various other social media platforms (Hitchcock, 2015b; Michaeli, 2015). Social workers can use PLNs to access information and resources when working off-site or in isolated practice settings or as a resource for working with complex situations or clients with rare conditions (Chen, Rittner, Manning, & Crofford, 2015; Smyth, 2016).

Case Study

#MACRO SOCIAL WORK

The hashtag #MacroSW, registered in 2012, represents "a collaboration of social workers, organizations, social work schools and individuals working to promote macro social work practice" (www.macrosw.com/about) using new technologies to advance dialogue and to explore emerging ideas. The practice of macro social work focuses on changing larger systems such as communities and organizations, and it encompasses a broad spectrum of actions and ideas, ranging from community organizing and education to legislative advocacy and policy analysis. Netting, Kettner, McMurtry, and Thomas (2012) define macro social work as "professionally guided intervention designed to bring about change in organizational, community, and policy arenas" (p. 5).

THE BACK STORY

Deona Hooper, founder of Social Work Helper (@swhelpercom; https://www.socialworkhelper.com), and Rachel West (@poliSW), founder of the Political Social Worker blog (http://www.politicalsocialworker.org) and member of the Association for Community Organization and Social Administration (ACOSA; @acosaorg; http://www.acosa.org/joomla) communications team, approached author Zgoda in January 2014 to start regular chats on Twitter to promote macro social work practice and to use the existing #MacroSW hashtag to create more opportunity for interaction. Other partners recruited for this collaborative effort in 2014 included a cross section of existing networks, social workers, and social work educators engaged in allied projects.

The first #MacroSW Twitter chat on March 13, 2014, focused on ACOSA's Rothman Report, which presented the need for macro-level content in social work education (Rothman, 2013; Zgoda, 2014). Approximately, 40 participants joined the chat (a transcript is available at https://storify.com/MSWatUSC/macrosw-chat-recap-3-13-14). In May 2014, the chat partners created the website for #MacroSW (https://macrosw.com) to further enrich the growing online community. The first blog post on the website was about #MacroSW's second chat on military family mental health advocacy on May 8, 2014 (#MacroSW, 2014). Since then, #MacroSW has hosted more than 100 live chat sessions. Other partners have joined the initiative, helping to coordinate the #MacroSW chats and to enrich the initiative's online presence. #MacroSW partners share the responsibility of moderating and participating in each weekly live chat, prepromoting the chats via their professional networks. Administrative duties, shared by the partners, include vetting chat topics, writing posts for the website, and recruiting participants and guest chat hosts.

#MacroSW (https://twitter.com/OfficialMacroSW) chats use Twitter, a microblogging platform, as the primary online location for member engagement(see Figure 13.1). Microblogging (limiting posts to 140 characters) can encourage participation, reflective thinking, and collaboration (Gao, Luo, & Zhang, 2012). Twitter users can follow other individuals and organizations, joining a feed of their posts, and gather information on a variety of topics. Tweets are posted and read via a website, smartphone or mobile application, tablet, or other device. Social science researchers, including those who investigate trends in demography, map public sentiment by community or track the development of civic engagement on social media, draw on Twitter streams as data (Bruns, & Stieglitz; 2012; Highfield, 2012; M. Smith, Raine, Shneiderman, & Himelbom, 2014). As a profession, social work must understand how Twitter and other forms of social media influence individuals, families, and communities, thinking critically about how to ethically and professionally use these tools to better client outcomes and to advance the profession.

FIGURE 13.1 Screenshot #MacroSW homepage on Twitter, April 13, 2017.

#MacroSW

#MacroSW: Social Action Series Starts 12/7/17

By Rachel L. West Storify Transcript The first part of a new series of chats on social action will take..

#Macro Social Work, #social action

#Macrosw Holiday Open Mic Night December 14, 2017

Here's the transcript of this chat. 2017. What a year! For most of us, it's been a year unlike any..

#MacroSW Chat for 11/30/2017: Professional Transparency in Social Work Practice

Chat archive. Read the Storify transcript here. For this week, #MacroSW will feature Elizabeth Flood, LSW, on the subject of..

FIGURE 13.2 #MacroSW Chat topics, Winter 2017.

Members can engage in asynchronous conversations by responding to each other's tweets over hours or days. The best ways to engage in a conversation on Twitter is to write and post tweets that include usernames or hashtags. Each user has a username starting with the @ symbol. If a username appears in a tweet, it will automatically show up on that user's timeline. If the username appears at the beginning of a tweet, it is called an @reply. If the username appears anywhere else in the tweet, it is called a mention. During a live Twitter chat, an @reply or mention will draw those users into the conversation and can allow two or more users to participate in a sidebar dialogue within the chat.

Through the open and fluid #MacroSW conversations on Twitter, social workers can expand their network of colleagues; investigate new topics and ways of thinking about an aspect of macro social work practice; and connect to resources, strategies, and research. This forum is not meant for in-depth conversation, but is instead a mechanism to incite topical dialogue that facilitates rapid access to a broad and rich online community of social work leaders and emerging new professionals. Figure 13.2 offers a snapshot of chat topics from the last months of 2017.

The website (www.macroSW.com) hosts information about the weekly chats, the partners in the community, and best practices for participating in a live chat (see also Hitchcock, 2015a).

LEARNING TO FACILITATE

To facilitate a live Twitter chat at #MacroSW, partners apply planning and group work skills in an online environment along with their working knowledge of the

Twitter platform. Those interested in moderating a chat should participate and observe other Twitter chats first, paying attention to how the chat hosts form and post their questions, encourage the flow of conversation, enforce the rules of the chat, and manage difficult or destructive participants. Asking questions of other moderators about their leadership style or reading how-to tips in forum discussions is another way to improve skill and comfort levels. Volunteering to cofacilitate a chat with a more seasoned moderator and then debriefing can also improve technology, etiquette, and social skills required for a live Twitter chat.

MODERATING A CHAT

To begin a live Twitter chat, moderators should plan carefully, thinking about the following questions:

1. What will be the purpose and topic of the chat?
2. Who is the audience for the chat?
3. How will the chat be organized and advertised?
4. What will be the rules of the chat and how will they be enforced?
5. What questions will be asked during the chat?
6. After the chat, how will the tweets be archived and how can this information be used to improve the next chat?

Best practices for live chats also include selecting a good hashtag, orienting potential participants to the chat, and archiving the chat. For a regular weekly chat, a unique hashtag is best, one that is not already being used or has multiple meanings. A hashtag for a one-time chat can include the year and/or location of the chat. A moderator can test possible tags by using the search function within the Twitter or Hashtags.org website and reviewing the types of tweets that are already associated with that hashtag.

HOSTING A CHAT

One of the best ways to educate and welcome participants to a chat is by posting a detailed description of the chat, weekly topics, and ground rules on a blog or website associated with the chat or on a third-party website that specializes in Twitter chats such as Twubs or TweetChat. These sites provide tools to advertise, organize, and subsequently archive a chat.

The textbox below shows a sample website post from #MacroSW. Depending on the chat's topic, the moderator might provide background information, links to news articles, or an embedded video or other graphic that describes and gives context to the issues and questions that might be discussed during the chat (See Box 13.1). Moderators should provide this information in advance of the chat along with guidelines on how to participate in live chats. Following the chat, moderators are encouraged to summarize, analyze, and archive the tweets

BOX 13.1 } Introduction to a #MacroSW chat.

FIGHTING AN ANTI-SOCIAL WORK AGENDA: THE POWER OF PROTEST #MACROSW CHAT 4/13/17 AT 9PM EST

At first glance, social work may not appear to be intrinsically linked to protest. After all, we're more likely to be found working behind a cluttered desk or our car between home visits. But in the earliest days of the profession social workers were integrated within the communities they served. Settlement houses were often used as meeting locations for community activists to organize strikes and other public demonstrations.

Since the election of Donald Trump, America has seen a resurgence in public activism in the form of mass protests and actions. Social workers of course have taken part in many of these actions as individuals or small groups, but our profession's collective presence has been limited. The current administration has taken many actions that are explicitly contrary to social work values. With calls from the NASW and other social work institutions to organize, oppose, resist, and educate in response to an anti-social work agenda, it is time for social workers to consider how we can take bolder action to resist unjust policies.

This discussion continues the #MacroSW organizing chat series. The first chat focused on understanding power as organized people and organized money. The second chat discussed how we can effectively build relationships to develop grassroots power. How can we now take these concepts to develop public demonstrations of our power? And to what end? In the third chat of the series, we will answer the following questions:

Q1: Have you ever taken part in an action (rally, protest, disruption, etc)? What was it? Describe the experience. #MacroSW

Q2: Was the action effective? Why or why not? If so, what did it achieve? #MacroSW

Q3: Are there specific forms of protest or tactics you think social workers should be engaging in? #MacroSW

Q4: Do you have plans to participate in an upcoming action? What is it? If not, what would you like to see in your area? #MacroSW

Excerpted from: Zgoda, K., & #MacroSW (2017).

and conversation from the chat in a simple blog post that reviews the major points of the conversations or a detailed report about the number and type of participants and number and quality of the tweets. A recent report by the Pew Research Center shows how data from Twitter can be used to map and analyze conversations based on the topic and participants (M. A. Smith et al., 2014). Again, third-party websites can be helpful. For example, the website Storify (http://www.storify.com) provides link offers for free and subscription-based Web services to create transcripts of live Twitter chats. Implicit in the process of documenting and assessing a Twitter conversation is the use of results to improve

TABLE 13.1 } MacroSW Chat Quantitative Data Summary 2014–2015

	Number of Tweets	Number of Unique Users
Mean	245	27
Median	194	20
Mode	360	11
Low Range	70	9
High Range	969	100

future interactions. #MacroSW regularly dedicates chat time to soliciting feedback, and uses quantitative data to analyze the reach and relevance of the chats, as seen in Table 13.1 above.

#MACROSW CURRENTLY

The #MacroSW community has steadily grown since 2014. Chats occurred bimonthly from 2014 until the fall of 2015. Due to public support and growth of #MacroSW volunteer partners, the chats now occur weekly on Thursdays from 9 to 10 PM EST. #MacroSW also reaches out to leaders in the social work profession and subject matter experts to guest host chats (see https://macrosw.com/guest-experts). In addition, #MacroSW has shared written content about the chats with both the *New Social Worker Magazine* (for example, see Thompson, 2017) and *Social Work Today* and on social media (http://www.socialworkers.com; http://www.socialworktoday.com). The chats are hosted and promoted by #MacroSW partners using social media and e-mail to social work listservs of the Association of Baccalaureate Social Work Program Directors (@BPDAssociation) and the Council on Social Work Education (@CSocialWorkEd). As of April 2017, the #MacroSW website had more than150 subscribers who receive e-mail announcements from the community, and the @OfficialMacroSW Twitter account has nearly 2,300 followers. (https://twitter.com/OfficialMacroSW).

The #MacroSW community provided feedback to the NASW on the draft *Technology Standards for Social Work Practice* in July 2016 (#MacroSW, Shelly, & Hitchcock, 2016). A transcript of the chat was curated and later delivered to NASW in response its call for feedback. This hour-long chat, which had more than 6,000,000 impressions from 1,644 tweets posted by 81 participants, is an example of how #MacroSW works as a community to influence and support direct practice. In addition, #MacroSW has sponsored five social work student-focused chats about income inequality. During these chats, social work educators from across the country encourage their students to join the live chat and engage in conversations with other students, educators, and practitioners from across the United States. Hitchcock and Young (2016) looked at how students responded to participating in these live chats and found that the #MacroSW chats offered opportunities for engaging students in the classroom around macro-level social work topics and connected students with the professional world outside of the classroom.

Finally, as an online community, #MacroSW helps social workers from various practice settings connect to each other to share experiences, questions, and resources related to a weekly topic. This provides an opportunity for social workers to engage in discussions about the knowledge, skills and values associated with macro-level social work practice. Using a systematic sample of #MacroSW chats, Table 13.1 summarizes chat data for 2014–2015. Chat attendance varies by topic, coincidence with other popular broadcasts, and time of year.

#MACRO SOCIAL WORK AS A PERSONAL LEARNING NETWORK

A variety of social media tools can be used to develop a PLN. For example, a social worker interested in learning more about macro social work practice might have a PLN that includes a Twitter account to follow prominent macro social work researchers and advocates, a podcast application to listen to a weekly podcast produced by a national social work management association, and a Facebook group of local macro social work practitioners to post comments and share links about new research and practice findings. A PLN is unique to the learner who creates it. Benefits of regular and active participation include enhancement of self-regulation skills related to learning, practice identifying reliable professional resources, greater facility with technology-based tools, and development of digital media literacy skills (Dabbagh & Kitsantas, 2012; Young, 2014).

Michaeli (2015) suggests the following steps for social work career development using social media such as Twitter: (1) determine your values (what you want to be known for), (2) build a track record and reputation to match what you want to be known for, (3) establish a LinkedIn profile, (4) consider blogging or creating an "about me" page, and (5) share content with others in e-authentic ways. Additionally, participation in #MacroSW is an opportunity for social workers to develop their professional identity:

> A strong brand can help you find great opportunities. How you portray your work and the issues you care about to the outside world shapes your career and reputation. . . . Creating a brand unique to you is about authentically sharing your strengths and passions and leveraging different outlets and venues to talk about your expertise. (#MacroSW & Battista-Frazee, 2016)

#MacroSW provides a way for social work students and their professors to participate in conversations, especially during the #MacroSW Media Nights, which use a film, article, or other form of media to discuss macro social work topics. Participants are encouraged to review the media before the chat. In 2016–2017, #MacroSW hosted eight Media Night chats on topics such as mass incarceration, disability rights, and macro-level social work ethics (https://macrosw.com/special-events).

Social workers and others come to #MacroSW chats for professional net-working, connection, and relationship building with others doing similar work. For example, a common theme reported by participants in the #MacroSW chats is that, with few macro social workers in practice, it is difficult to connect with others doing similar work, especially in rural areas.

TWITTER CHAT EFFECTIVENESS: AN OPEN QUESTION

Research detailing the effectiveness of Twitter chats is very limited. A recent survey by the Pew Research Center notes that individuals are more likely to engage in per-sonal and/or professional learning when they have access to technology such as smartphones, Internet access, laptops, and tablets (Horrigan, 2016). Specifically, Twitter has been shown to be an effective tool for supporting public discourse about such topics as race and politics (Anderson & Hilton, 2016; Rainie, 2014). Preliminary research findings from #MacroSW Partners Hitchcock and Zgoda suggest that chat participants regularly share resources, educate each other on the macro social work landscape, attempt to define and characterize macro social work practice, and engage in community-building conversation and networking. In terms of current social work practice, there are implications for connected learning, sharing content, and enriching the public discourse around macro social work practice.

Findings on the use of Twitter in classroom settings are limited, but some evi-dence suggests that this technology has potential for student learning. Hitchcock and Young (2016) report that students who participated in a #MacroSW class as-signment "enhanced their learning of the course content because they were able to connect with others outside of the classroom, learn what others outside of the classroom were thinking about poverty, and practice advocacy skills" (p. 8). In ad-dition, 93% of the students who completed the class assignment went from a nega-tive to a positive opinion of Twitter use in social work practice, with 83% reporting that they would continue to use Twitter for this purpose after the course ended. Saxton, Niyirora, Guo, and Waters (2015) reported that Twitter chat hashtag use that centered on public education, branding, call to action (advocacy efforts), and common values and goals increased the level of chat audience engagement and retweets.

Ethical Considerations

Online communities are an ever-evolving part of the human experience. Social workers and their clients need to learn skills to manage and partici-pate in civic life and online communities while professionals, businesses, and governments will need to develop policies and platforms to keep pace with the ever-changing technology environment. Moore's law suggests that microchip technology advances enough every 2 years to create significant changes in the software and hardware that supports online communities, raising concerns about ever-changing training requirements for both social workers and clients. Additionally, virtual communities are influenced by multiple disciplines: computer science, business and marketing, sociology, anthropology, and communication studies.

By engaging with social media platforms, a social worker can create opportunities for individuals to connect with others and find communities of support around a variety of problems or even to advocate for community change, creating virtual educational or task groups. While current ethical standards would not support therapeutic or clinical groups on Twitter or other public social media platforms, education-based chats such as answering questions on available community resources or moderating a chat with a local politician about a new policy development could be a valuable service to clients and communities. Community activists and groups can also use Twitter to communicate with each other, organizations, elected officials and governmental agencies. For example, #SaturdaySchool is a weekly Twitter chat hosted by Rhonda Ragsdale to address social justice issues, often using hashtag #socialjustice specific to particular issues (http://www.rhondaragsdale.com). In this way, social workers can promote social justice, raise awareness, or engage in digital activism for positive social change.

Individuals who participate in social media, such as live Twitter chats, should understand the public nature of communicating via social media networks. Comments in tweets are viewable by anyone with an account and can be easily shared on other social networking platforms, captured in a screenshot, and/or written about and discussed in more traditional media. Twitter provides privacy settings that limit access to posts, but live chats work best when a user's account is public. Most social work practitioners and educators agree that social media platforms are not a place to work and communicate directly with or about clients (Judd & Johnston, 2012; Reamer, 2009). Social media platforms such as Twitter represent uncharted territory for the social work profession, and important ethical and privacy dilemmas still need to be addressed (Strom-Gottfried, Thomas, & Anderson, 2014). In all such forums, social workers should maintain professional decorum that includes following the guidelines of the NASW Code of Ethics, NASW/Association of Social Work Boards technology guidelines (2005) and their own employer's policies and procedures (NASW, 2008).

Social Justice Implications

Increasingly, the ability to access, understand, and engage with digital content and environments is seen as an essential part of everyday life. Today, 87% of all adults and 97% of young adults (aged 18–29) use the Internet in a variety of ways—from communicating with friends and family or obtaining healthcare information to engaging with community organizations (Fox & Rainie, 2014). Those who do not have access to the Internet are disadvantaged in their ability to obtain information, to learn new skills and even to connect with needed services. Social workers will need to play a role in ensuring that disadvantaged and vulnerable populations not only have access to social media, but also can successfully use the Internet and social media to achieve health and well-being outcomes. Social workers can help orient clients, especially those who live in rural communities or are homebound, to create their own PLNs around issues of concern to them. Engaging the virtual world requires digital literacy skills such as being able to recognize credible sources of information, assessing the quality and reliability of content, and in turn, one's own responsibility in sharing or distributing information or advice. Social workers can help clients to interpret online content and provide education about the benefits and consequences of sharing and seeking information on Twitter and other social media platforms. This suggests that not only do social workers need to understand and apply digital literacy for their own benefit but they also need to be prepared to discuss and train clients about the importance and use of these skills.

Questions for Discussion

1. What online communities do you participate in and why?
2. Do you currently have a personal/professional learning network? If so, please describe it. If not, how would you go about developing one?
3. Have you participated in a Twitter chat? If so, describe the experience.
4. What role do social media such as Twitter play in community building?

Further Readings

#MacroSW Blog. https://macrosw.com/

Hitchcock, L., Zgoda, K., & Battista-Frazee, K. (2016). Hashtags for social work: Technology and Twitter chats. *The New Social Worker, 23*(2), 34. Retrieved from http://www.socialworker.com/feature-articles/technology-articles/hashtags-for-social-work-technology-and-twitter-chats/

Symplur. (n.d.). *The healthcare hashtag project.* Retrieved from https://www.symplur.com/healthcare-hashtags/

Thompson, V. (n.d.). *Ramp your voice homepage.* Retrieved from http://rampyourvoice.com/

Twitter. (n.d.). *Using hashtags on Twitter*. Retrieved from https://help.twitter.com/articles/49309?lang=en

Twitter. (n.d.). *@OfficialMacroSW Twitter Homepage*. Retrieved from https://twitter.com/OfficialMacroSW

Zgoda, K. (2009). How tweet it is: Social tweeters. *The New Social Worker, 16*(3). Retrieved from http://www.socialworker.com/home/Feature_Articles/Technology/How_Tweet_It_Is:_Social_Tweeters/

14 }

Going Forward

"Human progress is neither automatic nor inevitable. . . . Every step toward the goal of justice requires sacrifice, suffering, and struggle; the tireless exertions and passionate concern of dedicated individuals."
      —Martin Luther King Jr., *1929–1968*

Modern social work, or social work 2.0, will be challenged to deliver direct service by mobile devices, chat bots, and short message service (SMS); to advocate for just causes on a broad range of channels including social media, electronic messaging, and mobile apps; and to educate students and lifelong learners in face-to-face classrooms, hybrid settings, and virtual environments. In order for educators and professionals to engage these imperatives and master these competencies, we must adopt evolving technologies— becoming curious about their potential, thinking about their accelerating effect on culture and their role in the lives of clients, and interrogating the models that govern their use. The first principles of ethics and social justice guarantee that, going forward, social workers will face new responsibilities: translating principles into protocols for technology-enabled practice, assessing both the efficacy and client perception of the technologies we deploy, and advocating that a technologically charged society makes rights and resources equally available to all peoples and communities.

Technology, by Itself, Is Neutral

We inhabit a reality defined by technological proliferation. Accruing technological change shapes our material reality in discernable ways, yet less visibly, it reshapes human perception, transforming our relationships to time, to space, and to one another. While technology's promise of ongoing enhancement of human capacity perpetually captures our imagination, innovation does not necessarily inspire human progress toward the ideals of social justice. As Freeman Dyson and colleagues (2001) observed nearly two decades ago, the phenomenon of technological advance may prove ethically neutral over the arc of history. Long associated with the potential to advance human society—visible in the paradigm-altering introduction of the printing press and the technologies of clean water and medicine that can control epidemic disease—technology has also enabled the refinement of the human capacity for destruction via ever more powerful weapons of war and sabotage.

Contemporary technology shines with potential: it eases the friction of everyday life, enhances productivity, improves our ability to predict even complex scenarios, and democratizes the availability of knowledge. Yet the manufacture and refinement of hardware and software applications exacerbate inequality in material ways. Production and disposal of hardware degrade environmental conditions and reinforce the demand for cheap labor; more adept programming allows for the mechanization or outsourcing of jobs; and the wealth produced by the technology sector is unevenly distributed, reifying the income gap and stratifying populations by imprinting privilege onto geography. Despite its perpetually escalating capacity, technology by itself does not create solutions. As King states above, regardless of tools, progress toward justice never occurs without human intervention and commitment; rather it requires a sustained attention that translates into labor and action.

As a tool, technology can inspire a mythic worship, the belief that its mere application is a panacea that can eradicate social ills. Such enthusiastic scenarios often center on the potential of simple solutions to conditions of inequality, or on quick answers to the dilemma of what society owes its citizens. Entire villages in remote parts of the globe require only a portal to the Internet to acquire the skills and knowledge that will free future generations from poverty! Senior citizens need never be lonely again once caregiving robots come online! Underachieving urban schools can be invigorated and made effectual by adding laptops to every classroom! Yet, as Eubanks (2011) writes, an exclusive focus on technological development as an engine of greater equality and prosperity is "a dangerously under-examined species of magical thinking" (p. xv). The use of technology, suggests Kentaro Toyama, founder of the Technology for Emerging Markets group at Microsoft, magnifies existing material realities rather than transforming them. A pioneer in the use of information and communication technologies (ICTs) to further global development goals, Toyama writes that technology is "only an amplifier of human conditions," concluding that "social challenges are best met with deeply social solutions" (2015).

Indeed, many of the chapters in this book illustrate that technology-enhanced social work requires much the same labor as traditional social work—everything from engagement to termination at the individual level and the same needs assessment, stakeholder input, evaluation, and course correction at the agency or community level. The advent of new communication platforms has given voice to marginalized peoples and communities. However, some of the most salient global examples of sociopolitical movements that gained momentum through social media—the Arab Spring, the Black Lives Matter movement and #MeToo— have demonstrated that technology-enabled activism ultimately faces the same real-world obstacles as more established forms of advocacy and demonstration. Technology, by itself, cannot replace the primary human processes required to effect meaningful change.

e-Competence: A Route to Social Justice

A technological culture may redefine the rights to which every individual is entitled. Because so much of society is technologically mediated, access to technology is increasingly a human right. Initially, conceptions of technology-enabled social justice focused on equality of access—the ability of all people to use interactive devices and to connect to the Internet. This paradigm sought to remediate the "digital divide," or the distribution of technological tools along a familiar template of inequality in which poorer individuals and communities are far less able to access the benefits of new technologies. This model led to activism aimed at re-distribution, especially of hardware and broadband access. Yet this conception has evolved. The notion of digital divide is limited, based in a catalog of deficit among already marginalized communities, and outdated by the spread of mobile and wireless technologies across the globe, which has drastically altered the realities of ICT use (James, 2011; Berzin, Singer & Chan, 2015). In a 2016 Pew report, "Digital Readiness Gaps," Horrigan outlines a more contemporary conception of differential access:

> For many years concerns about "digital divides" centered primarily on whether people had *access* to digital technologies. Now, those worried about these issues also focus on the degree to which people succeed or struggle when they use technology to try to navigate their environments, solve problems, and make decisions. (2016)

The notion of the digital divide has thus evolved to include the ability of individuals and communities to make maximum use of technology: to use ICTs as a tool to realize individual goals and to achieve participation in communities and forums that foster social inclusion. A variety of terms map this concept, including "digital literacy," "digital engagement," "e-inclusion," and "e-competency." However, independent of specific vocabulary, all reflect the holistic notion that physical access to technology tools and the Internet is meaningful only when accompanied by the skills that allow people to make meaningful use of them.

Social Work and Technology: An Evolving Map of Values

The process of editing this book has allowed us, the editors, to interact with inspired professionals, to contemplate all of the technology we encounter every day through the lens of social justice, and to think deeply about how the discipline of social work can inform a fair and inclusive digital society. The process encouraged us to ask questions and to interrogate the assumptions we hold about both technology and social work. We can articulate many specific recommendations for how our field can act to further integrate technology; ultimately all reflect the following map of values. It is our belief that these core concepts—interrogated, refined, and augmented by active discussion—will enable new generation of practitioners to continue to work toward the fundamental values of social work and to ensure that the discipline makes a dynamic contribution to shaping a fast-changing society into one that offers opportunity and autonomy to all of its citizens:

- Technology, by itself, is neutral. Technology requires human input and advocacy to advance the values of a just society.
- In a digital society, access to technology and the skills to make meaningful use of its capacity are human rights.
- Social workers are uniquely positioned to advocate for technology that advances fairness and equality; and they are ethically obligated to do so.
- Technology does not preclude the traditional knowledge-base of social work: ethical and appropriate practice requires an informed hybrid of digital and analog skills.
- Technology, skillfully deployed, can foster and enhance vital human relationships, providing professionals new conduits of connection, and allowing clients to discover novel pathways to life-enhancing interaction with others.
- Standards for social work education and practice must be based in the principal that informed and appropriate use of technology is an ethical obligation.
- Technology evolves constantly, rendering lifelong learning necessary to ensure professional competence in social work.

Conclusion

It is our hope that the case studies you have encountered in this volume have intrigued you and ignited a sense of possibility. We hope also that they have charged you with a new sense of responsibility. Ethical and appropriate use of emerging technology tools requires both the effort of initial commitment and a career-long investment in curiosity to ensure competence. Going forward, social workers already in the field and those who aspire to join them will be responsible both for redefining the mechanics of practice and for articulating the role of social work in a world remade by technology.

If we fail to undertake the responsibility of incorporating technology into practice, clients may seek to access traditional social work services from sources such as for-profit virtual therapies that are fiscally or technically equipped to provide these resources more accessible, appropriately, or immediately. We must not force clients to choose between our services, which are informed by our Code of Ethics but eschew the convenience and power of technological tools, and those designed by others, which are technologically evolved, accessible, and useful, but unbound to informing principle.

We have made our case for the adoption of technology, with words, diagrams, and—perhaps most persuasively—real-life examples from practice. We want to know where you go with the material. We invite you to continue the discourse online. To share your own technology cases, visit www.laurigoldkind.net and click on "Instructor Resources Site." Good luck with the work.

"Strangers on this road we are on, We are not two we are one."

—DAVE DAVIES, *THE KINKS.*

Instructional Supports

This table describes the types of assignment that appear in this book. While all of these assignments address the interface between technology and social work practice, some take technology as a starting point, while others approach the assignment from the angle of a social problem or the needs of a specific population.

Each chapter is followed by:

1. Prompts for discussion that encourage students to reflect on the case example.
2. An assignment, drawn from this table, that asks students to think independently about the use of technology across practice contexts.

Assignment Type	Description	Prompts	Works with Chapter
Connecting	Learners research a tool, in order to describe the function/ benefit it offers and how it could be adapted to serve specific populations or to address particular issues.	Choose a technology tool. What does it do? What service or benefit does it offer? What technology or literacy skills are required to operate it? What is its cost? Does it augment or replace existing processes or services? Choose a population or issue and describe how the tool could be used to foster change.	Ch 6. Digital Story Telling Ch 4. mDad Ch 11. Blogging

Assignment Type	Description	Prompts	Works with Chapter
Critical Thinking	Learners assess a practice problem, and evaluate several tools to determine which offers the most appropriate benefit.	Choose a problem at the micro/mezzo/macro practice level. What three technology tools might be brought in to address this problem? How does each solution differ from the others?	Ch 9. GIS Ch 10. Social Media
Complementarity	Learners consider how analog activity interfaces with and supports effective implementation of technology tools for practice.	Choose an example of technology-enhanced social work. Consider what elements of the change process are best supported by analog or face-to-face skills, and which are best served by the use of technology. What does technology do well, and which human skills are critical to making the tool effective?	Ch 7. Data for Client Services Ch 5. Foster Care Youth Ch 3. Digital Music
Planning	Learners create a plan for implementing a technology tool, documenting the stages necessary for effective use.	Imagine that you are confronted with a challenging practice issue (at micro, mezzo, or macro level of practice). Select a technology tool to address this issue, and document a plan for implementation. What kinds of training and technical assistance would workers need in order to use this tool? What kinds of training would clients need? What are the indicators of success? How can you evaluate if the tool has been effective?	Ch 5. Foster Care Youth Ch 7. Data for Client Services

Ethics	Learners think critically about a technology tool in order to evaluate the ethical implications of its use. Equally important, learners are asked to think about the ethical implications of *not* using this tool with client populations.	Identify an example of the tool being used with your population (for example, if you are working in youth services, identify an example of an Integrated Data System [or a social media tool]) briefly describe the tool in use. Identify at least one possible ethical challenge and a remediation strategy for that challenge.	Ch 10. Social Media Ch 11. Blogging Ch 8. Integrated Data Systems
Experiencing Technology	Learners test a technology tool, learning, firsthand, about how the tool works and user experience of the technology.	Create an account and username and/or avatar in this platform. Write about your experience, commenting on the opportunities and challenges of this communication models, and on how this channel enriches or hinders communication with clients or other collaborators. What might be alternative channels to consider? How would you present this tool to clients?	Ch 2. Second Life Ch 13. Twitter for Professional Learning Communities Ch 11. Blogging

Additional Resources

The most recent reflection of the expanding role of technology in social work practice is the Council on Social Work Education (CSWE)'s *Envisioning the Future of Social Work, Report of the CSWE Futures Task Force April 2018*. This report describes four potential scenarios for the profession, built around two main dimensions: whether social workers lead just within social work or take on key leadership roles beyond social work, and whether social work "incrementally integrates technology into practice at all levels (evolution)" or "leverages new technologies to enhance practice at all levels (revolution)" (p. 6).

- https://cswe.org/About-CSWE/Governance/Board-of-Directors/2018-19-Strategic-Planning-Process/CSWE-FTF-Four-Futures-for-Social-Work-FINAL-2.aspx

The Task Force included representatives from the National Association of Social Workers (NASW), the Association of Social Work Boards (ASWB), and several deans, directors, and faculty from BSW and MSW programs. The report's Appendix (pp. 18–21) provides an informative listing of what are called "key drivers of change," both at the societal level and specific to social work, that together present the contemporary reality on which the four scenarios are built.

Other documents released in the past few years also point to growing interest in, and concern about, technology's role in social work practice. The increased number of licensure violations involving social media led the ASWB to commission an International Technology Task Force in 2013–2014. That group produced the *Model Regulatory Standards for Technology and Social Work Practice* (2015).

- https://www.aswb.org/wp-content/uploads/2015/03/ASWB-Model-Regulatory-Standards-for-Technology-and-Social-Work-Practice.pdf

These standards were incorporated into the ASWB's Model Social Work Practice Act in 2015. This latter document's purpose is "to provide a resource to legislatures and social work boards when addressing issues related to the public protection mission of regulating the practice of social work" (p. 1).

- https://www.aswb.org/wp-content/uploads/2013/10/Model_law.pdf

The collaboration around technology issues continued after the *Regulatory Standards* were released. The NASW convened a national work group together with ASWB, CSWE, and the Clinical Social Work Association (CSWA) to prepare a revision of the *NASW/ASWB 2005 Standards for Technology and Social Work Practice* to reflect the profound explosion of technology and social media in the intervening period.

- https://www.socialworkers.org/LinkClick.aspx?fileticket=lcTcdsHUcng% 3d&portalid=0

The updated standards have sections on providing information to the public; designing and delivering services; gathering, managing, and storing information; and social work education and supervision. While the new standards cover a wide range of issues and potential problem areas in the application of technology in social work education and practice, they fall short in creating a vision for the positive potential that technology-based and technology-supported tools may deliver in practice arenas. These possibilities are addressed more optimistically in *Envisioning the Future of Social Work.*

A more positive and less restrictive perspective on the possible advances stemming from technology can be found in the American Academy of Social Work and Social Welfare's Grand Challenge statement titled, *Practice Innovation Through Technology in the Digital Age* (Berzin, Singer, & Chan, 2015).

- http://aaswsw.org/wp-content/uploads/2013/10/Practice-Innovation-through-Technology-in-the-Digital-Age-A-Grand-Challenge-for-Social-Work-GC-Working-Paper-No-12.pdf.

This working paper addresses the potential of Information and Communication Technologies (ICTs) to transform much of what has become standard practice in social work, and it speaks to the emerging environment in which today's social work graduates are beginning their practice.

Two core documents are relevant in regard to their statements about technology. For the first time, the BSW and MSW accreditation standards (the 2015 Educational Policy and Accreditation Standards) of the CSWE identify "use technology ethically and appropriately to facilitate practice outcomes" as part of the competency to "Demonstrate Ethical and Professional Behavior" expected of all social workers.

- https://www.cswe.org/getattachment/Accreditation/Accreditation-Process/2015-EPAS/2015EPAS_Web_FINAL.pdf.aspx

Finally, it is worth noting that the 2017 revision of the NASW *Code of Ethics* speaks very clearly to the importance of technology competence (Standards 1.04 d and e) for those who use technology in practice.

- https://www.socialworkers.org/LinkClick.aspx?fileticket=ms_ArtLqzeI%3d&portalid=0

A number of journals, books, podcasts, and websites provide information, research results, and practice suggestions. This list is illustrative and by no means exhaustive.

The *Journal of Technology in Human Services* is probably the first place to search for current research on the use of technology both in social work education and social work practice. The journal long ago moved beyond studies that simply explored comparisons between technology-supported and traditional education approaches and now covers a wide range of subjects.

- https://www.tandfonline.com/loi/wths20

Current news stories, frequently including technology innovations, are standard fare in *The New Social Worker*. It describes itself as "the careers magazine for social work students, new graduates, and others who wish to learn and grow in their social work careers."

- www.socialworker.com/magazine

Another online source for news, videos, and other resources is the Social Work and Technology Google Plus Group.

- https://plus.google.com/communities/115588985317830085141

Two faculty-produced resources that focus on innovation in social work practice are the ***inSocialWork*** podcast series from the University of Buffalo School of Social Work (http://www.insocialwork.org/) and *The Social Work Podcast*, hosted by Jonathan Singer, PhD, LCSW (http://socialworkpodcast.blogspot.com/). Both cover a wide range of topics in research, practice, and technology. If you are interested in a contemporary interdisciplinary approach to tech-related topics, then the *Funny as Tech* podcasts is a great resource (https://www.funnyastech.com/).

While many additional resources for those interested in research are available online, we call attention to the *Association of Internet Researchers* (https://aoir.org/), in part because of its clearly stated commitment to "ensuring that research on and about the Internet is conducted in an ethical and professional manner."

Finally, for those interested in the use of technology to teach social work, two further resources stand out. The *Teaching and Learning in Social Work* blog has posts in a wide range of topics including "teaching with tech" and social media. The soon-to-be-released CSWE Press volume, *Teaching Social Work with Digital Technology,* edited by Laurel Hitchcock, Melanie Sage, and Nancy Smyth, features technology infused curricular offerings, including specific assignments.

Generalist Practice Textbooks Guide

DIGITAL SOCIAL WORK PRACTICE	Direct SW Practice: Theory and Skills (10th ed.). Hepworth, Rooney, et al.; Cengage (2017)	Understanding Generalist Practice (8th ed.). Kirst-Ashman & Hull; Cengage (2015)	The Skills of Helping (8th ed.). Shulman; Cengage (2016)	Generalist SW Practice (11th ed.). Zastrow; Oxford UP (2016)	Generalist Social Work Practice (8th ed.). Miley, O'Melia, & DuBois; Pearson (2017)	Direct Social Work Practice: Theories and Skills Ruffolo, Perron, & Voshel; Sage (2016)
Chapter 1: Introduction	1—Challenges of Social Work; 4—Operationalizing Cardinal Social Work values; ethics	1—Introducing Generalist Practice	1—An Interactional Approach to Helping	2—Social Work Values	1—Generalist Social Work Practice	2—Integrative Themes That Guide Practice with Individuals, Families, and Small Groups
Chapter 2: Second Life and Disabilities	5—Building Blocks of Communication: Conveying Empathy and Authenticity	9—Understanding Families: Family Assessment; 10—Working with Families	7—The Preliminary and Beginning Phases in Family Practice; 9—Variations in Family Practice	8—Social Work with Families	4—Strengths and Empowerment	3—From Evidence-Based Practice to Evidence-Informed Practice

DIGITAL SOCIAL WORK PRACTICE	Direct SW Practice: Theory and Skills (10th ed.). Hepworth, Rooney, et al.; Cengage (2017)	Understanding Generalist Practice (8th ed.). Kirst-Ashman & Hull; Cengage (2015)	The Skills of Helping (8th ed.). Shulman; Cengage (2016)	Generalist SW Practice (11th ed.). Zastrow; Oxford UP (2016)	Generalist Social Work Practice (8th ed.). Miley, O'Melia, & DuBois; Pearson (2017)	Direct Social Work Practice: Theories and Skills Ruffolo, Perron, & Voshel; Sage (2016)
Chapter 3: Therapeutic Electronic Music	12—Developing Goals and Formulating a Contract	2—Practice Skills for Working with Individuals	5—Skills in the Work Phase	5—Social Work with Individuals: Counseling	5—An Empowering Approach to Generalist Practice	5—Engagement and Relationship-Building Skills
Chapter 4: mDad: Mobile Fathering	15—Enhancing Family Functioning and Relationships	5—Engagement and Assessment in Generalist Practice (GP)	4—Beginnings and the Contracting Skills	8—Social Work with Families	8—Engagement: Defining Directions	3—From Evidence-Based Practice to Evidence-Informed Practice
Chapter 5: Digital Support for Aging Out Youth	8—Assessment: Exploring and Understanding Problems and Strengths (subsection on assessing children and older adults)	3—Practice Skills for Working with Groups	6—Endings and Transitions	6—Social Work with Groups: Types and Guidelines	13—Intervention: Creating Alliances	10—Additional Skills for Working with Families and Groups

Chapter 6: Digital Storytelling	9—Assessment: Intrapersonal, Interpersonal, and Environmental Factors	2—Practice Skills for Working with Individuals	2—Oppression Psychology, Resilience, and Social Work Practice; 13—Working with Individuals and the Group	4—Social Work with Individuals: Interviewing	9—Assessment: Identifying Strengths	7—Change Planning
Chapter 7: Data to Improve Client Services	1—Challenges of Social Work	16—Recording in Generalist Social Work Practice	15—Professional Impact and Helping Clients Negotiate the System	3—Assessment	10—Assessment: Assessing Resource Capabilities	6—Assessment in Social Work with Individuals and Families
Chapter 8: Interagency Data Sharing	8—Assessment: Exploring and Understanding Problems and Strengths (subsection on assessing children and older adults)	7—Examples of Implementation in Generalist Practice	15—Professional Impact and Helping Clients Negotiate the System	9—Social Work with Organizations	11—Assessment: Framing Solutions	9—Intervention Skills: Using Problem-Solving, Psychoeducational, and Multisystemic Intervention Approaches and Case/Care Management Skills in Working with Individuals and Families

DIGITAL SOCIAL WORK PRACTICE	Direct SW Practice: Theory and Skills (10th ed.). Hepworth, Rooney, et al.; Cengage (2017)	Understanding Generalist Practice (8th ed.). Kirst-Ashman & Hull; Cengage (2015)	The Skills of Helping (8th ed.). Shulman; Cengage (2016)	Generalist SW Practice (11th ed.). Zastrow; Oxford UP (2016)	Generalist Social Work Practice (8th ed.). Miley, O'Melia, & DuBois; Pearson (2017)	Direct Social Work Practice: Theories and Skills Ruffolo, Perron, & Voshel; Sage (2016)
Chapter 9: Mapping for Program Planning	14—Developing Resources, Advocacy, and Organizing as Intervention Strategies	6—Planning in Generalist Practice	15—Professional Impact and Helping Clients Negotiate the System	10—Social Work Community Practice	10—Assessment: Assessing Resource Capabilities	9—Intervention Skills: Using Problem-Solving, Psychoeducational, and Multisystemic Intervention Approaches and Case/Care Management Skills in Working with Individuals and Families
Chapter 10: Social Media in Agency Settings	14—Developing Resources, Advocacy, and Organizing as Intervention Strategies	14—Advocacy	15—Professional Impact and Helping Clients Negotiate the System	9—Social Work with Organizations	14—Intervention: Expanding Opportunities	4—Professional Values, Ethics, and Professional Use of Self

Chapter 11: Blogging Social Justice	18—Managing Barriers to Change	4—Skills for Working with Organizations and Communities	15—Professional Impact and Helping Clients Negotiate the System	12—Social Work Practice with Diverse Groups	14—Intervention: Expanding Opportunities	2—Integrative Themes That Guide Social Work Practice with Individuals, Families, and small Groups
Chapter 12: mGov—Mobile Benefits	14—Developing Resources, Advocacy, and Organizing as Intervention Strategies	7—Examples of Implementation in Generalist Practice	1—An Interactional Approach to Helping	1—Overview of Social Work Practice	12—Intervention: Activating Resources	9—Intervention Skills: Using Problem-Solving, Psychoeducational, and Multisystemic Intervention Approaches and Case/Care Skills in Working with Individuals and Families
Chapter 13: Twitter + Professional Learning Communities	18—Managing Barriers to Change	11—Values, Ethics, and the Resolution of Ethical Dilemmas	15—Professional impact and Helping Clients Negotiate the System	14 Surviving and Enjoying Social Work	13—Intervention: Creating Alliances	12—Lifelong Learning and Professional Development over the Life Course

DIGITAL SOCIAL WORK PRACTICE	Direct SW Practice: Theory and Skills (10th ed.). Hepworth, Rooney, et al.; Cengage (2017)	Understanding Generalist Practice (8th ed.). Kirst-Ashman & Hull; Cengage (2015)	The Skills of Helping (8th ed.). Shulman; Cengage (2016)	Generalist SW Practice (11th ed.). Zastrow; Oxford UP (2016)	Generalist Social Work Practice (8th ed.). Miley, O'Melia, & DuBois; Pearson (2017)	Direct Social Work Practice: Theories and Skills Ruffolo, Perron, & Voshel; Sage (2016)
14. Future Directions	19—The Final Phase: Evaluation and Termination	11—Values, Ethics, and the Resolution of Ethical Dilemmas	17—Evidence-Based Practice and Additional Social Work Models	14 Surviving and Enjoying Social Work	16—Intervention: Integrating Gains	12—Lifelong Learning and Professional Development over the Life Course

REFERENCES

#MacroSW. (2014, May 5). *Let's talk about Milfamily Mental Health Advocacy.* #MacroSW, May 8, 2014. Retrieved from https://macrosw.com/2014/05/05/milfamily-mental-health-advocacy-macrosw-5814/

#MacroSW & Battista-Frazee, K. (2016, May 4). *A personal brand is not just for rock stars but social workers too.* Retrieved from https://macrosw.com/2016/05/04/a-personal-brand-is-not-just-for-rock-stars-but-social-workers-too/

#MacroSW & Shelly, P. (2015, September 8). *Trauma-informed care.* #MacroSW Twitter Chat, September 10, 2015. Retrieved from https://macrosw.com/2015/09/08/traumainformedcare-the-next-macrosw-chat-on-sept-10-2015/

#MacroSW, Shelly, P., & Hitchcock, L. (2016, July 8). *Technology standards in social work practice: Give NASW feedback.* #MacroSW Chat, July 14, 2016. Retrieved from https://macrosw.com/2016/07/08/technology-standards-in-social-work-practice-give-nasw-feedback-macrosw-chat-07-14-16/

AAMC Institute for Improving Medical Education. (2007). *Effective use of educational Technology in medical education.* Retrieved from https://members.aamc.org/eweb/upload/effective%20use%20of%20educational.pdf

Abdel-Wahab, A. G., & El-Masry, A. A. A. (Eds.). (2011). *Mobile information communication technologies adoption in developing countries: Effects and implications.* Hersey, PA: IGI Global.

Adam, A. (2002). Exploring the gender question in critical information systems. *Journal of Information Technology, 17*(2), 59–67. doi:10.1080/02683960210145959

Adedoyin, A. C. A. (2016). Deploying virtual communities of practice as a digital tool in social work: A rapid review and critique of the literature. *Social Work Education, 35,* 357–370. http://doi.org/10.1080/02615479.2016.1154660

Aguilera, A., & Munoz, R. F. (2011). Text messaging as an adjunct to CBT in low-income populations: A usability and feasibility pilot study. *Professional Psychology: Research and Practice, 42,* 472–478. doi:10.1037/a0025499

Ailes, E., Newsome, K., Williams, J., McIntyre, A., Jamieson, D., Finelli, L., & Honein, M. (2014). CDC pregnancy flu line: Monitoring severe illness among pregnant women with influenza. *Maternal and Child Health Journal, 18,* 1578–1582.

Akard, T. F., Dietrich, M. S., Friedman, D. L., Hinds, P. S., Given, B., Wray, S., & Gilmer, M. J. (2015). Digital storytelling: An innovative legacy-making intervention for children with cancer. *Pediatric Blood and Cancer, 62,* 658–665. https://doi.org/10.1002/pbc.25337

Akbulut, A. Y., Kelle, P., Pawlowski, S. D., Schneider, H., & Looney, C. A. (2009). To share or not to share? Examining the factors influencing local agency electronic information sharing. *International Journal of Business Information Systems, 4,* 143–172.

Alexandra, D. (2008). Digital storytelling as transformative practice: Critical analysis and creative expression in the representation of migration in Ireland. *Journal of Media Practice, 9,* 100–112.

Allen, I. E., & Seaman, J. (2016). *Online report card: Tracking online education in the United States*. Oakland, CA: Babson Survey Research Group. Retrieved from http://onlinelearningsurvey.com/reports/onlinereportcard.pdf

Allshouse, W. B., Fitch, M. K., Hampton, K. H., Gesink, D. C., Doherty, I. A., Leone, P. A., . . . Miller, W. C. (2010). Geomasking sensitive health data and privacy protection: An evaluation using an E911 database. *Geocarto International, 25,* 443–452.

Alonzo, J. S. (2005). Restoring the ideal marketplace: How recognizing bloggers as journalists can save the press. *NYU Journal of Legislation and Public Policy, 9,* 751.

Amamoo-Otchere, E., & Akuetteh, B. (2005). Building disaster anticipation information into the Ghana development and poverty mapping and monitoring system. In P. van Oosterom, S. Zlatanova, & E. M. Fendel (Eds.), *Geo-information for Disaster Management* (pp. 809–818). Berlin, Heidelberg: Springer. Retrieved from https://link.springer.com/chapter/10.1007/3-540-27468-5_58#citeas

Anderson, A. (2015, April). 6 facts about Americans and their smartphones. *Pew Research Center*. Retrieved from http://www.pewresearch.org/fact-tank/2015/04/01/6-facts-about-americans-and-their-smartphones/

Anderson, K. M., & Cook, J. R. (2015). Challenges and opportunities of using digital storytelling as a trauma narrative intervention for traumatized children. *Advances in Social Work, 16*(1), 78–89.

Anderson, M., & Hilton, P. (2016). R. Retrieved from http://www.pewinternet.org/2016/08/15/social-media-conversations-about-race/

Angwin, J., Larson, J., Mattu, S., & Kirchner, L. (2016, May 23). Machine bias: There's software used across the country to predict future criminals. and it's biased against blacks. *Pro Publica*. Retrieved from https://www.propublica.org/article/machine-bias-risk-assessments-in-criminal-sentencing

Angus, L. E., & Greenberg, L. S. (2011). *Working with narrative in emotion-focused therapy: Changing stories, healing lives*. Washington, DC: American Psychological Association.

Anstadt, S. P., Bradley, S., Burnette, A., & Medley, L. L. (2013). Virtual worlds: Relationship between real life and experience in Second Life. *International Review of Research in Open and Distributed Learning, 14*(4), 160–180.

Anstadt, S. P., Bruster, B., & Girimurugan, S. B. (2016). Using virtual world simulators (Second Life) in social work course assignments. *International Journal of Learning Technology, 11*(1).

Anstadt, S. P., Burnette, A., & Bradley, S. (2011). Towards a research agenda for social work practice in virtual worlds. *Advances in Social Work, 12*(2), 289–300.

Apple, Inc. (2016). *iCloud: Erase your device*. Retrieved from https://support.apple.com/kb/ph2701?locale=en_US

Apple, Inc. (2017a). *Compare Mac models*. Retrieved from http://www.apple.com/mac/compare/

Apple, Inc. (2017b). *GarageBand for Mac*. Retrieved from http://www.apple.com/mac/garageband

Association of Social Work Boards. (2015). *Model regulatory standards for technology and social work practice*. Retrieved from https://www.aswb.org/wp-content/uploads/2015/03/ASWB-Model-Regulatory-Standards-for-Technology-and-Social-Work-Practice.pdf

Atabakhsh, H., Larson, C., Petersen, T., Violette, C., & Chen, H. (2004). Information sharing and collaboration policies within government agencies. In *International Conference on Intelligence and Security Informatics* (pp. 467–475). Berlin Heidelberg: Springer.

Atkinson, N. S., Saperstein, S. L., & Pleis, J. (2009). Using the Internet for health-related activities: Findings from a national probability sample. *Journal of Medical Internet Research, 11*(1), e4. Retrieved from http://doi.org/10.2196/jmir.1035

Auslander, G. K., & Cohen, M. E. (1992). Issues in the development of social work information systems: The case of hospital social work departments. *Administration in Social Work, 16*(2), 73–88.

Axelsson, A. (2002). The digital divide: Status differences in virtual environments. In R. Schroeder (Ed.), *The social life of avatars: Presence and interaction in shared virtual environments* (pp. 188–204). London, UK: Springer-Verlag.

Baggett, K. M., Davis, B., Feil, E. G., Sheeber, L. L., Landry, S. H., Carta, J. J., & Leve, C. (2010). Technologies for expanding the reach of evidence-based interventions: Preliminary results for promoting social-emotional development in early childhood. *Topics in Early Childhood Special Education, 29*, 226–238.

Bajaj, A., & Ram, S. (2003). IAIS: A methodology to enable inter-agency information sharing in eGovernment. *Journal of Database Management, 14*(4), 59.

Bakardjieva, M., & Feenberg, A. (2002). Community technology and democratic rationalization. *The Information Society, 18*(3), 181–192.

Baker, F., Wigram, T., Stott, D., & McFerran, K. (2008). Therapeutic songwriting in music therapy. Part I: Who are the therapists, who are the clients, and why is songwriting used? *Nordic Journal of Music Therapy, 17*, 105–123.

Baker, S., & Homan, S. (2007). Rap, recidivism and the creative self: A popular music programme for young offenders in detention. *Journal of Youth Studies, 10*, 459–476.

Bambina, A. D. (2007). *Online social support: The interplay of social networks and computer-mediated communication.* New York, NY: Cambria Press.

Bardone-Cone, A., Harney, M. B., Maldonado, C. R., Lawson, M. A., Robinson, P., Smith, R., & Tosh, A. (2010). Defining recovery from an eating disorder: Conceptualization, validation, and examination of psychosocial functioning and psychiatric comorbidity. *Behavioural Research and Therapy, 48*, 194–202.

Bargh, J. A., McKenna, K. Y.A., & Fitzsimmons, G. M. (2002). Can you see the real me? Activation and expression of the "true self" on the Internet. *Journal of Social Issues, 58*(1), 33–48.

Barnes, N. G., & Mattson, E. (2008). *Still setting the pace in social media: The first longitudinal study of usage by the largest US charities.* University of Massachusetts Dartmouth Center for Marketing Research.

Barsky, A. E. (2016). The ethics of app-assisted family mediation. *Conflict Resolution Quarterly, 34*(1), 31–42.

Barsky, A. E. (2017). Social work practice and technology: Ethical issues and policy responses. *Journal of Technology in Human Services, 35*(1), 8–19.

Barth, R. (1990). On their own: The experiences of youth after foster care. *Child and Adolescent Social Work, 7*, 419–440.

Bartholomew, M. K., Schoppe-Sullivan, S. J., Glassman, M., Kamp Dush, C. M., & Sullivan, J. (2012). New parents' Facebook use at the transition to parenthood. *Family Relations, 61*, 455–469. doi:10.1111/j.1741-3729.2012.00708.x

Battista-Frazee, K. (2015). *Your social work brand*. Retrieved July 2, 2016, from http://www.socialworker.com/feature-articles/your-social-work-brand

Battle, M., (2015, November 16). Estero resident poll shows satisfaction—and some concern. *Naples Daily News*. Retrieved from http://archive.naplesnews.com/news/government/estero-resident-poll-shows-satisfaction---and-some-concern-24b25d0d-dee9-6cdf-e053-0100007f324a-350782571.html

Bausch, P., Haughey, M., & Hourihan, M. (2002). Using blogs in business. We blog: Publishing online with weblogs, John Willey & Sons.

Bauer, S., Percevic, R., Okon, E., Meermann, R., & Kordy, H. (2003). Use of text messaging in the aftercare of patients with bulimia nervosa. *European Eating Disorders Review, 11*, 279–290.

Baumgarten, J. and Chui, M. (2009). *E-government 2.0. McKinsey Quarterly, 4*(2), 26–31. Retrieved from http://www.mckinsey.com/industries/public-sector/our-insights/e-government-20

Bayley, J., Wallace, L. M., & Choudhry, K. (2009). Fathers and parenting programmes: Barriers and best practice. *Community Practice, 82*, 28–31.

Bean, K. F., & Krcek, T. E., (2012). The integration of disability content into social work education: An examination of infused and dedicated models. *Advances in Social Work, 13*, 633–647.

Beer, S. (1985). *Diagnosing the system for organizations*. New York: John Wiley.

Bell A. P. (2014). Trial-by-fire: A case study of the musician–engineer hybrid role in the home studio. *Journal of Music, Technology and Education, 7*(3).

Bellamy, C., & Raab, C. (2005). Joined-up government and privacy in the United Kingdom: Managing tensions between data protection and social policy. Part II. *Public Administration, 83*, 393–415.

Benbenishty, R., & Oyserman, D. (1991). A clinical information system for foster care in Israel. *Child Welfare, 70*, 229–242.

Benbenishty, R., & Oyserman, D. (1995). Integrated information systems for human services: A conceptual framework, methodology and technology. *Computers in Human Services, 12*, 311–326.

Benbenishty, R., & Treistman, R. (1998). The development and evaluation of a hybrid decision support system for clinical decision making: The case of discharge from the military. *Social Work Research, 22*, 195–204.

Benford, S., Greenhalgh, C., Rodden, T., & Pycock, J. (2001). Collaborative virtual environments. *Communications of the ACM, 44*(7), 79–85.

Berzin, S. C., Singer, J., & Chan, C. (2015). *Practice innovation through technology in the digital age: A grand challenge for social work*. Working Paper No. 12, Grand Challenges for Social Work Initiative. Retrieved from http://aaswsw.org/wp-content/uploads/2013/10/Practice-Innovation-through-Technology-in-the-Digital-Age-A-Grand-Challenge-for-Social-Work-GC-Working-Paper-No-12.pdf

Bizer, C., Heath, T., & Berners-Lee, T. (2009). Linked data—the story so far. *International Journal on Semantic Web and Information Systems, 5*(3), 1–22.

Blanchard, A. L. (2004) Blogs as virtual communities: Identifying a sense of community in the Julie/Julia Project. In L. J. Gurak, S. Antonijevic, L. Johnson, C. Ratliff, and J. Reyman (Eds.), *Into the Blogosphere: Rhetoric, Community, and Culture of Weblogs*. Consulted March 2006, http://blog.lib.umn.edu/blogosphere/ blogs_as_virtual.html

Blanchard, A. L., & Horan, T. (1998). Social capital and virtual communities. *Social Science Computer Review, 16*(3), 293-307.

Blatt, A. (2012). Ethics and privacy issues in the use of GIS. *Journal of Map and Geography Libraries, 8*(1), 80-84.

Blau, I., & Caspi, A. (2010). Studying invisibly: Media naturalness and learning. In N. Kock (Ed.), *Evolutionary psychology and information systems research* (Vol. 24, pp. 193-216). Boston, MA: Springer US. Retrieved from http://link.springer.com/10.1007/978-1-4419-6139-6_9

Blood, R. (2000). Weblogs: A history and perspective. *Rebecca's Pocket, 7*(9), 2000.

Bloom, B. S. (1956). *Taxonomy of Educational Objectives, Handbook I: The Cognitive Domain.* New York, NY: David McKay.

Bloomfield, B. P., & McLean, C. (2003). Beyond the walls of the asylum: Information and organization in the provision of community mental health services. *Information and Organization, 13*(1), 53-84.

Boddy, J., & Dominelli, L. (2016). Social media and social work: The challenges of a new ethical space. *Australian Social Work, 70*(2), 172-184. https://doi.org/10.1080/0312407X.2016.1224907

Bogle, A. (2016). *Too many mental health apps put style over substance.* Retrieved from http://mashable.com/2016/11/30/mental-health-apps-little-evidence/ - HK.kexhvamq8

Boostrom, R. (2008). The social construction of virtual reality and the stigmatized identity of the newbie. *Journal of Virtual Worlds Research, 1*(2), 2-19.

Booth, C. (Ed.). (1902). *Life and labour of the people in London* (Vol. 1). London: Macmillan.

Boyd, D., & Ellison, N. B. (2007). Social network sites: Definition, history, and scholarship. *Journal of Computer-Mediated Communication, 13,* 210-230.

Boydell, K. M., Gladstone, B. M., Volpe, T., Allemang, B., & Stasiulis, E. (2012). The production and dissemination of knowledge: A scoping review of arts-based health research. *Forum Qualitative Sozialforschung/Forum: Qualitative Social Research, 13*(1), Art. 32.

Boydell, K. M., Pignatiello, A., Teshima, J., Hodgins, M., Willis, D., & Edwards, H. (2014). Using technology to deliver mental health services to children and youth: A scoping review. *Journal of the Canadian Academy of Child and Adolescent Psychiatry, 23*(2), 87-99.

Brabham, D. C., Ribisl, K. M., Kirchner, T. R., & Bernhardt, J. M. (2014). Crowdsourcing applications for public health. *American Journal of Preventive Medicine, 46*(2), 179-187.

Brady, S. R., McLeod, D. A., & Young, J. A. (2015). Developing ethical guidelines for creating social media technology policy in social work classrooms. *Advances in Social Work, 16*(1), 43-54.

Breslau, J., Aharoni, E., Pedersen, E.R., & Miller, L. L. (2015). A review of research on problematic Internet usage and well-being with recommendations for the U. S. Air Force. Retrieved July 1, 2016, from http://www.rand.org/pubs/research_reports/RR849.html

Briant, K. J., Halter, A., Marchello, N., Escareño, M., & Thompson, B. (2016). The power of digital storytelling as a culturally relevant health promotion tool. *Health Promotion Practice, 17*(6), 793-801. Retrieved from https://doi.org/10.1177/1524839916658023

Brock, A. (2007). 'A belief in humanity is a belief in colored men': Using culture to span the digital divide. *Journal of Computer Mediated Communication, 11,* 357-374.

Bromwich. (2015, August 2). A social network app for those battling addiction. *New York Times.* Retrieved from http://www.nytimes.com/2015/08/02/nyregion/a-social-network-app-for-those-battling-addiction.html?_r=0

Browning, D. (2012, May). Why cell phones are bad for parenting. *TIME*. Retrieved from http://ideas.time.com/2012/05/17/why-cell-phones-are-bad-for-parenting/

Bruns, A., & Stieglitz, S. (2012). Quantitative approaches to comparing communication patterns on Twitter. *Journal of Technology in Human Services, 30*, 160–185. https://doi.org/10.1080/15228835.2012.744249

BuiltWith. (2016, July). *Google Maps API usage statistics.* Retrieved from http://trends.builtwith.com/mapping/Google-Maps-API

Buquoi, B., McClure, C., Kotrlik, J. W., Machtmes, K., & Bunch, J. C. (2013). A national research survey of technology use in the BSW teaching and learning process. *Journal of Teaching in Social Work, 33*, 481–495.

Bureau of Labor Statistics. (2016, April 28). *College enrollment and work activity of 2015 high school graduates.* Report number USDL-16-0822. Retrieved from https://www.bls.gov/news.release/hsgec.nro.htm

Burg, J., Romney, J., & Schwartz, E. (2016). *Digital sound and music: Concepts, applications, and science.* Portland, OR: Franklin, Beedle & Associates.

Burns, M. N., Begale, M., Duffecy, J., Gergle, D., Karr, C. J., Giangrande, E., & Mohr, D. C. (2011). Harnessing context sensing to develop a mobile intervention for depression. *Journal of Medical Internet Research, 13*(3), e55. doi:10.2196/jmir.1838

Burton, J., & Van den Broek, D. (2009). Accountable and countable: Information management systems and the bureaucratization of social work. *British Journal of Social Work, 39*, 1326–1342.

Byrd, T. A., Cossick, K. L., & Zmud, R. W. (1992). A synthesis of research on requirements analysis and knowledge acquisition techniques. *MIS Quarterly, 16*(1), 117–138.

Cacioppo, J. T., Cacioppo, S., Gonzaga, G. C., Ogburn, E. L., & VanderWeele, T. J. (2013). Marital satisfaction and break-ups differ across on-line and off-line meeting venues. *Proceedings of the National Academy of Sciences, 110*, 10135–10140. http://doi.org/10.1073/pnas.1222447110

Canestraro, D. S., Pardo, T. A., Raup-Kounovsky, A. N., & Taratus, D. (2009). Regional telecommunication incident coordination: Sharing information for rapid response. *Information Polity, 14*, 113–126.

Carr, D. (2009). *Technology, inclusion and social practices in virtual worlds, a draft paper.* Retrieved March 18, 2017, from https://learningfromsocialworlds.wordpress.com/2009/05/26/draft-paper-voice-and-deaf-residents-in-sl/

Carr, N. (2011). *The shallows: What the Internet is doing to our brains.* New York, NY: W. W. Norton & Company.

Carta, J. J., Lefever, J. B., Bigelow, K., Borkowski, J., & Warren, S. F. (2013). Randomized trial of a cellular phone-enhanced home visitation parenting intervention. *Pediatrics, 132*, S167–S173 doi:10.1542/peds.2013-1021Q

Carter, A., Liddle, J., Hall, W., & Chenery, H. (2015). Mobile phones in research and treatment: Ethical guidelines and future directions *JMIR mHealth and uHealth, 3*(4), e95. doi:10.2196/mhealth.4538

Casey, B. J., Jones, R. M., & Hare, T. A. (2008). The adolescent brain. *Annals of the New York Academy of Sciences, 1124*, 111–126.

Center on Budget and Policy Priorities. (2015, November 17). *Policy futures: Chart book: Accomplishments of the safety net.* Retrieved from http://www.cbpp.org/research/poverty-and-inequality/chart-book-accomplishments-of-the-safety-net

Center on Budget and Policy Priorities. (2016, March 4). *Policy basics: Where do our federal tax dollars go?* Retrieved from www.cbpp.org/research/federal-budget/policy-basics-where-do-our-federal-tax-dollars-go

Chang, B. L., Bakken, S., Brown, S. S., Houston, T. K., Kreps, G. L., Kukafka, R., . . . Stavri, P. Z. (2013). Bridging the digital divide: Reaching vulnerable populations. *Journal of the American Medical Informatics Association, 11,* 448–457.

Chang, E., Park, K., & Choi, Y. (2016). Models and application of firefighting vulnerability. *Procedia—Social and Behavioral Sciences, 218,* 152–160.

Chapman, C. (2011). *A brief history of blogging.* Webdesigner Depot. Retrieved from https://www.webdesignerdepot.com/2011/03/a-brief-history-of-blogging/

Charara, S. (2016). Virtual worlds reborn: Can Second Life's second life democratize VR? *Wareable.* Retrieved July 1, 2016, from http://www.wareable.com/vr/second-life-project-sansar-beta-2016

Chau, M., Atabakhsh, H., Zeng, D., & Chen, H. (2001). Building an infrastructure for law enforcement information sharing and collaboration: Design issues and challenges. In *Proceedings of The National Conference on Digital Government Research.*

Checkland, P. (1999). *Soft systems methodology in action.* New York, NY: John Wiley & Sons.

Chen, Z., Gangopadhyay, A., Holden, S. H., Karabatis, G., & McGuire, M. P. (2007). Semantic integration of government data for water quality management. *Government Information Quarterly, 24*(4), 716–735.

Chen, Y.-L., Rittner, B., Manning, A., & Crofford, R. (2015). Early onset schizophrenia and school social work. *Journal of Social Work Practice, 29,* 271–286. https://doi.org/10.1080/02650533.2015.1014328

Chou, W. H., Hunt, Y. M., Beckjord, B. E., Moser, R. P., & Hesse, B. W. (2009). Social media use in the United States: Implications for health communication. *Journal of Medical Internet Research, 11*(4), 1–13.

Chrisman, N. (2006). *Charting the unknown: How computer mapping at Harvard became GIS.* Redlands, CA: ESRI Press.

Christenson, P. G., & Roberts, D. F. (1998). It's not only rock & roll: Popular music in the lives of adolescents. *Journal of Communication, 49,* 212–229.

Chun, Shulman, Sandoval, and Hovy. *Government 2.0.*

Churches, A. (2009). *Bloom's digital taxonomy.* Retrieved June, 2009, from http://edorigami.wikispaces.com/Bloom%27s-(-Digital+Taxonomy

Cihak, D., Fahrenkrog, C., Ayre, K. M., & Smith, C. (2010). The use of video modeling via a video iPod and a system of least prompts to improve transitional behaviors for students with autism spectrum disorders in the general education classroom. *Journal of Positive Behavior Interventions, 12,* 103–115.

Cnaan, R. A., & Parsloe, P. (1989). *The impact of information technology on social work practice.* New York, NY: Haworth Press.

Cobb, S. (1976). Social support as a moderator of life stress. *Psychosomatic Medicine, 38,* 300–314.

Cohn, A. M., Hunter-Reel, D., Hagman, B. T., & Mitchell, J. (2011). Promoting behavior change from alcohol use through mobile technology: The future of ecological momentary assessment. *Alcoholism: Clinical and Experimental Research, 35,* 2209–2215. doi:10.1111/j.1530-0277.2011.01571.x

Collier Senior Resources (CSR). (2016, October). *About us: History*. Retrieved from http://www.collierseniorresources.org/about/history/

Connor, D. J., & Gabel, S. L. (2010). Welcoming the unwelcome: Disability and diversity. In T. K. Chapman & N. Hobbel (Eds.), *Social justice pedagogy across the curriculum* (201–220). New York: Routledge.

Coulton, C. J., Goerge, R., Putnam-Hornstein, E., & de Haan, B. (2015). Harnessing big data for social good: A grand challenge for social work. American Academy of Social Work and Social Welfare, Paper No. 11.

Cook, N., & Winkler, S. L. (2016). Acceptance, usability and health applications of virtual worlds by older adults: A feasibility study. *JMIR Research Protocols, 1*(2). Retrieved July 1, 2016, from http://www.ncbi.nlm.nih.gov/pmc/articles/PMC4911513/

Coulton, C. (2005). The place of community in social work practice research: Conceptual and methodological developments. *Social Work Research, 29*(2), 73–86.

Council on Social Work Education. (2001). *Educational policy and accreditation standards*. Retrieved from https://www.cswe.org/Kentico82/getattachment/Accreditation/Candidacy/Candidacy-2001/2001EducationalPolicyandAccreditationStandards10-2004.pdf.aspx

Council on Social Work Education. (2008). *Educational policy and accreditation standards*. Retrieved from https://www.cswe.org/getattachment/Accreditation/Standards-and-Policies/2008-EPAS/2008EDUCATIONALPOLICYANDACCREDITATIONSTANDARDS(EPAS)-08-24-2012.pdf.aspx

Council on Social Work Education. (2015). *2015 educational policy and accreditation standards for baccalaureate and master's social work programs*. Retrieved from https://www.cswe.org/getattachment/Accreditation/Accreditation-Process/2015-EPAS/2015EPAS_Web_FINAL.pdf.aspx

Coursen, D., & Ferns, B. (2004). Modeling participant flows in human service programs. *Journal of Technology in Human Services, 22*(4), 55–71.

Courtney, M., Dworsky, A., Brown, A., Cary, C., Love, K., & Vorhies, V. (2011). *Midwest evaluation of the adult functioning of former foster youth: Outcomes at age 26*. Chapin Hall at the University of Chicago. Retrieved from http://www.chapinhall.org/sites/default/files/Midwest%20Evaluation_Report_4_10_12.pdf

Coyne, I., Chesney, T., Logan, B., & Madden, N. (2009). Griefing in a virtual community: An exploratory survey of Second Life residents. *Zeitschrift für Psychologie/Journal of Psychology, 217,* 214–221.

Crawford, E. A., Salloum, A., Andel, R., Murphy, T. K., & Storch, E. A. (2013). A pilot study of computer-assisted cognitive behavioral therapy for childhood anxiety in community mental health centers. *Journal of Cognitive Psychotherapy: An International Quarterly, 27,* 221–234. doi:10.1891/0889-8391.27.3.221

Crunkilton, D. D. (2009). Staff and client perspectives on the Journey Mapping online evaluation tool in a drug court program. *Evaluation and Program Planning, 32,* 119–128. doi:10.1016/j.evalprogplan.2008.11.001

Csiernik, R., Furze, P., Dromgole, L., & Rishchynski, G. M. (2006). Information technology and social work—The dark side or light side?. *Journal of Evidence-Based Social Work, 3*(3–4), 9–25.

Cueva, M., Kuhnley, R., Revels, L., Schoenberg, N. E., & Dignan, M. (2015). Digital storytelling: A tool for health promotion and cancer awareness in rural Alaskan communities. *International Journal of Circumpolar Health, 74,* 28781.

Culhane, D. P., Fantuzzo, J., Rouse, H. L., Tam, V., & Lukens, J. (2010). *Connecting the dots: The promise of integrated data systems for policy analysis and systems reform.* Philadelphia, PA: Actionable Intelligence for Social Policy.

Cummings, J. J., & Bailenson, J. N. (2016). How immersive is enough? A meta-analysis of the effect of immersive technology on user presence. *Media Psychology, 19*(2), 272–309.

Cummings, S. M., Chaffin, K. M., & Cockerham, C. (2015). Comparative analysis of an online and a traditional MSW program: Educational outcomes. *Journal of Social Work Education, 51,* 109–120. https://doi.org/10.1080/10437797.2015.977170

Curtis, A., Mills, J. W., & Leitner, M. (2006). Keeping an eye on privacy issues with geospatial data. *Nature, 441,* 150–161.

Dabbagh, N., & Kitsantas, A. (2012). Personal learning environments, social media, and self-regulated learning: A natural formula for connecting formal and informal learning. *The Internet and Higher Education, 15*(1), 3–8. https://doi.org/10.1016/j.iheduc.2011.06.002

Dalton, T. A., & Krout, R. E. (2005). Development of the grief process scale through music therapy songwriting with bereaved adolescents. *The Arts in Psychotherapy, 32,* 131–143.

Danielson, C. K., McCauley, J. L., Jones, A. M., Borkman, A. L., Miller, S., & Ruggiero, K. J. (2013). Feasibility of delivering evidence-based HIV/STI prevention programming to a community sample of African-American teen girls via the Internet. *AIDS Education and Prevention, 25,* 394–404.

Dare, T. (2013). *Predictive risk modelling and child maltreatment: Ethical challenges.* Children in Crisis. Hamilton: University of Waikato.

Davidson, L., Chinman, M., Sells, D., & Rowe, M. (2006). Peer support among adults with serious mental illness: A report from the field. *Schizophrenia Bulletin, 32,* 443–450.

Davis, R. (2006). *College access, financial aid, and college success for undergraduates from foster care. Report by the National Association of Student Financial Aid Administrators.* Retrieved from http://files.eric.ed.gov/fulltext/ED543361.pdf

Dawes, S. (2008). The evolution and continuing challenges of e-governance. *Public Administration Review, 68,* S5–S198.

Dawes, S. S. (1996). Interagency information sharing: Expected benefits, manageable risks. *Journal of Policy Analysis and Management, 15*(3), 377–394.

Day, A., Dworsky, A., Fogarty, K., & Damashek, A. (2011). An examination of postsecondary retention and graduation among foster care youth enrolled in a four-year university. *Children and Youth Services Review, 33,* 2335–2341.

Day, A., Riebschleger, J., Dworsky, A., Damashek, A., & Fogarty, K. (2012). Maximizing educational opportunities for youth aging out of foster care by engaging youth voices in a partnership for social change. *Children and Youth Services Review, 34,* 1007–1014.

Dearman, P. (2005). Computerized social casework recording: Autonomy and control in Australia's income support agency. *Labor Studies Journal, 30*(1), 47–65.

Dempsey, C. (2012). *History of GIS.* Retrieved from https://www.gislounge.com/history-of-gis/

DeHart, D., & Shapiro, C. (2016). Integrated administrative data & criminal justice research. *American Journal of Criminal Justice,* 1–20.

Depp, C. A., Mausbach, B., Granholm, E., Cardenas, V., Ben-Zeev, D., Patterson, T. L., . . . Jeste, D. V. (2010). Mobile interventions for severe mental illness: Design and preliminary data from three approaches. *Journal of Nervous and Mental Disease, 198,* 715–721. doi:10.1097/NMD.0b013e3181f49ea3

Desilver, D. (2013, May 20). *5 facts about Tumblr.* Pew Internet Report. Retrieved from http://www.pewresearch.org/fact-tank/2013/05/20/5-facts-about-tumblr/

Dewey, C. (2014, October 30). A complete history of the rise and fall—and reincarnation!—of the beloved '90s chatroom. *The Washington Post.* Retrieved from https://www.washingtonpost.com/news/the-intersect/wp/2014/10/30/a-complete-history-of-the-rise-and-fall-and-reincarnation-of-the-beloved-90s-chatroom/

Didehbani, N., Allen, T., Kandalaft, M., Krawczyk, D., & Chapman, S. (2016). Virtual reality social cognition training for children with high functioning autism. *Computers in Human Behavior, 62,* 703–711.

DiMicco, J. M. (2008). Motivations for social networking at work. *Proceedings of the 2008 ACM conference on Computer supported cooperative work* (pp. 711–720). San Diego: ACM.

Drezner, D. W. (2008). So You Want to Blog. . . . *APSA Guide to Publication.* (American Political Science Association, 2008. Retrieved January 1, 2009, from http://danieldrezner.com/research/APSAblogchapter. pdf

Dyson, F. J., Hansma, P. K., Roof, W. C., & Proctor, J. D. (2001). *Technology and social justice.* Irvine, CA: UCTV, Instructional Resources, University of California.

Eapen, Z. J., & Peterson, E. D. (2015). Can mobile health applications facilitate meaningful behavior change? Time for answers. *Journal of American Medical Association, 314,* 1236–1237.

Ecotec Research and Consulting. (2005). *Access, participation and progression in the arts for young people on Detention and Training Orders.* http://www.artscouncil.org.uk/media/uploads/documents/publications/detentionandtrainingorderspdf_phpIVpLCa.pdf.

Efimova, L., & Grudin, J. (2007). Crossing boundaries: A case study of employee blogging. In *Proceedings of the fortieth Hawaii international conference on system sciences (HICSS-40).* Los Alamitos: IEEE Press.

Eilam, M. (2012, May 25). *The shapes of stories, a Kurt Vonnegut infographic.* Retrieved July 18, 2016, from http://www.mayaeilam.com/2012/01/01/the-shapes-of-stories-a-kurt-vonnegut-infographic/

El-Atrash, A. (2016). Implications of the Segregation Wall on the two-state solution. *Journal of Borderlands Studies, 31*(3), 1–16.

Ellison, N. B., Steinfield, C., & Lampe, C. (2007). The benefits of Facebook "friends": Social capital and college students' use of online social network sites. *Journal of Computer-Mediated Communication, 12,* 1143–1168.

Emerson, J. (2015). *Supporting success: Improving higher education outcomes for students from foster care.* Casey Family Foundation Report. Retrieved from http://www.casey.org/Resources/Publications/HigherEdFramework.htm

Environmental Sciences Research Institute (ESRI). (2010). *Geocoding tutorial.* Retrieved from http://help.arcgis.com/en/arcgisdesktop/10.0/pdf/geocoding-tutorial.pdf

Environmental Sciences Research Institute (ESRI). (2010, August 18). *What is geocoding?* Retrieved from http://help.arcgis.com/en/arcgisdesktop/10.0/help/index.html#//00250000000100000.htm

Environmental Sciences Research Institute (ESRI). (2011). ArcGIS (Version 10.1) [Software]. Retrieved from https://www.esri.com/en-us/arcgis/products/index

Environmental Sciences Research Institute (ESRI). (2012a, April 4). *Buffer (analysis)*. Retrieved from http://help.arcgis.com/en/arcgisdesktop/10.0/help/index.html#// 000800000019000000 ESRI.

Environmental Systems Research Institute (ESRI). (2012b). *ArcGIS for desktop* (Version 10.1) [Software]. Retrieved from http://www.esri.com/software/arcgis/arcgis-for-desktop

Environmental Systems Research Institute (ESRI). (2013). *The language of spatial analysis*. Redlands, CA: Esri Press.

Epstein, I. (1977). *Research techniques for program planning, monitoring, and evaluation*. New York, NY: Columbia University Press.

Epstein, I. (2001). Using available clinical information in practice-based research: Mining for silver while dreaming of gold. *Social Work in Health Care, 33*(3–4), 15–32. doi:10.1300/ J010v33n03_03

Eubanks, V. (2011). *Digital dead end: Fighting for social justice in the information age*. MIT Press.

Evans, A. F., & Evans, R. A. (2001). Using case studies in urban theological education. In E. Villafañe, B. W. Jackson, R. A. Evans, & A. F. Evans (Eds.), *Transforming the city: Reframing education for urban ministry* (pp. 30–35). Grand Rapids, MI: Eerdmans.

Evans, W. D., Wallace, J. L., & Snider, J. (2012). Pilot evaluation of the text4baby mobile health program. *BMC Public Health, 12*(1), 1031–1041.

Ezell, M., & Levy, M. (2003). An evaluation of an arts program for incarcerated juvenile offenders. *Journal of Correctional Education, 54*(3), 108–114. Retrieved from http://www. jstor.org/stable/41971150

Farrell, H., & Drezner, D. W. (2008). The power and politics of blogs. *Public Choice, 134*(1–2), 15.

Fazel, S., Bains, P., & Doll, H. (2006). Substance abuse and dependence in prisoners: A systematic review. *Addiction, 101*, 181–191.

Feldman, M. B., & Meyer, I. H. (2007). Eating disorders in diverse lesbian, gay, and bisexual populations. *International Journal of Eating Disorders, 40*(3), 218–226.

Felke, T.P. (2014). Building capacity for the use of geographic information systems in social work planning, practice, and research. *Journal of Technology in Human Services, 32*(1–2), 81–92.

Fedock, G., Klein, S., Litt, J., & Kapnick, K. (2015). *Using Geographic Information Systems (GIS) to teach social work*. Paper presented at the Society for Social Work and Research Conference, New Orleans, LA. Retrieved from https://sswr.confex.com/sswr/2015/ webprogram/Paper22953.html

Fedorowicz, J., Gogan, J. L., & Williams, C. B. (2007). A collaborative network for first responders: Lessons from the CapWIN case. *Government Information Quarterly, 24*, 785–807.

Fernandez-Lopez, A., Rodriguez-Fortiz, M. J., Rodriguez-Almendros, M. L., & Martinez-Segura, M. J. (2013). Mobile learning technology based on iOS devices to support students with special education needs. *Computers and Education, 61*, 77–90.

Field, T., Martinez, A., Nawrocki, T., Pickens, J., Fox, N. A., & Schanberg, S. (1998). Music shifts frontal EEG in depressed adolescents. *Adolescence, 33*, 109–116.

Fildes, J. (2008, June 17). *"Oldest" computer music unveiled*. Retrieved January 11, 2017, from http://news.bbc.co.uk/2/hi/technology/7458479.stm

Fitch, D. (2005). The diffusion of information technology in the human services: Implications for social work education. *Journal of Teaching in Social Work, 25,* 191–204.

Fitch, D. (2007). Designing databases around decision making. In M. Cortes & K. Rafter (Eds.), *Nonprofits and technology: Emerging research for usable knowledge* (pp 135–147). Chicago, IL: Lyceum.

Fitch, D. (2010). Homeless management information system customization intervention. *Journal of Human Behavior in the Social Environment, 20,* 255–271.

Fitch, D., & Shaffer, J. (2007). An alternative database table design. *Journal of Technology in Human Services, 25*(3), 57–79.

Fjeldsoe, B. S., Marshall, A. L., & Miller, Y. D. (2009). Behavior change interventions delivered by mobile telephone short-message service. *American Journal of Preventive Medicine, 36,* 165–173.

Ford, P. J. (2001). Paralysis Lost: Impacts of virtual worlds on those with paralysis. *Social Theory and Practice, 27,* 661–680.

Foster, K. A., & Hipp, J. A. (2011). Defining neighborhood boundaries for social measurement: Advancing social work research. *Social Work Research, 35*(1), 25–35.

Fowler, J. (2016, May 11). GIS is the amazing, but often overlooked software for nonprofits! [web log post]. Retrieved from http://blog.roktech.net/blog/software-for-nonprofits

Fox, S., & Rainie, L. (2014). *The Web at 25.* Pew Research Center. Retrieved from http://www.pewinternet.org/2014/02/25/the-web-at-25-in-the-u-s

Franklin, V. L., Waller, A., Pagliari, C., & Greene, S. (2003). "Sweet Talk": Text messaging support for intensive insulin therapy for young people with diabetes. *Diabetes Technology and Therapeutics, 5,* 991–996.

Franklin, V. L., Waller, A., Pagliari, C., & Greene, S. A. (2006). A randomized controlled trial of Sweet Talk, a text-messaging system to support young people with diabetes. *Diabetic Medicine, 23,* 1332–1338. doi:10.1111/j.1464-5491.2006.01989.x

Freel, C., & Epstein, I. (1993). Principles for using management information data for programmatic decision making. *Child and Youth Services, 16*(1), 77–93. doi:10.1300/J024V16N01_05

Future Music. (2011). A brief history of GarageBand. Retrieved January 11, 2017, from http://www.musicradar.com/tuition/tech/a-brief-history-of-garageband-400471

Gabriel, D. (2016). Blogging while Black, British and female: A critical study on discursive activism. *Information, Communication and Society, 19,* 1622–1635.

Gal, N., Shifman, L., & Kampf, Z. (2016). "It Gets Better": Internet memes and the construction of collective identity. *New Media and Society, 18,* 1698–1714. https://doi.org/10.1177/1461444814568784

Gallo, C. (2016, September 22). *The digital evangelist leading Google's storytelling movement.* Retrieved September 24, 2016, from http://www.forbes.com/sites/carminegallo/2016/09/22/the-digital-evangelist-leading-googles-storytelling-movement/

Gambrill, E. (2008a). Evidence-based (informed) macro practice: Process and philosophy. *Journal of Evidence-Based Social Work, 5,* 423–452.

Gambrill, E. (2008b). Informed consent: Options and challenges. In M. C. Calder (Ed.), *The Carrot or the Stick* (pp. 37–55). Lyme Regis, England: Russell House Publishing.

Gangadharan, S. (2015). *The danger of high tech profiling using big data.* Retrieved April 23, 2017, from https://www.nytimes.com/roomfordebate/2014/08/06/is-big-data-spreading-inequality/the-dangers-of-high-tech-profiling-using-big-data

Gao, F., Luo, T., & Zhang, K. (2012). Tweeting for learning: A critical analysis of research on microblogging in education published in 2008–2011. *British Journal of Educational Technology, 43,* 783–801. doi: 10.1111/j.1467-8535.2012.01357.x

Gatica-Rojas, V., & Méndez-Rebolledo, G. (2014). Virtual reality interface devices in the reorganization of neural networks in the brain of patients with neurological diseases. *Neural Regeneration Research, 9,* 888.

Gazmararian, J. A., Elon, L., Yang, B., Graham, M., & Parker, R. (2013). Text4baby program: An opportunity to reach underserved pregnant and postpartum women? *Maternal and Child Health Journal, 18*(1), 223–232.

Geiss, G. R., & Viswanathan, N. (1986). *Human edge: Information technology and helping people.* New York, NY: Haworth Press.

Gelman, C. R., & Tosone, C. (2010). Teaching social workers to harness technology and inter-disciplinary collaboration for community service. *British Journal of Social Work, 40,* 226–238. https://doi.org/10.1093/bjsw/bcn081

Giedd, J. N., Blumenthal, J., Jeffries, N. O., Castellanos, F. X., Liu, H., Zijdenbos, A., & Rapoport, J. L. (1999). Brain development during childhood and adolescence: A longitudinal MRI study. *Nature Neuroscience, 2,* 861–863.

Giffords, E. (2009). The Internet and social work: The next generation. *Families in Society: The Journal of Contemporary Social Services, 90,* 413–418.

Gilbert, R. L., Murphy, N. A., Krueger, A. B., Ludwig, A. R., & Efron, T. Y. (2013). Psychological benefits of participation in three-dimensional virtual worlds for individuals with real-world disabilities. *International Journal of Disability, Development and Education, 60,* 208–224.

Gil de Zúñiga, H., Puig-i-Abril, E., & Rojas, H. (2009). Weblogs, traditional sources online and political participation: An assessment of how the Internet is changing the political environment. *New Media & Society, 11*(4), 553–574.

Gil-García, J. R., & Pardo, T. A. (2005). E-government success factors: Mapping practical tools to theoretical foundations. *Government Information Quarterly, 22,* 187–216.

Gillingham, P. (2011). Computer-based information systems and human service organizations: Emerging problems and future possibilities. *Australian Social Work, 64,* 299–312.

Gillingham, P. (2014). Repositioning electronic information systems in human service organizations. *Human Service Organizations: Management, Leadership and Governance, 38,* 125–134.

Ginossar, T., & Nelson, S. (2010). Reducing the health and digital divide: A model for using community-based participatory research approach to e-health interventions in low-income Hispanic communities. *Journal of Computer-Mediated Communication, 15,* 530–551.

Giota, K. G., & Kleftaras, G. (2014). Mental health apps: Innovations, risks, and ethical considerations. *E-Health Telecommunication Systems and Networks, 3,* 19–23. doi:10.4236/etsn.2014.33003

GISGeography. (2016, July 23). *Mapping out the GIS software landscape.* Retrieved from http://gisgeography.com/mapping-out-gis-software-landscape/

Gjesfjeld, C. D. & Jung, J. K. (2011). How far?: Using geographical information systems (GIS) to examine maternity care access for expectant mothers in a rural state. *Social work health care, 50*(9), 682–693.

Glastonbury, B. (1993). *Human welfare and technology.* Netherlands: Van Gorcum.

Glastonbury, B. (1996). *Dreams and realities.* Helsinki: Stakes.

Glastonbury, B., LaMendola, W., & Toole, S. (Eds.). (1988). *Information technology and the human services.* London: John Wiley & Sons.

GO-Globe. (2015, May). *Mobile apps usage: Statistics and trends.* Retrieved from http://www.go-globe.com/blog/mobile-apps-usage/

Gold, C., Wigram, T., & Elefant, C. (2006). Music therapy for autistic spectrum disorder. *Cochrane Database of Systematic Reviews, 2006*(2). Art. No.: CD004381. doi: 10.1002/14651858.CD004381.pub2.

Golder, S. A., & Donath, J. (2004). Social roles in electronic communities. *Internet Research, 5,* 19–22.

Goldkind, L. (2014). E-advocacy in human services: The impact of organizational conditions and characteristics on electronic advocacy activities among nonprofits. *Journal of Policy Practice, 13*(4), 300–315.

Goldkind, L. (2015). Social media and social service: Are nonprofits plugged in to the digital age. *Human Service Organizations: Management, Leadership, and Governance, 39,* 380–396.

Goldkind, L., & McNutt, J. (2014). Social media & social change: Nonprofits and using social media strategies to meet advocacy goals. In A. M. Lucia-Casademunt & J. A. Ariza-Montes (Eds.), *Social Media and Networking: Concepts, Methodologies, Tools, and Applications* (pp. 11–27). Hershey, PA: IGI Global.

Goldkind, L., Wolf, L., & Jones, J. (2016). Late adapters? How social workers acquire knowledge and skills about technology tools. *Journal of Technology in Human Services, 34,* 338–358.

Gopnik, A. (2012). What's wrong with the teenage mind? *Wall Street Journal,* 28–29.

Granholm, E., Ben-Zeev, D., Link, P. C., Bradshaw, K. R., & Holden, J. L. (2012). Mobile Assessment and Treatment for Schizophrenia (MATS): A pilot trial of an interactive text-messaging intervention for medication adherence, socialization, and auditory hallucinations. *Schizophrenia Bulletin, 38,* 414–425. doi:10.1093/schbul/sbr155

Grasso, A. J., & Epstein, I. (1993). Introduction: The need for a new model of information utilization in human service agencies. *Child and Youth Services, 16*(1), 1–13. doi:10.1300/J024V16N01_01

Grimes, J. M., Fleischmann, K.R., & Jaeger, P. T. (2010). "Research ethics in virtual worlds." In C. Wankel & S. K. Malleck (Eds.), *Emerging ethical issues of life in virtual worlds* (pp. 75–100). Charlotte, NC: Information Age Publishing.

Grobman, L., & Mankita, S. (2016). A true history of social workers online. Retrieved from http://www.socialworker.com/feature-articles/technology-articles/true-history-of-social-workers-online/

Gubrium, A. (2009). Digital storytelling: An emergent method for health promotion research and practice. *Health Promotion Practice, 10,* 186–191. https://doi.org/10.1177/1524839909332600

Gubrium, A. C., Hill, A. L., & Flicker, S. (2014). A situated practice of ethics for participatory visual and digital methods in public health research and practice: A focus on digital storytelling. *American Journal of Public Health, 104,* 1606–1614. https://doi.org/10.2105/AJPH.2013.301310

Guerra, J. (2015, January 5). From foster care to freshman year. *National Public Radio, All Things Considered.* Retrieved from http://www.npr.org/sections/ed/2015/01/05/368436717/from-foster-care-to-freshman-year

Gustavsson, N., & MacEachron, A. (2008). Creating foster care youth biographies: A role for the Internet. *Journal of Technology in Human Services, 26*(1), 45–55. https://doi.org/10.1300/J017v26n01_03

Hamill, A. C., & Stein, C. H. (2011). Culture and empowerment in the Deaf community: An analysis of Internet weblogs. *Journal of Community and Applied Social Psychology, 21,* 388–406.

Hampton, K. H., Fitch, M. K., Allshouse, W. B., Doherty, I. A., Gesink, D. C., Leone, P. A., . . . Miller, W. C. (2010). Mapping health data: Improved privacy protection with donut method geomasking. *American Journal of Epidemiology, 172,* 1062–1069.

Hamre, B., Oyler, C., & Bejoian, L. (2006). Guest editors' introduction. *Equity and Excellence in Education, 39*(2), 91–100.

Hansgen, Kristopher B.E. (2016). Crime Mapping In Law Enforcement: Identifying Analytical Tools, Methods, And Outputs. *Culminating Projects in Criminal Justice,* 4. http://repository.stcloudstate.edu/cjs_etds/4

Hara, N., Shachaf, P., & Stoerger, S. (2009). Online communities of practice typology revisited. *Journal of Information Science, 35,* 740–757.

Hargittai, E. (2002). Second-level digital divide: Differences in people's online skills, *First Monday, 7*(4). Retrieved from http://firstmonday.org/issues/issue7_4/hargittai/index.html

Harlow, E., & Webb, S. A. (Eds.). (2003). *Information and communication technologies in the welfare services.* Philadelphia: Jessica Kingsley.

Hart, T., Ahlers-Schmidt, C. R., Chesser, A., Jones, J., Williams, K. S., & Wittler, R. R. (2011). Physician impressions of using text messaging technology to increase vaccination compliance. *Telemedicine and e-Health, 17,* 427–430. doi:10.1089/tmj.2010.0221

Hass, M., & Graydon, K. (2009). Sources of resiliency among successful foster youth, *Children and Youth Services Review, 31,* 457–463.

Hawkins, B. L., & Oblinge, D. G. (2006). The myth about the digital divide. *Educause Review, 41*(4), 12–13.

Hawn, C. (2009). Take two aspirin and tweet me in the morning: How twitter, Facebook, and other social media are reshaping health care, *Health Affairs, 28,* 361–368.

Hendricks, C. B., Robinson, B., Bradley, L. J., & Davis, K. (1999). Using music techniques to treat adolescent depression. *Journal of Humanistic Counseling, 38*(1), 39.

Heron, K. E., & Smyth, J. M. (2010). Ecological momentary interventions: Incorporating mobile technology into pyschosocial and health behavior treatments. *British Journal of Health Psychology, 15*(1), 1–39. doi:10.1348/135910709X466063.

Herring, S. C., Scheidt, L. A., Kouper, I., & Wright, E. (2007). Longitudinal content analysis of blogs: 2003–2004. In M. Tremayne (Ed.), *Blogging, citizenship and the future of media.* New York, NY: Routledge, 3–20.

Herrington, J., Reeves, T. C., & Oliver, R. (2014). Authentic learning environments. In J. M. Spector, M. D. Merrill, J. Elen, & M. J. Bishop (Eds.), *Handbook of research on educational communications and technology* (pp. 401–412). New York, NY: Springer. Retrieved from http://link.springer.com/chapter/10.1007/978-1-4614-3185-5_32

Hershey, C. L., Doocy, S., Anderson, J., Haskew, C., Spiegel, P., & Moss, W. J. (2011). Incidence and risk factors for malaria, pneumonia, and diarrhea in children under 5 in UNHCR refugee camps: A retrospective study. *Conflict and Health, 5,* 24–33.

Hess, D. (2012). Walking to the bust stop: Perceived versus actual walking distance to bus stops for older adults. *Transportation, 39,* 247–266.

Hetling, A., & Zhang, H. (2010). Domestic violence, poverty, and social services: Does location matter? *Social Science Quarterly, 91*(5), 1144–1163.

Highfield, T. (2012). Talking of many things: Using topical networks to study discussions in social media. *Journal of Technology in Human Services, 30,* 204–218. https://doi.org/10.1080/15228835.2012.746894

Hile, M. (1997). The history and function of the Target Cities management information systems. *Computers in Human Services, 14*(3/4), 1–8.

Hines, A. M., Merdinger, J., & Wyatt, P. (2005). Former foster youth attending college: Resilience and the transition to young adulthood. *American Journal of Orthopsychiatry, 75,* 381–394.

Hitchcock, L. I. (2015a, January 8). *How to participate in a Live Twitter Chat—Tips for social workers.* Retrieved from http://www.laureliversonhitchcock.org/2015/01/08/how-to-participate-in-a-live-twitter-chat-tips-for-social-workers/

Hitchcock, L. I. (2015b, July 2). *Personal learning networks for social workers.* Retrieved from http://www.laureliversonhitchcock.org/2015/07/01/personal-learning-networks-for-social-workers/

Hitchcock, L. I., & Young, J. A. (2016). Tweet, tweet!: Using live twitter chats in social work education. *Social Work Education, 35,* 457–468. https://doi.org/10.1080/02615479.2015.1136273

Hodgins, M., & Boydell, K. (2014). Interrogating ourselves: Reflections on arts-based health research. *Forum Qualitative Sozialforschung/Forum: Qualitative Social Research, 15*(1), Art. 10.

Hoefer, R. A., Hoefer, R. M., & Tobias, R. A. (1994). Geographic information systems and human services. *Journal of Community Practice, 1,* 113–128.

Holmes, A., Fox, E. B., Wieder, B., & Zubak-Skees, C. (2016, May 12). *Rich people have access to high speed Internet; many poor people still don't.* Retrieved from the Center for Public Integrity: https://www.publicintegrity.org/2016/05/012/19659/rich-people-have-access-high-speed-internet-many-poor-people-still-dont

Holmstrom, L., Karp, D., & Gray, P. (2002). Why laundry, not Hegel? Social class, transition to college, and pathways to adulthood. *Symbolic Interaction, 25,* 437–462.

Horrigan, J. (2016). *Digital readiness gaps.* Pew Research Center. Retrieved from: http://www.pewinternet.org/2016/09/20/digital-readiness-gaps/

Horrigan, J. B. (2016, March 22). *Lifelong learning and technology.* Retrieved from http://www.pewinternet.org/2016/03/22/lifelong-learning-and-technology/

Horton, M. J. (2015). *Six sobriety apps you should know about.* Retrieved from https://www.addiction.com/12575/six-sobriety-apps-you-should-know-about/

Howard, T. M. (2009). *GarageBand '08 power!: The comprehensive recording and podcasting.* Palo Alto, CA: Howard Cengage Learning.

Howell, J. C., Kelly, M. R., Palmer, J., & Mangum, R. L. (2004). Integrating child welfare, juvenile justice, and other agencies in a continuum of services. *Child Welfare, 83,* 143–156.

Hughes, J., & McLewin, A. M. A. (2005). *Doing the arts justice: A review of research literature*. Theory and Practice, DCMS, the Department for Education and Skills, and Arts Council.

Hunt, T. (2015, August). Smartphones are hurting our children—but the real culprit is bad parenting. *The Telegraph*. Retrieved from http://www.telegraph.co.uk/education/ educationnews/11784092/Smartphones-are-hurting-our-children-but-the-real-culprit-is-bad-parenting.html

Iceland, J., & Steinmetz, E. (2003). The effects of using census block groups instead of census tracts when examining residential housing patterns. In *Racial and ethnic residential segregation in the United States: 1980–2000*. US Census Bureau, Census Special Report, CENSR-3. Washington, DC: US Government Printing Office.

Information Solutions Group. (2008). *Survey: "Disabled gamers" comprise 20% of casual video games audience*. Retrieved July 1, 2016, from http://www.prnewswire.com/ news-releases/survey-disabled-gamers-comprise-20-of-casual-video-games-audience-57442172.html

International Telecommunication Union. (2016). *Measuring the information society report*. Geneva, Switzerland: International Telecommunication Union. Retrieved from http://www.itu.int/en/ITU-D/Statistics/Documents/publications/misr2016/MISR2016-w4.pdf

IRS Oversight Board. Retrieved March 13, 2017, from https://www.treasury.gov/IRSOB/ reports/Documents/IRSOB-E-File%202013.pdf

Iseke, J., & Moore, S. (2011). Community-based indigenous digital storytelling with elders and youth. *American Indian Culture and Research Journal, 35*(4), 19–38.

Ivanitskaya, L., O'Boyle, I., & Casey, A. (2006). Health information literacy and competencies of information age students: Results from the interactive online research readiness self-assessment, *Journal of Medical Internet Research 8*(2), e6.

Ivanov, M., & Yankov, Y. (2016). Application of geographic information systems in crisis management. *Land Forces Academy Review, 21*, 170–176.

Jakobsson, M. (1999). Why Bill was killed: Understanding social interaction in virtual worlds. In A. Nijholt, et al. (Eds.), *Interactions in virtual worlds. Proceedings of the fifteenth Twente workshop on language technology*. Enschede, The Netherlands: Twente University.

James, J. (2011). Are changes in the digital divide consistent with global equality or inequality? *The Information Society, 27*(2), 121–128.

Jenkins, J., & Ogden, J. (2012). Becoming "whole" again: A qualitative study of women's views of recovering from anorexia nervosa. *European Eating Disorders Review, 20*, e23–e31.

Jerz, D. G. (2003, 17 February 2003). On the trail of the Memex: Vannevar Bush, Weblogs and the Google Galaxy. Retrieved 31 December, 2003, from http://www.dichtungdigital. org/2003/issue/1/jerz/index.htm

Johnson, S. (2007). *The ghost map: The story of London's most terrifying epidemic and how it changed science, cities, and the modern world*. New York, NY: Riverhead.

Johnson, T. J., Kaye, B. K., Bichard, S. L., & Wong, W. J. (2007). Every blog has its day: Politically-interested Internet users' perceptions of blog credibility. *Journal of Computer-Mediated Communication, 13*, 100–122.

Jones, R., & Malson, H. (2013). A critical exploration of lesbian perspectives on eating disorders. *Psychology and Sexuality, 4*(1), 62–74. http://doi.org/10.1080/19419899.2011.603349

Jordan, E. T., Ray, E. M., Johnson, P., & Evans, W. D. (2011). Text4Baby: Using text messaging to improve maternal and newborn health. *Nursing for Women's Health, 15,* 206–212. doi:10.1111/j.1751-486X.2011.01635.x

Jordan, K. (2014). Initial trends in enrollment and completion of massive open online courses. *International Review of Research in Open and Distance Learning, 15,* 133–160.

Joubert, L., & Epstein, I. (2005). Multi-disciplinary data-mining in allied health practice: Another perspective on Australian research and evaluation [Editorial]. *Journal of Social Work Research and Evaluation, 6,* 139–141.

Judd, R. G., & Johnston, L. B. (2012). Ethical consequences of using social network sites for students in professional social work programs. *Journal of Social Work Values and Ethics, 9*(1), 5–8.

Kahn, R., & Kellner, D. (2004). New media and Internet activism: From the "Battle of Seattle" to blogging. *New Media and Society, 6*(1), 87–95.

Kalinka, C. J., Fincham, F. D., & Hirsch, A. H. (2012). A randomized clinical trial of online-biblio relationship education for expectant couples. *Journal of Family Psychology, 26,* 159.

Kandalaft, M. R., Didehbani, N., Krawczyk, D. C. et al. (2013). Virtual reality social cognition training for young adults with high-functioning autism. *Journal of Autism and Developmental Disorders, 43,* 34–44. doi:10.1007/s10803-012-1544-6

Kanter, B., Fine, A., & Zuckerberg, R. (2010). *The networked nonprofit: Connecting with social media to drive change.* San Francisco: Jossey-Bass.

Kao, D., Torres, L. R., Guerrero, E. G., Mauldin, R., & Bordnick, P. S. (2014). Spatial accessibility of drug treatment facilities and the effects on locus of control, drug abuse, and service use among heroin-injecting Mexican American men. *International Journal of Drug Policy, 25,* 598–607.

Kaplan, A. M., & Haenlein, M. (2010). Users of the world, unite! The challenges and opportunities of social media. *Business Horizons, 53*(1), 59–68.

Karp, D., Holmstrom, L., & Gray, P. (1998). Leaving home for college: Expectations for selective reconstruction of self. *Symbolic Interaction, 21,* 253–276.

Kaufman, D. R., Patel, V. L., Hilliman, C., Morin, P. C., Pevzner, J., Weinstock, R. S., . . . Starren, J. (2003). Usability in the real world: Assessing medical information technologies in patients' homes. *Journal of Biomedical Informatics, 36,* 45–60.

Keigher, S. M., & Stevens, P. E. (2011). Catch 22: Women with HIV on Wisconsin's temporary assistance to needy families (TANF) program: A qualitative narrative analysis. *Journal of HIV/AIDS & Social Services, 10*(1), 68–86.

Kelley, M. (2011). Collaborative digital techniques and urban neighborhood revitalization. *Social Work, 56*(2), 185–188.

Kemper, T., Jenerowicz, M., Gueguen, L., Poli, D., & Soille, P. (2011). Monitoring changes in the Menik Farm IDP camps in Sri Lanka using multi-temporal very high-resolution satellite data. *International Journal of Digital Earth, 4*(1), 91–106.

Kernsmith, P. D., & Kernsmith, R. M. (2008). A safe place for predators: Online treatment of recovering sex offenders. *Journal of Technology in Human Services, 26,* 223–238. doi:10.1080/15228830802096598

Khanna, P. (2008). Icyou: How social media is the new resource for online health information. *Medscape Journal of Medicine, 10,* 113.

Kietzmann, J. H., Hermkens, K., McCarthy, I. P., & Silvestre, B. S. (2011). Social media? Get serious! Understanding the functional building blocks of social media. *Business Horizons, 54*(3), 241–251.

Kim, A. J. (2000). *Community building on the web: Secret strategies for successful online communities.* Berkeley, CA: Peachpit Press.

Kimball, E., & Kim, J. (2013). Virtual boundaries: Ethical considerations for use of social media in social work. *Social Work, 58,* 185–8.

Kingsley, C., & Goldsmith S. (2013). Getting big data to the good guys. Data smart city solutions. Retrieved from http://datasmart.ash.harvard.edu/news/article/getting-big-data-to-the-good-guys-140

Klasnja, P., & Pratt, W. (2012). Healthcare in the pocket: Mapping the space of mobile-phone health interventions. *Journal of Biomedical Informatics, 45,* 184–198.

Kim S., & Ulfarsson, G. (2004). Travel mode choice of the elderly: Effects of personal, household, neighborhood, and trip characteristics. *Transportation Research Record, 1894,* 117–126.

Koch-Weser, S., Bradshaw, Y. S., Gualtieri, L., & Gallagher, S. S. (2010). The Internet as a health information source: Findings from the 2007 Health Information National Trends Survey and implications for health communication. *Journal of Health Communication, 15*(suppl. 3), 279–293.

Kolmes, K., & Taube, D. O. (2014). Seeking and finding our clients on the Internet: Boundary considerations in cyberspace. *Professional Psychology: Research and Practice, 45*(1), 3.

Kondrat, M. E. (2008). Person-in-environment. In T. Mizrahi & L. E. Davis (Eds.), *Encyclopedia of social work* (Vol. 3, 20th ed., pp. 348–354). Washington, DC: NASW Press.

Konrath, S., Falk, E., Fuhrel-Forbis, A., Liu, M., Swain, J., Tolman, R., . . . Walton, M. (2015). Can text messages increase empathy and prosocial behavior? The development and initial validation of text to connect *PLoS ONE 10*(9), 1–27. doi:10.1371/journal. pone.0137585

Krishna, S., Boren, S. A., & Balas, E. A. (2009). Healthcare via cell phones: A systematic review. *Telemedicine and e-Health, 15,* 231–240.

Krueger, A. (2013). *People with disabilities in virtual worlds: Who, how, why, and what's next?* Selected Papers of Internet Research 14.0. Denver, CO: Association of Internet Research.

Krueger, A., & Boellstorff, T. (2015). *Disability and the familiarity of the virtual.* Presentation at the annual meeting of the American Anthropological Association, Denver, CO.

Krueger, A., & Stineman, M. (2011). Assistive technology interoperability between virtual and real worlds. *Journal of Virtual Worlds Research, 4*(3), 2–8.

Kruger, R., & van Zijl, L. (2015). Virtual world accessibility with the Perspective Viewer. In G. Kouroupetroglou (Ed.), *Proceedings of ICEAPVI.* 12–14 February 2015, Athens, Greece.

Kushchu, I., & Kuscu, H. (2003, July). From e-government to M-government: Facing the inevitable. In *The 3rd European conference on e-government* (pp. 253–260). Dublin, Ireland: MCIL Trinity College.

Kuzmich, J., Jr. (2014). DAW workstations: Customizing beyond the bundles. *School Band and Orchestra,* 46–48.

Kvasny, L. (2005). The role of the habitus in shaping discourses about the digital divide. *Journal of Computer Mediated Communication, 10*(2). Doi: 10.1111/j.1083-6101.2005.tb00242.x

Kvasny, L. (2006). Let the sisters speak: Understanding information technology from the standpoint of the "other." *ACM SIGMIS Database, 37*(4), 13–25.

Kvasny, L., & Payton, F. (2018). African American youth tumbling toward mental health support-seeking and positive academic outcomes. In W. Tierney, Z. Corwin, & A. Ochsner (Eds.), *Diversifying digital learning: Online literacy and educational opportunity* (pp. 151–171). Baltimore, MD: Johns Hopkins University Press.

Kvasny, L., & Payton, F. C. (2008). African Americans and the digital divide. In M. Khosrow-Pour (Ed.), *Encyclopedia of information science and technology* (pp. 78–82). Hershey, PA: Idea Group Publishing.

Kvasny, L., & Warren, J. (2006). The representation and performance of menu-driven identities in online health portals. In E. Trauth (Ed.), *Encyclopedia of information technology and gender* (pp. 745–751). Hershey, PA: Idea Group Publishing.

KZero. (n.d.). *Age ranges and gender analysis.* Retrieved July 1, 2016, from http://www.kzero.co.uk/blog/age-ranges-and-gender-analysis/

Labov, W. (1997). Some further steps in narrative analysis. *Journal of Narrative and Life History, 7,* 395–415. http://dx.doi.org/10.1075/jnlh.7.49som

Lai, L. S., & Turban, E. (2008). Groups formation and operations in the Web 2.0 environment and social networks. *Group Decision and negotiation, 17,* 387–402.

Laird, M. (2010). *Social media fundraising: Facebook friend or foe? A case study of Oregon nonprofit organizations*, Doctoral dissertation, University of Oregon.

Lam, W. (2005). Barriers to e-government integration. *Journal of Enterprise Information Management, 18,* 511–530.

LaMarre, A., & Rice, C. (2015). Normal eating is counter-cultural: Embodied experiences of eating disorder recovery. *Journal of Community and Applied Social Psychology, 26,* 136–149.

LaMarre, A., & Rice, C. (2016). Embodying critical and corporeal methodology: Digital storytelling with young women in eating disorder recovery. *Forum: Qualitative Social Research, 17*(2), Art. 7.

LaMarre, A., Rice, C., & Bear, M. (2015). Unrecoverable? Prescriptions and possibilities for eating disorder recovery. In N. Khanlou, & B. Pilkington (Eds.), *Women's mental health: International perspectives on resistance and resilience in community and society* (pp. 145–160). Toronto, ON: Springer Press.

Lambert, J. (2010). *Digital storytelling cookbook.* San Francisco, CA: Digital Diner Press.

LaMendola, W., Glastonbury, B., & Toole, S. (Eds.). (1989). *A casebook of computer applications in the social and human services.* New York, NY: Haworth Press.

Landman, M. S., Shelton, J., Kaufmann, R. M., & Dattilo, J. B. (2010). Guidelines for maintaining a professional compass in the era of social networking. *Journal of Surgical Education, 67,* 381–386.

Landsbergen, D., Jr., & Wolken G., Jr. (2001). Realizing the promise: Government information systems and the fourth generation of information technology. *Public Administration Review, 61,* 206–220.

Larose, S., & Boivin, M. (1998). Attachment of parents, social support expectations, and socioemotional adjustment during the high school-college transition. *Journal of Research on Adolescence, 8*(1), 1–27.

Lave, J., & Wenger, E. (1991). *Situated learning: Legitimate peripheral participation* (1st edition). Cambridge, UK; New York, NY: Cambridge University Press.

Leavy, P. (2009). *Method meets art: Arts-based research practice.* New York, NY: Guilford Press.

Lee, J. Y., & Harathi, S. (2016). Using mHealth in social work practice with low-income Hispanic patients. *Health and Social Work, 41*(1). doi:10.1093/hsw/hlv078

Lee, R., & Kvasny, L. (2014). Understanding the role of social media in online health: A global perspective on online social support, *First Monday, 19(1–6).* Retrieved from http://firstmonday.org/ojs/index.php/fm/article/view/4048/3805

Lee, S. J., Hoffman, G., & Harris, D. (2016). Community-based participatory research (CBPR) needs assessment of parenting support to fathers. *Children and Youth Services Review, 66,* 76–84.

Lee, S. J., Neugut, T. B., Rosenblum, K. L., Tolman, R. M., Travis, W. J., & Walker, M. H. (2013). Sources of parenting support in early fatherhood: Perspectives of United States Air Force members. *Children and Youth Services Review, 35,* 908–915. doi:10.1016/j.childyouth.2013.02.012

Lee, S. J., & Walsh, T. B. (2015). Using technology in social work practice: The mDad (Mobile Device Assisted Dad) case study. *Advances in Social Work, 16,* 107–124.

Lee, S. J., Yelick, A., Brisebois, K., & Banks, K. L. (2011). Low-income fathers' barriers to participation in family and parenting programs. *Journal of Family Strengths, 11*(1), 1–16. Retrieved from http://digitalcommons.library.tmc.edu/jfs/vol11/iss11/12

Lefevre, M. (2004). Playing with sound: The therapeutic use of music in direct work with children. *Child and Family Social Work, 9,* 333–345.

Leiner, B. M., Cerf, V. G., Clark, D., Kahn, R. E., Kleinrock, L., Lynch, D. C., . . . Blumberg, S. J. (2012). *Brief history of the Internet.* Reston, VA: Internet Society. Retrieved from http://www.internetsociety.org/internet/what-internet/history-internet/brief-history-internet#Leiner

Lenhart, A., Duggan, M., Perrin, A., Stepler, R., Rainie, L., & Parker, K. (2015, April 9). *Teens, social media and technology overview 2015.* Retrieved from http://www.pewinternet.org/2015/04/09/teens-social-media-technology-2015

Levitin, D., & Tirovolas, A. (2009). Current advances in the cognitive neuroscience of music. *Annals of the New York Academy of Sciences, 1156,* 211–231.

Levy, F., Leboucher, P., Rautureau, G., Komano, O., Millet, B., & Jouvent, R. (2016). Fear of falling: Efficacy of virtual reality associated with serious games in elderly people. *Neuropsychiatric Disease and Treatment, 12,* 877.

Lewan, D. (2016). *Foresee e-government satisfaction index, Q1 2016.* Retrieved March 1, 2017, from https://www.fcg.gov/sites/fcg.opengov.ibmcloud.com/files/eGov-Q1-2016.pdf

Liang, X., Wang, Q., Yang, X., Cao, J., Chen, J., Mo, X., . . . Gu, D. (2011). Effect of mobile phone intervention for diabetes on glycaemic control: A meta-analysis. *Diabetic Medicine, 28,* 455–463. doi:10.1111/j.1464-5491.2010.03180.x

Linden Lab. (2009). *Linden Lab announces co-winners of inaugural Linden Prize.* Retrieved July 1, 2016, from http://www.lindenlab.com/releases/linden-lab-announces-co-winners-of-inaugural-linden-prize

Lipschutz, R. (2011). *Ethics corner: Ethics and disability.* Retrieved July 1, 2016, from http://naswil.org/news/chapter-news/featured/ethics-corner-ethics-and-disability/

Lightfoot, M., Comulada, S., & Stover, G. (2007). Computerized HIV preventive intervention for adolescents: Indications of efficacy. *American Journal of Public Health, 97,* 1027–1030.

Loewy, J. V. (2011, March). *Music in the treatment of acute, chronic and procedural pain.* Paper presented at Music, Science and Medicine: Frontiers in Biomedical Research and Clinical Applications, New York, NY.

Lopez, Y. (2014, April). First senior center opens in Collier County. *WGCU News.* Retrieved from http://news.wgcu.org/post/first-senior-center-opens-collier-county

Lovejoy, K., & Saxton, G. D. (2012). Information, community, and action: How nonprofit organizations use social media. *Journal of Computer-Mediated Communication, 17*(3), 337–353.

Lubas, M. M., & De Leo, G. (2014). Grief support groups in second life. *Annual Review of Cybertherapy and Telemedicine 2014: Positive Change, 118,* 118–122.

Lysiak, J. (2015, March 6). CHR Partners with FGCU on affordable housing assessment. *The Island Sun.* Retrieved from http://www.islandsunnews.com/Island%20Sun%20 2015-03-06.pdf

MacDonald, D. E. (2011). Impossible bodies, invisible battles: Feminist perspectives on the psychological research on and treatment of eating disorders in queer women. *Journal of Gay and Lesbian Social Services, 23,* 452–464.

Ma, Z., Sun, A., & Cong, G. (2013). On predicting the popularity of newly emerging hashtags in twitter. *Journal of the American Society for Information Science and Technology, 64,* 1399–1410.

Madway, G. (2010). *Twitter remakes website, adds new features.* Retrieved November, 5, 2010. https://www.reuters.com/article/twitter/update-1-twitter-remakes-website-adds-new-features-idUSN1411135520100915

Maier, R., & Hädrich, T. (2011). *Knowledge management systems.* New York, NY: Springer.

Manderscheid, R. W., & Henderson, M. J. (2004). From many into one: An integrated information agenda for mental health. *Behavioral Healthcare Tomorrow, 13,* 38–41.

Marcus, H. (2015, June 17). Senior lunch and more program to see much needed expansion. *Naples Daily News.* Retrieved from http://archive.naplesnews.com/news/local/senior-lunch-and-more-program-to-see-much-needed-expansion-ep-1142249748-337624051.html

Markus, M. L. (1983). Power, politics and MIS implementation. *Communications of the ACM, 26,* 430–444.

Martin, T. (2012). Assessing mHealth: Opportunities and barriers to patient engagement. *Journal of Health Care for the Poor and Underserved, 23,* 935–941. doi:10.1353/hpu.2012.0087

McAllister, M., Brien, D., Flynn, T., & Alexander, J. (2014). Exploring the educative potential of eating disorder memoirs. *Journal of Mental Health Training, Education and Practice, 9*(2), 69–78.

McClure, E. A., Acquavita, S. P., Harding, E., & Stitzer, M. L. (2012). Utilization of communication technology by patients enrolled in substance abuse treatment. *Drug Alcohol Dependence, 129,* 145–150.

McFarland, L. A., & Ployhart, R. E. (2015). Social media: A contextual framework to guide research and practice. *Journal of Applied Psychology, 100*(6), 1653.

McFerran, K. (2010). *Adolescents, music and music therapy: Methods and techniques for clinicians, educators and students.* London, UK: Jessica Kingsley.

McFerran, K., Baker, F., Patton, G. C., & Sawyer, S. M. (2006). A retrospective lyrical analysis of songs written by adolescents with anorexia nervosa. *European Eating Disorders Review, 14,* 397–403.

McFerran, K., & Sheridan, J. (2004). Exploring the value of opportunities for choice and control in music therapy within a paediatric hospice setting. *Australian Journal of Music Therapy, 15*(2004), 18.

McNutt, J. G., & Boland, K. M. (1999). Electronic advocacy by nonprofit organizations in social welfare policy. *Nonprofit and Voluntary Sector Quarterly, 28*(4), 432–451.

Mestre, D. (1995). *Immersion and presence.* Retrieved July 1, 2016 from www.ism.univmed.fr/mestre/projects/virtual%20reality/Pres_2005.pdf

Michaeli, D. (2015, June 22). *Episode 170: How social media expands social work career choices.* SocialWork® Podcast Series. [Audio Podcast]. Retrieved from http://www.insocialwork.org/episode.asp?ep=170

Mihailidis, P., & Cohen, J. (2013). Exploring curation as a core competency in digital and media literacy education. *Journal of Interactive Media in Education, 2013*(1). https://doi.org/10.5334/2013-02

Mihailidis, P., & Thevenin, B. (2013). Media literacy as a core competency for engaged citizenship in participatory democracy. *American Behavioral Scientist, 57*(11), 1611–1622.

Miller, C. R., & Shepherd, D. (2004). Blogging as social action: A genre analysis of the weblog. *Into the blogosphere: Rhetoric, community, and culture of weblogs, 18*(1), 1–24.

Milward, J., Day, E., Wadsworth, E., Strang, J., & Lynskey, M. (2015). Mobile phone ownership, usage and readiness to use by patients in drug treatment *Drug and Alcohol Dependence, 146,* 111–115 doi:10.1016/j.drugalcdep.2014.11.001

Miranda, D., & Claes, M. (2009). Music listening, coping, peer affiliation and depression in adolescence. *Psychology of Music, 37,* 215–233.

Mishna, F., Bogo, M., Root, J., & Fantus, S. (2014). Here to Stay: Cyber Communication as a Complement in Social Work Practice. *Families in Society: The Journal of Contemporary Social Services, 95,* 179–186. https://doi.org/10.1606/1044-3894.2014.95.23

Montague, E., & Perchonok, J. (2012). Health and wellness technology use by historically underserved health consumers: A systematic review. *Journal of Medical Internet Research, 14*(3), e78.

Moon, M. J. (2002. July/August). The evolution of e-government among municipalities: Rhetoric or reality. *Public Administration Review, 62,* 424–246.

Morris, M. E., Kathawala, Q., Leen, T. K., Gorenstein, E. E., Guilak, F., Labhard, M., & Deleeuw, W. (2010). Mobile therapy: Case study evaluations of a cell phone application for emotional self-awareness. *Journal of Medical Internet Research, 12*(2), e10. doi:10.2196/jmir.1371

Muller, A. R., Roder, M., & Fingerle, M. (2014). Child sexual abuse prevention goes online: Introducing "Cool and Safe" and its effects. *Computers and Education, 78,* 60–65.

Naeem, F., Gire, N., Xiang, S., Yang, M., Syed, Y., Shokraneh, F., . . . Farooq, S. (2016). Reporting and understanding the safety and adverse effect profile of mobile apps for psychosocial interventions: An update. *World Journal of Psychiatry, 6,* 187–191. doi:10.5498/wjp.v6.i2.187

Nah, S., & Saxton, G. D. (2013). Modeling the adoption and use of social media by nonprofit organizations. *New Media & Society, 15*(2), 294–313.

Nance, M. (2008). Helping foster care youth access college: Education has not been on the radar for child agencies until recently, say child advocates. *Diverse Issues in Higher Education, 24,* 12.

Nardi, B. A., Schiano, D. J., Gumbrecht, M., & Swartz, L. (2004). Why we blog. *Communications of the ACM, 47,* 41–46.

National Association of Social Workers (NASW). (1993). *Standards for the practice of social work with adolescents.* Retrieved from http://www.socialworkers.org/practice/standards/sw_adolescents.asp

National Association of Social Workers (NASW). (2008). *Code of ethics of the National Association of Social Workers.* Retrieved July 1, 2016, from https://www.socialworkers.org/pubs/code/default.asp

National Association of Social Workers (NASW). (2013). *Standards for social work practice in child welfare.* Retrieved from https://www.socialworkers.org/practice/standards/childwelfarestandards2012.pdf

National Association of Social Workers (NASW), Council on Social Work Educaiton, and Association of Social Work Boards. (2017). *Standards For Technology In Social Work Practice.* Retrieved June 6, 2018, from https://www.socialworkers.org/practice/practice-standards-guidelines

National Association of Social Workers and Association of Social Work Boards. (2005). *NASW and ASWB Standards for technology and social work practice.* Retrieved from http://www.socialworkers.org/practice/standards/NASWTechnologyStandards.pdf

National Association of Social Workers, Association of Social Work Boards. (2005). *Standards for technology and social work practice.* https://www.aswb.org/wp-content/uploads/2013/10/TechnologySWPractice.pdf

National Association of Social Workers, Association of Social Work Boards, Council on Social Work Education and Clinical Social Work Association. (2017). *Standards for technology and social work practice.* http://www.socialworkers.org/includes/newIncludes/homepage/PRA-BRO-33617.TechStandards_FINAL_POSTING.pdf

National League for Nursing. (2008). *Preparing the next generation of nurses to practice in a technology-rich environment: An informatics agenda.* Retrieved from http://www.nln.org/docs/default-source/professional-development-programs/preparing-the-next-generation-of-nurses.pdf?sfvrsn=6

National Research Council. (2007). "Appendix E: A short history of e-government." *Social security administration electronic service provision: A strategic assessment.* Washington, DC: The National Academies Press. doi: 10.17226/11920

National Working Group on Foster Care and Education. (2014, January). *Research highlights on education and foster care.* Retrieved from http://cdn.fc2success.org/wp-content/uploads/2012/05/National-Fact-Sheet-on-the-Educational-Outcomes-of-Children-in-Foster-Care-Jan-2014.pdf

Nelson, E. L., Barnard, M., & Cain, S. (2003). Treating childhood depression over videoconferencing. *Telemedicine Journal and e-Health, 9,* 49–55.

Netting, F. E., Kettner, P., McMurtry, S., & Thomas, M. T. (2012). *Social work macro practice* (5th ed.). Boston, MA: Pearson Education, Inc.

New York City Public Advocate Office. (2003). *New York City working families unlawfully denied access to food stamps.* New York, NY: Public Advocate Office.

Nicholas, D. B., Fellner, K. D., Frank, M., Small, M., Hetherington, R., Slater, R., & Daneman, D. (2012). Evaluation of an online education and support intervention for adolescents with diabetes. *Social Work in Health Care, 9,* 815–827. doi: 10.1080/00981389.2012.699507

Nielsen. (2015). *Smartphone owners are as diverse as their devices.* Retrieved from http://www.nielsen.com/us/en/insights/news/2015/smartphone-owners-are-as-diverse-as-their-devices.html

North, A C., Hargreaves, D. J., & O'Neill, S. A. (2000). "The importance of music to adolescents." *British Journal of Educational Psychology, 70,* 255–272.

Ogden, T. N., & Starita, L. (2009). Social networking and mid-size non-profits: What's the use. *Philanthropy Action, 4,* 1–21.

Olajuyigbe, A., Omole, K., Bayode, T., & Adenigba, A. (2016). Crime mapping and analysis in the core area of Akure, Nigeria. In O. J. Ebohon, D. A. Ayeni, C. O. Egbu, & F. K. Omole (Eds.), *Proceedings from the Joint International Conference (JIC): 21st Century Human Habitat: Issues, Sustainability and Development.* Akure, Nigeria: The Joint International Conference Editorial Committee.

Olson-McBride, L., & Page, T. F. (2012). Song to self: Promoting a therapeutic dialogue with high-risk youths through poetry and popular music. *Social Work with Groups, 35,* 124–137.

Ondersma, S. J., Grekin, E. R., & Svikis, D. S. (2011). The potential for technology in brief interventions for substance use, and during-session prediction of computer-delivered brief intervention response. *Substance Use and Misuse, 46*(1), 77–86. doi:10.3109/10826084.2011.521372

Ondersma, S. J., Svikis, D. S., & Schuster, C. R. (2007). Computer-based brief intervention: A randomized trial with postpartum women. *American Journal of Preventive Medicine, 32,* 231–238. doi:10.1016/j.amepre.2006.11.003

O'Reilly, T. (2009). *Gov 2.0: It's all about the platform.* https://techcrunch.com/2009/09/04/gov-20-its-all-about-the-platform/

Organisation for Economic Co-operation and Development. (2016). *OECD data.* Retrieved from https://data.oecd.org/socialexp/social-spending.htm

Ovadia, S. (2014). ResearchGate and Academia.edu: Academic social networks. *Behavioral and Social Sciences Librarian, 33,* 165–169. https://doi.org/10.1080/01639269.2014.934093

Oyserman, D., & Benbenishty, R. (1997). Developing and implementing the integrated information system for foster care and adoption. *Computers in Human Services, 14*(1), 1–20.

Pacifici, C., White, L, Cummings, K., & Nelson, C. (2005). Vstreet.com: A web-based community for at-risk teens. *Child Welfare, 84*(1), 25–45. doi:10.1016/j.pec.2006.03.001

Panos, P. T., Panos, A., Cox, S. E., Roby, J. L., & Matheson, K. W. (2002). Ethical issues concerning the use of videoconferencing to supervise international social work field practicum students. *Journal of Social Work Education, 38*(3), 421–437.

Dawes, S., Cresswell, A. M., Pardo, T. A., & Thompson, F. (2004, May). Modeling the social and technical processes of interorganizational information integration. In *Proceedings of the 2004 annual national conference on Digital government research* (p. 85). Digital Government Society of North America.

Pardo, T. A., Cresswell, A. M., Thompson, F., & Zhang, J. (2006). Knowledge sharing in cross-boundary information system development in the public sector. *Information Technology and Management, 7,* 293–313.

Pardo, T., & Tayi, G. (2007). Interorganizational information integration: A key enabler for digital government. *Government Information Quarterly, 24*(4), 691–715.

Parks, A. C., Della Porta, M. D., Pierce, R. S., Zilca, R., & Lyubomirsky, S. (2012). Pursuing happiness in everyday life: The characteristics and behaviors of online happiness seekers *Emotion, 28,* 1–13. doi:doi: 10.1037/a0028587

Parsons, C., (2008). Second Life offers healing, therapeutic options for users. *San Francisco Chronicle.* Retrieved March 18, 2017, from http://www.sfgate.com/living/article/Second-Life-offers-healing-therapeutic-options-3277221.php

Pasquinelli, E. (2010) The illusion of reality: Cognitive aspects and ethical drawbacks. In C. Wankel & S. Malleck (Eds.), *Emerging ethical issues of life in virtual worlds* (pp. 197–216). North Carolina: Information Age Publishing.

Patten, C. A., Croghan, I. T., Meis, T. M., Decker, P. A., Pingree, S., Colligan, R. C., & Gustafson, D. H. (2006). Randomized clinical trial of an Internet-based versus brief office intervention for adolescent smoking cessation. *Patient Education and Counseling, 64,* 249–258.

Paul, E., & Brier, S. (2001). Friendsickness in the transition to college: Precollege predictors and college adjustment correlates. *Journal of Counseling and Development, 79*(1), 77–89.

Pavlik, J. V. (2015). Fueling a third paradigm of education: The pedagogical implications of digital, social and mobile media. *Contemporary Educational Technology, 6,* 113–125.

Pazzanese, C. (2016). Don't trust that algorithm. *Harvard University Gazette.* Retrieved March 22, 2017, from http://news.harvard.edu/gazette/story/2016/10/dont-trust-that-algorithm/

Pearce, C., Blackburn, B. R., & Symborski, C. (2015). Virtual Worlds Survey Report: A trans-world study of non-game virtual worlds—Demographics, attitudes, and preferences. Retrieved July 1, 2016, from http://cpandfriends.com/wp-content/uploads/2015/03/vwsurveyreport_final_publicationedition1.pdf

Pearsall, B. (2010). Predictive policing: The future of law enforcement. *National Institute of Justice Journal, 266*(1), 16–19.

Pedell, S., Miller, T., Vetere, F., Sterling, L., & Howard, S. (2014). Socially-oriented requirements engineering: Software engineering meets ethnography. *Perspectives on Culture and Agent-Based Simulations* (pp. 191–210). Cham: Springer.

Peressini, T., & Engeland, J. (2004). The homelessness individuals and families information system: A case study in Canadian capacity building. *Canadian Journal of Urban Research, 13,* 347–361.

Perron, B. E., Taylor, H. O., Glass, J. E., & Margerum-Leys, J. (2010). Information and communication technologies in social work. *Advances in Social Work, 11*(2), 67.

Pew Research Center. (2017a). *Mobile fact sheet.* Retrieved from http://www.pewinternet.org/fact-sheet/mobile/

Pew Research Center. (2017b, January 12). *Social media fact sheet.* Retrieved from http://www.pewinternet.org/fact-sheet/social-media/

Phethean, C., Tiropanis, T., & Harris, L. (2013, May). Rethinking measurements of social media use by charities: A mixed methods approach. In *Proceedings of the 5th annual ACM web science conference* (pp. 296–305). New York, NY: ACM.

Plachecki, L. (2013, July 23). *How to make social media demographics work for you.* Retrieved from http://2060digital.com/how-to-make-social-media-demographics-work-for-you/

Powell, J., Inglis, N., Ronnie, J., & Large, S. (2011). The characteristics and motivations of on-line health information seekers: Cross-sectional survey and qualitative interview study. *Journal of Medical Internet Research, 13*(1), e20.

Prentice, J. L., & Dobson, K. S. (2014). A review of the risks and benefits associated with mobile phone applications for psychological interventions. *Canadian Psychology, 55,* 282–290.

Purcell, K., Buchanan, J., & Friedrich, L. (2013, July 16). *The impact of digital tools on student writing and how writing is taught in schools.* Retrieved from http://www.pewinternet.org/2013/07/16/the-impact-of-digital-tools-on-student-writing-and-how-writing-is-taught-in-schools/

Quanbeck, A., Chih, M. Y., Isham, A., Johnson, R., & Gustafson, D. (2014). Mobile delivery of treatment for alcohol use disorders: A review of the literature. *Alcohol Research, 36*, 111–122.

Queralt, M., & Witte, A. D. (1998). A map for you? Geographic information systems in the social services. *Social Work, 43*, 455–469.

Queralt, M., & Witte, A. D. (1999). Estimating unmet need for services: A middling approach. *Social Service Review, 73*, 524–559.

Quinn, A., & Fitch, D. (2014). A conceptual framework for contextualizing information technology competencies. *Journal of Technology in Human Services, 32*, 133–148.

Rabin, C., & Bock, B. (2011). Desired features of smartphone applications promoting physical activity. *Telemedicine and e-Health, 17*, 801–803.

Rafferty, J., Steyaert, J., & Colombi, D. (1996). *Human services in the information age.* New York, NY: Haworth Press.

Rainger, P. (2005). Accessibility and mobile learning. In A. Kukulska-Hulme & J. Traxler (Eds.), *Mobile learning: A handbook for educators and trainers* (pp. 57–69). Abingdon, UK: Routledge.

Rainie, L. (2013). *Cell phone ownership hits 90% of adults.* San Diego, CA: Pew Research.

Rainie, L. (2014). *The six types of Twitter conversations.* Retrieved from http://www.pewresearch.org/fact-tank/2014/02/20/the-six-types-of-twitter-conversations/

Rainie, L. (2017). *Digital divides-feeding America.* Pew Research Center. Retrieved from http://www.pewinternet.org/2017/02/09/digital-divides-feeding-america/.

Rainie, L, & Anderson, J. (2017). *Code-dependent: Pros and cons of the algorithm age.* Pew Research Center. Retrieved from http://www.pewinternet.org/2017/02/08/code-dependent-pros-and-cons-of-the-algorithm-age

Rajabi, A., Ghasemzadeh, A., Ashrafpouri, Z., & Saadat, M. (2012). Effects of counseling by mobile phone short message service (SMS) on reducing aggressive behavior in adolescence. *Procedia-Social and Behavioral Sciences, 46*, 1138–1142.

Ramburuth, P., & Daniel, S. (2011). Integrating experiential learning and cases in international business. *Journal of Teaching in International Business, 22*(1), 38–50.

Ramey, K. (2013). What is technology-meaning of technology and its use Retrieved from http://www.useoftechnology.com/what-is-technology/

Ramey, K. (2014). How to use technology—100 provided ways to use technology. Retrieved from http://www.useoftechnology.com/how-to-use-technology/

Randviir, E. P., Illingworth, S. M., Baker, M. J., Cude, M., & Banks, C. E. (2015). Twittering about research: A case study of the world's first twitter poster competition. *F1000Research, 4*, 798. https://doi.org/10.12688/f1000research.6992.3

Reamer, F. G. (1987). Informed consent in social work. *Social Work, 32*, 425–429.

Reamer, F. G. (2009). Eye on ethics: Novel boundary challenges social networking. *Social Work Today.* Retrieved from http://www.socialworktoday.com/news/eoe_111309.shtml

Reamer, F. G. (2013). Social work in a digital age: Ethical and risk management challenges. *Social Work, 58*, 163–172. https://doi.org/10.1093/sw/swt003

Reamer, F. G. (2015). *New technology standards for social work: Ethical implications.* http://www.socialworktoday.com/news/eoe_073015.shtml

Rebecca, B. (1998). *It takes a Nation: A new agenda for fighting poverty.* Princeton, NJ: Princeton University Press.

Redmond, M. E. (2003). School social work information systems (SSWIS): A relational database for school social workers. *Journal of Technology in Human Services, 21*, 161–175.

Reetz, D. R., Krylowicz, R., Bershad, C., Lawrence, J. M., & Mistler, B. (2016). The association for university and college counseling center director's annual survey. Retrieved from http://www.aucccd.org/assets/documents/aucccd%202015%20monograph%20-%20public%20version.pdf

Reisch, M., & Andrews, J. (2002). *The road not taken: A radical history of social work.* London, UK: Routledge.

Reinsmith-Jones, K., Kibbe, S., Crayton, T., & Campbell, E (2015). Use of Second Life in social work education: Virtual world experiences and their effect on students. *Journal of Social Work Education, 51*(1).

Reger, G. M., Holloway, K. M., Candy, C., Rothbaum, B. O., Difede, J., Rizzo, A. A., & Gahm, G. A. (2011). Effectiveness of virtual reality exposure therapy for active duty soldiers in a military mental health clinic. *Journal of Traumatic Stress, 24*(1), 93–96.

Reyna, V. F., & Farley, F. (2006). Risk and rationality in adolescent decision making: Implications for theory, practice, and public policy. *Psychological Science in the Public Interest, 7*(1), 1–44.

Reynolds, B. C., & Reynolds, B. C. (1942). *Learning and teaching in the practice of social work.* New York, NY: Rinehart.

Rheingold, H. (1993). *The virtual community: Homesteading on the electronic frontier* (1st ed.). Menlo Park, CA: Addison-Wesley.

Rice, C., Chandler, E., & Changfoot, N. (2016). Imagining otherwise: The ephemeral spaces of envisioning new meanings. C. Kelly & M. Orsini (Eds.), *Mobilizing Metaphor: Art, Culture and Disability Activism in Canada* (pp. 54–75). Vancouver, BC: UBC Press.

Rice, C., Chandler, E., Harrison, E. Ferrari, M., & Liddiard, K. (2015). Project Re•Vision: Disability at the edges of representation. *Disability and Society, 30,* 513–527.

Rice, C., Chandler, E., Liddiard, K., Rinaldi, J., & Harrison, E. (2016). The pedagogical possibilities for unruly bodies. *Gender and Education.* doi: 10.1080/09540253.2016.1247947.

Rice, C., & Mundel, I. (2018). Multimedia storytelling methodology: Notes on access and inclusion in neoliberal times. *Canadian Journal of Disability Studies, 55*(2), 211–231.

Richardson, W., & Manacebelli, R. (2011). *Personal learning networks: Using the power of connections to transform education.* Bloomington, IN: Solution Tree Press. Retrieved from http://soltreemrls3.s3-website-us-west-2.amazonaws.com/solution-tree.com/media/pdf/study_guides/Personal_Learning_Networks.pdf

Rickson, J., & Watkins, W. G. (2003). Music therapy to promote prosocial behaviors in aggressive adolescent boys: a pilot study. *Journal of Music Therapy, 40,* 283–301.

Roback, A. J. (2013, February). Uncovering motives for social networking site use among practitioners at non-profit organizations. In *Proceedings of the 2013 conference on computer supported cooperative work companion* (pp. 77–80). New York, NY: ACM.

Robinson, A. C., Kerski, J., Long, E. C., Luo, H., DiBiase, D., & Lee, A. (2015). Maps and the geospatial revolution: Teaching a massive open online course (MOOC) in geography. *Journal of Geography in Higher Education, 39*(1), 65–82.

Roblyer, M. D., McDaniel, M., Webb, M., Herman, J., & Witty, J. V. (2010). Findings on Facebook in higher education: A comparison of college faculty and student uses and perceptions of social networking sites. *The Internet and Higher Education, 13,* 134–140. https://doi.org/10.1016/j.iheduc.2010.03.002

Rolls, K., Hansen, M., Jackson, D., & Elliott, D. (2016). How health care professionals use social media to create virtual communities: An integrative review. *Journal of Medical Internet Research, 18*(6). https://doi.org/10.2196/jmir.5312

Rossiter, M., & Garcia, P. A. (2010). Digital storytelling: A new player on the narrative field. *New Directions for Adult and Continuing Education, 126,* 37–48.

Rothman, J. (2013). *Education for macro intervention: A survey of problems and prospects.* Retrieved from https://www.acosa.org/joomla/rothman-report

Rotondi, A. J., Hass, G. L., Anderson, C. M., Newhill, C. E., Spring, M. B., Ganguli, R., . . . Rosenstock, J. B. (2005). A clinical trial to test the feasibility of a telehealth psychoeducational intervention for persons with schizophrenia and their families: Intervention and 3-month findings. *Rehabilitation Psychology, 50,* 325–336. doi:10.1037/0090-5550.50.4.325

Russell, T. L. (2001). *The no significant difference phenomenon* (5th ed.). Chicago, IL: The International Distance Education Certification Center. Retrieved from http://www.nosignificantdifference.org/

Saarikallio, S. (2007). *Music as mood regulation in adolescence.* Jyväskylä, Finland: University of Jyväskylä.

Safire, W. (2002). Blog: Do a million hits make a word. *New York Times,* 28.

Saguy, A., & Gruys, K. (2010). Morality and health: News media constructions of overweight and eating disorders. *Social Problems, 57,* 231–250.

Sandars, J., & Murray, C. (2011). Digital storytelling to facilitate reflective learning in medical students. *Medical Education, 45,* 649. https://doi.org/10.1111/j.1365-2923.2011.03991.x

Santana, A. D. (2014). Virtuous or vitriolic. *Journalism Practice, 8*(1), 18–33. https://doi.org/10.1080/17512786.2013.813194

Savaya, R., Spiro, S., Waysman, M., & Golan, M. (2004). Issues in the development of a computerized clinical information system for a network of juvenile homes. *Administration in Social Work, 28,* 63–79.

Saxton, G. D., & Guo, C. (2012). Conceptualizing web-based stakeholder communication: The organizational website as a stakeholder relations tool.

Saxton, G. D., Niyirora, J. N., Guo, C., & Waters, R. D. (2015). #AdvocatingForChange: The strategic use of hashtags in social media advocacy. *Advances in Social Work 16,* 154–169.

Saxton, G. D., & Wang, L. (2014). The social network effect: The determinants of giving through social media. *Nonprofit and Voluntary Sector Quarterly, 43*(5), 850–868.

Schadler, T., Bernoff, J., & Ask, J. (2014). *The mobile mind shift: Engineer your business to win in the mobile moment.* Austin, TX: Greenleaf Book Group.

Schlaug, G. (2009). Listening to and making music facilitates brain recovery processes. *Annals of the New York Academy of Sciences, 1169,* 372–373.

Schiano, D. J., & White, S. (1998). The first noble truth of CyberSpace: People are people (even when they MOO). In C.-M. Karat, A. Lund, J. Coutaz, & J. Karat (Eds.), *Proceedings of the ACM CHI Human Factors in Computing Systems Conference* (pp. 352–359). Los Angeles.

Schmidt, J. (2007). Blogging practices: An analytical framework. *Journal of Computer-Mediated Communication, 12,* 1409–1427.

Schoech, R., & Arangio, T. (1979). Computers in the human services. *Social Work, 24,* 96–102.

Schoech, R., Quinn, A., & Rycraft, J. R. (2000). Data mining in child welfare. *Child Welfare, 79,* 633–650.

Schultze, U. (2010). Embodiment and presence in virtual worlds: A review. *Journal of Information Technology, 25,* 434–449.

Schwartz, S. L., Wiley, J. L., & Kaplan, C. D. (2016). Community building in a virtual teaching environment. *Advances in Social Work, 17*(1), 15–30. https://doi.org/10.18060/20875

Sedenberg, E., & Hoffmann, A. L. (2016). *Recovering the History of Informed Consent for Data Science and Internet Industry Research Ethics.* arXiv preprint arXiv:1609.03266.

Selwyn, N. (2004). Reconsidering political and popular understandings of the digital divide. *New Media and Society, 6,* 341–362.

Semke, J. I., & Nurius, P. (1991). Information structure, information technology, and the human services organizational environment. *Social Work, 36,* 353–358.

Shams, L., & Seitz, A. R. (2008). Benefits of multisensory learning. *Trends in Cognitive Sciences, 12,* 411–417. https://doi.org/10.1016/j.tics.2008.07.006

Shapiro, J. R., Bauer, S., Andrews, E., Pisetsky, E., Bulik-Sullivan, B., Hamer, R. M., & Bulik, C. M. (2010). Mobile therapy: Use of text-messaging in the treatment of bulimia nervosa. *International Journal of Eating Disorders, 43,* 513–519. doi:10.1002/eat.20744

Shaw, I., G., R., & Warf, B. (2009). Worlds of affect: Virtual geographies of video games. *Environment and Planning, A, 41,* 1332–1343.

Shorkey, C. T., & Uebel, M. (2014). History and development of instructional technology and media in social work education. *Journal of Social Work Education, 50,* 247–261. http://doi.org/10.1080/10437797.2014.885248

Sillesen, L. B. (2014). Is this the webs first blog? *Columbia Journalism Review.* Retrieved from http://archives.cjr.org/behind_the_news/justin_hall_blog_web.php 4-11-17.

Singer, J. (n.d.). *Social Work and Technology Google Plus Group.* Retrieved from: https://plus.google.com/communities/115588985317830085141

Sly, J. R., Miller, S. J., & Jandorf, L. (2014). The digital divide and health disparities: A pilot study examining the use of short message service (SMS) for colonoscopy reminders. *Journal of Racial and Ethnic Health Disparities, 1,* 231–237. doi:10.1007/s40615-014-0029-z

Smith, A. (2016, January 12). *Record shares of Americans now own smartphones, have home broadband.* Pew Research Center. Retrieved from http://www.pewresearch.org/fact-tank/2017/01/12/evolution-of-technology/

Smith, G. H. (2006). *Remembering Garrett: One family's battle with a child's depression* (1st Carroll & Graf ed). New York, NY: Carroll & Graf.

Smith, J., & Wertlieb, E. (2005). Do first-year college students' expectations align with their first-year experiences? *NASPA Journal, 42,* 153–174.

Smith, K. (2010). The use of virtual worlds among people with disabilities. In *Proceedings of the International Conference on Universal Technologies*(pp. 15–21). Oslo, Norway.

Smith, M. A., Raine, L., Shneiderman, B., & Himelbom, I. (2014). *Mapping twitter topic networks: From polarized crowds to community clusters.* Pew Research Center. Retrieved from http://www.pewinternet.org/files/2014/02/PIP_Mapping-Twitter-networks_022014.pdf

Smyth, N. J. (2011). *Virtual worlds as immersive treatment settings: The PTSD Sim.* Retrieved from https://njsmyth.wordpress.com/2011/03/25/virtual-worlds-as-immersive-treatment-settings-the-ptsd-sim/

Smyth, N. J. (2015). *Social worker's guide to social media* [infographic]. Retrieved July 1, 2016, from http://socialwork.buffalo.edu/social-media-guide.html

Šorgo, A., Bartol, T., Dolničar, D., & Boh Podgornik, B. (2016). Attributes of digital natives as predictors of information literacy in higher education. *British Journal of Educational Technology, 48*(3), 749–767. doi:10.1111/bjet.12451

Standen, P. J., & Brown, D. J. (2006). Virtual reality and its role in removing the barriers that turn cognitive impairments into intellectual disability. *Virtual Reality, 10,* 241–252.

Standen, P. J., & Cromby, J. J. (1995). *Can students with developmental disability use virtual reality to learn skills which will transfer to the real world?* Paper presented at the 3rd International Conference on Virtual Reality and Persons with Disabilities. San Francisco, CA.

Stein, R. (2007). Limits, inhibitions disappear online. *Seattle Times* online. Retrieved May 20, 2008, from http://seattletimes.nwsource.com/html/nationworld/2003931084_netavatar07.html

Steinberg, L., & Silk, J. S. (2002). Parenting adolescents. *Handbook of Parenting, 1,* 103–133.

Stendal, K. (2013). *Virtual world affordances for people with lifelong disability.* PhD thesis, University of Agder, Department of Information Systems. University of Agder, Kristiansand, Norway.

Stendal, K., Balandin, S., & Molka-Danielsen, J. (2011). Virtual worlds: A new opportunity for people with lifelong disability? *Journal of Intellectual and Developmental Disability, 36*(1), 80–83.

Stern, G. (1966). Myth and reality in the American college. *AAUP Bulletin, 52,* 408–414.

Stewart, S., Hansen, T. S., & Carey, T. A. (2010). Opportunities for people with disabilities in the virtual world of Second Life. *Rehabilitation Nursing, 35,* 254–259.

Steyaert, J., Colombi, D., & Rafferty, J. (1996). *Human services and information technology: An international perspective.* Brookfield, VT: Ashgate.

Strecher, V. J., McClure, J. B., Alexander, G. L., Chakraborty, B., Nair, V. N., Konkel, J. M., . . . Pomerleau, O. F. (2008). Web-based smoking-cessation programs: Results of a randomized trial. *American Journal of Preventive Medicine, 34,* 373–381. doi:10.1016/j.amepre.2007.12.024

Strom-Gottfried, K., Thomas, M. S., & Anderson, H. (2014). Social work and social media: Reconciling ethical standards and emerging technologies. *Journal of Social Work Values and Ethics, 11*(1), 54–65.

Sullivan, C. (2015). *Digital identity: An emergent legal concept.* Adelaide, Australia: University of Adelaide Press. Retrieved from http://www.oapen.org/search?identifier=560114

Tandy, C., Vernon, R., & Lynch, D. (2016). Teaching student interviewing competencies through Second Life. *Journal of Social Work Education—Taylor and Francis Online.* Retrieved July 1, 2016, from http://www.tandfonline.com/doi/full/10.1080/10437797.2016.1198292

Taylor, T. L. (2002). Living digitally: Embodiment in virtual worlds. In R. Schroeder (Ed.), *The social life of avatars: Presence and intersection in shared virtual environments* (pp. 40–62). London: Springer-Verlag.

Teixeira, S. (2016). Qualitative geographic information systems (GIS): An untapped research approach for social work. *Qualitative Social Work.* Advance online publication.

Thackeray, R. N., Neiger, B. L., & Hanson, C. L. (2008). Enhancing promotional strategies within social marketing programs: Use of Web 2.0 social media. *Social Marketing and Health Communication, 9,* 338–343.

Thoits, P. (1995). Stress, coping, and social support processes: Where are we? What next? *Journal of Health and Social Behavior, 35*, 53–79.

Thompson, G. A., McFerran, K. S., & Gold, C. (2014). Family-centred music therapy to promote social engagement in young children with severe autism spectrum disorder: A randomized controlled study. *Child: Care, Health and Development, 40*, 840–852.

Thompson, V. (2017, April 4). #MacroSW: What is the role of allies? The Macro social work approach to understanding disability and online disability advocacy. Retrieved from http://www.socialworker.com/api/content/b75acffe-18b4-11e7-ac04-0aea2a882f79/

Thraen, I. M., Frasier, L., Cochella, C., Yaffe, J., & Goede, P. (2008). The use of TeleCAM as a remote web-based application for child maltreatment assessment, peer review, and case documentation. *Child Maltreatment, 13*, 368–376. doi:10.1177/1077559508318068

Thriveport. (2016). Moodnotes (2.2.1) [Mobile application software]. Retrieved from https://itunes.apple.com/us/app/moodnotes-thought-journal/id1019230398?mt=8

Tredinnick, L. (2006). *Digital information contexts: Theoretical approaches to understanding digital information*. Norwalk, CT: Elsevier.

Tribou, R. (2014, March 7). Florida has billionaires galore. *The Orlando Sentinel*. Retrieved from http://www.orlandosentinel.com/features/the-list/os-florida-billionaires-list-20140307-post.html

Turkle, S. (2012). *Alone together: Why we expect more from technology and less from each other*. New York, NY: Basic Books.

Turnbull, G. (2002). The state of the blog. We've got Blog: How Weblogs are changing our culture, 78–88.

Tzilos, G. K., Sokol, R. J., & Ondersma, S. J. (2011). A randomized Phase I trial of a brief computer-delivered intervention for alcohol use during pregnancy. *Journal of Women's Health, 20*, 1517–1524.

Ulrich, W. (2003). Beyond methodology choice: Critical systems thinking as critically systemic discourse. *Journal of the Operational Research Society, 54*, 325–342.

United Nations. *E-government survey 2014*. https://publicadministration.un.org/egovkb/portals/egovkb/documents/un/2014-survey/e-gov_complete_survey-2014.pdf

United Nations. *E-government survey 2016*. https://publicadministration.un.org/egovkb/en-us/reports/un-e-government-survey-2016

Unrau, Y., Font, S., & Rawls, G. (2012). Readiness for college engagement among students who have aged out of foster care. *Children and Youth Services Review, 34*(2012), 76–83.

URISA. (2003). *GIS Code of ethics*. Retrieved from http://www.urisa.org/about-us/gis-code-of-ethics/

US Census Bureau. (2012, December 6). *Geographic terms and concepts—census tract*. Retrieved from https://www.census.gov/geo/reference/gtc/gtc_ct.html

US Census Bureau. (2013). *American Community Survey 3-year estimates—Collier County, Florida census tracts*.

US Department of Education. (2015, June 26). *Family Educational Rights and Privacy Act (FERPA)* [Guides]. Retrieved September 18, 2016, from http://www2.ed.gov/policy/gen/guid/fpco/ferpa/index.html

US Department of Health and Human Services. (n.d.). *Office of adolescent health*. Retrieved from https://www.hhs.gov/ash/oah/adolescent-development/index.html.

US Department of Health and Human Services (HHS). (2016). *The HIPAA privacy rule*. Retrieved July 1, 2016, from http://www.hhs.gov/hipaa/for-professionals/privacy/

US Department of Health and Human Services, Administration for Children and Families, Administration on Children, Youth and Families, Children's Bureau, (2016). *The AFCARS report, Preliminary FY 2015 Estimates as of June 2016, No. 23.* http://www.acf.hhs.gov/programs/cb

US General Services Administration. (2017). *Learn about Section 508 requirements and responsibilities.* Retrieved April 4, 2017, from https://www.section508.gov/content/learn

Ussher, J. (2010). Are we medicalizing women's misery? A critical review of women's higher rates of reported depression. *Feminism and Psychology, 20*(1), 9–35.

van Uden-Kraan, C. F., Drossaert, C. H., Taal, E., Seydel, E. R., & van de Laar, M. A. (2009). Participation in online patient support groups endorses patients' empowerment. *Patient Education and Counseling, 74,* 61–69.

van Uden-Kraan, C. F., Drossaert, C. H., Taal, E., Shaw, B. R., Seydel, E. R., & van de Laar, M. A. (2008). Empowering processes and outcomes of participation in online support groups for patients with breast cancer, arthritis, or fibromyalgia. *Qualitative Health Research, 18*(3), 405–417.

Varney, S. (2015, May). *Number of seniors threatened by hunger has doubled since 2001, and it's going to get worse.* Retrieved from http://www.pbs.org/newshour/bb/number-hungry-seniors-doubled-since-2001-going-get-worse/

Vaughn, M. (2014). History of DAW. *logitunes blog.* Retrieved from http://logitunes.com/blog/history-of-daw/

Verdi, M. P., & Kulhavy, R. W. (2002). Learning with maps and texts: An overview. *Educational Psychology Review, 14*(1), 27–46.

Vernon, R., Lewis, L., & Lynch, D. (2009). Virtual worlds and social work education: Potentials for "Second Life." *Advances in Social Work, 10,* 176–192.

Vest, G., Pruett, K., & Holmgren, B. (n.d.). *Social advocacy, brokering and networking with PCs.* Retrieved from http://www.socialworksearch.com/research/researchgv.shtml#

Vonnegut, K. (2006). *Palm Sunday: An autobiographical collage.* New York, NY: Dial Press Trade Paperbacks.

Vonnegut, K., & Simon, D. (2007). *A man without a country* (Random House Trade pbk. ed.). New York: Random House Trade Paperbacks.

Voshel, E. H., & Wesala, A. (2015). Social media and social work ethics: Determining best practices in an ambiguous reality. *Journal of Social Work Values and Ethics, 12*(1), 67–76.

Wallace, S., Parsons, S., Westbury, A., White, K., White, K., & Bailey, A. (2010). Sense of presence and atypical social judgments in immersive virtual environments. *Autism, 14,* 199–213.

Walzer, D. A. (2016). Software-based scoring and sound design. *Music Educators Journal, 103*(1), 19–26.

Wang, B. (2015). Analyzing and predicting risks of infectious diseases by geographic information science. *Hong Kong Polytechnic University Institutional Research Archives.* Retrieved at http://hdl.handle.net/10397/35307

Wang, C., & Burris, M. A. (1997). Photovoice: Concept, methodology, and use for participatory needs assessment. *Health Education and Behavior, 24,* 369–387.

Wasley, P. (2009). More charities are on social networks–but few have raised much. *The Chronicle of Philanthropy.*

Waters, R., Burnett, E., Lamm A., & Lucas, J. (2009) Engaging stakeholders through social networking: How nonprofit organizations are using Facebook. *Public Relations Review, 35,* 102–106.

We Are Social. (n.d.). *Digital in 2016.* Retrieved from http://wearesocial.com/uk/special-reports/digital-in-2016

Wellman, B., Haase, A. Q., Witte, J., & Hampton, K. (2001). Does the Internet increase, decrease, or supplement social capital? Social networks, participation, and community commitment. *American Behavioral Scientist, 45*(3), 436–455.

Welty, W. (1989). Discussion method teaching. *Change,* July/August, 40–49.

Wenger-Trayner, E., & Wenger-Trayner, B. (n.d.). *Levels of participation.* Retrieved from http://wenger-trayner.com/project/levels-of-participation/

Wexler, L., Gubrium, A., Griffin, M., & DiFulvio, G. (2013). Promoting positive youth development and highlighting reasons for living in Northwest Alaska through digital storytelling. *Health Promotion Practice, 14,* 617–623. https://doi.org/10.1177/1524839912462390

Whittaker, R., Borland, R., Bullen, C., Lin, R., McRobbie, H., & Rodgers, A. (2009). Mobile phone-based interventions for smoking cessation. *Cochrane Database System Reviews, 4*(4), CD006611.

Whittaker, R., Matoff-Stepp, S., Meehan, J., Kendrick, J., Jordan, E., Stange, P., . . . Rhee, K. (2012). Text4baby: Development and implementation of a national text messaging health information service. *American Journal of Public Health, 102,* 2207–2213.

Wiggins, L., Nower, L., Mayers, R. S., & Peterson, A. (2010). A geospatial statistical analysis of the density of lottery outlets within ethnically concentrated neighborhoods. *Journal of Community Psychology, 38*(4), 486–496.

Wilke, D. J., King, E., Ashmore, M., & Stanley, C. (2016). Can clinical skills be taught online? Comparing skill development between online and F2F students using a blinded review. *Journal of Social Work Education, 52,* 484–492. https://doi.org/10.1080/10437797.2016.1215276

Willem, A., & Buelens, M. (2007). Knowledge sharing in public sector organizations: The effect of organizational characteristics on interdepartmental knowledge sharing. *Journal of Public Administration Research and Theory, 17,* 581–606.

Williams, D., Martins, N. Consalvo, M., & Ivory, J. D. (2009). The virtual census: Presentations of gender, race and age in video games. *New Media and Society, 11,* 815–834.

Williamson, B. (2016). Digital education governance: data visualization, predictive analytics, and "real-time" policy instruments. *Journal of Education Policy, 31,* 123–141.

Wilson, F. A. (1997). The truth is out there: The search for emancipatory principles in information systems design. *Information Technology and People, 10,* 187–204.

Winerip, M. (2013, October 30). Out of foster care, into college. *New York Times,* Education Life Section. Retrieved from http://www.nytimes.com/2013/11/03/education/edlife/extra-support-can-make-all-the-difference-for-foster-youth.html

Wolf, L., & Goldkind, L. (2016). Digital native meet friendly visitor: A Flexner-inspired call to digital action. *Journal of Social Work Education, 52*(suppl. 1), S99–S109. https://doi.org/10.1080/10437797.2016.1174643

Wolf, L., & Wolf, T. (2011). *Music and health care.* London: Carnegie Hall & WolfBrown.

Wolford, B. (2014, September). Nowhere to go: The struggle of impoverished seniors in Naples. *GulfshoreLife.* Retrieved from http://www.gulfshorelife.com/September-2014/Naples-affordable-housing-senior-poverty-Section-8-Jewish-Family-and-Community-Services-of-Southwest-Florida-Collier-County-poor-seniors-Housing-Human-and-Veteran-Services/

Wong, Y. I., & Hillier, A. (2001). Evaluating a community-based homelessness prevention program: A geographic information system approach. *Administration in Social Work, 25*(4), 21–45.

Wordpress. (2016, December 23). *Types of blogs.* Retrieved from https://wordpress.com/types-of-blogs/

World Wide Web Consortium (W3C). (2016). *Accessibility.* Retrieved July 1, 2016, from https://www.w3.org/standards/webdesign/accessibility

Wunderlich, G., & Norwood, J. (2006). *Food insecurity and hunger in the United States.* Washington, DC: National Academy of Sciences.

Yamashita, T., & Kunkel, S. (2012). Geographic access to healthy and unhealthy foods for the older population in a U. S. metropolitan area. *Journal of Applied Gerontology, 31,* 287–313.

Yang, T. M., & Maxwell, T. A. (2011). Information-sharing in public organizations: A literature review of interpersonal, intra-organizational and inter-organizational success factors. *Government Information Quarterly, 28,* 164–175.

Young, G. (2010). Virtually real emotions and the paradox of fiction: Implications for the use of virtual environments in psychological research. *Philosophical Psychology, 23*(1), 1–21.

Young, J. (2013). A conceptual understanding of organizational identity in the social media environment. *Advances in Social Work, 14,* 518–530.

Young, J. (2014). iPolicy: Exploring and evaluating the use of iPads in a social welfare policy course. *Journal of Technology in Human Services, 32*(1–2), 39–53.

Young, J. A. (2015). Assessing new media literacies in social work education: The development and validation of a comprehensive assessment instrument. *Journal of Technology in Human Services, 33*(1), 72–86. https://doi.org/10.1080/15228835.2014.998577

Yu, J., Taverner, N., & Madden, K. (2011). Young people's views on sharing health-related stories on the Internet. *Health and Social Care in the Community, 19,* 326–334. https://doi.org/10.1111/j.1365-2524.2010.00987.x

Yuen, E. K., Herbert, J. D., Forman, E. M., Goetter, E. M., Comer, R., & Bradley, J. C. (2013). Treatment of social anxiety disorder using online virtual environments in second life. *Behavior Therapy, 44*(1), 51–61.

Zakour, M., & Harrell, E. (2004). Access to disaster services: Social work interventions for vulnerable populations. *Journal of Social Service Research, 30*(2), 27–54.

Zgoda, K. (2011). SW 2.0: Going where the client is: Exploring virtual clinical social work practice. *The New Social Worker.* Retrieved July 1, 2016, from http://www.socialworker.com/feature-articles/technology-articles/SW_2.0%3A_Going_Where_the_Client_Is%3A_Exploring_Virtual_Clinical_Social_Work_Practice/

Zgoda, K. (2014, March 13). #MacroSW twitter chats start tonight at 9pm EST! Retrieved from https://karenzgoda.org/2014/03/13/macrosw-twitter-chats-start-tonight-at-9pm-est/

Zhang, J., & Dawes, S. S. (2006). Expectations and perceptions of benefits, barriers, and success in public sector knowledge networks. *Public Performance and Management Review, 29,* 433–466.

Zhang, J., Dawes, S. S., & Sarkis, J. (2005). Exploring stakeholders' expectations of the benefits and barriers of e-government knowledge sharing, *Journal of Enterprise Information Management, 18*(5), 548–567.

Zhang, S., Freundschuh, S. M., Lenzer, K., & Zandbergen, P. A. (2015). The location swapping method for geomasking. *Cartography and Geographic Information Science, 44*(1), 22–34.

Zheng, L., Yang, T. M., Pardo, T., & Jiang, Y. (2009, January). Understanding the "boundary" in information sharing and integration. In *42nd Hawaii International Conference on System Sciences, 2009. HICSS'09* (pp. 1–10). IEEE.

Zickuhr, K. & Smith, A. (2012). *Digital differences*. Retrieved July 1, 2016, from http://www.pewinternet.org/2012/04/13/digital-differences/

Ziv, S. (2015, May 29). Technology's latest quest: Tracking mental health. *Newsweek*. Retrieved from http://www.newsweek.com/2014/11/21/technologys-latest-quest-tracking-mental-health-283944.html

Zoppo, A. (2015, August 30). College programs provide help for "aged out" foster care students. *USA Today*. Retrieved from http://college.usatoday.com/2015/08/30/college-programs-provide-help-for-aged-out-foster-care-students/

Zorn, T. E., Flanagin, A. J., & Shoham, M. D. (2011). Institutional and noninstitutional influences on information and communication technology adoption and use among nonprofit organizations. *Human Communication Research, 37*(1), 1–33. doi:10.1111=j.1468- 2958.2010.01387

Zur, O. (2010). To Google or not to Google . . . our clients? When psychotherapists and other mental health care providers search their clients on the web. *Independent Practitioner, 30*(3), 144–148.

Zur, O. (2012). Therapeutic ethics in the digital age. *Psychotherapy Networker, 36*(4), 26–36.

INDEX